Science of God

Srinivasan Kannan

PARTRIDGE
A Penguin Random House Company

To order additional copies of this book, contact
Partridge India
000 800 10062 62
www.partridgepublishing.com/india
orders.india@partridgepublishing.com

Acharya
Sri U.Ve. KKVA Kumaravenkatachar Swamy
Mudaliyandan Thirumaligai

Sri U. Ve. A.K.E Srinivasan
Kooram

Contents

Dedication:

This book is dedicated to the Lotus feet of our revered Acharyan Sri.U.Ve. K.K.V.A. Kumara Venkatachar Swamy, Mudaliyandan Swamy Thirumaligai; and our father, Sri.U.Ve. A.K.E. Srinivasan.

Acknowledgement and Thanks:

Our mother Smt. Champakavalli has always been a source of knowledge, guiding me whenever I sought clarifications, for she is well versed in Divyaprabandham, sacred granthas and commentaries (vyAkhyAnams) of all Acharyas, which was bestowed upon her by our father.

Sri Balakrishnan, my brother-in-law, encouraged me whenever the write ups were emailed to him and Mrs. Geetha Balakrishnan, my sister, has been a source of inspiration, for she has been blessed with insight about the 4000 psalms of Divyaprabandham and the divine granthas of Acharyas. We would often discuss some of the intrinsic nuances of the meanings of our sacred scriptures.

Sri Badrinath, Bangalore, a disciple of our Acharya, who read through this work to share his views in the final outcome of the book.

Sri Azhagiya Manavalan, Mudikondan, a close family friend, who urged me to write this book whenever I spoke to him about topics related to God.

And my wife Usha, and our kids Krishna and Madhuri, who supported in making this book possible, coming up with questions to send me into thinking to finding logical answers.

To all of them, I owe my debt of gratitude and thanks.

adiyen Dasarathi Dasan
Srinivasan Kannan
B-504, Mantri Greens,
#1, Sampige Road,
Malleswaram,
Bangalore—560003

Mobile "0-81979 66493"
Email—kannan@highdefinition.in; s.kannans@gmail.com"

Synopsis:

We often wonder as to who we are, why we are born, what is the purpose of life, especially human life? The questions are endless. We also wonder about our world, and this universe. We do not know much about how this universe formed or about its functioning. Due to our natural intelligence, we are able to ponder whether there is some power that is causing all that exists in this universe including us, because we know that we did not cause anything that exists here; neither us nor the universe. Then it should also make us contemplate if we are anyway related to that power, who is the cause for everything.

Knowledge is Science and knowledge is our nature. Knowing about God is the greatest knowledge there is. When we know of God, we can know of everything there is in creation.

We mostly identify the self (Atma) with our body, thinking that we and the body are one and the same, and in the bargain, spend a whole life in ignorance without avail. For some, questions spring up much earlier in life and may find the right answers and for most others, life would end even before questions arise.

Those who realize the self would know that it is rare to get human life and it would be such a waste if we don't use this life to its potential.

It is in our nature to seek happiness and joy in everything we do, but we are not happy even after attaining the state we thought would bring us happiness. We die dissatisfied; holding on to several unfulfilled desires, wishing to live on if it was possible; and unsure of the future course of existence after death. We are in this world, going through life and death in some 8.4 million bodies, since eternity; looking for that elusive bliss, one that

is unlimited, unending and ever-growing; one similar to what
Chandogya Upanishad 7-23-1 describes—
"yo vai bhUmA tat sukham"—
"he who experiences plentitude that is infinite bliss"; or

Azhwar describes—
"appozhudaikku appozhudu en ArA amudamE"—
*"The unending bliss of the Lord we experience, would be
increasing every moment"* and

"nalam anthamillador nAdu puguvIr".-
"we would attain that world where there is no end to bliss".

If we could not find that bliss so far, it is unlikely that we will find
it henceforth. Simply, that bliss is not available here. Here is the
hitch. The joy we experience in this world is merely the pleasure
of our body, joy of the senses and happiness of the mind. Our
senses and mind themselves do not enjoy; it is the Atma who is
seeking the enjoyment. But what the atma is seeking is divine
bliss (parama-ananda) and not the transient material enjoyment
of senses and mind.

We seek that divine bliss due to our nature and origin. We
originated from God, having certain similarities with Him, but
acquired bodies from this non sentient universe out of our own
choice. Naturally, the quality of joy experienced in this non
sentient world would also be of the same nature as this world—
limited, momentary, declining, perishable and changing. But we
are divine, eternal, unchanging. Logically, we seek similar bliss
that matches with our own nature which is available only at our
source when we attain immortality in the eternal world. Our origin
is of the nature of 'divine Bliss' or 'Anandamaya', who is also
known as the Supreme God.

Though our desire for choosing this world was to experience joy
and independence, we have got grief and imprisonment, caught

up in the realm of this prakruti (universe), instead. We chose this world to experience freedom, but are bound by the birth-death cycles in mortal bodies, instead. We have no control over our birth, or choosing our parents or choosing how and when to die or over events during our life. Choice alone is in our power. Our attempt is to attain something but the resultant outcome is something else, except sometimes things happen as desired, due to our good karma.

Those who sought to find answers would know that there are just three entities in all—*We, the immortal souls*; this *material universe* from which we obtained our bodies; and *the supreme God*, who is the common factor in everything there is; He is the origin for this universe and us.

Though we can see our bodies and this universe, we are unable to see either the self (atma) or the supreme Lord (Paramatma) because both are subtle, divine and invisible. So how do we know of something that cannot be seen? What cannot be seen can only be realized through knowledge. For that matter, nearly 96% of this universe is invisible as it comprises of 73% of dark energy and 23% of dark matter. If non sentient matter and energy of this world cannot be seen, we should not be bewildered that the Soul and the Supreme Lord, both of whom are divine, cannot be seen by material eyes or perceived by material senses we possess.

This is where the Lord's kindness comes to our aid. He has made us (souls) naturally knowledgeable, He dwells inside the souls giving us the power for everything we do using our body-senses-mind-intellect, but without involvement. He has given us the Vedas and sacred scriptures which alone has the knowledge of the Atma and Paramatma. Any amount of scientific research cannot reveal either the soul or the supreme Lord. The Lord has created this universe because we chose to experience such an existence. Not only has he given us knowledge in scriptures; he has also incarnated from time to time, and also sent many divine souls from the eternal world to take birth here to bestow upon us the requisite knowledge; either for our happy existence here or to attaining His abode, where He grants us a state similar to His own; sharing with us His infinite divine bliss.

What would it be like, to be an immortal? In a way we can understand, we would all be like the superman without any limitations or weaknesses of the super hero of the comic book or we would be truly the children of God, experiencing His divine Person.

However, immortality can be granted only by the Lord for it is not in our jurisdiction to grant salvation to ourselves, just as we cannot grant visa to ourselves for visiting another country that requires a visa.

Vedas affirm that the only way to transcending birth-death cycles and to attaining immortality is by knowing the Lord. Vedas also declare that the Lord cannot be known by any means, for He is infinite in all respects. However, He can be known when He reveals Himself, when we seek Him with unconditional devotion.

Taittiriyopanishad—
Anandam brahmanO vidvAn"
"yato vAcho nivartante aprApya manasa saha,

"to knowing that bliss of Brahman,
"speech and mind turn back without reaching its end"
mind and speech cannot reach the end of bliss of Brahman
as He is infinite.

Svetasvataropanishad 3-8
"vEdAhamEtam purusham mahAntam AdityavarNam tamasah parastAt;
tamEva viditvA'timrutyumEti nAnyah panthA vidyatE'yanAya"

"I know this great Purusha, who is of the effulgence of the sun and who is beyond matter; Knowing Him alone can one go beyond death (mortality). To attaining that there is no other path"

Katopanishad 2-23
"nAyamAtmA pravachnEna labhyo na mEdhayA na bahunA
*   SrutEna;*
yamEvaisha vruNutE tEna labhyah tasyaisha AtmA vivruNutE
*   tanUm svAm"*

"This Supreme Self (paramatma) is not attainable either by thinking or by meditation or by hearing. He is attainable by him whom He (the Lord) chooses and to him this Supreme Self reveals His form".

More importantly, we should seek the Lord, taking refuge with an Acharya who would guide us to attaining our goal. Lord Krishna declares that He considers Acharyas much above Himself and grants them his own nature.

Devotion is a state in which we do not seek anything from the Lord, we seek to serve Him in ways it pleases Him. The best way to serve God here is to serve humanity. How does serving people tantamount to serving the Lord? Simple, the Lord is the indweller of every atma. A devotee would realize that the atma in every person is similar to him. Thus, the devotee serves the Lord by serving people.

Some of us are privileged and well positioned, either born wealthy or able to earn our way becoming rich due to opportunities, which is purely owing to our past and present karma. Only those who do not have to worry about poverty, hunger and starvation can possibly find time for self realization or knowing God. The poor and under privileged cannot think of self realization or God, for their only goal is to find their next meal. The greatest service to God is when we support someone to rise from the state of poverty and become a devotee so that he too can attain immortality. So it is all the more important that we share our excess resources with the needy of the society.

Success, wealth, power and every achievement in a mortal body would have to end. One, who realizes this truth, would live a happy life here as well as make that effort to reaching out to the Lord. '*Seshatvam*' or subservience to the Lord is our prime nature due to our inherent relationship with God.

This book is an effort to compile knowledge acquired from various sources, realizations and experiences that strengthen the fact that it is truly God's '*nirhEtuka krupa*', or unconditional benign grace, which enables each one of us to seeking a learned Acharya or Guru, who selflessly devotes his life for our attaining the glory of immortality.

Submission:

If I look back at the events of our life as a family, make an honest assessment of what we are today in relation to what we deserve, be it in terms of material gains or the understanding purely by the grace of the Acharya, I cannot miss realizing the Lord's 'nirhetuka krupa' (unconditional grace) at every stage in life. With that knowledge, comes the state of fearlessness and sense of joy never experienced before. This is the right stage to developing 'vairagya' or losing taste for things which is perceived as the very purpose of life for most. Developing distaste to worldly matters is a consequence of our natural love for the Lord and His people here. In this state, we don't seem to want to seek anything, yet, life seems to be going well, as though by arrangement, on autopilot mode. If we develop dispassion for worldly matters, it is purely by realizing God's love, which is unmistakable and overwhelming.

We as a family, have experienced paucity of resources for some years, as well as the luxuries and comforts later on, which is the goal for attainment for all of us. However, 'happiness' has been a constant throughout. We do not see a difference even when we acquired more resources than needed. This is where we get to realize the grace of God and Acharya. *You have nothing, yet you don't miss anything. You have everything, yet life keeps you in the same happiness, except that we get used to greater physical comforts and are able to do little things for others, which is God enabled.*

We cannot miss the realization that human life so fragile. It is like a bubble that is formed to burst anytime. Yet, we do bad things in our effort to acquire wealth and power in wrong ways, as though, we are here to live eternally.

When we realize the truth about the Lord and experience His grace, it fills us with the sense that there is nothing to be achieved here except being of use to family, friends and society. If it was merely owing to past karma, we should still be caught up in the events and outcomes, helplessly. When the realization dawns upon, you see the difference clearly. There were instances when I would persevere and make a conscious effort to make things happen, but would fail repeatedly. And at other times, things would fall in place even without the effort as though to reveal the unseeable divine grace, when we let go of the notion of the self being the doer. Everything that happened couldn't have been better.

I must confess that I am only beginning to understand about God, for God cannot be fully known, nor can one exhaust knowing about Him. Life is much more meaningful, when we realize God's benevolence and live life, including Him in everything we do.

In the process of completing this work, we have been enabled to adopt a charitable trust school in a small village of Tamilnadu. Proceeds from the sales of this book would be used for running this school.

Honestly, I have been motivated to express things based on real life experiences and understanding, which benefited me immensely. The least I can do is to make an effort to spread the message for the benefit of the readers as well. After all, everyone deserves to live a happy life. The real benefit, more than gaining material wealth, is realizing our eternal relationship with our true Father, God.

We have known that there are some people who live life beyond compare. In that, even those who think of them as their adversaries would also acknowledge that they are blemishless. In the case of Lord Rama, even those He killed; openly sung His glories. At least, Lord Rama is the supreme Lord and He naturally possesses only infinite auspicious attributes and no defilement can exist in the Lord.

Koorathazhwan is another who is affirmed by all, as one without an equal, for his kindness and compassion, and transcending the pride of three statuses—vidya madam, dhana madam and abhijAtyamadam (pride of knowledge, wealth and royalty). Azhwan surpassed Rama; for no one ever considered Azhwan as an adversary. Everyone agreed that Azhwan had only virtues; none could find a fault in him.

We could not miss the benevolent grace of our Acharya who has no equal when it comes to kindness, either. He was sometimes truly a superhuman; in the way one would refer to the attributes of Rama being of the nature of 'atimanushatvam', our Acharya too was such a person in the human form, for he could find no fault even in a known sinner. He looked at everyone as related through the Lord, including his own family.

I cannot remember, even if I had seen Rama during His incarnation and Azhwan during his. However, apart from our Acharya, I know one person who stands out as someone who cannot be faulted, for no one so far uttered one wrong thing he had said or done. If there is any reason for me to feel good about having been born in a mortal body, it is that I am blessed to be the son of such a father, who lived a life beyond compare and whom no one considered as an adversary nor anyone ever had a trivial grievance about what he said or did. He was kindness personified. It is said that during drought, being a landlord, he would share the food grain stock with some of the poor of the village. Even after two generations after his passing away, the surviving elders of the village still adore and revere him, confessing that it was not usual even for a noble man to be like him, for he excelled in every respect. Selflessness and care for other's well being probably stood out in him more than any other man of his time and place.

I made a mention of these two glorious men, apart from Lord Rama and Azhwan, for we have people finding fault even in a Mahatma Gandhi and such. It is rare to find people who are virtuous and free from blame. However, here were the two known men who lived a life of near perfection, for only the Lord is truly perfect.

All true devotees are kind people, transcending to a state in which they are fulfilled and seek nothing, either from this world or from the Lord, except to be of use to both, in any state. If anything, they would work righteously to provide for their needs and that of dependents.

I am convinced that there is a logical, perceivable and even scientific answer to all questions about God and Soul, in the sacred scriptures; which can be realized; for God cannot be shown or taught. If anyone wants to feel God, it is possible by thinking of God, with unconditional devotion. He or she can experience the bliss bestowed by God from within. This is unmistakably more real than all other realities we perceive in our lives. We must realize that we cannot connect with God of our own effort, but He would connect with us, when we truly seek Him. It is essential to know the self, our origin and seek to attain the source we belong to, *for we cannot separate ourselves from our origin*. We will, when we fall in love with God, which is the ultimate devotion. Hope this work triggers that love for God in the readers. And if we can strive to realize our eternal relationship with God, it would be worth our life as humans.

Sarvam Sri KrishnArpaNamastu

adiyen Dasarathi dasan
Srinivasan kannan

Chapter One

We, the immortals

Did you know that the real you, are an Immortal? For that matter, you, I and all the people in the world, all the living beings are immortals. It is our own doing why we are in a mortal body! After knowing this, should we not know how we can obtain an immortal body as well?

As a first step, we must know who we are, what our true identity is, our origin, nature, and attributes. We identify ourselves with our respective bodies. We think we are the body. We do not realize the fact that we are the atma/soul/power/life that is keeping this body alive. Our bodies are alive till we stay inside; they are dead the moment we leave.

Obviously, it would be in our benefit to know as to what we are doing in this mortal body? Why have we obtained a perishable body? If we are immortals, shouldn't we be in an immortal body as well?

The very purpose of sharing this understanding that "I" (atma) have acquired over a period of a lifetime is to let everyone derive the potential benefit there is with this knowledge, just as I have benefited immensely. This thought is in line with the famous saying in tamizh *"yAn petra inbam, peruga vaiyagam"*—"May the joy I experienced, be experienced by all in the world"—sharing this knowledge with everyone to make a difference to those who can absorb the essence of the knowledge and practice it. They can see the benefits soon enough. For even those who do not relate to these values or would like to try it out just in case it might work, without the conviction, may still see the positive impact when practiced. Once they do, they will hold on to it. Those who do not want to try, worried about the possible ill effects, can be assured that there are no negative effects in following a lifestyle based on these thoughts. For, it does not cost anything at all, materially or emotionally. There is no need to change in the way we live, we can continue to do everything that we always loved doing, but just with a proper understanding about what we do and why we do them. This would bring about a purpose and reasoning to all our actions; being in a state of *consciousness* in everything we do, always being aware. With the awareness comes a lasting fulfillment and fearlessness about the unknown adverse consequences. There should be no adverse consequence when we do everything in total consciousness and hence the cause itself would be good and so would be the effect. There are only positives coming from this.

Atma is eternal.

Great sages, Rishis, Saints, Azhwars and Acharyas have taken birth here to bestow upon us the true knowledge about the 'jivatma' and its relationship with the Lord and how we can attain immortality. When we acquire this knowledge, it enables our progression towards immortality.

The joy of seeing others benefit is in itself a great reward. There is a big difference between sharing knowledge that can lead to finding eternal solutions than sharing ones material wealth that can provide temporary relief within this life. While the latter is considered a great service, nothing can be greater than the former. After all, life for the Soul does not end with this body.

Surely enough, everything that has a beginning, must end. But the Soul neither has a beginning nor an end. Life does not end for the Atma with the death of a body; it is a continuous process till he chooses to end this process, consciously. The true nature of the Atma is explained in Gita thus:

Gita 2-18—
    "antavanta imE dehAnityasyoktAh SarIriNah . . ."

"These bodies with the embodied self are said to have an end while the Atma itself is eternal, indestructible and incomprehensible"

Gita 2-20—
    "na jAyatE mriyatE vA kadAchinnAyam bhUtvA . . ."

"The Atma is never born, it never dies, having come into being, it never ceases to be. Unborn, eternal, abiding and primeval, Atma is not slain when the body is slain"

Gita 2-22—
    "vAsAmsi jIrNAni yathA vihAya navAni gruhNAti . . ."

"Just as a man takes off worn-out garments and puts on the new ones, so does the embodied Atma cast off worn-out bodies and enter into new ones"

Gita 2-28—
    "avyaktAdIni bhUtAni vyakta madhyAni bhArata . . ."

"Beings have an unknown beginning, a known middle and an unknown end. What is there to grieve over in all this?"

Needless to say, souls deserve to be in a body that they don't have to change. *Immortal soul in an immortal body makes the right combination!* And that is possible.

It is contrary to the inherent nature of the Atma, who is an immortal, to have chosen to go through mortal life cycles, by a choice made in an impulse to experience the changing world; has gotten himself into the vicious cycle of birth and death. Surely he is not relishing this mortality experience which also comes with its share of many qualitative diseases such as— kama (desire), krodha (untamed anger), lobha (avarice), moha (obsession), madha (haughtiness), matsarya (jealousy/envy) combined with pain, sorrow, suffering, fear, intolerance, grief etc. *Though mortality brings with it, its share of pain and suffering; there is a potential to experience momentary pleasure due to contact with sense objects, which, we perceive as happiness. But this is not the real happiness that we are all seeking.*

We may ask as to why it should be a problem to go through mortal life cycles. For some, it may seem to work well, as they might not have seen much suffering in their life or if they did have their share of both happy moments and problems; they were able to bear the swinging moments of joy and sorrow due to their prime state of endurance. But things may, and will change very quickly, with in a life. No one is guaranteed of only happy moments. Those who think they have the best of life, are saying so because they have not experienced the superior happiness, transcendental in nature. We are like a frog in a well, thinking that the well is the whole universe and there is nothing beyond. But those who know that there is a better state of existence would also understand what the others are missing. Even great personalities have gone through ups and downs. A Steve Jobs or a Princess Diana and many like them had things going their way till some things changed. I am sure Steve Jobs would have liked to live longer, if not for ever; and keep doing what came to him naturally. He even spoke about life being short and was constantly bothered by the fact that life in this body had to end so soon.

I can assure that many of us would like to live forever, if it was in our control to do so; if we did not have to grow old; if it was possible to be in youth forever, wealthy, strong and healthy, everything going well eternally. *Our inclination to live on decreases as the body grows old, our vision and organs failing; our mind active and wishing to experience so much more but our body not co-operating, even the brain failing; then we begin to lose interest in life as the body becomes frail; we prefer to let go of this body as it becomes unbearable to endure the misery of old age and the inability associated with it. It is the condition of the body and its deteriorating functionality that deters us from wanting to go on living.* If not for that, if we could indulge in nonstop pleasures, we would much prefer to be in that state than think of dying. But even the most pleasurable life here is not the happiness that we want to experience. What we want is just not available here, in this world.

Human life is so fragile. There is a very thin line between life and death. From the moment we are born, we progress towards death. Every minute we keep advancing towards death. Every day spent takes us closer to death, as though we have taken birth merely to die. Though we die many times in between as the body keeps changing, total death of the body occurs only when the Soul departs from the body.

We may then ask, as to what is the proof that there is life after death or proof that there is birth and death continuously for the same Soul. The proof is simple and easy if we can comprehend—that since our birth in this body, our body has been witnessing many births and deaths—our red blood cells die and new ones are born every few days, all of our body parts including the hardest part—the skeleton—are totally replaced in 6 months. Literally every 6 months our old body is dead and new one is born—I will have died and re-born 200 times in this life if I live for 100 years! We can even see the physical changes in our body from infancy to childhood—to teenage-youth—to middle age and old age. All these stages that we witness are death and birth taking place periodically. But we are not aware of it. It is the Soul that keeps the continuity going, thinking he is in the same body since birth. Similarly, when the body becomes dysfunctional or when the Soul completes his term in the body, he has to relinquish this body and will go on to get another, based on his entitlement (karma). The Atma will not have the knowledge of his previous body after getting into a new body, just as we are not aware of several deaths and rebirths in our body with in this life.

Gita 2/13—
   "dEhinosminyathAdEhE kaumAram yauvanam jarA . . ."

"Just as the Atma (soul) associated with a body passes through childhood, youth and old age (pertaining to the body), so too (at death of the body) the Soul passes into another body. A wise man is not deluded by this".

If this is hard to see, then we may not be able to understand many realities that are true and happening but we are not aware of and will stay that way.

Matter and Divine

We know that the earth is rotating on its axis with a surface speed of 1670 km/hour (1040 miles/hour) at the equator, which is the reason for our day and night; and it is floating in space, revolving around the sun at an astonishing speed of about 107000 km/hour (66600 miles per hour), which is how we get our seasons. We cannot feel either the rotation or the revolution around the sun or the speeds. We know of gravity but cannot feel its difference till we are taken to a no gravity zone, or to another planet to feel the differential gravity or to our moon where relative gravity is 6 times less than (17% of weight on earth) that on earth. We would never have known this truth till the scientists showed us live videos and pictures of these realities.

Earth and Sun are very insignificant in size, in comparison to the larger scheme of things in the universe. The same scientists who could show us certain aspects of earth and solar system do not have a clue about the origin, and functioning of the universe. They have recently claimed to have found the existence of dark energy everywhere, but also claim that the dark energy cannot be seen. They do not know anything about it except that it exists. We accept their word because they are scientists who have given us proof for many other things. Yet this could be a hypothesis or it could be true. Learning is a continuous, ongoing process. The reason why we are able to see the Earth, Sun and the way they function is because of the potential of the body we are in. Ours is a material body and so are the Earth, planets, Sun and stars in the universe. Our body and this universe are made from the same 5 elements of nature. There is compatibility for a physical body being used to know of the physical universe. Even in that, we need the help of certain gadgets to see. We use telescope to see distant galaxies as they are not visible to the human eye. We can see micro organisms only through microscope.

When it comes to the capabilities of our senses and body, it is a package that has limitations. We cannot know of the soul or God using our mind and senses. Souls and God are divine and superior in nature than the material senses and material worlds. The Soul is not made from the elements of nature that are non-sentient. Hence, it is beyond the non sentient to know of the divine Soul or God. Our body is like a machine that can perform certain functions and it cannot function by itself. It needs a power that can make it function and the Soul is that power.

Though we do not know much about even the physical universe; when it comes to God, we are mislead into thinking that someone should show God as a proof of His existence. If material eye cannot see the material world that is beyond its scope, how can we expect to be able to see God who is divine and not material? *Only divine can see divine, feel divine and experience divine.* Souls are divine, *sentient* beings and are part or *amsh* or potency of that Supreme Power we call God (not a fractional part as Paramatman is indivisible). It is possible only for the Soul to experience God. For us to realize this, we need to make an effort seeking God's grace, and God alone can empower us to know about Him. We are not willing to do anything for that ultimate state of being in a divine, eternal body that matches with our own nature. In the divine body, the Soul will not have constraints that it experiences in a material body. A Soul in a divine body can see, feel and experience both matter and divine.

It would be amazing, rather amusing to realize that we are all of the same age or ageless for that matter. I am referring to the Atma and not about our bodies. Even God is not elder to us when it comes to age. We (all the souls) and God are of the same age or ageless. Both God and souls are unborn and will never cease to be. For that matter even this universe is eternal, except that it goes through changes of formation and dissolution; similar to the birth and death of the bodies we acquire.

When we say 'God', we are inclined to call it religion. In reality, God and about God does not have to be religion or philosophy. *Knowledge about God is the greatest science there can be and God is the Supreme Scientist.*

We don't have to call Him God if we have a problem with that, we can call Him anything we want, a superman (without the limitations of the comic hero we know), if that sounds better. The religions and philosophies have evolved to enable humans to understand God better. Divine souls, who are messengers of God, took birth here to enlighten us about the transcendental knowledge that can lead to higher state of existence. Many, who trusted their grace and followed their prescribed ways of life, have attained the ultimate state that each one of us wants. Some others disillusioned, believed this world is where they belong and this life is all there is, convinced in their perception, continued with their journey of repeated births and deaths. Yet others that did not have faith in the message, as they could not perceive beyond a physical level, showed much disregard for religion and God.

Some, who are religious, are intolerant towards others following a different religion. Their behaviour is due to ignorance. Neither it is religion nor would any God associate with them. *To be religious means to show extreme love and care about God and His creation. All living beings are His creation and originate from Him. If we love God, we should also love everyone belonging to God and related to God.* *True religion is a way of life filled with compassion for everyone.*

Living beings are conscient beings. They have feelings, emotions; can feel pain and pleasure which is purely due to their association with the body. Some of us are less privileged due to our past karma. However, if some of us are better placed to take care of our needs and in addition be able to help relieve others from pain and suffering, we shall do so. We could get into a problem situation anytime soon and would wish for help from others. *God does not involve directly in helping us; he reaches out to us within the karmic framework, through others.*

We have seen that when pain becomes unbearable, a person becomes unconscious. Why is it so? It is so due to God's kindness. He does not want us to experience extreme pain that goes beyond our endurance levels. We remain conscious till pain is bearable.

We show so much importance in keeping everyone comfortable physically and emotionally, because that is what life in this body is all about. Hospitality and warmth are part of a big business today. People are willing to spend a lot of money just for that experience of being wanted in a place, for the physical and mental comfort. *Life is all about being happy, feeing good in a nice way without causing hurt, harm, pain and suffering to*

the self or the others. At the same time, I cannot claim to be
happy by doing bad things to others.

Sense gratification and happiness

Being happy is not a state of indulging in pleasure seeking
activities. Physical comfort is different from pleasure. However
keeping one physically comfortable is important; for physical
discomfort could be painful and the focus is to avoid pain.

Happiness is a state of mind; we can be in a state of constant
happiness without having to do anything physically. To connect
our happiness to physical pleasures is to limit ourselves to
certain happiness. Anything physical has a limitation. Why
should we limit our happiness to what our body can do? It is due
to ignorance that we associate sense gratification to being in a
state of happiness. You do not feel pain by not indulging in sense
gratification. Physical pleasures are momentary; they have a
limitation and can also result in pain if extended.

We can recognize each living being as the Atma who is the
enjoyer; who is the experiencer in all bodies; understand the true
nature and potential of Atma being a natural seeker of happiness;
one who is knowledgeable and who originates from God. And we
are all part of the same God.

Gita 5/18—
  "vidya vinaya sampannE brAhmaNE gavi hastini . . ."

"The sages look with an equal eye—a person endowed with
learning and humility, a brahmana, a cow, an elephant, a dog and
a dog-eater".

People with correct understanding know the real nature of the
Atma in all beings, though they are perceived in different bodies.

The dissimilarity is observed because of their different bodies which they have obtained due to karma; but the souls in all the bodies are same as the self. And the same God resides in all of them.

Each living being feels good just as I feel good when in happiness and by the same token, he can suffer pain just as I do. All great men have always said "do unto others what you would like them to do unto you". All our lives we work so hard in order to avoid pain for the self, family and friends closely associated with us. That is also the reason why we have a legal system in place to punish those who cause pain and suffering to others, physically or emotionally. Life is all about feeling good and happy. Every living being should try to contribute to the others' happiness. If that is not possible, at least, shall not intentionally disturb their happiness. If we develop mutual care, then there would be no crime, hate and envy in the world.

True love is universal

The so called love between men and women, not bound by the lifetime marriage, when a man says to a woman "I love you" or the woman to a man, is not the true love in the real sense. It is an expression by two selfish people, of lust and infatuation for seeking physical pleasure, when they engage in illicit relationships, in the name of love. We can see that it is not the same when parents say the same thing to kids and kids to them. *True love is an unconditional affection and care for the other person's well being without any sense gratification or pleasure for the self with that person.* Marriage is a lifetime companionship of understanding, support, trust, friendship, reliability and unconditional love. Love is not meant to be expressed only to the physical aspects between the husband and wife. A married couple can be in love even without physical contact. Their love will not increase or decrease based on their ability to seek sense gratification. True love and marriage is forever, for a full life time; which is the reason there would be no divorce in a true marriage.

True love can be shown towards every one. You can love a friend, you can love your mother, father, brother, son and daughter; you can love your country and countrymen, the whole of humanity and creation, and God. You do not expect any sense gratification from any of these people. And such true affection shall be extended to one and all without exception. It really costs nothing to be affectionate to all. Today, the word love is more often used to signify physical pleasure sought between man and woman. Their love can end and turn into hate, the moment the degree of pleasure diminishes.

The relationships that we acquire in this world are only through the body and will be gone soon as the body falls. But the relationships of the souls are eternal, coming from the same source. Relationships of the body are external; my father in this life is in another body. I recognize my father with his body and not the Soul. But God, who is our real Father, is our innerself. He has never been separate from us even for a moment and will stay that way for eternity. Now think for a moment; if the relationships we identify with bodies that are temporary and will be gone after death are greater, or God who is always with us and will remain so, forever? God loves us more than we can love Him. Our relatives love us only based on our usefulness. Even a trivial issue such as a difference of opinion can bring in dislike; at least momentarily.

If we are all universally related to each other, then why is that we show special affection for our own families and not to others? We take birth in families owing to our past guna (nature) and karma (deeds). We are duty bound and obligated to take care of our dependants. Likewise every person is duty bound to provide for the needs of his dependants. Does that mean we have no duty to others not related to us by birth? No, once we are able to take care of all our family needs, we must also consider helping others, with the excess resources in our possession, because not everyone is privileged or positioned to take care of his family needs.

True relationships

Relationships are the essence of life, be it in this world, or with God. The whole world exists on account of relationships. All of humanity lives for the sake of relationships. Even animals and birds that can perceive relationships find their motivation to survive and fight, in preserving and protecting relationships. Relationship is the very purpose around which the structure of our families, societies, nations and the world on the whole is built and functioning. However, the relationships in the mortal world are temporary, inconsistent, and varying. Our eternal relationship is with the Supreme Lord alone. My father in this life might not have been my father in the previous life or may not be in the next. Similarly, all our relationships change in every life, for we might be born as animals or other species. Each one of us is related differently to so many—as a son/daughter, brother, friend, father, husband etc.

True relationships are not based on what favours or benefits we can get. Sri Pillailokacharyar gives us insight on relationships to be practiced, in Srivachanabhushanam—112, thus—

> **"guNakruta dAsyattilum kAttil swarUpa prayuktamAna dAsyamirE pradhAnam"**

"Abiding by natural relationship unconditionally is essential than based on benefits or usefulness out of the relationship"

Relationships are classified under "swarUpa prayukta dAsyam" (unconditional relationship, based on the nature of relationship) or *"guNa kruta dAsyam"* (conditional relationship based on benefits and usefulness out of the relationship).

*Srivachanabhushanam 113—**"anasUyaikku pirAtti aruLicheyda vArttaiyai smarippadu"**—"remember the words uttered by Divine Mother Sita to Anasuya"*

Rightfully, we are expected to practice 'swarUpa prayukta dAsyam" (unconditional relationship). One who abides by the relationship based on the nature of the relationship, remaining unchanged in his perception about the person, regardless of the benefits from him or her. However, if a relative is evil minded and hurting or harming the peace, we can decide to stay away from such a person, without hate and enmity. It is very important to be associated with virtuous people even if they are not our relatives and stay away from those who are wicked even if they are our relatives, as we are easily influenced in acquiring either good or bad qualities due to our association with people.

I shall obey and respect my parents, unconditionally, irrespective of their virtues and qualities; whether rich or poor, good looking or ugly, whether they do things I expect of them or not, whether they have social status or not. Does not matter what they are, they are still my parents. This is also true for all other relationships and those not related to us as well. All those who are not related to us physically, are related to us through God.

Parahlada respected and loved his father Hiranyakashipu for being his father; however, he did not accept his father's ways and conveyed to him the truth fearlessly that he was wrong. If a father is sinful, a son shall not abide as guided by the father, yet show the dignity and respect that his father deserves.

This is exactly what Mother Sita explains to Sati Anasuya in Sri Ramayana when the latter suggests to Sita that her pAtivratyam (being a devout wife) to Rama was convenient as Rama was "shodaSa guNa paripUrNah",—"endowed with 16 perfect virtues". Rama was a perfect man in all respects; there are only glorious attributes in Him, devoid of defilement. Even those who considered Him as their enemy, those who were killed by Rama, sung His glories openly, and hence it does not take an effort to practice "swarUpa prayukta dAsyam" to Him. After all, Rama is the 'embodiment' of Dharma. Same with Krishna, "Krishnam dharmam sanAtanam"

Valmiki asks Narada if there was any one in this world, with the following virtues—"*kah nu asmin sAmpratam lokE guNavAn, kascha vIryavAn, dharmajnascha, krutajnascha, satya vAkhyo, drudhavratah. ChAritrENacha koyuktah, sarva bhUteshu kohitah, vidvAn kah, kassamarthascha, kaschaika priyadarsanah. AtmavAn ko jitakrodhah, dyutimAn ko anasUyakah, kasya bibyati dEvascha jAtaroshasya samyuge*".

Here Valmiki lists out the 16 qualities

1. gunavan (virtuous)
2. viryavan (invincible, undefeatable/ valiant)
3. dharmajnah (righteous, conscientious)
4. krutajnah (grateful)
5. satyavakhyah (truth-teller, or would fulfill his word)
6. drudhavratah (self-determined, steadfast, resolute)
7. charitrena yuktah (of impeccable character, blemishless)
8. sarvabhuteshu hitah (benign well wisher of all beings)
9. vidvan (omniscient, all-knowing)
10. samartah (omnipotent, all-capable)
11. priyadarshanah (bewitching, captivating, pleasant looking),
12. atmavan (master of all beings),
13. jitakrodhah (who has conquered anger)
14. dyutiman (of—lustrous, resplendent, glowing personality)
15. anasuyakah (un-envious) and
16. bibyati devah (even feared by the gods (devas).

Narada confirms to Valmiki that the merits which he has extolled are many and unattainable even for great emperors, let alone ordinary humans. Rama alone possesses the virtues he mentioned.

Anasuya continues—"When you have a husband like Rama, it is very convenient to be in your position practicing your natural relationship with a perfect man, and yet you get the glory of being a 'pativrata'".

Sita explains that her unconditional devotion to Rama was not based on His qualities or status; she would still be the same to Him even if He was ugly, if he was not a king, not having all the virtues. In the same way, Rama accepted Guha (hunter), Sugriva (monkey king), and Vibhishana (a rakshasa and brother of Ravana) as His brothers, unconditionally, irrespective of their status in comparison to His own. So did Krishna, who accepted Sudhama, and all his gopala and gopika friends.

We normally love and show affection when people do things we want; say things we like. We deal with God in the same way as well. We worship God because we think He can take care of our problems. We should worship Him because of our eternal relationship with Him, not because of the benefits we can derive from Him.

If we maintain relationships based on usefulness, our affection is only to the extent of their usefulness and not with them.

Our problem is that we look at people and relationships like products. We are used to 'use-and throw' when it comes to products and we deal with people and relationships in the same way. Use people till they are beneficial; disregard them when they are not.

Body-universe & Soul-God

Our non-sentient material body is compatible with this non-sentient material universe and the sentient Soul is compatible with the super sentient, divine God. *God formed this universe for the benefit of the bodies we take, and the Soul having certain similarities with God Himself, would benefit being with Him.*

Our bodies are made of the same matter that the universe comprises of. But the souls belong to the superior sentient power of God. The goal for all souls should naturally be to acquire a divine body that can match with its own nature and potential. Outcome—unlimited, unending, ever-growing divine joy in the company of the supreme God. Sri Azhagiyamanavala Perumal Nayanar (acharyahrudayam 1-10) sums up in one sutra as to how we can either choose to live in this material world or with God thus:

". . . achidayanAnAdi sambandhangaL"

"**achit**" signifies our bodies and this world; '**ayana**" denotes God. We can choose what we want. Naturally, we have done whatever was needed to remain in this world. However, we have to do what it takes to seek God, if we want to be with God.

It is natural for the eternal Soul to aspire for immortality.

Each one of us originates (like a drop of water in the ocean, with its distinct identity intact) from that supreme power, God. The prime identity of the Supreme Lord is 'Anandamaya'; of the nature of 'infinite bliss'; and the identity of the Atman is 'vijnanamaya', of the nature of 'knowledge'. The definition of science is 'to know', science is 'knowledge'. Atma is naturally intelligent and knowledgeable, which is the reason why we are on a constant quest for knowing, learning, discovering, inventing;

exploring etc.—about us and about our universe. We can know to some extent about our physical universe, using the limited capabilities of our senses and mind, but not about the Atma or Paramatma, on our own.

The potential of the Atma is much beyond this material universe and it should be our goal to soar higher and beyond this universe, knowing our true potential and attaining what we deserve; reaching where we belong.

We do not know all about our universe as a lot of it is still invisible matter and energy. But it is not easy for us to comprehend about Souls or God as both are invisible, immutable. At least, even if we cannot see the Soul, we can feel that we are the life, the driving force in our body. The soul keeps the body alive even when in a state of coma or brain dead, without the consciousness.

What is the proof for our existence in our respective bodies—a person answered thus "I think, therefore I am"; implying that if not for my existence, there can be no thoughts or actions using the body. The correct answer though is "I am, therefore I think", meaning that I exist even without thinking; however, there can be no thoughts without me, because I am the thinker. To think or doing actions is a choice I make, I am not dependent on the body for my existence.

Proof of God's existence

We are aware of our existence in the body. But we cannot realize or know of God using our non sentient mind and senses. However, the Soul can communicate with God through his mind seeking Him. Though we cannot hear God, He knows our thoughts. Though we cannot see Him, He is seeing us, always.

Svetasvatara Upanishad—3-19 declares Lord's capabilities thus:

> *"apANipAdo javano grahItA paSyatya chakshuh*
> *sa SruNotya karNah . . ."*

"Without hands or feet He is swift in movement and he grasps, He sees without eyes. He hears without ears. He knows all that is to be known. There is none who knows Him. They say He is the first cause and the Great Self"

This verse explains that the Supreme Lord is omniscient and infinite in His capabilities and functions without the limitations of senses and mind which we possess with limited perceptibility. *There is no soul and body differentiation in God. He, His body, His senses and mind are all one and the same, unlike the souls which are different from the bodies they acquire.* That's why scriptures declare that His body is divine and same as Himself, termed as "divya mangala vigrahaya". There is no such a thing as embodied God or Paramatma, for He is His body and His body is He.

Sri Thondaradippodi azhwar confesses to the Lord in his thirumAlai

> *"uLLuvAruLLattellAm udanirudaridiyennu*
> *veLgippoyennuLLE nAn vilavarachirithittEnE"*—

"You are right there in everyone's heart knowing our thoughts, even before our mind can process the thoughts. On knowing this, I could not withhold my hilarity, for I thought I could evade you".

There is an illustration in the Upanishads about how the Soul and God function, when the Soul assumes a body.

-Svetasvataropanishad—4-6

*"dwA suparnA sayujA sakhAyA samAnam vruksham
parishasvajAte . . ."*

"Two birds of similar qualities which are inseparable from each
other are perched on the same tree. One enjoys the pippala fruit
and the other is witnessing without enjoying the fruit";

Here the two birds are—jivatma and paramatma.

There is a distinction between the Jivatma and Paramatma.
Though both are connected with prakruti, the jivatma is involved
in enjoying his association with the bodies (prakruti) while the
Paramatma is not. The similarity indicated between Jivatma and
Paramatma here relates to the fact that they are both endowed
with knowledge (of varying degree though) and both are eternal
and unchanging. 'Pippalam' is the effect of karma—to which the
jivatma is subjected to, where as the Paramatma is not, as He is
beyond karma.

One bird (atma) is actively participating and enjoying the fruits of the tree and the other bird (God) who is the innerself of the Atma, is merely an observer, witnessing the activities of the bird (atma). He does not participate in the activities nor enjoys the fruits. The tree here is the human body.

The same Upanishad further states 4-7—"*samAnE vrukshE purusho nimaghnah anIsayA sochati muhyamAnah . . .*"

"Being deluded by prakruti, the atma grieves as he is involved in the same tree. When he realizes the presence of the Lord in him who is distinct from him, and who is pleased when atma sees this entire world as the glory of that Lord, he becomes free from grief"

Since Jivatma considers the body as the self, suffers the effects of karma and when the Atma realizes the presence of Paratmatma who is distinct from the self, who is the upholder, controller and master (*dhAraka, niyantA* and *seshI*) the Lord is pleased with the *subservience* and worship of the Atma. When the Atma becomes aware that this universe is the effect of His omnipotence, such a Soul becomes free from grief.

Imagine someone who has never tasted anything sweet, you cannot describe or express the 'sweet taste' to him. Even if you do, he would not know the taste. The only way for him to know is to taste something sweet. Effectively, experiencing God's grace is also something similar; it cannot be shown or explained. If you follow the prescribed way of life, you can experience it yourself. There is no other way. And by following the prescribed lifestyle, you do not have to give up on anything you like. In fact your life now becomes much more enjoyable and will also get you the best life ahead, after this.

One may ask—what if all this is utter nonsense about God and His existence? Why should we waste our time and effort in pursuit of something that we don't even know exists? And how possibly can that make our lives better?

The greatest mystery is that, though the human body has 9 gates (exits—two eye sockets, two nostrils, two ears, mouth and two excretory outlets) the invisible life (soul) could escape from the body through any of these gates, but does not. It leaves the body only when the body becomes dysfunctional or when the Soul completes its term in the body. It is the Soul that supports the body, keeping it alive, making it function; from an insect to an elephant. So we do not have a dispute here about the Soul being the power that keeps the body alive. The disagreement could only be about God as we are unable to see Him, feel Him, and experience Him normally, like we can feel the self in the body.

What is the proof for God's existence? We do know that we breathe without our conscious effort. We neither do anything to feel hungry nor are we involved in digesting the food. Our heart beats by itself pumping blood and energy to all parts of the body without our active participation. **Every vital part in the body functions without our involvement, even during sleep. This is proof enough that there is another Superior Power that enables everything in our body.** That apart, the presiding gods of nature, work nonstop in keeping our body functioning. **We are not alive in the body with our effort nor can we stop our death despite all our effort.**

We have the power of choice to using our mind, senses and body to function, but empowered by the Lord dwelling in the Soul. Whatever we do as a choice is with our involvement. Our staying alive in the body; and the body functioning even without our active participation is due to the presence of God in us. It is similar to our switching on to get the bulb glowing. I would say the bulb is glowing because I switched it on. However, if the bulb continues to glow even when I switch it off, what would we say? The bulb glows even when I switch if off, because there is another power that constantly supplies energy and keeps the bulb glowing even when we switch off; similar to all key factors working when we sleep. We are not alive in the body because of our choice and will to stay alive but because of the will and power of the Lord keeping us alive and functioning. It is the Lord who protects us in the body, keeping our immune system and self healing mechanism working nonstop.

We are functioning in our bodies by the power of the Lord who is our inneself; He is the one who enables us to using our bodies, senses, mind and intellect. With this realization, our impression would change, accepting the presence of the Lord in us. Just as we can feel the self, we should include the Lord in every thought, action, to realize His presence in us. This is termed as '**Abhimukhyatavam**' (turning towards God) which is the improved stage of '**advEsham**' (not turning away from God) and when we get the realization that God is our innerself, we would experience that bliss. We can see a total change from then on in our life.

Chapter Two

How is God the cause for this universe and us?

We often question as to why there should be a God and why He should be the reason for the existence of worlds and creatures including humans. Even the greatest of human minds have this doubt, in that they are not sure if their understanding is correct. Is it human weakness to think of God as the reason for everything existing? At least that's what one of the greatest scientists, Albert Einstein, thinks in his letter thus; "**The word God is for me nothing more than the expression and product of human weaknesses**". By the same token, if we say that the '**Soul**' in all the bodies of humans and other species, is the reason for their being alive; is that an expression of our weakness to think so? Are all the living beings that are being born, living a lifetime, happening without the Soul in them?

Only a questioning mind can understand and perceive God to an extent. *Realization of God is not forced upon anyone, nor can it be realized by force, nor can one understand God following blindly. Only a person with an open mind can understand about God.*

No scientific experiment can show us the Soul or God, for both are divine and beyond the realm and scope of this non sentient world. Soul and God can only be realized through knowledge of sacred scriptures.

What is the proof that there is a cause for our universe? Could the universe not have formed by itself, exist by itself and perish by itself. And go through the cycle of formation, existence and dissolution, repeatedly, endlessly as well? And there are several factors (laws of universe or universal properties) for the universe to exist and function, such as, gravity (which does not apply at sub-atomic levels!!), mass, space, etc. if you remove one thing from the equation, the universe cannot function! Is it possible for the non-sentient universe to form these laws for its own existence and functioning?

If someone told us that the buildings and everything that is made or built in the world happened by themselves and no one built them, would we accept? If someone declares that the masterpieces of art, the great paintings happened without any artist creating them, is it not questionable? This is true for all the non living things for they cannot either cause or function by themselves. They are lifeless, they have no potential or capability to cause themselves or function on their own. Non living things have no knowledge or intelligence. A thing without knowledge or intelligence cannot cause itself or anything else.

The computers and robots did not come about by themselves; they did not become functional by writing up their own programming, for they are inanimate, lifeless things. Even the programs are lifeless. The computers and robots function because they have been programmed to function in a certain way. This universe is also programmed with all its energies and properties to function in the way it does.

We have to be living beings in order to make, build or programme. Only living beings can reproduce, cause, create and function; non living things cannot.

The nature of the Soul is knowledge and intelligence while the physical matter of this universe or things we build, have no knowledge and are lifeless.

We are able to see the bodies of programmers, but not their individual souls in their respective bodies. Likewise, in the case of the maker of this world, who is the all pervading inner-soul of this universe, we are unable to see Him. What we see as universe is indeed the creator's body.

We know that we did not cause this universe or ourselves. Obviously, it would have to be a distinctly superior living power than us, with super intelligence and super knowledge that could have caused this universe and the souls into existence. And that super power must be omnipotent, omniscient and omnipresent with infinite capabilities to have been able to cause infinite numbers of souls and this infinite universe. And that super power must have been unborn, without beginning or end. He would have existed even before the universes, souls and beings were caused by Him, from Him.

If I told that theory of relativity was not derived by Einstein or Wright brothers did not invent the airplane, they would take umbrage with such a statement. Now who would be upset? The body of Einstein? Even if he is alive, his body is not capable of any feelings or emotions. It would have been the Soul, due to its association with the body, who would have felt offended when someone disclaims the truth. However, I would not be able to see the soul of Einstein even if he is alive in his body now, so can I say that all his inventions and similar other inventions by all the scientists happened by themselves for no one could see the real 'soul' in them. Or had we retained their dead bodies after their souls departed, to come up with more inventions, would they, really? We have preserved Einstein's brains; can it function now without the soul in his body? Realistically, their bodies are lifeless by themselves or dead the moment the souls exited their bodies. Bodies by themselves cannot do anything except decay. The ones who were the reason for all the activities of their bodies cannot be seen. Just because we cannot see the souls, does that prove that their bodies were functioning without the soul in them?

Simple logic and scientific thinking would tell us that a Soul cannot function without a body; the body on its own is lifeless matter. Similarly, this physical universe is lifeless matter on its own and it is functioning because of the power of the supreme Lord in it, who is all pervasive.

However, God would not be offended when we deny His existence or for not acknowledging His being the cause of this universe due to our ignorance. We cannot see Him, for He is in unmanifest form dwelling in every atom, every sub-atomic particle of His world, including the souls. Just as we cannot see the soul in a living, functional body, we cannot see God in this living functioning universe. There will be a time when this universe will disappear or die. Then we cannot see the universe either, till a new universe is born.

The souls are similar to God for they originate from Him and yet, God is distinctly superior and different to the souls.

The proof that someone caused this universe is in the fact that this universe is inanimate and lifeless matter and hence cannot come to exist by itself. The fact that our bodies are made from the same matter and elements that this universe is made of, is evident that our bodies and universe are not different from one another. Just as the souls keep the body alive and functioning, the indwelling God keeps this universe alive and functioning.

Universe manifested from God who is also the innerself of the manifest universe. God is independent and absolute, while the universe and souls are dependent on Him to exist and function. God is inseparable from the universe and souls, for He is in them, as well as outside of them. In all the states—formation, functioning or merged into God—they are inseparable from God.

When the souls and universe merge into God, He exists alone as far as this changing universe is concerned, for there is an immortal world as well! Though He is our source, our eternal Father, we are not willing to accept His role in causing us or the universe. That's how much gracious He is. He lets us say anything about Him, even deny His existence. He knows only one thing, to love us, care for us, provide for us to be happy and well off. He created this universe, indeed, for our sake, as we sought to experience change and independent existence.

If all this is hard to understand and realize, I am afraid we are belying the basic nature of the soul—knowledge and intelligence. Our problem is that we go into denial mode the moment something is beyond our comprehension. We tend to negate the existence of anything we cannot understand or perceive or control. God is divine and infinite in all respects and hence cannot be perceived by us without His Grace. We can know only so much about Him for He cannot be fully known. So far, we seem to know only about 4% of this universe. If we can make an effort to know of the self first, it would be possible to know about the universe or God.

Eternal journey in the mortal world.

If we consider the countless number of years the soul has spent journeying in different bodies, relatively, it is like giving a person only a fraction of a second as duration he would get to stay in a house and he would have to move on to another house the next fraction of a second, and so on. If I was told that I have to change homes every fraction of a second, I would say that I might as well not stay in such a house at all.

Based on our nature, we would prefer to avoid being in this situation and work towards owning a house, without any bother of moving out. If we can relate to the time we spend in bodies of humans, animals, insects etc to the total duration of one cycle of creation of a Brahma and his worlds, which is about 309.173 trillion earthly years, the time we spend in different bodies is insignificantly minuscule. And even this cycle of creation and dissolution of the worlds and of Brahma, is cyclical and unending.

If we own the house but only for a fraction of a second and then the house would become dysfunctional and we would get another house which may be better or worse, based on the quality of life we live in the earlier house, again, only for a moment; we would be unhappy with the quality of the house if it is worse than the earlier one, and if it is better than the previous house, the duration of stay being momentary, still a big worry.

Considering each of the 8.4 million bodies as a house we acquire, in that, the similar body we re-obtain would be different qualitatively, each and every time. For instance, we could get a human body countless times. But the quality of life, happiness or suffering would not be the same every time. Not only do we have to suffer life in different bodies, but also we would not have the same potential and experience in the same type of body, repeatedly. *So there is no 'body' that can keep us happy totally; nor would we get a 'body' that we can keep forever.*

One may say that it is this change that he likes to experience in different bodies or different experiences in the same type of body but with different potential, each time. However, he should realize that he has been going through just that for eternity, until now. We have experienced life in all types of bodies, billions of times. Imagine our every day as new life in a new body without the memory of the previous day. We may have some great days, some normal and some painful days. When our day is full of joyous moments, we feel greatly motivated to experience much more of the same, every day. However, when the next day ends up being an utterly painful one, everything going wrong morning to evening, even the night becoming dreadful depriving us of good sleep, we don't feel inspired about life, fearing the next day would be the same or could be even worse. For, experiencing pain and suffering is against the nature of the Atma, who naturally desires to experience unending joy. Only immortality can ensure that state of happiness.

Sri Azhagiyamanavalaperumal Nayanar states in his unequalled grantham "acharyahrudayam" thus—

> "**kAruNikanAna sarvEswaran arivila manisar uNarvennum sudarviLakkEtti . . . . NirmaiyinAl aruL seidAn**".

'The Lord out of benign grace, has given us—'the lacking in knowledge humans'—the sacred knowledge of the Vedas to realize our nature, to discriminate between good and evil, right and wrong, for our benefit, owing to His fluidic benevolence'.

It's alright if we have no way of knowing how to attain immortality. But God, out of unmatched kindness, has made us naturally intelligent; He has provided us with all the knowledge in the scriptures. He has personally incarnated to reveal His supreme nature. He has sent divine Azhwars and Acharyas from time to time to guide us. He has given us the ability to differentiate between right and wrong, do's and don'ts. If we fail to recognize what is in our benefit, after all this, we are ourselves the reason for the suffering we go through.

All our problems are self inflicted. If we make that resolve to effectively live life to our potential, we would not only be happy every moment of this life, but also attain immortality, which is the ultimate state we naturally seek.

Our plight is similar to the students who do not pass through, citing various reasons for their failures. They have the same intelligence just as the ones who pass through. They have the same study materials and guidance from the teachers that the good students have. The only difference is that they don't do what the good students do. The good students do their work promptly without being distracted by the temptations and attractions that would lead them astray; while the students who fail would come up with many reasons for not doing what they ought to have done.

In essence, God gave us the option to choose the world and life we wanted. We chose this world and hence are here. We have everything we need, we can know everything there is to know, yet we don't care to do what ought to be done and end up suffering the effects of our wrong choices and wrong actions.

Attaining immortality is not much different than passing through a degree course. In a college, there is grading based on the marks obtained. But with God, everyone who scores the minimum marks would go through. A student scoring a perfect 100 and a student scoring 50 would be promoted to immortality. This is how it works with devotion and love for God. YasodA, the mother of Krishna on one hand, who scores a perfect 100, which is a rarity and pUtanA, the ogress who feeds the infant Krishna, poisoned breast milk with the intent to kill Him—are both given the same 'paramapadam' (immortality). When asked how it was justified that Yasoda who has no equal, gets the same state of paramapadam as Putana the rakshasi (ogress), whose intent was killing Krishna?

Krishna agrees that there is no comparison. However, 'for the devotion of Putana who comes to feed Him, was pure and motherly, for there was no adulteration in her devotion. Her mind and Soul were totally devoted to Krishna alone. Though her intent was to kill Him, she deserved the eternal world. By granting her immortality He had paid her back, and does not remain indebted to her. However, even after granting Yasoda the paramapadam, He remains eternally indebted to her. Immortality is the highest and the best He can grant anyone.

It is easier to be a good person

It takes less effort to be righteous, and enjoying the effects of good karma than be a bad person, doing forbidden acts, inflicting pain and suffering to others and then suffering the painful effects of our karma.

It is easy to be a good person. To be a bad person, we need greater resolve to face the perilous outcome of our actions, knowing full well that the consequences would have to be borne sooner or later and with an element of uncertainty as well. Sinful persons would have to live life in constant fear. For some, it becomes a habit when they become seasoned sinners. But that does not help their cause. Eventually, they would have to suffer much more. When suffering becomes extreme, they too would wish to change, when they get the realization that it is their own doing that is the reason for their suffering. We cannot dodge God's laws of karma. We are accountable for every choice, every thought and every deed and *God does not decide what we should choose nor does He interfere when we face consequences*.

We know it is easy to speak the truth than to lie. Lying is difficult; for we have to come up with non real, imaginary situations in our mind, making up what doesn't exist, eventually leading to a confused state of mind, for we might have to fabricate several such lies in order to justify the preceding one. Then lying becomes a habit. We may even end up with loss of memory, for we might forget the truth ourselves. We would start believing the lie as the truth. We could even lose track of our own lies, in an illusion to convince ourselves as to which one of our lies could be a better truth that suits our ego and helps our situation. In the bargain we become our own adversary. No one causes our destruction more than the self.

Refrain from doing prohibited acts

Stealing is wrong and one shall not steal. Some people would not steal because of the fear of punishment and so, they try doing the crime in a way they can avoid being held by law. To them stealing is not considered a sin and would do it if they can get away.

There is a saying in tamizh *"kaLavum kattru mara"*—true translation would mean "learn even to steal, and forget it". Most speakers' have interpreted the essence of this saying thus—"steal once to know what it is to steal, and then give up stealing". If it is so, would it be proper to say that we are advocated to do everything once, including stealing, and then give up? Truly that is not the contention of this proverb. If it were so, we would be tempted to try even other things as killing and the list can become endless. Are we justified in doing a wrong act to learn it is wrong and then give it up? We know pretty well that stealing is wrong and it shall not be done. Then what is the true essence of this saying? Does it limit its scope only to stealing?

In reality, this proverb is about all acts *'ought not to be done'*. Stealing is quoted as an example. What it really means is that we should become aware of what is right and wrong. "Know what is wrong and forget doing it" is the true essence of this saying.

For someone who distinguishes between good and bad, right and wrong, would not steal a million dollars, even with the confirmed knowledge that no one will ever catch him with the crime. That is the essence of righteousness. If we do a crime and think that no one will know, we are being ignorant. There is God right inside us who would know of every thought, speech and action. We might escape from others, but not God.

It is in our wellbeing if we refrain from the following:

- ➢ Extra marital and illicit relationships
- ➢ Becoming addicted to alcohol, drugs and such
- ➢ Meat eating by killing animals etc.
- ➢ gambling

There is a line in Sanskrit about being truthful "*satyam brUyAt, priyam brUyAt, na brUyAt satyamapriyam, priyam cha nAnrutam brUyAt Esha dharmah sanAtanah*"

Speak only truth, but in a way that it is pleasing and harmless to others. Never speak the truth that may potentially harm others. Also, never speak untruth which might be pleasant, though. This is the path of timeless dharma.

How we present truth is as vital as the truth itself. It should be reported pleasantly so as not to hurt or cause harm to the person who receives the message. At the same time, we shall never speak a non-truth even if it can please others. This is important because we would lie for two reasons. One to save the self from ill effects of something we have done and two, to gain advantage from others who would fall for our lies to favour us.

We have even taken birth as gods in heaven and in the world of Brahma, which is considered the highest and best existence in the created world. The degree of happiness is several times more (beyond our comprehension) in heaven and other celestial worlds. Just for an idea—the body odor of celestial beings would smell fragrant unlike the foul smell emitted by us. Yet, even their happiness is material happiness and not divine bliss that all of us want. We would have even experienced being the king of the gods (Indra) in heaven, in one or more lives. Though the pleasures would be much longer lasting in the heavens, souls are still the same, going through fear in every body. Even the gods of the heaven possess the despicable qualities we have, such as kAma, krodha, lobha, moha, madha and mAtsarya.

KAma (desire for sense gratification, wealth acquisition, and power) is the cause for all our suffering. If we are successful in desire fulfillment, our desires multiply leading to intense greed (**Lobha**), which is even more dangerous for it would proliferate our kAma, having tasted success once. Surely, at some point of time, with the multiplied degree of desire, fulfillment would suffer a failure. It is then that kAma gives birth to **Krodha** (untamed anger).

When' kama' tastes success, it leads to 'Lobha' (intense kAma), if we fail to achieve as desired, it leads to 'krodha'.

'Krodha' tasting success or failure would both lead to '**moha**' (loss of consciousness). A person in this state does not see reasoning or discrimination of right and wrong. He would acquire by force, if unattainable otherwise. If he fails, the mind of an angry person would suffer delusion.

A man tasting success with his 'moha' enters the stage of '**madha**' (haughtiness or overbearing pride). In this stage he just takes whatever he wishes to acquire without the fear of consequence. When 'madha' rules supreme, a person cannot bear the sight of another in an enviable position. He would not hesitate to destroy them when his 'madha' turns into '**mAtsarya**' (envy, jealousy). He would suspect even a pious person as a competitor to his own state, ends up harming those he suspects to be better off than him for being his rival.

If a kid such as Druva does penance, the king of heaven is worried of losing his kingdom. He has to send his powerful gods to disturb his penance, for he does not know the purpose of Druva's penance. Should any one acquire any power anywhere in the world; the king of the heavens goes through sleepless nights. To him, every powerful person would have acquired the power to plan a coup on the heavenly throne.

A deluded Brahma

We can understand how even a Brahma can behave below ordinary when smitten by envy, from this story during Krishna's incarnation. Krishna, Balarama and all his cowherd friends, take the cows and calves to the gracing fields. Krishna was keeping them in divine bliss, playing his flute or they would engage in playing some game or the other, or they would eat sitting together. Krishna would share with his friends—butter, yogurt rice with varieties of tasty pickles, and all of them seemed to experience the divine bliss that is possible only in the eternal world.

Watching this, Brahma felt envious, for this was his creation and even Krishna was in his created world. Brahma wanted to show to them his superiority, for all the beings of this world were caused by his power. He could not comprehend the nature of joy they were sharing with each other, which even he has never experienced. He was able to feel that they were experiencing bliss of another level, unknown to him. While they were playing a game, Brahma makes them all vanish by his power. All the cowherds, all the cows and their calves, except Krishna and Balarama, vanished from the scene. Krishna knows of Brahma's thought instantly for He is the antaryami residing in all the Souls including that of the Brahma. He then manifests Himself as all the missing cows and cowherds and they continue playing as though everything was normal. Krishna also manifests as the Brahma in the satya loka. Brahma who was waiting to see Krishna's reaction to the disappearance of all the cows and cowherd friends; was baffled to see every cowherd, cow and calf reappear in their position as though nothing had changed. Only he knows that he made them disappear. His intent was to baffle Krishna; instead, he was mystified as to how they could re-appear, for he was the one who had the powers to create in this world. Brahma also knew that all those cowherds and cows he had hidden in a cave were still there. Now there were two of everyone.

What happened next was too much of an embarrassment for Brahma. Completely taken aback by things going out of control, he decided to go back to his world, satya loka. The gate keepers stopped him saying that the real Brahma was already inside and that he must be an imposter and he cannot enter satya loka. Brahma realized this was the result of his misadventure with Krishna. He was filled with shame and fear for what he had done. He did what he did because he could not bear the sight of Krishna sharing that divine bliss with the cowherds which even Brahma had never experienced. He realizes his mistake and surrenders to the Lord and asks to be forgiven for his misdemeanor. As always, God is ever willing to accept our shortcomings. Brahma had met his punishment when his own guards called him an imposter. Brahma also realized that Krishna was the supreme power of all the worlds, including his.

Krishna wills for everything to return to their original state. Meanwhile, in Brindavan, Krishna's brother Balarama mentions to Krishna that for the last few days he felt Krishna in every cowherd and every cow in Brindavan. They all seemed to him as Krishna, though in different bodies. Was that an illusion or was he so obsessed with Krishna's affection that he started seeing Him in everyone including the cows? In fact it was a transcendental feeling as though he was experiencing a divine bliss; and everything changed to normal now. Krishna does not mention anything to anyone, for whatever he does would be beyond anyone's comprehension. For, He is the sole Paramatma. Everyone including Balarama was a jivatma and it would mean to compound their delusion if He explains who He is.

Even with the power of immortality that the gods of the heavens are endowed with, they are vulnerable. They live in fear of losing whatever they possess. They are not undefeatable. They are immortal only for that cycle of creation and there would be a new heaven in the next cycle of creation and a new king of heavens would take charge along with his team of new gods. One of us could be the next Indra or Brahma if we choose to be, backed by karma entitlement. But beware; we shall not be tempted into wishing for such a life of gods. It is an unenviable state, getting which we could repent, for there is no re-course if we dislike that state, at least for that cycle of time which is quite a long period in human terms. Even Indra is not content with his existence, constantly desiring for more and better state of happiness. At least, we can get close to the supreme God, when we get the realization that He dwells right inside us, anytime we make that choice. He is ever waiting for that move from us, eager to bestow upon His benign grace, and grant us immortality, which even the gods of this world cannot attain without taking a human birth. The gods won't make the choice we can, to reaching the supreme Lord. They are attached to their existence. Their long life, in a way, is self inflicted curse.

Based on the nature of the soul, getting an immortal body would be like living in our own home that's ever-lasting, with the awareness that we would experience only the best that would not be taken away. That is what all of us want. But we have to do whatever is needed to get there.

Live life happily.

Soul can experience joy in four different ways—
    a> pleasure (at a physical level)
    b> enjoyment (perception through senses)
    c> happiness (state of mind)
    d> bliss, (the ultimate state the Atma seeks)—bliss is what the atma experiences directly. In that, we have 'bliss of the atma' and the 'divine bliss of the Paramatma'.

Pleasure—is the perception at a physical level. We derive pleasure using our body and sense organs, through seeing, hearing, smelling, tasting and touching. We may end up experiencing pain as well using these mediums. For instance, if I love watching movies, I may suffer eye pain due to excessive watching. Both pleasure and pain are temporary with both qualitative and quantitative limitation. There is no such thing as unlimited pleasure or pain.

Enjoyment—is perceived by the senses. We can experience joy even in dreams, while the physical sense organs are inactive.

Happiness—is a state of mind and can remain undisturbed if not attached to seeking sense gratification and physical pleasure. Happiness can be longer lasting for a righteous person of steadfast mind.

Bliss—is the direct experience of the Atman (Soul) transcending the happiness of the mind or enjoyment of the senses or the pleasures using the sense organs. The bliss the atman can experience in this world occur when in deep sleep and in devotion. The bliss during deep sleep cannot be felt as the Atma does not experience the bliss in a conscious state. However, we feel good when we wake up. We also experience the bliss when in devotion—praying, worshipping, or deeply engrossed thinking about the Lord's glories or connecting with the deity in a temple or chanting hymns etc. In both states of deep sleep bliss and bliss during devotion, it is the indwelling Lord who bestows bliss upon the Atman but without His involvement.

The divine bliss can be experienced only when we attain immortality. The bliss in this world is without involvement from the Lord and the divine bliss is an experience with our conscious participation and involvement by the Lord. None of us have ever experienced the divine bliss, for we have been in the mortal world by choice, forever, so far and divine bliss of the Lord is not available here.

What is happiness? Happiness is different for different people. But most would agree that it is a state in which you do not wish to seek anything, nor would you oppose anything that happens as a natural consequence. *You remain happy constantly, neither seeking nor forsaking.* A truly happy person would reach a stage, in which he would not even seek happiness, for he has transcended even that state. It is like the richest man, who does not care if he is the richest or not. One can lose all his wealth but happiness would not be lost, for it is not connected to any event or emotion. Happiness is not reduced or diminished when shared.

True happiness is beyond all emotions. You remain unaffected by situations. A happy person would respond to desirable or undesirable outcomes equally. At the same time, a happy person would not refrain from doing his duties merely because he has no interest in the results.

Lord Rama delightfully accepted when He was asked to go to the forest for 14 years in exile, just a day after He was declared to be coronated as the King.

We should not attach the self to our activities or the results. Most of us become unhappy due to our expectations not being fulfilled. We are very attached to our relationships, expecting everyone to respond in a particular way. Even if there is a slight variation in what they say or do, affects our state of happiness.

In fact, most righteous people would be happy, for happiness is a state achieved doing our duties correctly. We would have a reason to be aggrieved when we realize that we failed in doing our duty.

In reality, we cannot make someone happy, as that is not in our control. However, we can make someone unhappy by doing things they don't like; we must refrain from contributing to someone's unhappiness by our actions or speech or behaviour.

Happiness is a stage beyond 'rAga or dwEsha'. Raga is our attachment to what we like; dwEsha is repugnance or what we dislike, turning into hatred or enmity. We are conditioned to like what we want and hate what we don't. In reality, everything is 'raga'. Even dwesha is 'raga' for we become attached to the unwanted. We develop 'raga' to dwesha.

If we analyze the two qualities—raga and dwesha, both mean the same thing as far as we are concerned. Raga is our attachment to our desires leading to obsession and delusion; dwesha is also an obsession to the undesired. If we like a person too much, we think of him or her constantly which develops into attachment to that person. By the same token, if we dislike a person too much, we cannot forget thinking about him, due to our negative attachment. We have to remain untouched by both raga and dwesha of this world, if we truly want to nurture devotion to the Lord. Instead we must develop 'vairagya' or dispassion to the worldly matters and divert our attachment to the Lord. Both raga and dwesha to this world bind us to repeated birth/death cycles. Instead, if we develop attachment to the Lord, it would lead us to attaining the Lord. Even those who were attached to Krishna in a negative sense, such as a Kamsa and Sisupala etc, attained the supreme abode of the Lord.

We need to understand that 'vairagya' or dispassion is to remain same in all situations—it is not a state in which we dislike or like any one or any outcome. We treat everyone and every situation with equanimity, remaining unperturbed in all situations. In other words, we remain happy, without being affected by events and results treating everyone fondly.

This world can neither cause us to like or dislike, for it is a non-living thing. The non sentient world and materials from it cannot respond. It is a one way attachment by us. Whatever happiness or sorrow, it is our own doing and not caused by this world.

We are trying to derive happiness from things that cannot give us happiness. We have seen infants suck their own thumb imagining that they are sucking in mother's milk. The babies experience an imaginary happiness sucking their thumb but in reality there is no milk coming from the thumb. Even adults are not different. Even if there is no real happiness, we become illusioned to seeking happiness from activities leading to addictions that are potentially harmful.

We become happy or unhappy based on the results for every action, thought and expectation. But that happiness is only momentary for our wants and expectations keep changing.

Anxiety about the future would rob us of happiness now. If we are smart, we have to realize that the future is truly not in our control; all that we can do is live in the present, in this moment. And every next moment would become 'present moment' as we come to pass that moment. We could be happier, if we can consciously learn to leave the worries of our past behind. With each passing day, we can become better and this would be a continuous process, as there is no state of perfection in this mortal world. The situation is not going to change by our worrying. When we worry, we become inefficient in doing whatever we do.

Some of us would have every resource in life, yet would have lots of unwanted problems as well. Our purpose of acquiring so much money and wealth was to be able live life without problems. So, merely being able to become wealthy, does not guarantee a problem-free life. However, it is also true that we cannot achieve anything in poverty. If we intend helping others, we must be more resourceful. If someone asks a rich man what he wants in life, more than asking for something, he would ask for problems taken out of his life. After acquiring wealth, we realize that wealth cannot solve all our problems.

To know our own state, we must learn to become an observer of the self. Look at the self as an impartial outsider. We would soon be able to assess the self for every thought, speech and deed. This would also give us the opportunity to analyze our own strengths and weaknesses and to transform our weaknesses into strengths.

With practice we would be able to treat issues, identifying them as different from the self or people related to the issues. It would help maintain cordial relationship with everyone. We would find amicable solution to issues without hurting or blaming them and avoid putting the relationship in jeopardy. The person who committed a mistake can change so as to not repeat the mistakes. Good or bad are the adjectives we associate to the effects of what people do and not directly to them.

If we want to avoid disputes, all that we have to do is put ourself in the other person's position to realize their perspective instead of vehemently holding on to ours.

We think of God only when in trouble

We have become so unmindful that we have even started looking at people as pleasure objects, which is the reason why we have so many cruel incidents against women. We look at them as objects of sense gratification. According to scriptures women shall be revered in all our relationships with them—as a mother, as a sister, as a wife, as a daughter or as a friend. Better than that would be to look at them as the 'Atma' in whom the Paramatma dwells eternally. Our mother represents all women in the world. How can we cause any indignity to any girl or woman? After all every lady is someone's mother or wife or sister or daughter. Above all, the Lord has created women to personify kindness, patience, sacrifice, and unconditional affection. Our very existence is a testimony to our eternal indebtedness to our mothers, which we must never fail to honour.

In a way, most of us behave like children in the wrong sense. Most kids would forget about parents or home when they are engrossed in playing. The moment they get hurt or are unable to play for some reason, they come crying to the mother seeking help. Similarly, people like us who are deeply attached to this samsaram, materials, wealth and desire fulfillment, do not think of our 'mother/father/friend—all in one-person—God, when we are successful in doing what we like. We think of Him only when in trouble. We need His help only to have our desires and wants fulfilled endlessly. If we are able to manage on our own, we don't think of Him at all.

For the skeptics, existence of God depends on how much of their problems are resolved, somehow or by someone as though God-sent. If we are unable to find a solution, we tend to deny the existence of God, as though God exists just for the purpose of attending to our problems. In a way, we look at God as an unpaid servant who is there just to take care of our wants.

People in delusion, having reached a stage beyond discriminating right and wrong, would anyways not bother about God when they unleash all sorts of atrocities on others. But the same people when in trouble would ask, if God really exists, why isn't He helping them? We need God when we are unable to find a solution ourselves. If we can take care of ourselves, we don't need God.

We must understand that everything in this karmic world works based on the laws of karma alone and God will not interfere in the karmic world. Precisely, that is the reason why He remains invisible (avyaka) though He is all pervading. The logic is simple. We sought this world and God gave us this world. If we want anything in this world, there is no point in seeking it from God.

Karma takes care of functioning of this world. Though all the power comes from the Lord, for everything, He does everything without involvement; by will alone. If we truly wish God to involve in our lives, we have to renounce fruits of karma, seeking Him alone. *We cannot mix up between karma and God, for He is beyond karma.*

Other than the supreme Lord, Souls are the only sentient, intelligent beings. It would be unbecoming of the Atma to seek happiness through and from the inanimate entities. We can seek happiness in the company of other devotees when their goal is selfless.

Gita 10-9—
"macchitta madgataprANA bodhayantah parasparam . . ."

"devotees with their minds focused on Me, with their praNas (breath) centered in Me, inspiring one another and always speaking of Me, live in bliss at all times"

Sri Pillailokacharyar declares that we often commit four types of 'apachAra' or sins which are prohibited. In this he has not included 'krutya-akaranam'. Krutya-akaranam implies failing to do what ought to be done. For instance if I don't help someone, it is not an offense, though I am expected to help. But if I harm someone, which is prohibited, I cannot escape consequences. It also implies that if we don't do good things for others, we would be forgiven, but we cannot do bad things.

'akrutya-karaNam' (doing what ought not to be done)— includes—abusing and causing injury to others, praising the undeserving; having illicit relationships; stealing other's wealth; lying; eating banned substances, doing forbidden acts and causing pain and suffering to others by thought, speech or deed, etc.

bhagavadapachAra (wrongdoing to God) includes—not realizing the supreme Lord's nature and our inherent relationship with Him; assuming Him to be one of any other gods, assuming Him to be human when He incarnates (Rama, Krishna); analyzing the material cause in an idol of the temple not realizing the presence of the Lord in the idol, stealing anything belonging to a temple (for it belongs to everyone), thinking that the atma is one's own (truly, the Lord owns all the souls) etc ,

bhAgavatapachAra (wrongdoing to devotees/people)—treating any devotee with contempt out of ego; showing disrespect.

asahyApachara (wrongdoing owing to intolerance)—showing aversion to devotees and God, treating issues relating to them with disdain, showing disrespect to acharyas and their disciples.

If we can practice to avoid the four modes of wrongdoing, it would enable our progression to devotion.

There can be no greater happiness, than seeing everyone happy. Imagine existence of a society with these ideals, every person caring for the others, totally free from crime, hate, intolerance and violence. It sounds like the description of the days of Krishna and His cowherd friends, gopikas and everyone in Brindavan living in eternal bliss. In such a society, there is just one class of people. All of humanity of this world co-existing as one family; like '**vasudhaiva kutumbakam**'.

Isavasyopanishad—6, expounds with clarity
  "yastu sarvANi bhUtAni AtmanyEvAnupasyati . . ."

"he who can see all entities in Supreme self and
that Supreme self in all entities does not abuse anyone"

This is confirmed in the Gita 6/30—
  "yo mAm pasyati sarvatra, sarvam cha mayi pasyati . . ."

"One who sees Me in every self and sees every self in Me,
I am not lost to him and He is not lost to Me"

Every disparity, discrimination in society is manmade. The sacred
scriptures do not advocate the social discrimination we follow
today. If there are scriptures suggesting discrimination, surely
these scriptures have been altered by certain vested interests to
suit their mean goal.

Mohandas Karamchand Gandhi became a Mahatma by his
deeds, by what he did for the country and by how much he
influenced humanity of the world, following the path of truth and
non violence. He was influenced by the teachings of Bhagawad
Gita. He was a true devotee of Lord Rama. Evidently, his last
words were 'Hey Ram'! He would refer to the Gita for solutions
to every real life problem. He was totally guided by the doctrines
prescribed in the Gita. He called all the downtrodden people that
the upper class of the society discarded for being poor, as the
'hari-jan', 'vaishNav jan' (children of God, people of God) and he
truly practiced his faith to the core.

Sri Ramanuja called everyone a 'bhAgawata' (of God, belonging
to God, dear to God).

More than the evil of the caste system is the inequity and
inequality prevalent in our societies. There are just two classes
of people today, the haves and the have-nots. All the have-nots
automatically become the backward class of the society. The gap
between the rich and poor is ever increasing like the universe
that is ever expanding. Whatever economic growth and progress
that is achieved, is not inclusive to all. If our GDP grows by 8%,
most of it is reaped by the rich, making them richer by so much.

Imagine the top 1% of the population gaining major part of the
8% of the total national growth. In simple terms, if we are a 2
trillion dollar economy, 8% GDP growth would be 160 billion

dollars and 80% of it would go to the top 1% of the rich instead of benefiting the whole population. The remaining 20% would be reaped by the 30% of the middle class who are well educated and employed. The poor get nothing but having to struggle for survival due to unchecked inflation, while their already-below—the—poverty—line-income declines further. In addition, the rich enjoy the profits of the 2 trillion GDP, and the growth benefit is merely the change added to their ever growing wealth. In a fair capitalistic society, the benefits of growth would be enjoyed by the entire country; while the rich would grow richer, there would be no one below the poverty line, as the overall standards of living would improve for the whole population.

Que—how is the soul propelled into action? What causes his losing control over his senses and body?

Ans—We make choices, sometimes driven by our ego (Ahamkara); *ego is a state of self estimation, assuming priority and preference for the self over all other realities and other beings, including God.* We fail to recognize that the self (atma) and the body are different; with ego driving the self, going totally uncontrolled. Impelled by ego, when we taste pleasure due to contact with sense objects, we lose our conscious nature to reasoning and discrimination of right and wrong; and without that realization we cause pain and suffering to other people when they happen to come in the way of our seeking enjoyment. Since God does not control, bind, force any soul, He lets the soul do what he wishes. And we end up making choices that are made to satisfy our ego which may become counterproductive for the self. Ego becomes so powerful that it supersedes all rationale and would be bent upon proving to the self of its supremacy. In this state, one makes all sorts of choices that are detrimental to his well being, totally becoming a slave of the ego and senses. All this is driven by desire to experience pleasures. It goes in circles—and the self is ever caught up in this world, believing that this is the purpose of his existence.

It is important to know that only as humans do we have the independence to choice and action. Only as humans can we exhaust most of our karma and also practice true devotion to attain immortality. The other two—gods and animals/birds etc. are lives in which the soul can only exhaust part karma. Either as gods or as animals, we go through a programmed life.

We are all devotees in one way or the other, for devotion is a state of what the mind seeks the most. When we seek pleasures from the material world and relationships, we are devotees of this world and people we seek pleasures from. The purpose of true devotion is to seek nothing for the self. When we are devoted to the people of this world, we are selfish. If we become devoted to God, our devotion is undivided and there would be no change from that state. But our devotion to this world and people is divided and keeps changing. We dislike things that we once wanted. We seek new things every time. We are upset with people when they don't respond in a way we like them to. We break friendships, marriages and even at work people are replaced due to disagreements owing to undesired responses. Sometimes we replace people even when they are good; merely because they did not do what we wanted of them. Ego sets our devotion to this world.

When a person is devoted to becoming rich, he attains that goal better than anyone else. But he changes his devotion to something else after attaining the goal, as the goal he thought he wanted most, might not serve his purpose after attaining. We would not have this problem with God; once you taste the experience of being devout, you would not want to change, guaranteed. The reason why devotion to God works well is because God is also trying to do His bit reaching out to us, but we cannot feel or realize this till we attain the state of devotion.

The moment we learn to become unaffected by raga and dwesha (likes and dislikes); we can attain 'antah-karaNa suddhi' or purity of mind and heart. We would then be able to establish God in our mind. And God has been waiting for this moment for eternity. Soon enough, He would do His part to give us the realization of His being our innerself. That would bring us pure joy in everything we do. And we would do everything better than before.

True sign of being rich

A man being wealthy and rich would be measured solely by how much he has given away helping others and not by how much he has safekept. The richest in the world would still be considered poor if he has not used his wealth to help others. Keeping it away for the use of future generations exceeding the needs of immediate dependants is foolish as we would be gone and so would our dependents but the wealth would not be of use to anyone. If we are in a position to help others while we are alive, we should, for we would be useless after death, except that if we are evil, others would take a sigh of relief that the evil person is gone and he cannot trouble them anymore.

The wealth we earned working hard with the intention to make our lives better, can do us harm if we don't use it wisely. We can misuse the wealth even for self destruction, acquiring addictions and engaging in illegal activities.

There is a story about how obsession to owning unlimited wealth can cause delusion. There lived a very wealthy man, probably richest of his times. He would constantly engage in doing special 'yajnas' (fire sacrifices for acquiring more wealth or kamya karma). Whether it was due to the yajna or his good karma and business opportunities, he was making lots of money. Despite increasing his wealth year after year, he was still a worried man. The rishis who conducted the yajna were wondering what could be the reason for his fretting. After completing the yajna, one of the rishis mentions to the rich man that from his foresight (divya-drishti) he can assure him that his wealth will not decline for at least 7 generations, so he should stop worrying if that was his concern. After this assurance from the rishi, he seemed more worried and responded saying that he would have to work harder to make much more money as he is worried about the wealth for the eighth generation! This exactly is the state of mind of many rich men and corrupt people today that they have to stash away billions in some foreign banks. The rich man in the story never acquired wealth illegitimately. Everything was legally earned. However, many of today's rich have no sense of right and wrong. All their focus is to keep accumulating countless amounts of money in every illegal way possible.

Now, going back to the rich man in the story, seeing his plight, the rishi takes pity on him and takes him to the king who was practicing philanthropy regularly. They arrived at the right time as the king was giving away a lot of wealth, land, cows, food grains etc. to the needy. There were no poor in his kingdom for he was a pious king and all the people lived a content life. There were some people who sought gold, land, cows and food grains for their family weddings or the yearly carnival in their villages etc. The king paid respects to the rishi and invites them to have a seat. While they were witnessing, the king gave away things to every one based on what they sought. Then, it was the turn of a resplendent old brahmana, dressed in simple clothing, who asked for a handful of flour. The king suggested sending a cartload of wheat flour with his men to his place and the man refused saying he needs merely a handful of flour. The king felt uneasy, for everyone sought and accepted aplenty but this man who seemed like a divine person is refusing to accept more. He requested the elderly man to accept a bag of flour at least, so that it would serve his purpose for a month at least and merely a fistful of flour was too little. The old man insisted that he needs only so much and takes a fistful of flour and walks away thanking the king. Meanwhile, the rishi and the rich man were watching the brahmana. The rich man commented that he had not seen a greater fool than the brahmana for refusing to accept more than a fistful of flour, knowing full well that he would need it for months and years at least and there was no logic in refusing more than a fistful. The rishi suggests that they should follow the brahmana and see what he does next.

They went after the brahmana, who went to his hermitage, kept the flour on a plate, went to the river, took his bath, returned to his hut, offered his daily prayers, prepared two rotis out of the flour, offered it to the Lord and ate it. He was then reading or chanting or writing something, and in the evening he received a huge audience at his place that seemed to assemble every day at his hermitage. He gave them lectures on devotion and related topics. Several people also sought his counseling to resolve their problems, clarifying their doubts on various mundane and devotional aspects. He seemed to expel doubts convincingly.

Out of curiosity the rich man wanted to know from the brahmana, why he refused more flour and did not seek anything else such as gold, cows, land, in addition, which the king would have gladly given. They asked the old man.

He answered that he accepted only so much flour because he only needs so much for a day. He does not store food or wealth for the next day because he is not sure if he might be alive tomorrow. He is already 160 years old (he looked some 70 years old). He has been living this way for decades and he never went without food even for a day. He had realized that the body we acquire here was God given. The same Lord also dwells inside every atma to empower using the body, senses, intellect etc. So everything belongs to the Lord who is taking care of his needs, so far. If he kept more for himself, he would be depriving others of what was rightfully theirs. He does not worry if he would be able to get handful of flour next day for the Lord who has provided him with everything thus far, would also take care of his needs henceforth. He has been bestowed with divine happiness throughout his life and he would spend rest of his life in being useful to the society, imparting knowledge and devotion to everyone. Even if he had acquired lots of wealth, his needs would still be the same and the unused wealth would be a sheer waste lying with him, for there are lots of people, who can survive on these wasted resources. We earn and acquire wealth in order to be happy and content. If all the wealth in the world cannot give us the happiness we really want, it shows that there is something wrong in the way we live life in constant fear and worry. If we employ the resources for good use, sharing excess wealth with those who need it, that is the purpose of earning wealth.

On gaining this knowledge, the rich man returns to his place, gives away most of his unused wealth to the needy people. He also realized that he has been able to experience true happiness for the first time. At the same time, he continued to make more money without losing his status of being wealthy and spent rest his life happily and fearlessly, becoming a philanthropist.

"paropakArah puNyAya, pApAya parapIdanam"

"Helping others is nobility while causing pain and suffering to others is sin"

We worship the Lord, gods of nature such as the sun god, the rain god, animals such as a cow, even trees, as they all exist only to give. We have special respect for parents, gurus, teachers, saints, rishis, great souls and mahatmas—there is one thing common in all of them, which is the reason why we worship them. All of them give, and give unconditionally. *It shows that giving is such a great quality and power that each one of us is capable of, in some way or the other.* By the same token, we dislike those who take away what belongs to others. We can give, because we are part of that Lord who knows only to give. Kindness and compassion are the essential qualities in humans who give. All our lives would be filled with bliss and fearlessness, if we did not decimate our nature and exhibited kindness and affection to one another.

Even a poor man who gives away a part of his possession is considered that much rich for he is able to give. A rich man who has never given is still poorer than the poor. We normally have a tendency to waste resources when it comes to the self; we show extravagance in spending on parties and functions or expensive holidays, and in displaying our luxurious lifestyle just to feed our false ego.

We should give away only useful things

We often think of giving some of our possessions to the needy. But we prefer to give away things that are of no use to us. In other words, we want to get rid of a thing or two which has outlived its usage for us and hence would like to find someone who would accept it and credit ourself of 'philanthropy'. It is important to give what is valuable to us, what is important and useful to us, to the needy. That indeed is real giving. Giving something that we would like to dispose off is not a nice thing to do.

Katopanishad reveals the story of Nachiketas, son of Vajrasravas who performs viswajit sacrifice. Giving away possessions to the priests and others was part of the sacrifice. Vajrasravas gives away cows that were past their use, barren and frail. Seeing this, Nachiketas was impelled to ask his father, who would he give him away to (as his father was giving away things that were useless) and his father was angry to hear from his son such a question and he shot back saying he would be given away to mrityu (death). What has been said cannot be undone. Nachiketas heads straight to Yama, the god of death and waited to see him, going without food for three nights. Yama was impressed and grants him three boons saying that he stayed without food for three nights in his abode. Nachiketas prays that his father be free from anxiety and feel fondly towards him as a first boon; secondly, he wanted taught the Agni vidya by which he can gain knowledge and devotion to attain the eternal world (moksha) and by the third boon asks for knowledge about the nature of moksha. Yama dissuades him from the third boon, offering instead wealth, long life, comforts, happiness and earthly benefits including the rule over the whole of earth, as the supreme king. Nachiketas declines any transitory temptations (sense gratification) in the mortal world, but insists to know of the immortality after death. Yama was pleased with his determination and teaches him all about nature of the Atma and Paramatma and ways to attaining Paramatma who is the eternal Father of all souls. Nachaketas learns that attaining immortality is eternal and irrevocable. No other power, position, wealth and enjoyment in any world can be same as attaining immortality, nor are they everlasting.

True service

Happiness and joy is not caused by speech alone, we have to translate it into action, doing what we can, relieving others from pain and suffering. It does not help if we merely express sympathy, only actually helping would. A helping hand is more sacred than praying minds—like the famous Mother Teresa saying "helping hands are better than praying lips". It is true that we are not God, and cannot take care of everyone's problems or protect the whole world from suffering. But when we attain a position to help others, we should not lose that opportunity, for even that position is God enabled.

We do not have to go in search of people needing help. The least we can do is to help when opportunities come our way. There is a story from Mahabharata. Just after the rajasuya yaga, Yudhishtira gives away lots of wealth, land, cows etc to people. He still had more things to be given away but there were no seekers. He would have been happier if he could have given away everything he had set aside for philanthropy.

Next day, a brahmana comes to Yudhishtira seeking help. Yudhistira happened to be busy doing something and requests the brahmana to come the next day, assuring him, he would get whatever he sought. Bhima, his younger brother, who was a witness to this incidence, tells Yudhishtira that indeed he was the greatest in the whole world for he knew the future with certainty. He was so sure he would be able to give the Brahmana something tomorrow. He knew he would be alive tomorrow and so would be the brahmana. However, the scriptures affirmed that "the future is not ours to see", there was no one in the world who knew the future with certainty.

On one hand, Yudhishtira was unhappy because he could not give away everything he had set aside for giving. And here was an opportunity when a brahmana came to him seeking help. All that he had to do is take a moment to give him whatever he wanted. That would have served two purposes. The brahmana would have got what he wanted, as also he would have provided Yudhishtira the opportunity to be able to give. *The scriptures declare that the seeker is indeed helping the giver by seeking. Otherwise, the giver fails in his mission to give. The seeker bestows a great deal of good karma to the giver by seeking. The giver is indebted to the seeker for enabling him to give.*

Yudhishtira being the 'dharma raja' realized his error in judgment and gives him many things. Yudhishtira felt immense joy after that. It was indeed 'Yama dharma raja' who had come to test Yudhishtira. Bhima, his brother, guided his brother at the right time from the blunder of missing out on an opportunity to give.

Definition of success is how much we have contributed to others' well being. If we have been able to help at least one person in our life, based on our ability and disposition, we would feel fulfilled. *Success is not measured by our wealth accumulation, but by the good deeds done for the benefit of the others. Obviously, we bring nothing with us into this world other than the package of past karma and take nothing with us when we die, other than more karma accumulated in that life.*

In order to be prosperous, we have to make money and the purpose of making money is to use it judiciously, ensuring that we extract optimum value from every cent / rupee spent. Making money and using the money—would have to be done righteously. How can spending money become unrighteous? After all if we make money legitimately, how does it matter how we spend it? Is it a crime to spend hard earned money to fulfill our passions?

Let's say, due to good karma, some of us are in a position to make more money than most others. So, it would make every extra cent I have, so much more precious, for the others don't have the same opportunity as I, to make that extra cent. Now if I spend such extra cents without taking benefit of it, we have to call it 'waste of precious money' which is in a way unrighteous. It is only right to extract full value of money whether spent on the self or the others. Our wealth would be much more valuable when spent for the right purposes and right causes. If we get into the habit of senseless lavish spending, we would be wasting our valuable resources for nothing.

For instance, if I spend rs.25000/—on eating at an expensive star hotel wasting a lot of food, I would consider it a waste of hard earned money. It would not be a waste if I order items I could eat and the expense would also be small. The same amount could feed 250 people, a wholesome meal each; and we would have gotten full value of money, spent wisely.

We can list out many ways how money is wasted in India where majority of the population live in poverty, just because money comes easy for some.

One other aspect of those who are extremely rich with a trait of extravagance in spending is that *"they would know the price of everything and value of nothing"*. Merely not indulging in extravagant spending does not help. It is important to use the excess resources for the benefit of the needy.

I remember a friend once telling me about a garment exporter, who traveled frequently to meet with his customers abroad in Europe and North America. Though he could afford business class, he would travel economy class to Europe, so that he could use the fare savings to be given to charity. I am sure he would have enjoyed the economy trips much more than the trips he went business class, for every rupee he saved to give away went a long way in helping many poor students.

There is one more incidence that's fresh in memory—just a couple of days after the catastrophic tsunami on Dec 26, 2004, we saw many people who donated little, but were spoken about at length on TV shows, about their great gesture. Some of them were inspiring so that more people would be influenced to contribute; but some of them were merely seeking publicity.

A few of us lead by a Srivaishnava Swamy visited the tsunami affected areas and chose to do whatever we could to one village. This Swamy did so much work silently that his service was perhaps more effective in terms of value and solution. He organized rice, books, and school uniforms for some kids. The lady from the village, who was a school teacher and also the secretary of the village panchayat, was one of the more sensible persons we had met. She suggested that the urgent need of the hour was to provide fishing nets as they were young healthy fishermen who were ready to go to work from the very next day, but all their nets were totally damaged or gone. They had their boats intact. she said *"Lord is their employer, the sea is their factory*, and they have the boats, if you buy them fishing nets, they would go back to work from the very next day" she also pleaded 'please don't give them money or free food as that would make them lazy for life. They would waste the money to drink alcohol and would get used to eating free food'. We were fortunate enough to order and procure fishing nets within two weeks or so and distribute to the village without any fuss or publicity. Each big net was good for one boat of 4-5 fishermen. They would fish in teams of 4 or 5, catching fish worth 35000—50000 rupees each trip of 2-3 days. We believe this was the fastest help delivered to any village. That apart, many organizations and government of Tamilnadu did great job in the recovery programmes for all the affected people; but their help would reach people a bit later for it would involve bureaucracy; going through systems and procedures. A Srivaishnava Jeer swamy also arranged to have duplex homes built for some, in the quickest possible time. Reportedly, an actor from Mumbai did a lot of good work, silently. There were some who did less work or nothing, but were keen on publicity. There were many others who did effective work, silently.

So, if we truly value our earning and wealth, we have to put it to good use, ensuring that every rupee is spent wisely for the right purpose and not wasted just because it is in our power to waste money.

Experience happiness in helping others

Once a relative mentioned to me that he seems to have everything, yet he was not happy about the way his life was going. He felt that he was missing something in life and not sure if he should be doing something else to find a purpose to life. I suggested to him to think in terms helping others as giving brings great joy. Just taking care of our own needs on a daily basis brings certain monotony to it and it can indeed be too boring. I suggested to him that helping poor students is a good beginning.

He knew there are so many who need help. All that he should do is not turn away when an opportunity comes his way. Based on his financial resources he could possibly sponsor one or two children for education, every year. Even if he wanted to help more, he could not as he has limitations as to how much money he could spare. *It is important to do as much as possible; for every bit is precious when it comes to using it for the sake of others.*

His reply was truly startling. He felt that there are billions who needed help and there was no point just helping one or few people, and it would not be possible to help all of them and hence might as well not bother about helping, as it would not serve the purpose.

It is ignorance to think that either we should help all the people in the world or we would not try helping even one person. One who thinks he should run the whole world, wants to become God, play God, but does not want to do anything. We come across situations in our own life, failing to be able to solve a problem despite all the resources at our disposal. When that is how insignificant and fragile and helpless each one of us is, how can we claim to want to take care of the whole world?

God is pleased when some of us are able to help the others here within the karmic framework because He does not get involved in this world directly but would enable us when we show interest in helping others. We would be serving God when we undertake to help the needy, becoming His true representatives. The reason is scientific. We have come to this karmic world to experience and enjoy karma. When we help the others here, it is He who empowers us to succeed in our mission to help.

Every rupee we give enhances the value of money in our possession and vice versa. There is a saying in Kannada '*kottiddu tanagE, bachittiddu pararigE*' 'whatever is given in charity remains in our credit and whatever is hidden away, will end up in others' hands.

We can feel that there is a built-in conscience in all of us. Whenever we are about to do something wrong, we do feel guilty and uneasy about it the first few times. We can feel within as to what is right. If we let our conscience decide the course of action to be pursued, we would invariably end up doing the right thing. If we make a choice to kill our conscience and proceed doing what we wanted, we end up doing the wrong thing.

What differentiates humans from animals is the superior knowledge and conscience. Some animals are superior to humans in some aspects. Humans cannot match an elephant in strength; humans are no match for the scent perception of the dogs. Eagles have greater eye sight, owls' possess infra-red and night vision, the felines have better sighting in the nights; bulls and horses are bestowed with better endurance; the birds can fly, the fish can remain underwater. A cheetah outruns humans by many times.

Except for humans it is not normal for other species to die of heart attack. Animals don't commit suicide. They react instinctively based on face value. They behave true to the nature of the bodies they acquire. Animals have no remorse, they just live a lifetime using the potential of their respective bodies. *Only humans can be perverse, vulgar. Animals do not understand both*

Animals don't suffer because they have no desires and wants. They are fulfilled by meeting their needs and instincts. Animals are never disappointed with their life. Humans suffer because we don't stop at fulfilling our needs. We have unlimited wants and in the bargain we are taking away what rightfully belongs to the others.

Two classes of people in our society are guaranteed of great life in their next birth that may eventually lead them to attaining God, even if they are not devotees in this life—*Soldiers and Farmers*. All those who develop a flair for serving humanity would eventually become great devotees, for, that is the first basic requirement that God recognizes in a devotee.

Sri Kulasekara azhwar seeks from God thus in his mukundamala —27

> "*majjanmanah phalamidam madhukaitabhAre . . .*
> *. . . . bhrutyasya bhrutya iti mAm smara lokanAtha*"

"All that I seek from You for having been born is only this "please facilitate me to serve your devotees (society) as I stand last in the line serving everyone"

And Sri Kulasekara azhwar, who was a king, was wishing to serve the people of his kingdom. A true devotee looks at everyone as God's child. Just as God does not distinguish between one another, a true devotee does not see any difference in people. They see their Lord dwelling inside everyone's heart.

True devotee never perishes.

For the sake of an argument, even if we don't succeed in realizing God's grace by following a prescribed lifestyle, there is no loss. There is only gain either way. If we succeed, there is double gain; if we don't, we would still have the best of everything in this life which is anyway our goal. We can see the benefit soon as we attain the state of unwavering realization. 'SraddhA' or unshakable trust and faith are essential to realizing the Lord's grace. It is not suggested to follow a blind belief, but by scientific approach to realizing the presence of the Lord.

Those who are experiencing a good life, do so because of their good karma. They would experience good things in life till the effects of good karma are exhausted. We can never do only good karma unless we are devoted. Eventually, effects of bad karma will catch up with us, as karma is always a blend of good, neutral and bad. If we become a devotee, we would enjoy the grace of the Lord, in doing only good karma.

Arjuna gets similar doubt about succeeding in his effort to practice yoga that would lead to devotion; what if he fails in performing as prescribed.

Gita—6/37
"ayatih shradhayopEto yogAchchalitamAnasah . . ."

"If a person, who is possessed of faith but has put in only inadequate effort, finds his mind wandering away, fails to attain perfection; what way does he go?"

Krishna declares without uncertainty. Gita 6/40—
"pArtha naivEha nAmuttra vinASastasya vidyatE . . ."

"Neither in this world, nor in the next, is there devastation for him. For, no one who does good, ever comes to an evil end".

Gita 6/41—
"prApya puNya krutAm lokAnushitvA SASvatlh samAh,

"He who has fallen away from this yoga is born again in the house of pure and prosperous after having attained worlds of doers of good deeds and dwelt there for many long years".

The Lord re-affirms in Gita 9/30—

"api chEtsu durAchAro bhajate mAm ananyabhAk . . ."

"If even the most sinful man worships Me with undivided devotion, he must be regarded as holy, for he has rightly resolved".

Gita 9/31—

"kshipram bhavati dharmAtmA sasvacchAntim nigacchati . . ."

"Quickly he becomes a dharmatma (righteous) and obtains unending peace. I affirm (guarantee) that my devotee never perishes"

This is a blanket declaration by the Lord that even a sinner who is resolute to becoming righteous, soon becomes a 'dharmatma' who would never be sinful again. And such a person will not perish; for the Lord knows best when a person resolves consciously, desiring to be righteous and devout. Such a person would have seen both being sinful, or being righteous and devout; he would have experienced both states. Being sinful, he would have experienced the ill effects of sins. Being a devotee would mean to be fearless, unaffected by events; ever happy. Why would anyone want to go back to fearful and suffering ways after tasting the luxuries of devotion? At least the material wealth may decline, but the power of devotion would only keep ever increasing.

A devotee would influence everyone, sharing the imperishable virtue of devotion he has been bestowed with. Sri Andal affirms in her Thiruppavai—27 thus "*kUdi irunthu kulirnthu*". That true bliss is in togetherness, inclusive to all. *There is no prosperity or joy in isolation.* Here prosperity signifies attaining a state of serving the Lord eternally.

If one of us has been able to realize our true nature and relationship with God, we could make a difference in the lives of others, spreading this knowledge and joy there is with knowing God, who is our eternal Father.

Fearlessness is a great trait and is hard to attain. Even the greatest of personalities have the fear of losing; fear of the unknown consequences. If we adapt to a devout lifestyle, not only do we profit materially due to our clear state of mind, but also enjoy everything much more than we would have, otherwise. Experientially, it would make an overwhelming difference to the way we live life, doing everything conscientiously. Events that would otherwise cause anxiety and stress would not disturb our tranquility.

As a second benefit, if we succeed in realizing God's grace, it is guaranteed that He would not fail us. Even if we succeed to some extent, God would contribute greatly to our becoming totally successful. It is not just us who are seeking God; God is seeking us much more than us. If due to our inadequacies, for some reason, we don't succeed in this life, surely we would take it further in the next life. It would not be in vain. Either way, it is a win, win situation. On the other hand, it costs nothing, not a penny. So what have we got to lose by trying? But there is unlimited gain, if we succeed. And succeed we will, either in this life or in the next and both this life and the next would be glorious ones qualitatively.

We should know that all our actions would meet us in the form of an equal and opposite reaction when actions are done for our sake (*kAmya karma*). If we renounce fruits of karma (*nishkAma karma*), doing them as an offering to God, the consequences would not affect us, for we would only do good deeds, without desire for the fruits. His grace would enable us to endure all adverse situations, if any, of past bad karma. Difficult situations would pass like child's play. I can assure that we would get out of even worst situations as though by arrangement; for a solution would have been out of our reach for such situations if not for God's grace. I have personally experienced many situations that would seem like a miracle but yet they occurred realistically. God would enable us to find solutions within the karmic framework. Krishna recommends the simplest of ways to be a devotee and yet derive maximum benefits for our deeds without the fear of adverse consequences—

Gita 9/27—

    "yatkaroshi, yadaSnAsi, yajjuhoshi, dadAsi yat . . ."

"Whatsoever you do, whatsoever you eat, whatsoever sacrifices you offer, whatsoever you give away, whatsoever austerity you practice, do that as an offering to Me".

Being devoted to God does not give us immunity from effects of past karma. We would have problems, but a devotee having a strong mind and faith in God, would overcome problems better than being a non-devotee, as God would not support any wrong doing.

Chapter Three

Prevention is better than cure.

Science today is progressing at a fast pace. Medical science has shown tremendous advances in curing ailments and diseases. Yet, for some ailments we do not have a cure and can only treat symptomatically. We can merely prolong the suffering and nothing more. Despite so much progress, we still cannot create any of the human parts as it were, naturally. Only artificial substitution is possible. We cannot create blood, cell, tissue or bone at the laboratory, why we cannot even create a nail or hair that we cut to dispose of periodically.

If we were smarter, we should be thinking in terms of preventing diseases. However, we keep advising everyone that "*prevention is better than cure*". If all of us can live a full lifetime healthy, we would not need any drugs. Surely, there is a need for medical assistance for injuries from accidents, childbirth and certain other cases. However, diseases caused due to lack of immunity can be prevented by developing immunity. Above all, medicines we take can cause a side effect which is a big bother in itself.

We must realize that our bodies are made in such a way that there is a self healing mechanism. All that we have to do is not abuse our bodies with drugs, alcohol and chemicalized food. We see adulteration in every product for more profits. We see even milk products for infants adulterated.

Taittiriyopanishad states—

"annAdvai prajAh prajAyantE, yAh kAscha prithvIm sritAh . . ."

"All the people on earth are born from food and they live on food;
In the end they merge into food. Food is verily the greatest of all
creatures. Therefore it is called the medicine for all" Let *food be
thy medicine and medicine be thy food.*

Maybe the chemicals and fertilizers that we use in growing all
our food, fruits and vegetables is destroying our immunity and
making us susceptible to any and every infection. We do see
around us, some ordinary men and women who live their full
lifetime without any health problems. Maybe we should live a
systematic lifestyle with disciplined eating, trained breathing,
sufficient exercising, yoga and meditation; daily prayer
sessions—staying free from addictions—might be the answer.

A lot of money, time, man-power and resources are being
invested in finding newer and advanced health care solutions.
**What we should really be investing in is 'health', instead of
'health care'.** *If we spend even a fraction of what is spent on
health care, on maintaining good health, we would all be happier
and richer people.*

If you study the ancient scriptures on health, for instance
'ayurveda', the essence is on 'good health' and not 'health care'.
Ayurveda literally means, 'knowledge of life', in other words,
health is life. So essentially, ayurveda is the knowledge of health.
We need to know and do more on what it takes to stay healthy
instead of spending trillions of dollars in finding cures and health
care solutions. Prevention is the solution. Staying healthy is the
prevention.

Disciplined routine would ensure that we enjoy life much more,
spend less and remain energetic all through the day and more
importantly, we can sleep well in the nights. Most people, that

are not healthy, are unable to sleep well. They spend more time in taking medicines and visiting doctors and feeling weak all the time, losing valuable time of life in pain and agony. Penny wise, pound foolish is an apt simile when it comes to how we neglect our health and end up wasting more time and money in trying to recover from ailments. Life becomes miserable when we are not healthy

We eat food and drink fluids in order to live a healthy life. It defeats the purpose if the food and drink we consume can make us unhealthy. It is important to eat and drink only what keeps the body healthy. We invent new ways to remain intoxicated, killing even the little bit of consciousness in us. We can enjoy every moment when our mind and body are in peak condition. We can experience the joy of life when we are fully conscious.

Our body is like a machine. If it is kept idle it rusts. If kept in optimum, disciplined and controlled usage, and well serviced, it remains free of problems and is always ready for use. *One good thing about our body is that we can never overuse its potential.*

With the population growth expected to touch 9.00 billion by around 2050, we might not have enough quality food for the whole population. There would be scarcity of energy and drinking water as well. What is the purpose of all the scientific progress and economic growth that benefits only the top layer of the society? Industrial progress has seen tremendous jump in the recent decades. If we cannot ensure that every man, woman and child gets the basic minimum, what is the purpose of all the development? True development is when no one goes without food, water, energy, housing, education, employment and healthcare. If that was achieved, there would be some purpose to all these achievements and progress we are making.

Most of our problems with paucity of resources have to do with consumption levels, especially of the rich and upper class of the society. We consume much more than our needs and most of it is wasted. As a result, majority of the population would be deprived of their needs. If we could follow the ancient system of recycling all the resources, we would not have to face situations we have today. The word 'consumerism' also implies destruction of resources that need to be preserved. We have to learn to use resources without destroying them. Use them in a way that they are re-cycled, re-used, renewed and sustained so that there would be no dearth of resources.

Each one of us wants more than there is in the world; but there is only one world. In this state, even the world is not enough, even for one person! Our world has sufficient resources to meet the needs of all its creatures, including humans. Yet, many of us who have everything are still a dissatisfied lot, and many others are deprived of their needs.

According to the food productivity report in early 2013—the world today has enough food for 12 billion people. We are just over 7.00 billion people. Yet, over 1.5 billion people can hardly eat one meal a day!! And many of them go without food altogether! Isn't it a crime that we have so much more available, yet more than a fifth of the world population is starving despite the excess availability?

The only solution is to ensure that a fair system is in place; of equal opportunities for all, every one having access to quality education and employment that would bring them adequate incomes to take care of their basic needs. This would also bring them pride and joy and also keep them busy, contributing to the progress and growth of the society and economies at large.

We must realize that education alone does not make us better humans. Education along with moral values can create a dream world for peaceful and prosperous co-existence, while the same knowledge without the discipline or morality can devastate peace and harmony. We cannot put the fear of law in the minds of people to discourage them from committing crimes. *We can prevent crime only by inculcating high values; self control and discipline; from childhood.*

As elders and parents, it is our moral duty to guide the children to nurturing righteousness; we must correct them if they are wrong then and there, in a way they can realize their mistake and avoid repeating such mistakes. It is important that we should not allow children to do their first mistake. If they are allowed once, we cannot justify stopping them later on. It is important that we must never lie as a principle and surely not in the presence of children. If they see us do wrong things, we cannot question them when they lie or do wrong things. We must lead by example in every aspect. It is important to have children join us in daily prayers. Daily worship is essential for them to develop self control, righteousness and love for people and God.

If we have a system teaching high human values based on kindness and compassion from childhood, there would be very few incidents of crime in the society. Being righteous, is built on the basic premise of caring for the well being of the others and not doing anything that may potentially cause pain and suffering to others.

We can see that the US is an intelligent and prosperous society and yet is struggling to control gun related crimes. They can have hundred laws and background checks but when people go beyond the reasoning state, even those who qualified to acquire guns legally, would commit the crime and then prepare to deal with the law. One who follows basic values of dharma and righteousness would not commit a crime because it is not in him to hurt anyone; just as a man cannot fly, he cannot kill.

Guns, even in the possession of good people could prove to be dangerous because all it takes is one moment of uncontrolled rage to pull the trigger. If they truly want to prevent gun related deaths, the only solution is to abolish possession of guns by private citizens. Even a good man will justify after killing someone, that he had to kill in self defense or it was a mistake.

Peace can exist only in prosperity. Knowledge and righteousness are the essence for success in life. Those that are deprived of knowledge end up either being impoverished or choosing unlawful means to fulfill their needs. Hence it is imperative that sensible and smart societies shall empower their people with quality education and moral values, resulting in a society of righteous and learned people.

Create an ideal society

On one hand we say that all of humanity is one family. If we really mean it, we must also try and practice that notion at least to some extent. Let's say we are a well to do family. In that family, is it possible that one or two in the family are rich; and rest of them are poor and starving. No. Every member of the family is equally rich, eating the same food, gets the same facilities.

Similarly, in a society or nation, if we consider all the people as one family, we cannot remain mere spectators, watching poor people starving and dying. It is not suggested that we bring home all the population. The least we should do is to share with them, out of what we are willing to waste on our unwanted extravagances.

An ideal society would be—free from the caste system that's being fervently followed in today's societies; free from racism which has reached fanatical heights. There is a sense of brutality and ruthlessness in many societies today, comparable only to the savage nature seen in the wilderness. The reason for the caste system prevalent in countries like India is mainly due to the politicians that would want to divide the society to garner support of communities in the name of religion and caste; what is popularly known as 'vote-bank-politics'. The solution is to ensure that no one declares his caste in the birth certificate. Why should there be any forward caste or a backward caste or dalits? The criteria for government aid should be extended to all the economically weaker sections of the society. There should be no minority community based on caste or religion. There should be one common code for all the citizens.

What we need is capitalism with a human touch, of kindness and compassion so that everyone gets to reap the benefit of economic growth. We don't need to be super economists to know how a prosperous economy keeps growing continuously. It starts with quality education for all, empowering them with knowledge and skill development. Knowledge gets them employment, employment generates productivity and income. With income, people would be able to buy the products they can use; which in turn increases productivity, resulting in more employment. Most of the population would be tax payers. And there would be no poverty in such an economy.

Most European countries that were ravaged by world wars have shown tremendous economic growth after the war. Post war period has seen phenomenal developments in Japan. Countries like Singapore, South Korea, Taiwan and few others that were in a much worse condition than India in 1947 have become developed countries while India is still rated amongst some of the poor countries in the world. They have become advanced societies in a matter of 25-30 years, due to honest, well educated, qualified, competent and corrupt free politicians leading their countries. They have reached a peak in a remarkably short time.

Though India obtained independence in 1947, even after 66 years, we are still one of the poor nations in the world. More than

70% of the population lives in poverty. Nearly 65% of the poor in the villages defecate in the open. Even the definition of poverty line in India is laughable. It is declared in mid 2013 that a person earning more than Rs.27/—(0.45 US cents) per day qualifies for above poverty line status! They have assumed that a person just needs food and nothing more. If a person spends all of rs.27/— on his food alone, even which is insufficient, what would he do for housing, clothing, education, healthcare, commuting and other expenses for the whole family? There are families in which only one person brings home the income and all of them have to live within that income. Child mortality, lack of healthcare and sanitation, illiteracy, lack of basic infrastructure—roads, water, and energy has to be tackled from scratch. We can take a sigh of relief for the fact that the poor here can breathe, as air cannot be robbed from them. It should not have taken us more than 3 decades to have attained the status of a developed nation had we been lead by honest, educated, competent leaders. *The sign of true progress is, it does not matter if most people are rich in a country, but not even one family should suffer poverty.*

It should encourage us knowing that India can only progress from here on, for we have stagnated at the bottom. There is tremendous potential for growth as only around 20% of the population is somewhat well to do, which means that 80% of the population would need good quality housing, education, healthcare, energy and water, infrastructure, etc. If anything, we can only progress from here on. On the other hand, the developed countries, can only grow by another 15-20% on the whole; for 85% of the population is already well off.

- A person acquiring wealth, becoming rich, without earning it will not know the value of money.

- Education without character and morality could lead to criminality

- Seeking sense gratification and pleasures without the control over senses and mind would lead to addiction and crime. It is important to remain moderate in all our activities with conscience directing all actions.

- Power in the hands of politicians without righteousness would lead the whole nation to ruin, corruption and atrocity ruling supreme.

- Businesses focused on profits without ethics, integrity, and transparency will end in illegitimate dealings, giving rise to corruption and malpractices.

- Scientific breakthroughs solely for making money without the human factor will not benefit humanity.

I don't have to get married to a person of different caste just to show I respect all castes. I don't have to visit their places of worship to prove that I revere their religion, nor should I expect them to follow my religion. I don't have to embrace everyone to show I see similarity in everyone, instead treat everyone with kindness in my interactions with them; conduct with humility, respecting them as equals.

Caste discrimination cannot be overcome by inter-caste marriages. When marriages end in a sour note even within the families of same culture and caste due to different up-bringing, how can it last a lifetime from different cultures, castes? Marriages will work only between two people coming from the families of similar values and mindset.

Inter-caste marriage is like asking an aspirant for engineering course to attend accountancy classes for full duration; a scientist to take up clerical job for life. Marriages in earlier times lasted a full life time as they would find the support of both families and society, even if there were problems after marriage.

Types of people

What we see in people is based on their physical appearance—
some black, some brown, some fair and white—but if you open
up the skin, it is the same flesh, blood and bones. No one is
superior based on the type of body he possesses. Great people
were recognized as great men and women based on their
conduct and how much they cared for the others. *If there should
be a system to identify people, let us classify them based on
what good they have done for others—*

We know there are different types of people—

> ➤ Ones who help others, even if it could bring upon them
> any harm, they are the **great souls, unselfish.**

> ➤ One more set of people who would be glad to help others
> if that does not cause them any inconvenience. However,
> they would not harm anyone. They are **neutral** types

> ➤ One who is unto himself, without bothering others, at the
> same time he does not help anyone even though he is
> capable of helping. We should call them **selfish.**

> ➤ Some people who would harm others in order to achieve
> their goals, because it is in their power. These are **evil
> doers or sinners**. Dictators, corrupt people, people
> misusing position of power in politics etc.

> ➤ Some others—who are bent upon causing harm to others
> with the wrong understanding that they are doing this for a
> larger good. In this case they also hurt themselves which they
> do not mind. They are **ignorant, deluded and obsessed.**

> ➤ Yet others would not tolerate others prospering, even if
> they are themselves prosperous. They are **envious** types.

➤ And some that are not well off but cannot bear the thought of others doing well. These are **intolerant.** There is a story—two friends do penance seeking Brahma's appearance. Impressed with their penance Brahma appears before the first one and asks what his wish was. The first person directs Brahma to visit his friend first and to grant him twice as much of whatever his friend asks for. Brahma goes to the second person, who wants to know what the first one wanted and brahma tells him the first ones wishes. The second person asks that he may lose one eye, one leg and one hand with the intention that the first person would lose both the eyes, legs and hands.

➤ One more type—would not want to help anyone even if they are capable of. It is just that they enjoy watching others suffer. They would contribute if it is in their power to enhance the suffering—they are **sadists.**

It is important to realize that there are no part solutions to any problem. We have to come up with a total, sustainable remedy to eradicate any problem in the society. It is like treating a person for cold once, and then he would have fever; next time some other infection. He would continue to need medications as some ailment or the other would keep cropping up. The root cause is lack of immunity. The only solution is to ensure that he develops immunity. This should be the right approach to finding lasting solutions to all our problems. We have to correct the problems at the roots. Be it caste system, poverty, crime, terrorism, racism and corruption—anything that is detrimental to peaceful living and economic progress.

The sign of a developed society is in the quality of facilities available to all the citizens; especially public education and health care has to be the best there is and even the rich should prefer to send their kids to public schools and get healthcare done at public hospitals. If this can be achieved, there would be no poverty in that country. Obviously this can be done only by the government. Canada has successfully shown, how!

Many of the social reformers, philanthropists, economists and thinkers come up with a part solution to the problems prevalent today. Some think that helping the poor with free healthcare and medicine to eradicate certain diseases such as—HIV, malaria and polio would take care of all their problems. Yet some think providing with sanitation would help. Some others suggest solving a part of their needs. No one, so far has come up with a wholesome, comprehensive solution to the problems of the poor people of the world today. All the solutions envisaged so far only meet a part of their requirement. The poor do not have just one problem of either healthcare or sanitation. Their problem is their very survival. They do not have homes; they need food, clothing, healthcare, education, employment. Those who get healthcare would still die of starvation as no one is taking care of their food requirements. It is not practical for even all the wealthy in the world to take care of their needs eternally, as these are poor people and their future generations will remain poor as well.

Poverty is the root cause for all the problems. The total solution is to provide good quality education to all the children of this generation, till they graduate. Along with education, we shall instill in them moral values to live righteous life. We shall also take care of their food, clothing, healthcare needs. This would have to be done in a de-centralized manner, simultaneously in all the countries. Support them for a whole generation (for 20-25 years) so that they would all be empowered suitably to earn their living with dignity. Once they attain economic independence, all their other problems would be resolved automatically. They would not need support or aid for their future generations as well. This may also find solutions to increasing crime, hate, terror, religious intolerance etc. Humans would look at humans fondly. It sounds like a dream, but it is possible if we can take this up as a challenge by adopting one village first, as a model. Surely, even small people can come together to accomplish such a dream into reality.

How can there be righteousness when some of leaders holding powerful positions and the wealthy corporate are themselves corrupt? Corruption has reached monstrous levels in India that even the judiciary has lost credibility of being clean, as few of them have sown the seeds of corruption even in judiciary. Corruption is so rampant today, that it has assumed cancerous proportions; comparable only to the blood cancer. Each and every one of us is responsible for this; no one can claim to be excluded for this mess. The result would be ominous—either for the patient to die (in this case the whole country facing untold suffering) or the only cure is to replace the entire cancerous blood in the body, transfusing pure blood (entire population becoming righteous and honest)

Creating an ideal society is not a farfetched fantasy. We have known of societies functioning in harmony. It would be possible if the leaders and prominent personalities of the society live a clean life, leading by example. Existence of a 'Rama rajya' in an earlier millennium is a testimony that we can try and emulate something close, if not achieving a society that is perfect in all respects. In an ideal society, the *judiciary and legal department would be on perpetual vacation as they would not be active due to lack of any sort of crime.* Entire society would be self sufficient with all sections of the society employing their skills to economic prosperity. The whole population lives affectionately, without fear.

Even the Mahatma dreamt of establishing such a society as 'rama-rajya' in India after independence, for, the inherent nature of our people is *piety* and *dharma.* Even lying was considered a great sin and a liar would hide his face in shame and soon would become truthful after having realized it was wrong to lie. India is a deteriorating society losing its very core values of morality, character and dharma, based on which it flourished earlier.

Heaven on earth!

"*vidyA dadAti vinayam, vinayadyAti pAtratAm, pAtratvAt-dhanamApnoti,dhanAd-dharmam tatassukham*"—

"Education inculcates humility/character/discipline; humility inherits worthiness; with worthiness comes wealth/money/status; and wealth in the possession of such wise men would be used for philanthropy (dharma) which ensures happy living for everyone".

As stated in 'hitopadesha', we must build a strong structure of our society based on education and knowledge founded on dharma. In order to transform a society into people of kind and law abiding citizens, we need to have qualified teachers and professors at the helm of affairs. We need to pay our teachers and professors well; making them among the top paying jobs. Great minds must think of taking up teaching profession for the rewards it can offer, in terms of high remuneration and even greater motivation would be the impact they can make in creating an intelligent and learned society on the principles of high morals.

The deprived are able to see the top layer of the population living extravagantly luxuriously and would aspire for such a lifestyle as well, but it is too late for them to start from the beginning as they would be past that stage. The only way to become rich overnight is through display of muscle power, politics, corruption, drugs, underworld, mafia and extortion. As we can see, you don't need to be educated or qualified to do these activities.

Well educated Indians are rated amongst most intelligent people in the world, yet many of our politicians are uneducated, and some with criminal background as well. *There is a basic minimum qualification required for any job except for becoming a politician in India.*

Every elected member must be suitably competent and qualified in the line of portfolio he wishes to head; he shall be free from criminal past. Position in politics should not be viewed as a coveted seat of power. Only those who are truly interested to serve and driven by high moral values should take up political careers. We must set high standards for candidate selection, like it is done to appoint CEO's of the top multi-national corporations of the world today. If we show so much importance in the selection process of a candidate to lead an MNC, how much more criteria should be examined in the selection of political candidates, who would eventually be leading a country? It should be the highest paid job. That way the whole country would benefit by having an able person and his team of intellectuals guided by high sense of morality and ethics, at the helm of affairs, leading the country to prosperity and peaceful co-existence.

A true leader would create conducive atmosphere for industries and businesses to prosper, trigger wealth creation for the whole population, drive inclusive growth and development, provide basic amenities and infrastructure in all areas. The poorest would be well earning middle class who would not need any freebies.

There should be impartial verification system to assess the quality of governance and if anyone is found short in delivering, for any reason, must relinquish the post immediately. *There must be accountability not only for clean governance but also for performance.* If a whole government is found incompetent to govern, must give up their positions for a new team, even if it is in the middle of the contracted term. Should run the government like a service provider; the team that serves better and finds a clean record of zero grievances shall be rewarded financially and would qualify for re-election.

The elected leaders must be conscious to realize that they have chosen to serve the people and not to rule. If we eliminate corruption in government, there can no question of corruption in the corporate world or in private life of the people.

Politicians today invent new methods to influence the populace in the name of secularism. Probably that is the reason why they strive to keep most of the population illiterate and uneducated for several decades even after independence, so that for generations they can take advantage of their naivety and ignorance, and keep getting re-elected. *True secularism is to empower the entire population to attaining economic stature, so that they would never have to depend on the government for freebies and subsidies*. They should all be proud tax payers who can contribute to the growth and development on a continuous basis. Every citizen must feel a sense of belonging in the society and every citizen must feel he is an important member contributing to the growth and progress of the country, which indeed he is. The truth is even the poor people pay their taxes in whatever products they buy, including food. So it is all the more important to ensure that they get proper infrastructure and facilities considered essential for a dignified living.

If there is corruption in the developed countries, it is only after they provide the best quality infrastructure. Many Indian politicians seem to swallow most of the budget allocated for nation building. They think tax payers money is meant for their private use or in their foreign bank accounts.

A Canadian customer once told me a joke about the extent of corruption in India, in comparison with the developed western societies. An Indian politician visits his counterpart in the US. The host invites him to a private lunch at his luxurious home in a sprawling expanse of hundred acres, having a golf course, swimming pool and a massive house with the best of everything. The Indian politician had never seen anything like it and was awestruck at the wealth possessed by his US counterpart. He was curious to know how it was possible for a politician who has no other business income to acquire so much wealth. The American confesses—"did you see the new high ways and bridges, airports, during your stay here? The Indian says, "Yes, they are truly high tech roads and flyovers, everywhere. It is truly amazing your country can build such quality roads". The American hints "ten per cent, and the result is what you see and I am done for life". The Indian commends him for his great achievement and invites him to come to India.

After some 5-6 years, the American comes to India and the Indian politician who was a minister, takes him to his house. He takes him on a tour of his property covering hundreds of acres. They drove around in a lush green well maintained landscape, boasting of all varieties of trees and plants and flowers, golf course, polo course, several swimming pools, hundreds of security guards positioned in their places and when they come to the main house, the American could not believe what he saw. He was standing in front of a magnificent palatial structure. Inside, the palace was filled with silver and golden adornments, furniture fitted with precious stones that was out of this world; walls with golden borders and paintings. Everything was on a royal scale, and he had a huge vault filled with all currencies of the world, and expensive diamond jewelry. The American couldn't resist any more and asks him "how? You didn't seem to have all this when you visited me in the US". The Indian was very proud and said, "We travelled all over the country, did you see all the national highways, dams, airports, power projects? The American said 'no, there weren't any". The Indian smiles agreeing, "That's how". Then the Indian also gives him a piece of advice. "What you see here is only a part of the whole; we keep most of our wealth abroad, just in case there is a problem in the future". I am not the only one; most of us have made it big. It is relative to the portfolio and powers we have in the government".

As a matter of fact, even black money is earned money except that proper taxes are not paid for such incomes. However, corrupt money is red money, which is much worse than killing, for millions are deprived due to corruption at the political levels involving billions and trillions of dollars, with which the whole country can remain prosperous.

It is also true that not all honest men and women can become capable political leaders. As a matter of fact, people should persuade good and able personalities to take up politics. It is not an easy job and not everyone can successfully deliver. It would be easier to discredit good politicians giving some reason or the other, but to go there and deliver is indeed a herculean task.

In the ultimate analysis—what do people want? Everyone needs two or three meals a day and in order to provide food, shelter, clothing for the self and family, man has to be better educated, seek better paying jobs so that he can live a comfortable life. We look at education as a means to make money and not as a learning process. For that matter, be it education, business, politics, healthcare or anything else, finally, everything comes down to money. And before we can realize as to who we are and why we have taken birth, what is the goal of human life, what we should be doing to transcend beyond fulfilling our daily requirements, we come to the end of our lives and it goes on and on endlessly—taking births in different bodies and dying to get into other bodies.

Chapter Four

Nature of food

Food influences our thoughts and self control, for our body is made of the food we eat. Food is converted in to blood, muscles, bones, energy and semen in the body. Countless number of souls enter our body through food and fluids we consume. Every blood cell has a soul in it.

Humans are both vegetarians and meat eaters. Some societies eat meat as they cannot grow food. Some others, who have access to vegetarian food, eat meat because they like the experience of eating meat (driven by taste) even if it might not be healthy for them. There are some who are strict vegetarians. Even in vegetarian diet, there are few vegetables that are considered 'rajasika' (aggressive) in nature. Though milk is not a vegetarian (not grown on ground), it is considered satvika (soft) in nature.

Food is categorized in Gita as:
  ➤ Satvika (soft natured)
  ➤ Rajasika (induces aggression)
  ➤ Tamasika (inducing laziness, sleep, ignorance and delusion)

Satvika food—consists of vegetarian and milk / milk products—that are soft in nature, not smelling or tasting too strong, not too harsh, easy to digest, causing no ill effects after eating—easy to eat, pleasant looking. Even some vegetables like onion, garlic, drumstick, raddish are considered rajasika in nature.

Rajasika food is too spicy, heavy to digest, very pungent and harsh with a strong taste of bitter and sour as well.

Tamasika food is that which is stale, emitting bad smell, that has lost its natural taste, decaying due to not consuming soon after preparation; not easy to digest, and can cause illness if not used to such food.

We can see the effect of food unmistakably in our body odour. *We know that the new born babies and infants live on mother's milk alone, which is the reason they smell good, unlike the adults who emit bad odour. We smell bad because we eat all sorts of things.* The moment kids start eating non sattvik food, they start emitting bad odour. Those who follow a sattvik diet smell relatively better.

There is a double benefit in being a vegetarian. For one, our digestive system is made for the vegetarian diets to maintaining a healthy mind and body. And the second reason is more important—that we would not be causing resultant pain and suffering when we kill animals/birds, fish, poultry for meat. We do not cause pain and suffering by consuming milk and vegetarian food. That is the reason why cows are respected and even worshipped, for they are like our second mother. We also worship nature for being a source of food. Even in obtaining milk from the cow, we must be conscious to leave enough milk for the calf, without depriving it of its rightful share.

We consider hurting or killing humans a crime, for it causes pain, suffering, and anguish, not only to the person being killed, but also to his family and friends.

Some people contend that we cannot kill what we have not caused. However, are they justified in killing those animals they nurture in farms where they facilitate breeding of pigs, sheep, chicken etc? It is to be noted that we do not create these beings, but are merely the facilitators. So, can we justify killing even the farm animals?

If we can feel pain and suffering when harmed physically, it is not different with animals, birds, fish and all other creatures in a physical functional body. We are also ending life for a soul in a functional body. It must be hurting the animals and birds, much as it hurts us when killed. Even animals feel the anguish of losing their close ones when they die. They have the sense of affection and sense of belonging. Even they have the instinct of fear of death and do not like being killed. *Just as we would all die one day, yet do not like to be killed before our natural death, animals too love being who they are and would like to live their full life till they eventually die a natural death. Some may argue that there are methods to kill animals without causing pain. In that case, can we kill humans without causing pain, by putting them to sleep?* It is not merely pain alone that is in question; we also cause them the anguish of death. They do not want to die. And we have no right to end their life.

George Bernard Shaw once said "animals *are my friends and I don't eat my friends*". He also mentioned that we should not eat meat because our stomach is not a burial ground for dead animals.

When we have an alternative source for our food, it makes sense to avoid killing or causing pain to these animals and birds. After all even Jesus Christ's—one of the Ten Commandments is—"thou shall not kill". Jesus did not specify thou shall not kill only humans. It means that one must not kill any living being in a functional body; that would feel the pain and fear of being killed, just like humans. All the beings in a functional body have a natural bondage of relationships. The perception of fear of dying, and the will to protect or defend to stay alive, is in their inherent nature.

But then, milk and milk products are not really a vegetarian source, as it comes from the body of the cows and not grown on ground. Milk from the body of a cow has millions of micro organisms like in water, which are invisible. When we drink milk those bacteria and micro organisms present in the milk would enter our body. In any case, they would not be hurt or killed by our consuming milk, as they do not have a functional physical body. There is no pain caused to them nor do they die when we drink liquids or water.

Even when we breathe in and out—we inhale 10 to the power of 23 micro organisms that are living organisms but without a functional body and hence we are not hurting them or killing them.

Now it is arguable whether vegetarians don't kill the plants (spinach, root vegetables etc), even if they can claim to 'not killing' when they use other vegetables, fruits, flowers as the plants continue to live. Even the food grains are harvested after the plants complete their life.

Plants are immobile living beings. They do not experience pain in any of their parts—roots, stem, branches, flowers, fruits, seeds, leaves etc. By eating food grown on ground (vegetation), we do not hurt them like we would hurt an animal. There is no pain caused to the vegetables, fruits or seeds and grains. Upanishads declare that plant life is part of this prakruti, meant as food source for humans and other herbivores.

God cares more than anyone else about every embodied soul and hence He created the plant life in a way they do not experience any pain or suffering. Scientific experiments have confirmed that the plant life has no nervous system or brain and there is no perception of pain or pleasure for them. They simply exist, in a state of 'suspended animation', dependant on this nature for their survival—such as the sun light, water, oxygen, carbon-di-oxide etc. Plants multiply by the help of wind, water, birds, animals and humans enabling their growth. When we walk on grass, we do not hurt them. All the plants, in their entirety, are like our hair and nail which grows, but has no pain or pleasure perception. Above all, they are created by God as a source of food.

Some may argue that eggs are also like plants, but in reality, eggs are like unborn babies in the formation stage. The hen is anguished when it loses its eggs. There is bondage between the mother and egg which is the reason they protect their eggs, incubate the eggs till they hatch. There is a relationship, affection which is destroyed when they are not allowed to hatch. Even the farm eggs that do not hatch are loved by their mother hens.

When we soak beans and other seeds in water for longer hours, the souls in them use the potential ingredients growing into a sprout. If the seeds are stored in proper conditions, they remain intact for millions of years in the same state of suspended animation. Hence eating vegetarian food and milk/dairy products is considered better and meat eating to be avoided at least by those who have vegetarian food available. Eventually, whatever pain and suffering we cause to other living beings, would have to be faced as consequences. Whether we can feel it now or not, it is a phenomenon that would catch up with each one of us. There is no escape.

Control over senses

Our senses bother us when we become addicted. Like the Mahatma said "see no evil, speak no evil, hear no evil"; and we could add 'touch no evil' 'taste no evil' to this list, for most crimes are committed for gratifying the sense of touch and addictions are caused due to the sense of intoxication. *Funnily, we are supposed to possess 'sense objects' but in the manner we are using them, they are rendered 'senseless objects'!*

In short, we must avoid any addiction; remaining in control of providing our body, its needs. We should do everything in moderation; be it eating, sense gratification, sleeping, working etc.

Gita 6/16 suggests how a person can be in control of his senses practicing yoga—"*nAtyasnatastu yogo'sti na chaikAntamanasnatah . . .*"

"*yoga is not for him who over-eats, nor for him who fasts excessively; not for him who sleeps too much, nor for him that stays awake too long*"

Gita 6/17—
   "*yuktAhAravihArasya yuktachEshtasya karmasu . . .*"

"*yoga destroys sorrows for him who is temperate in food and recreation, who is temperate in actions, who is temperate in sleep and wakefulness.*

Gita also gives us a way to find true happiness—6/21—
   "*sukhamAtyantikam yattad budhigrAhyamatIndriyam . . .*"

"*One would know that infinite happiness which can be grasped by the intellect, but is beyond the grasp of the senses. Established, one does not swerve from that condition*"

We are never satisfied when it comes to enjoyment and would always want more ('give me more' or 'ye dil maangE more')— and wanting more enjoyment is a constant. But wanting more is a state of mind. Mind has no limits to how much it can seek; however, our body has constraints to how much it can take. Even the mind does not experience the happiness directly. It is the atma that uses the mind, senses and body for happiness. Atma can remain happy without employing any of these agencies. We can employ these agencies and yet remain unaffected.

Katopanishad explains our body structure with great clarity—

3-3 *"AtmAnam rathinam viddhi sarIram rathamEva tu . . ."*

"know the atma as the master of the chariot and the body as the chariot itself, know the intellect to be the charioteer and the mind as the reins"

3-4 *"indriyANi hayAnAhuhu vishayAn tEshu gocharAn . . ."*

"the senses are the horses and their objects are the paths on which they tread. It is said that the individual atma associated with the body, senses and the mind is the enjoyer"

3-5 *"yastvavijnAnavAn bhavati ayuktEna manasA sadA . . ."*

"the sense organs of that person who is ignorant for ever with his mind uncontrolled, become uncontrollable just like wild horses for the charioteer"

3-10—
indriyEbhyah parAhyarthA, arthEbyascha param manaha . . ."

"the sense objects are superior to the sense organs, the mind is superior to the sense objects; intellect is superior to the mind and the great atma is superior than that intellect.

3-11—
"mahatah paramavyaktam avyaktAt purushah paraha . . ."

"the unmanifest (maya/prakruti) is greater than the atma, the Supreme Paramatma is greater than the prakruti (maya).
There is nothing greater than Purusha (paramatman).
It is the ultimate means and it is the final goal.

3-13—

yachchEdvAngmanasI prAjnaha
tadyachchEjjnAna Atmani . . ."

"A knowledgeable man must integrate his speech with his mind and mind with his intellect which is united in his soul. He must integrate the intellect with the great soul and that soul with the Supreme Self (paramatman).

- Sabdha, sparsa, rUpa, rasa and gandha (sound, touch, sight, taste and smell) are the five essential senses along with the body parts, we use for momentary pleasures. Senses are primarily the input agencies for knowledge and perception. If we use them judiciously to doing our righteous duties, not only would we acquire knowledge, we would also experience happiness.

Sri Kulasekara azhwar suggests in his Mukundamala thus—

JihvE kIrtaya kEsavam muraripum, cheto bhaja srIdharam . . ,
. . . jighra ghrANa mukundapAdatulasi mUrdhan
*   namAdhokshajam"*

Use the tongue to praise the Lord Kesava, mind to worship MurAri, employ the hands to serve the Lord Sridhara, ears—please listen to Acchuta's stories of divine acts, eyes—feast on seeing the divine beauty of Krishna, let the nose smell the tulasi from Mukunda's lotus feet, use the head to prostrate before the Lord.

In short, we have acquired this human body to realize our eternal relationship with the Lord and should use the body/senses/mind to reaching Him.

Sri Pillailokachariar gives an insight about us:

"sarva prakArattAlum nAsa hEtuvAna ahankarattukkum,
adinudaya kAryamAna vishayaprAvaNyattukkum viLainilam
tAnAgayAlE . . ."

He confirms that it is our ego that is the reason for our downfall and it is ego that is the sowing field for prompting attachment to sense gratification and desire fulfillment.

In order to realize and overcome that state, we have to look at:

➢ *tannaikkandAI satruvaikkandArpolEyum*—*the self as the 'enemy'*, we are obsessed about maximum sense gratification, wealth acquisition, and fulfilling boundless desires, even unrighteously. This would result in having to go through repeated births and deaths in mortal bodies, having to suffer the consequences of our karma. This makes us our own enemy.

➢ *avattukku vartakamAna samsArigaLaikkandAI sarppattaikkandArpolEyum*—*people who encourage us to reckless indulgence in pleasures as 'serpents'*—there are some vested interests, who would encourage us to indulge in activities even if wrong. They are not in a position to either uplift themselves or us. With such people, we have to do what we do when we encounter a serpent—stay away.

➢ *Avattukku nivarttakamAna srivaishNavargaLaikkandAI bandukkaLaikkandArpolEyum*—*people (srivaishnavas) who guide us to the right path, as 'true relatives'*,—devotees would always be interested in our well-being and would be honest in their perspectives about right and wrong. Though they are not our blood relations, they are selfless and mean well for us.

➢ *IswaranaikkandAI pitAvaikkandArpolEyum*—*God as the eternal father*. With this realization, we would untie our attachment to this world and progress towards gaining eternal relationship with Him.

➢ *AchAryanaikkandal pasiyan sottaikkandArpolEyum*—*Acharya as food for a person who is hungry*. As long as we are in a body, we would be working towards providing food for the body. When we develop hunger for reaching the Lord, Acharya provides us the means to attaining our goal.

Thus he becomes the very life sustaining source for the Atma to attaining immortality just as food sustains the body.

Karma is mixed, and the effects would also be in three ways— good, neutral and bad. Even if we intend doing noble deeds, we would have also done neutral and bad karma without control, for neither actions nor results are in our control.

Gita—18/12—
"anishtamishtam misram cha trividham karmaNaha phalam . . ."

"Undesirable, desirable and mixed—thus threefold is the fruit of deeds (actions) that accrues after death to those who have not renounced karma. But to those who have renounced, there is no consequence of karma whatsoever".

When we start a business, our intention is to make money. No one does business to lose money or merely to break even. However, we have no control over the profits or losses or even breaking even. Similarly, when we translate our noble intentions into action, we end up doing bad things as well, without control over the execution.

Good or bad is what we do for the others. Neutral karma is what we do for the self in fulfilling our obligatory duties. **We have to remove the self out of the equation when accounting for good or bad karma.** *It is not about the self. We are self centered in everything, in doing karma or in devotion to God. If we remove the notion of the self and for the self, we would be successful in this world as well as in attaining God.*

Isavasyopanishad—2
"kurvannEvEha karmANi jijIvishEt satam samAh . . ."

"One should desire to live a hundred years just performing nishkAma karmas (as accessory to devotion). For an aspirant

there is no other way. Karma will not stick to such a person (who knows of Brahman)

Gita-14/5—
  "sattvam rajastama iti guNAha prakrutisambhavAha . . ."

"sattva, rajas and tamas are the gunas that arise from the prakruti. They bind the immutable self (atma) in the body"

Gita 14/6—
  "tatra sattvam nirmaltvAt-prakAsakamanAmayam . . ."

"of these, sattva, being pure, is luminous and free from malady. It binds, by attachment to pleasure and knowledge"

Gita 14/7—
  "rajo rAgAtmakam viddhi trushNAsangasamudbhavam . . ."

"know that rajas is of the nature of passion springing from thirst and attachment. It binds the embodied soul with attachment to work"

Gita 14/8—
  "tamastvajnAnajam viddhimohanam sarva dEhinAm . . ."

"know that tamas is born of false knowledge and deludes all embodied souls. It binds with negligence, indolence and sleep"

Sattva is a better nature and yet it binds the soul to repeated life cycles in the mortal world. Hence Krishna suggests rising above the three gunas—

Gita 14/19—
"nAnyam guNEbhayah kartAram yadA drashtAnupasyati . . ."

"when one sees none else other than the gunas as the agent, and knows what transcends the gunas, he attains similar to My state"

When the Atma realizes that he is not the agent of actions and knows his nature to be of knowledge/consciousness and that all actions are by contact with the gunas springing from karma, he attains a state similar to God.

Gita 4/26—
  "mAm cha yo'vyabhichArENa bhaktiyogEna sEvatE . . ."

"He who with unswerving bhakti yoga, serves Me, he, crossing beyond the gunas, becomes entitled to the state of Brahman"

This sloka clarifies, transcending gunas cannot be attained merely by knowing the difference between the prakruti (body) and the self (atma) and that the atma is not the agent of actions but is bound due to the contact with the gunas. Only by pure devotion to the Lord, one can surpass gunas, which are otherwise invincible.

Gita 7/14—
  "daivI hyEsha guNamayI mama mAyA duratyayA . . ."

"This divine maya of mine consisting of the three gunas is hard to overcome, but those who take refuge in Me (by devotion) alone shall reach beyond the Maya"

sattva guna is the nature of good person, who is righteous and noble but yet is attached to his deeds—it binds, by attachment to pleasure and knowledge. As a result, he would take good births or take birth in heaven and other worlds (even as gods) for better levels of enjoyment as a reward for his noble deeds. But even that would end soon and we have to take birth again in this world to exhaust balance karma.

rajasa guna—is the nature of a neutral person, doing everything for a benefit. He would be bound to this world, but would not be entitled to better lives in heaven and such.

tamasa guna induces evil nature in people, who would harm others for their selfish purposes without the realization nor would they care about their actions or the outcomes. Such persons would have to take birth in hell to suffer the consequences of their evil deeds and soon, they too would have to return to earth taking different bodies.

However, it is also to be noted that every person has a blend of all three gunas unless he is conscious in nurturing pure sattva. No one is totally sattvik or rajasik or tamasik. Blend of all gunas would give us corresponding effects in this world.

Develop association with virtuous people

If we associate with noble and pious people, we tend to absorb noble qualities. Similarly if we associate with evil doers, we acquire evil qualities.

Sri Manavalamamuni mentions aptly in his 'upadesa rattinamalai'

".... nalla guNamudayor tangaLudan kUdiyiruppArkku,
guNamaduvEyAm sErttikondu"

".... tlyagunAmudayor tangaLudan kUdiyiruppArkku
guNamaduvEyam serivukondu"

When we develop a tendency of finding faults in everyone, we start acquiring those faults ourselves for that is what our mind has absorbed. When we are able to see good qualities and virtues in every one, we become influenced by such qualities as well. *We must always look for good qualities in every person, not their deficiencies. No one is perfect and by the same token no one is totally bad.*

Chapter Five

Even simple devotees can attain God.

We chose to come to this mortal world, desirous of experiencing total freedom and enjoyment, doing whatever we liked; but ended up being bound by the limitations of the mortal bodies that we have to change more frequently than to our liking. We chose this world in order to experience joy in every possible way, but ended up suffering pain as well. We have been bound by the power of this world since eternity and we have no way of getting out, on our own. Our only saviour is God, who can get us out of this eternal misery. All that we need to do is seek Him with devotion.

Ramanuja in his 'Sriranga gadya—sukti 5' enlists some of the infinite auspicious qualities of the Lord. Azhwars and Acharyas contend that a devotee cannot exhaust experiencing even one of the Lord's attributes, as each one is infinite in nature. So all that a devotee can do is wonder at His magnificence in all aspects. Ramanuja quotes a few of them—

"aujjvalya (splendorous), saundarya (wholly beautiful), saugandhya (divinely fragrant), saukumArya (tenderly gentle), lavaNya (charming), yauvvana (ever youthful), jnAna (omniscient), bala (powerful), aiswarya (all prosperous), vIrya (valorous), sakti (mighty), tEja (radiant), sausllya (virtuous), vAtsalya (lovingly affectionate), mArdhava (soft), Arjava (honest), sauhArdda (tender hearted), sAmya (extends likeness, sameness), kAruNya (kind and compassionate), mAdhurya (gracefully sweet),gambIrya (majestic / dignified), audArya (magnanimous) , chAturya (dexterity), sthairya (steadfastness), dhairya (brave), saurya (gallant), parAkrama (valour/prowess), satyakAma (truth-loving; truthful), satyasankalpa (one whose purpose is fulfilled, His will becomes reality) etc. etc.

It is also said that all these qualities are merely an expression by us to relate to His auspicious attributes, for He is beyond all expressions.

Knowing that the Lord, who is our true Father, possesses such supremely magnificent attributes in itself should be an attraction for each one of us to seek to remain with such a Father. We don't have to look at Him as the Supreme Lord. We can think of Him in any way we wish to relate to Him; which He truly is in every sense. It is that unconditional love that binds Him to us. We should not seek Him for what He can do for us or how we can benefit by Him.

Neither Yasoda nor the gopikas looked at Him as the supreme Lord. He was merely Krishna, their most beloved in human form. They expected nothing from Krishna except to serving Him. They sought no favours from Him. Even when Krishna revealed the universe in his mouth when Yasoda asks Him to open His mouth to show if he had eaten mud, she felt momentarily mystified about Him, wondering if He was some great power who has taken birth as Krishna.

Knowing her state of wonder, Krishna erases such thoughts from her mind using His yoga maya. He liked being loved as Krishna, not as the supreme God. The moment we think of Him as the Lord of this universe, we create a barrier between Him and us. He doesn't like any gap between us and Him.

Azhwar is overwhelmed by the "Lord's simplicity and easy access to His devotees, whilst He remains beyond comprehension even to the greatest of sages and gods "*pattudai adiyavarkkeLiyavan pirargaLukkariya vittagan"*. Simply put, the Lord goes seeking simplest of devotees while even the gods including Brahma cannot perceive God, though he was directly created by the Lord.

Sri Poigai-azhwar declares in—mudal tiruvandAdi—57
    ". . . nErE kadikkamalattuLLirundum kANgilAn
    kaNNan adikkamalam tannai ayan"

"Even though Brahma was created by the Lord and is so close to Him, Yet he finds the Lotus feet of the Lord beyond his reach".

Thirumangai-azhwar explains in his Thirunedunthandagam-21
    "maivaNNa narunkunji kuzhalpin tAzha . . . .
    avvaNNattavar nilaimai kandum tozhI,
    avarai nAm dEvarennanjinomE"

Azhwar, becoming a 'nayaki', expresses with the friend, regretting that "The Lord came right in front of me and I stayed away fearing that He was the supreme Lord, by His appearance" it implies that we all miss the chance to get close to the Lord thinking of Him as someone distantly different and not related to us, someone who is beyond our reach; which becomes a reason for us to create a distance between us and the Lord.

In reality He is much easier to approach than our own relatives, friends and neighbors. If the mother of the president of a country distances herself due to the respect for her son's position, she would not be able to bestow upon her son the kind of love and affection she could when she looks at him as her son and not as the President. I might fear to approach my father out of respect and we might have similar apprehensions about many people that we are related to or close to. We may keep a distance with a very rich friend who is a celebrity because of the status difference. If we are employees of a large company, we may keep a distance from the owner of the company. But with God, we don't have to think of any of these criteria to approaching Him. *God is the greatest though; He is also the simplest and easiest to approach*, if we care to seek Him. We don't have to go in search of Him anywhere, He is right inside us. Since, not everyone can feel the indwelling Lord, that's exactly why He incarnates in a divine form, for us to relate to Him.

Everyone loved Krishna for all the out-of-the-world acts he performed. He did everything for the joy of the people. He takes incarnations for our sake, for our delight, though He has nothing to achieve. It is merely a pretext when He says that He comes here to establish dharma and punish the evil doers and protect the righteous. If not for this kindness, we would not be able to experience His divinity while in the mortal world. We enjoy His divine acts for hundreds of thousands of years, even after He ends His incarnations. He does not want us to miss any opportunity that can lead us to experiencing divine bliss. He tries every which way possible to reach out to us. We, on our own, are not capable of reaching the eternal world, nor can we experience His divine acts if He does not take birth amongst us. We would be ever deprived of proximity to His real presence. It is out of unconditional love that He comes to us. Even today, when we go to Brindavan, we say this is the place where Krishna spent his childhood years, when we see 'govardhan hill', we are delighted to see the hill he lifted up on one finger to protect the people of Brindavan from the fury of Indra, raining nonstop for a week. Similarly, we relate to all the places Rama traveled during his incarnation nearly 1.2 million years ago! We are able to relive those glorious moments even today.

Lord Rama gives us the insight of how much He loves even a Ravana and there is no such a thing as enmity for the Lord. Soon after Ravana's death, Rama directs Vibhishana to perform last rites to his brother's body. Vibhishana was upset with the atrocities Ravana had committed throughout his life. Ravana was a Brahmana who was a learned scholar, who had complete knowledge of dharma sastras. Yet he disregarded the righteous path due to the powerful boons he had obtained from Brahma that made him invincible. In Vibhishana's view abducting mother Sita was unpardonable. He had tried on several occasions to persuade Ravana to return Sita to Rama and seek his forgiveness. Everyone, including Kumbhakarna advised Ravana in the same lines but he would not accede, for he was convinced that by being the most powerful he could do anything he wanted and that there was no one who could stop him.

Rama recognizes that Vibhishana's anger for Ravana was not about Ravana's ill-treatment to him but for the wrong done to Mother Sita and Himself. Vibhishana was a true devotee who cared for the well being of his Lord. Rama suggests to Vibhishana that He would perform the last rites if Vibhishana did not, though he was duty bound. Ravana was bad all his life till he was alive, but now he is no more and he shall not hold his body responsible for all the atrocities he had committed.

Vibhishana questions Rama's logic as to how He could be so magnanimous towards someone who had caused untold suffering to his wife and Himself; someone who had transgressed all barriers of righteousness and treated Him with deadly hostility? How could Rama be kind to someone who doesn't deserve such compassion from anyone?

Rama explains fondly to dispel Vibhishana's improper understanding. Though Ravana considered Rama as his enemy till he was alive, Rama never looked at him as an enemy, even when he was alive. In fact, during their first meeting in the battlefield, Ravana stood defeated. Rama asks him to go home and return the next day. Rama had sent messengers earlier offering peace, but he would not accept. Rama offered him his hand in friendship suggesting Ravana could return Sita respectfully and he would accept Ravana as a friend and an equal which Ravana did not accept owing to his false pride and ego.

Rama was prevented from offering friendship by Ravana till he was alive. Now that he was gone, Ravana could not prevent Rama from extending courtesies in performing his last rites and he would do them gladly. He had no animosity when he was alive, nor now, when he is dead.

Eventually Vibhishana realizes his ignorance and performs last rites for Ravana's body. This is how the Lord guides every devotee when he would be about to fail in his righteous duties. When He incarnates He guides them personally. Other times, He guides by sending divine souls to take birth amongst us and within the karmic framework. To God, dharma stands above all else; dharma in simple terms is what we do for the well being of everyone. *We can ensure dharma only when we perform our duties, for we could cause harm to others by not doing our duties; like a doctor who refuses to treat patients.*

Rama's greatness was openly praised even by those who violated dharma; those who were graced to death by Rama. A **mArIcha** (rakshasa/demon) who delightfully chooses to die in the hands of Rama, describes Him thus "**rAmo vigrahavAn dharmah**"—"Rama is the embodiment of dharma".

Nammazhwar in his Thiruvaimozhi 7-5-1 states "**karpAr irAmabirAnai-allAl mattum karparo**?"—Azhwar wonders as to how the people of this world could be interested in knowing about the worldly matters that would eventually bind them to mortality and misery, instead of indulging in the divine ecstasy of experiencing the Lord's infinitely auspicious virtues that one cannot exhaust experiencing?

Azhwar also suggests that if one manages to know about Rama, knows so much there is to know. Knowing about Him would mean to have known all the Vedas, Upanishads, dharma sastras. There is nothing else left to be known.

For eternity, thus far, we have got used to taking from every quarter and everyone, including God. We have known only seeking and receiving. It is not such a delightful experience to be a recipient always. We must learn to give as well. We cannot give God anything in kind; all that we can give Him is our pure, unconditional love. We have not left even the nature untouched. We take so much from nature that even inexhaustible resources would be totally destroyed at the rate we are using them up. We have evolved to become totally selfish but that can change if we resolve to change. For, we are capable of giving, to humanity, to nature and even to God. In that, we must learn to give without the ownership, after all, everything is God given.

Each one of us has something special and different we can give. Each one is blessed with something in which he is better than the others and he can make a difference with his specialty.

Sastras give us the knowledge of what is good for us, but we must on our part, aspire to serving God and doing what pleases Him most. He is doing everything He needs to do; we shall do what we have to do, as well. Seeking anything from God, would limit us to getting just that. God, on His own might have other ideas, much beyond our comprehension. If we ask Bill Gates merely for 1000 dollars for a charitable cause, he would give us what we seek. However, if left to him, he might have considered giving millions of dollars, knowing that it is a worthwhile cause.

We have to believe, only when in doubt.

The common expression when we say—do you believe in God or God's existence—answer to this question in the affirmative or otherwise, is as absurd as the question itself. *When someone says that he believes there is God, is saying so in doubt, and is unsure.*

When it is possible for us to know and realize something, why should we consider believing? *You have to believe only if there is a doubt in the first place.* It is like a person with a deficient vision suspecting a rope to be a snake, believing the rope to be a snake. That is the reason why *there is something called "blind belief". There is no such a thing as 'blind knowledge'; because knowledge in fact, dispels 'blind belief'*

It would be a great feeling to realize that each one of us represents everything that is there in the universe. We comprise of all the three main entities; **we**, the individual souls, **the universe** and our beloved **Lord**. How?

> a> **We** are the **atma**, the power that is keeping our bodies alive.
>
> b> **The universe**—this universe is made up of five basic elements—AkAsa (sky, open space, ether), vAyu (air) Agni (fire/heat), Apa (water), prithvi (earth, and all the matter of this universe). Our body is part of this universe for we obtained our bodies from this universe.
>
> c> **Paramatma**—God—is the innerself of everything sentient and non sentient. Jivatma is sentient and this prakruti/ universe is non sentient matter.

We (the individual atma) possess part of this universe in our body and the Lord in His totality inside us; part of the universe because universe is matter; changing and perishable, so is our body; and God in His entirety because, He is indivisible, eternal and infinite.

Our perception of this world is not much different from the story of 4 blind men checking out an elephant; each one perceives the elephant to be something else based on his understanding, by each one touching different part of the elephant. We as humans have limited perceptibility, though our overall ability to perceive is better than all other species.

We are dependent on our senses and sense organs to perceive everything in our lives, including this world around us. Even for someone with a perfect functioning of all senses and organs, there is a limitation to our vision, hearing, smell, taste and touch. In that we use these senses differently and hence our understanding is relative to how we perceive.

Divine, sentient and non-sentient

God is divine, His body is divine, and everything about Him is divine. The Supreme Lord possesses countless infinite powers, and they are never separate from Him—

> ➢ Swarupa Sakti (His own Self in glorious form, powers and virtues)
> ➢ Jiva Sakti (or Para Sakti)—Para means superior power.
> ➢ Yoga Maya Sakti (Apara Sakti) in two ways—antaranga (internal) and bahiranga (external)

Swarupa Sakti refers to His nature of being 'Anandamaya' while possessing a resplendent divine form, infinitely auspicious glories, being omniscient, omnipotent and omnipresent.

'Para'—is the Divine consort, Mother of all souls, who is popularly known as 'Peria Piratti' or 'Mahalakshmi', who resides in Him eternally, from whom the souls are released into this universe based on their karma. Hence, the Divine Mother is also a jivatma.

Yoga Maya Sakti—in that He uses the 'antaranga sakti' (internal power) to incarnate and for other divine acts. And 'bahiranga sakti' (external power) to manifest the material universe etc.

> **'para' or 'akshara'** or imperishable and unchanging is the superior, sentient (chEtana) power. The atma

is born from God by His Para power and hence has some similarities with Himself, yet there are many dis-similarities as well.

'apara' is the **yoga maya** power from which the universe (prakruti) manifests and the manifest universe is non-sentient (achEtana, lacking knowledge, lacking consciousness). There are no similarities here with either the Atma or the Paramatma. The manifest universe is also known as '**kshara**'—perishable, changing.

Paramatma is all pervasive. He is the inner-atma of both sentient and non sentient. *Literally there is one source for everything and that is Paramatman. And there is only one of Him.*

If the atmas were direct part (amsh) of God Himself, they would have had all the qualities and powers of God and there would have been no difference. We would not be seeking the elusive bliss/Ananda, nor would we be subjected to karma and suffering acquiring mortal bodies. Hence we are His indirect 'amsh'

Atma is part of the supreme God like the rays of the sun are part of the sun, for God is indivisible, whole, complete and infinite in all respects. Sun's rays do bear some of the nature and characteristics of the sun while they are not directly the sun or the divided part of the sun.

This statement in Upanishads expounds the wholeness and indivisible nature of the supreme Lord.

"pUrNamadah, pUrNamidam, pUrNAt pUrNamudachyatE;
pUrNasya pUrNamAdAya pUrNamEvAvasishyatE"

The souls are bound by the prakruti when they take birth in this changing universe. To understand this based on physics, it is like escaping the gravity on earth—you would need a thrust that can propel you into space at a speed of over 7 miles per second (over 24000 miles per hour).

We are still coming to terms in trying to understand our universe. In one of the theories, scientists assumed that after the big bang, the universe started expanding rapidly and now assumedly after some 13.8 billion years; its expansion is slowing down. This was the theory until recently. And now they think those physicists were wrong in saying so. Today's truth is, the universe is still expanding rapidly and not slowing down. In fact it is expanding faster than before!

They assumed the universe will end in a big crunch; because the universe formed from a big bang and a big bang has to end in a big crunch. But that does not seem like a possibility now. If the universe is expanding rapidly, much faster than before, and will go on that way, how will it end in a big crunch? It can end in big crunch only if it starts contracting and not by expanding. By expanding it can only end by vaporizing into nothingness, exhausting all the gases, energy and matter, like the black holes. This new theory also defies the laws of gravity based on which the universe should contract but does not seem like a possibility now.

According to them today—about 4% of the universe is matter, structured by atoms—which includes the galaxies, stars, planets and humans; about 23% of the universe is invisible dark matter which helps in the formation of galaxies and stars and planets; and 73% of the universe is 'dark energy' which is invisible, intangible and they have no clue whatsoever about it. And probably this dark energy is the repelling force for galaxies to move away from one another; which is why the universe is expanding faster than before. The repelling power of dark energy is greater than the gravity of all the galaxies! We know that the objects having mass have relative gravity. We do not know if the dark energy has any mass, if so, how does it repel the bodies possessing mass to expand? Now they are trying to learn as to when this dark energy formed. They had no idea it existed, until recently.

The problem is each group of scientists comes up with a theory based on their knowledge in a specialized area of understanding, restricted by their strong conviction. Science confirms that nothing can travel faster than light, and light is the fastest that can travel at about 300000 km per second (some 9.50 trillion km a year or about 6.0 trillion miles a year), while in their own theory on big bang, they claim that the universe expanded up to 100000 light years a moment after big bang. When they say a moment—maybe they meant few seconds—so here they are contradicting their own theory that light is the fastest. They have to admit that the impact of big bang has been faster than the speed of light by close to 100000 x 365.25 x 84600 seconds. They are off by some 3.09 trillion times!! If they meant few seconds, assuming it was 3 seconds, they are off by a trillion times.

We shall have to wait till they come up with some new theory, again.

After the big bang blast off, all the matter from the big bang would have been blown away in all directions and everything would end up closer to the edge all around and nothing would remain at the point of impact or around its proximity. If everything settles down forming into galaxies and star systems at the edge, there would be a big vacant space in the middle, as the universe is expanding even after some 13.8 billion years after big bang. If this is true, the vacant space in the middle must be increasing continuously and all galaxies should be pushing and moving away as well, creating more space, like the balloon inflating nonstop and the emptiness or inner space, ever growing.

If we are (earth/sun/milky way galaxy) some 13.8 billion light years away from the impact of the big bang, we know that there are galaxies beyond the Milky Way as well. Similarly, maybe there are many galaxies several billion light years apart on all sides from big bang (big bang is the centre (point A); we are 13.8 billion light years from the point of big bang (point 'b') and there would be many other galaxies beyond us (point c); a→ b→ c. Similarly, exactly the same would have happened all around the point of big bang, in all directions, which means that we should be some 27.6 billion light years away from the galaxies on the opposite side of big bang, similar to our own position. Galaxies on the other side of big bang, -c←; more galaxies like our own—b; the point of big bang ←a. (c← b← a — a→   -b→   -c)

If big bang was true, we should be seeing no galaxies around the big bang area. There should be empty space of billions of light years in the middle, of no visible matter. Big bang happened only once. It was not a continuous, series of big bangs of varying impacts, for us to see galaxies around there.

We see many infant galaxies forming (what we see is always the past, by the extent of time it has taken for light from them to reach us) all over the universe and there will be more galaxies forming in the future, but we would know of them only later, as the light from them will reach us much later in the distant future.

The biggest noticeable flaw with the big bang theory, when they say that we are looking back in to the past by 13.8 billion years at the early universe, in its infancy at the stages of formation, that are close to the big bang event, moments after big bang, cannot be a matter of fact. For the simple reason that we were the big bang and we changed into the universe we are today. And we would have traveled all the way from the point of big bang to where we are now. How could we possibly be looking into our own past? We were the ones who came all the way from the point of big bang. If we are looking at the past, we should be looking at ourselves, which is not a reality.

On the funny side, a 5 year old kid once asked that he wants to see himself, as he was an infant, when he was shown his pictures as a baby. We said, we have only pictures to show and it was not possible to see him as he was even a moment ago, let alone as an infant. That he gradually transformed into a 5 year old from being a new born and an infant. We explained to him that all of us were once infants, we kept growing up and there is only one of each of us. Or we can show him another infant or more infants but they are not him. To think that we can physically see ourselves as we were in the past, we should be able to see so many of each one of us, because we kept changing every moment. Similarly, if we were the big bang, we would not be able to see that part of us or big bang itself. Nor for that matter, can we see every stage of change from big bang to what the universe is today. We could possibly see other star systems and galaxies and not anything related to big bang.

Or, claiming to be seeing an egg after it has been hatched into a bird. We can either have the egg or the bird, not both.

How can they not realize that the very next moment after the big bang happened, it transformed into matter and gases forming our universe. This infinite universe exists because the singularity of big bang does not exist after it happened; because big bang itself was an event lasting only for a moment. For that matter we should not be seeing even early universe, which is evidently our own past and we have come to our position, changing every moment of the 13.8 billion years it has taken us to get to a position where we are now.

We see the sun 8 minutes in the past always because, we exist and so does the sun. However, we cannot see the sun as he was yesterday or earlier than that or as he was forming. If we see other galaxies such as Andromeda some two million light years away because, we exist and so does Andromeda. We cannot say the same of the big bang for it happened and became the universe. Both big bang and universe cannot exist simultaneously, not even the traces of big bang can be witnessed as it transformed from singularity into the universe. Or there should have been many continuous big bang events of varying impacts, originating from the same point for them to form so many younger galaxies in that proximity.

Even the 13.8 billion years is questionable for all our assumptions are based on speed of light which is a constant. But there are variables we have to account for—initial expansion after impact being trillion times faster than light and later on the expansion slower than light. Knowing Calculus might be of help? Or we could be looking at galaxies on the other side of the point of big bang? In that case the point of big bang has to be half of 13.8 billion light years?

Even if someone argues that we are seeing the light coming from the big bang as it happened 13.8 billion years ago, even then we can see that light only for one moment, because big bang event lasted only for a moment. It is still questionable that we can see light from the big bang even for a moment, because the light from big bang would have passed our position much before our part of the universe expanded arriving where we are today. In that case, we cannot see light of big bang even for a moment.

Some theories suggest that the big bang is not really an explosion, but *infinitely enormous heat of singularity* which released gases—hydrogen, helium and matter that expanded and then cooled down as they formed into galaxies. If it was a release from the point of singularity, the initial expansion at trillion times faster than light, would not be possible? Or if all gases cooled to become galaxies, universe should have started contracting instead of continuously expanding. But even that is questionable for new galaxies are not forming from just one spot of this assumed singularity. We can see galaxies being formed at many places. So are there many points of infinite singularity?

We have also seen galaxies and stars dying or becoming neutron stars or collapsing into black holes, and new galaxies forming at different locations.

Science does not talk about the presence of singularity at many places. Or how the universe will end?

Just as the universe is infinite, we could come up with infinite number of theories about the universe, but all of them could be hypotheses. The 13.8 billion years being the age of the universe is too weak. More likely hypothesis should be that there never was a beginning in the way we are assuming. Formation and dissolution would not be happening with a big bang and big crunch.

According to scriptures, the lifetime of Brahma, the architect/creator (not GOD) is about 309.173 trillion earthly years. That is the life time for a brahmanda to dissolve before the next manifestation of a new brahmanda. And there are countless brahmandas in the universe.

Formation of universe

The Upanishads expound clearly about the formation of the universe.

Taittiriyopanishad—*kAraNatvAtmatvAdi vivaraNam*—

> *"so'akAmayata, bahusyAm prajAyEyEti, sa tapo'*
> *tapyata . . ."*

"He, The Anandamaya (supreme Lord), willed, 'May I become many', May I manifest'. He deliberated. He, having thus deliberated, created all this, all that exists. Having created all that, that Brahman entered into that itself. Having entered into it, that became conscient and the inconscient; the defined and the undefined; the host of sentients (that forms the ground of non-sentients) and the non-sentients (that are dependent); the non-inert, and the inert; the true (atma) and the changing (matter). The true Brahman entered all this that exists (this concludes, Brahman is neither the atma nor the universe but is the indweller of both). Therefore it is said that this universe has that true Brahman in it".

"All this was in the beginning unmanifested Brahman (without expression of names and forms). From that the manifested came into existence. That Brahman created all this from Itself. Hence, Brahman is called the one of good deed".

The supreme God of the nature of Anandamaya willed (by sankalpa) the creation of both collective and individual (chEtana (sentient souls) and achEtana (non-sentient matter, the universe, forming ether and other elements).

And He formed many of the gods, humans and others. 'sat' signifies the sentient souls which are unchanging, in subtle, unmanifest form. 'tyat' means non-sentient matter which is subject to change on account of giving up of the preceding state. The achEtana (non-sentient) having jAti (birth), guNA (quality) and kriya (action) and the chEtana (sentient souls) who is devoid of jAti, guNa etc. are the ground (adhAra/support) for the non-sentient. Satyam signifies the Brahman/God who is the innerself of all entities, sentient and non-sentient, eternally. Brahman is both the material cause and instrumental cause for creation which is termed as 'sukrutam'—the effect of itself.

If we look at the formation of the universe from the Upanishads' point of view, Supreme Lord is the source for all that exists. He formed this universe by a mere sankalpa or will. If we look at God as the origin for the universe, then there are no limitations to what could have happened. *There was no need for a big bang explosion which would negate its own existence after the event.*

If we take the big bang that occurred from the point of singularity as the only source which formed into our universe, there is a hitch. Only one of them can exist; either the singularity or the universe.

And more importantly, there are no answers to the question how the singularity itself existed or formed before the big bang? What was the origin or source for the singularity before big bang? How will the universe end and re-form again?

However, God and the manifest universe, both exist, except that He is invisible to the eyes of this prakruti for He is divine and aprAkrutik.

Human Science has yet to come up with a unified theory for the formation and functioning of the universe. True answers about the universe can come from knowing the self first; than by searching into distant spaces.

Our constraint is that we want to explore the whole universe, but the speeds at which we can possibly travel (a space shuttle can travel at about 26000 miles per hour) it would take us forever just to be able to reach out to the boundaries of our solar system. Cosmic and inter-galactic distances are measured in light years. The expanse (diameter) of our milky way galaxy is about 100000 light years (light can travel about 6.00 trillion miles in a year and a space shuttle would take about 26000 years to travel the distance, light can travel in one year). And nothing can travel close to the speed of light because light is in wave lengths without mass. Even at the speed of light it would take 100000 years just to go from one end to the other in our own galaxy. Our neighbour galaxy—Andromeda—is about 2.5 million light years from earth. Alpha centaury is the closest star system to our sun at some 4.37 light years and scientists are suggesting that it may have habitable planets. To know, we have to get there but with the speeds of our space travel, it would take us 4.37x26000 years to get there. That apart, we do not know if we can survive the unknown conditions. For instance, though we can travel the distance up to our sun, we would be burnt up.

We could explore all the spaces and extent of our universe if we did not have the constraint of going beyond the dimensions— space, speed, time and distance which are the barriers we have to transcend. If we could appear in every place by the potential of the mind, we would not be traveling at all; we would be there in the spot we choose, instantaneously. We can realize the potential of the mind, if we can think of all the places we have visited on earth. We can visit every place we have seen, instantaneously by our mind. If I have traveled all over the world, it is possible for me to be in New York's Manhattan at the very instant I think of the place; from there to Melbourne at that same moment, as there is no speed or time or distance involved. We have to go beyond the physical barriers to be able to experience many things in our universe but all this is possible only in theory, when in a material body. But in a divine, immortal body, we would have no barriers or constraints.

As on July 4 2012—at CERN, Geneva, great physicists (a team of thousands of physicists from all over the world) have declared to the world that they have successfully discovered the elusive 'god-particle'. In their discovery they have confirmed that the god-particle cannot be seen. *A comparison as to what the Higgs Boson is, as portrayed by one of the Indian students taking part in that discovery is that "if the universe is full of a field called Higgs Field, the particles are called Higgs Bosons. Relatively speaking, if a swimming pool is the universe, a water molecule ($H2O$) is an equivalent to a Higgs Boson. Just as we cannot see water molecules in a swimming pool, we cannot see this Higgs Boson particle in the Higgs Field.* This idea originated some 48 years ago and was pursued upon to establish the large hadron collider.

We accept when the physicists say that the god-particle cannot be seen, without a question. However, we deny the existence of God when it is said that He remains invisible to this world.

Gita 9-4 confirms "***mayA tatamidam sarvam jagadavyakta mUrtina***" "this entire universe is pervaded by Me in an unmanifest form or invisible form" *it is evident that He has a form even in His invisible state.*

It would be interesting to know, based on a US scientists' conversation on the CNN channel soon after the discovery of the god-particle, that the US worked on a similar project during the cold war period and spent more than 10 billion dollars. It seems, they had built the hadron collider and were almost ready to conduct the proton collisions. US congress abandoned the project with the end of the cold war in the 90s and declined to fund the project to take it further. They probably shelved the project as the main intent was to build more powerful weaponry to show their upper hand and did not pursue with the end of the cold war. Or, that the outcome was not going to be useful for anything else, say, for the larger benefit of the people in their country, other than producing more destructive weapons than the existing ones."

It is declared in the Upanishads and Gita in not so uncertain terms that the energy field of prakruti (the unseeable 'maya') is 'avyakta'—invisible.

By discovering the unseeable god particle they have not understood how the universe formed. Anything they say would be accepted by the world; being laymen, we do not know anything specifically technical.

Discoveries in bits and pieces put together cannot give us the knowledge of the whole. Scientists can now think of collision of a god-particle against another god-particle to see if something comes of it. If it does, they may call it 'life' or even 'God'—but still it would not solve their mystery of how the universe formed nor would they know God or the Soul.

Greater than the god-particle discovery are the seeds that give us food. When you sow paddy removing the husk, it would not grow; it catches on to life only in the paddy form. What do we understand from this? That God's universe already has everything needed for its functioning. We have been all along ignorant of certain factors and when we suddenly discover an unknown, we think we have overtaken God or have understood everything. *With each learning and discovery, we must know that we know so little, only to the extent of the tiniest god-particle, while there is still so much as the whole universe, that is infinite, to be unfolded.*

Know the self first to know God or universe.

The first step to knowing about God or universe; is to know the self. Without a clear understanding and realization of the self, we cannot know of the other two.

A learned scholar was about to lecture a large audience on spirituality, specifically about self realization. There were several dignitaries sharing the stage with him. The spiritual leader who as a routine would start asking questions to reveal if the audience knew their true identity? While doing so, all the persons gathered would also get to know their true identity.

The scholar greets the first one—sir, please tell me about yourself.

Man—revered sir, I am Krishna, son of . . .

Scholar—sir, that is the name given to you, tell me about yourself. On hearing this, the man was confused, but recovers thinking he knows what to say.

Man—sir, I am a business man, the scholar smiles at him

Scholar—sir, that is your profession, please tell who you are.

Man—now more confused, thinks for a while and says "sir, I am a human being, a man; I hope that answers your question correctly".

Scholar—now seemingly amused with this response, says—"that is the species you are and the gender you are referring to, please identify yourself.

Man—quickly responds saying "I am a qualified engineer".

Scholar—laughingly, "like you said in your words—that is the qualification"

Man—thinks he was better off giving him all the details in one go. Sir I am Krishna, son of so and so, aged 36 years, a husband to my wife and father to two children, an engineering graduate and doing business.

The scholar was amused to realize Krishna did not know his identity and asking him more questions would not help his cause and fondly tells him that he was referring to his relationships, age of his body, his gender, his qualification, his profession and status in the society etc.; everything except his true identity. Being a human being refers to his body; being a man refers to his gender, being 36 years old refers to the age of his body, being married and having a wife and children refers to his relationships, being a degree holder refers to his qualification and being a businessman refers to his profession or job. None of these can be attributed to his true identity.

Then the scholar—explains—"you are the Soul (Atma) just as I am a Soul and so are all these men, women and children assembled here—each one of us is an Atma in our respective bodies. The scholar continues, "Does this make sense to you? Are you able to relate to what I am saying?" The Man acknowledges affirmatively with a face mirroring his inner clarity that he has no confusion about who he was, now.

Scholar—you see, this is my hand, when I say this, what do you understand; that I am not the hand. When I say this is my watch, you realize that I am not the watch, but the watch is worn on my hand. Similarly when I say this is my head or my body, you can see that I am not my head or my body. With this understanding we can realize that we are not our body, but we reside in the body, using the body to its potential doing what we wish to do.

He goes on. "Please tell me now, if you know, whether the human brain is intelligent? Krishna thinks for a brief moment and answers "yes, I think so". The scholar smiles at him, shaking his head, to express that he was incorrect. He explains "you said, you think so" it is evident from your answer that you are the thinker; similarly you are the one who uses the brain and rest of your body. You use your brain to think, the brain cannot think by itself. It is merely a hardware that has no intelligence. The brain by itself cannot do anything; it is a tool with tremendous capability. It is the intelligent Atma that uses the brain.

To test if your brain is intelligent or not, take it off your head and keep it aside, see if it can think? It cannot. It is not much different from your hand except that it is a tool with different capabilities. Your hand can not function if disconnected from your body. You are the one who makes it function. And the brain is not different, you use the brain to think and process information and memorize etc. it is a hardware with the processing capabilities, but at the same time, you cannot use your hand to think, nor the brain to do the tasks of a hand. They are body parts with different capabilities and the Atma uses the body and its parts based on their respective capabilities. Do you understand now? Krishna nods in agreement.

The speaker goes on—just as you have been able to realize that you are the Atma and not the body, with this awareness, comes a greater realization that the Paramatma is indeed the inner-atma residing in you and you the atma, are His body. This is the truth though; it is not easy to experience this reality. We can realize this truth, if we can understand that even without our active involvement, our heart works nonstop circulating blood, we feel hungry and the food is digested, all our vital organs function, and everything works even when we are sleeping. This is the proof that it is the Lord dwelling in us who is the real reason how our body functions even without our involvement. The realization of the presence of the Lord in us comes with purity of mind and heart as a first step. *(antah-karaNa suddhi)*.

What do we really seek in this world?

The Scholar then asks him—"what do you want in life, why did you come to this lecture?

Man—Sir, I want all the good things in life, I want lots of money, wealth, health and happiness for myself and my family and relatives. I have come to this lecture with the hope that by the grace of God, through your guidance, I can find answers to solving my problems and can lead a good, happy life.

The Scholar—smiles at him and says *"thankfully you did not say forever"*. I am sure that's what all the 7 billion people on this planet would want as well, and a few of them may want a bit more—power, fame, popularity, fanfare and control over others etc. Some of them would even want to live forever. Imagine, if it was possible for us to communicate with all the animals, birds, fish, insects—all the living beings—they would probably say the same thing? Even in your wish, you can see that you are selfish. You did not say you wanted the whole world to have all the good things. Your wish is exclusive to yourself and family!

But we should also know that merely by wishing for things we like, does not entitle us to having them. Everything in life comes by working for them, earning them. There is a need for effort in the right direction. A sportsman, a marathon runner or sprinter trains hard for 6-8 hours a day, forgoing many things he likes, to be able to achieve his goal, to be the best marathon runner or sprinter. He would not eat or drink many items he may like, as that may prove to be counter-productive in his performance as an athlete. Similarly, all those who want to achieve greater heights in their respective fields, would have to devote time and effort every day, towards achieving their goal.

We can well understand that we have to work towards our goal in this world and that the goal cannot be achieved by merely wishing, without doing anything. Many of us would truly think and wish that we could do less and expect the most; most times disappointed with the outcome, not realizing that we are the ones that have contributed to that outcome.

However, when it comes to knowing God, we think it should happen in an instant, without any effort on our part. Just as we need to work for our goals in this world, we should also practice prescribed methods towards realizing the self and our true relationship with God. All that we have to do is yearn for Him, seek Him; and that is not even an effort, it is merely a mental process. Since God resides in us, He is the first to know of our thoughts.

It is said that the human body is rarely obtained, by going through birth/death cycle in all sorts' of bodies. And when we get a human body due to the progressive good effect of karma over millions of life cycles, we should not miss the opportunity to realize the self, and our relationship with God. For, it is possible to realize the self and God only in a human body, as animal bodies have no potential for such realizations.

The goal of going to school is to learn, become educated. The goal of doing business is to make money, legitimately, of course. Similarly, *the goal of a human birth should be—not to be born again in a mortal body and to attain immortality.*

Broadly there are two things that we all need taken care of in all our lives. On the one hand, we would want to be free from all problems, difficulties, pain, suffering, fear, losses etc.—'anishta nivrutti' or 'duhkha nivrutti'—relief from the undesired or relief from grief; and on the other hand we would want fulfillment of all our desires and wants; 'ishta prApti' or 'ananda prApti'—fulfilling the desired or attaining 'bliss'.

Merely getting out of pain, suffering, or relief from grief does not give us the happiness that we seek. We need to have all our desires fulfilled to feel happy. Our need for God, His existence is all about these two aspects—*we shall have no problems and all desires fulfilled.*

Not only do we seek to be free from problems, but also seek to attain state of undisturbed joy. If I am in pain, getting relieved of pain does not bring me pleasure. However, when I experience pleasure, there is no pain. If I owe people money, by being able to repay the debt does not make me rich. I need to acquire wealth in order to be rich. So they are two different things. Getting rid of grief is like repaying debts, it still does not make me wealthy or happy. 'Duhkha nivrutti' does not bring me happiness; however, 'Ananda prapti' would mean that while I would have attained imperishable joy, I also become insulated from grief. Attaining immortality alone will get us that divine bliss much beyond any grief.

It is out of fear that we think of God (in doubt though), what if He really exists and can take care of us or what if He would punish us for not worshipping? Once in a while, as a co-incidence, when things work out the way we wanted, we attribute it to God's involvement. If things don't work out as desired, we are advised to pray and make offerings to God and in return, our wishes would be fulfilled. Even non believers tend to pray God when they are in trouble, as their selfishness drives them hard to give up their non-belief. We deal with God on a give and take basis; strike a business deal with Him, though, in reality, we don't give anything, but expect a great deal in return from God. But you can be sure that God would have nothing to do with such people. If God grants us our wishes based on our prayers, many of us would not exist. Most people would want good things for themselves and would wish for others to be removed from the face of the earth, as they cannot see others flourish. If everyone's wishes come true there would be no one here.

If God's involvement in the lives of non devotees is true, then many criminals, wrongdoers, who offer a share in cash, gold or jewelry to temples, should not be in jail. But some of them are, as their good karma has run out of stock. God does not seem to have come to their rescue? Why? In the first place it was their illusion that God would involve in their karmic routine. If they were successful in evading law, it was their karmic effect that delayed the inevitable. There are many who make God their business partner. Not all of them make their profits legally. If God were to involve or favor us based on how much we can pray or how much we can offer in kind, no one would suffer consequences for their evil deeds. And no one would follow a virtuous lifestyle either. Everyone would be a sinner, and all that he has to do to protect himself from the consequences is to pray and offer God a share from his ill gotten wealth.

If God is involved in granting everything we seek, there would be no poor in this world. For, everyone would be equally richest as that is what all of us seem to want in common. We should not be suffering ailments and health problems, we would not be dying in ways we do now. If praying God or visiting temples would resolve all our problems, so many accidents should not be taking place on the way to or return from the temples. It just shows that all of us are neither true devotees, nor is God involved in what is happening to us.

However, it is also true that God is directly involved in taking care of His true devotees like a PrahlAda. Prahlada did not seek anything from the Lord. Lord Narasimha was so pleased with Prahlada's unwavering devotion, that the child remained steadfast even after witnessing the salvation of his father Hiranyakashipu, by the Lord. The Lord offered granting Prahlada some boons, which Prahlada declines. On His insistence that it would please Him, as a first boon, Prahlada prays that he should not have to ask for anything from God, ever. As a second boon, he seeks to ever remain in unconditional devotion (subservience) to the Lord even if he acquires a body of an insect.

It is important to note that Prahlada does not say he would ever remain in a state, not seeking anything from the Lord, but is asking the Lord to keep him in that state; which is a revelation that everything we are able to do is God enabled, by His power, remaining within us, eternally. *We on our own do not have the capability to do anything, except making choices.* The second boon explicitly conveys that we should not ask our Lord to grant even immortality. If it pleases the Lord to keep us in the body of an insect, even then, we shall remain devoted to Him and seek to be useful to Him. We are his property and He owns us and He can use us any which way he likes. The Lord has given us that independence to choose which we have misused to harming ourselves.

Similarly, Purandaradasa says "dAsana mAdiko yenna"; make me your subservient devotee". He did not say, he will become a devotee, but is asking God to make him His devotee.

There is no devotion equal to Prahlada's, but if we aspire to become one, God would support us. He would grace us the same way He graced Prahlada.

Chapter Six

---

*Knowledge about God has to be
self realized, guided by a guru.*

Knowledge of the self and relation of the self with God is possible only through an authentic teacher or guru, and by pursuit of knowledge as guided by the teacher.

Srivachanabhushanam—
431—"**AchAryan iruvarkkum upakArakan**"—the Acharya benevolently favours both the sishya and the Lord. It is the Acharya, who selflessly prepares a disciple, and guides him to be devout. Acharya does not seek any benefit for himself. He is involved in eternal subservience to the Lord.

433—"**Isvaran tAnum AchAryatvattai Asaippattirukkum**"—Even the Lord desires being an Acharya; this refers to the Lord incarnating as an 'acharya' and 'sishya' in *bhadrikasram* to reveal the 'Thirumantram' to humanity.

434—**Agai-irE guruparamparai-ilE anvayittadum, srigltai-yayum abhayapradhAnamum aruLicheidadum**—the guruparampara link starts and ends with the Lord as He is both the Acharya and also becomes the disciple of Sri Manavalamamuni, thus completing the link. He enjoys the role of an Acharya to Arjuna revealing to him the sacred knowledge of Gita and giving him assurance of His protection.

437—*bhagavallAbham AchAryanAlE*—attainment of God is through the Acharya

438—*AchAryalAbham bhagavAnAlE*—It is the Lord's benign grace (*nirhEtuka krupa*) that enables one to taking refuge with an Acharya.

From the above suktis, it is evident that the Lord seeks the souls, for they belong to Him and a Soul when in realization that he belongs to the Lord, also seeks the Lord. They both have inherent interest in attaining each other. However, it is the Acharya, who is also a Soul, gracefully makes it possible for the souls to attain God. He is the one truly, ever in service of the Lord.

Krishna enlightens Udhava in a conversation—that He considers the acharyas as Himself, He grants them His own nature and hence devotees shall look upon all great saints, gurus as the supreme Lord Himself.

The only way to find answers is by asking questions; knowledge can be gained only by inquest; as we learn from the story in *Taittiriyopanishad*—of the sage *VaruNa* and his son *Bhrugu*. After completing his learning, Bhrugu feels inadequate in his understanding about God. He goes up to his father and asks— Venerable sir, please teach me Brahman (God). Varuna does not describe Brahman as 'such and such' to his son; instead he kindles his inquiring mind saying "*annam, prANam, chakshuhu, kshotram, mano vAchamiti, tam hovAcha*". "*food, vital airs, the eye, the ear, the mind, the speech are Brahman*. (also because Brahman cannot be described but only realized through enquiry and penance). Varuna's response implied that literally everything is pervaded by Brahman. One would have to delve deep to understand even little about Brahman.

Varuna said further—

"yato vA imAni bhUtAni jAyantE; yEna jAtAni jIvanti; yat prayantyabhisamvisanti; tad vijijnAsasva; tad bhramEti; sa tapo'tapyata; sa tapastaptvA.

"desire to know that from which all these beings are born, that by which they live and that towards which they move and enter into. That is Brahman".

Saying thus, Varuna asks his son to enquire through penance.

This is the most crucial knowledge from the Upanishads about the souls. It establishes the origin of the Atma, how it remains a living being eternally and into whom it merges or with whom it remains in eternal bliss. 'yato vA imAni bhUtAni jAyantE'— establishes that souls are born from Brahman. 'yEna jAtAni jIvanti'—establishes how they remain a living, conscious, and knowledgeable beings eternally (because the Lord remains as the indweller of every soul, keeping it a living/conscious being), and into whom it merges at the end of dissolution of the mortal worlds—again the supreme Lord.

There is no other source of knowledge about the soul in this world; for no inference or understanding by human science can reveal the Soul to us. The Soul cannot be seen by any one or shown by any equipment.

Bhrugu returns after practicing penance, thinks 'food' (annam) as Brahman and asks his father "is it food?" as all the beings are born of food and live upon food and move towards food and enter into it.

VaruNa—suggests he should return to doing penance directing him thus:

"*tapasA brahma vijijnAsasva; tapo brahmEti*"—

"desire to know Brahman through penance, Penance is Brahman".

Bhrugu does penance again and comes back saying "having practiced penance, I believe 'prANa' (vital air) is Brahman, as all beings are born of prANa and live through prANa, ...

VaruNa asks his son to go back to penance again—the son practices penance for a third time and declares to his father that "he practiced penance and feels that **mind** is Brahman as all beings are born of mind and live through the mind, move toward the mind and enter into it.

VaruNa tells him to do more penance. After doing more penance he informs his father that he is convinced that 'vijnAna' or knowledge or 'Atma' (knowledge is the nature of Atma) is Brahman as all beings are born from knowledge and live by knowledge and move towards knowledge and enter into it.

VaruNa informs his son that he has to do more penance if he wants to realize Brahman, the son faithfully goes back to doing more penance and comes back declaring—

"Anando brahmEti vyajAnAt;
AnandAdhyEva khalvimAni bhUtAni jAyantE;
AnandEna jAtAni jIvanti;
Anadam prayantyabhisamvisantIti"—

*"having practiced penance, **realized** 'bliss or Ananda" as Brahman, for indeed all beings are born from bliss and having been born, they live on account of bliss and move towards bliss and enter into it".*

And indeed Brahman is 'ananda'. (We are familiar with the Upanishad words **"rasovai saha"**, *Brahman is bliss.* '**esha hy eva anandayati'**, "this verily bestows bliss". *"sat-chit-**Ananda** swarUapAya"*

Bhrugu first thinks that food was God as food is the cause of origination of all beings here, but he was not convinced with this understanding and went to his father for confirmation. His father promptly asks him to continue his tapas as knowledge of God (Brahmavidya) can be realized only through practice of penance and not by explanation. The fact of real "reason" (kAraNatva) mentioned of in respect of food and others indicate some kind of similarity between them and the 'Real Cause'. PrANa is more subtle than food, mind subtler than prana and knowledge (Atma) even subtler than mind. But it is Ananda (bliss) that is the subtle most (Anor-anIyAn) of which all the functions of creation, sustenance and destruction belong to and at the same time Ananda is all pervasive. It is decisive that Anandamaya alone is the sole cause of creation, sustenance and dissolution of this universe. The Atma is not the creator of himself. If he were to be the cause, he would not have subjected himself to suffering nor would he seek happiness. The Creator (God) is therefore someone distinctly different from the Atma and that Creator has *pure joy* in creating this universe and hence *God is wholeness of infinite bliss or Anandamaya.*

We can relate to the 'joy' factor in everything we do. Every human feels happy when he is able to accomplish any task, produce any product, come up with a new invention; literally in everything we do. It is evident that we are driven by 'joy' our entire lifetime. However, we may not be successful in being happy all the time, except during sleep. Though we are not doing anything to seek happiness, we attain that peace and bliss during sleep, and that bliss is caused by the Anandamaya, the Paramatman who is the indweller of the Jivatman. This is the direct proof that we are not alone in our body, and we are not the reason for the joy we experience during sleep even without our consciousness.

Now let us ask ourselves the question—what do we want in our lives, and why do we do things that we do every day in our life, what is the purpose of our non-stop action; be it work, play, sleep—anything and everything that we do. Obviously there is something that we want, seeking which we do everything. Let's for the sake of argument say—that we do everything to make money—in that case, we should stop at making money. Just making money does not seem to serve the purpose; money is merely a means to achieving our other wants and goals that keep changing. We need money in order to buy things we want; which we think would make us happy possessing or using.

Now, let us apply joy / happiness as the purpose of life for all the living beings and it seems to make sense. We feel happy by the thought of achieving or possessing things that we aspire for. But soon as our wish is accomplished, we are not satisfied with what we have; we look for more and different things. It is endless. We do not seem to have happiness stay with us, it becomes a thing of the past and we need to do more things, acquire more things seeking that elusive happiness. It would be nice to pause for a moment, and think—as to who wants to be happy? Is it the mind, senses and body or the self?

Are we all happy in the real sense? If yes, then why do we continue to seek happiness? If we are happy, we should stop seeking happiness? So then, it would seem that we are not happy in the real sense. Then what is the true definition of happiness? Is it merely being in a state of having fun, or is it indulging in sense gratification? Surely these states cannot last for long; they are momentary, limited and diminishing, if persisted. Then happiness is relative to different people. A person, who has no cycle, would say he would be very happy if he could get to ride a cycle going places instead of walking and indeed does feel happy when he possesses one. He soon loses his sense of happiness as he has seen someone riding on a motorcycle and decides that he would be better off possessing a motor cycle and is already unhappy about the cycle that he once thought would serve his purpose. Soon after, he would only be happy driving around in a car; and it can go and on. Even the richest man is constantly looking for things that will make him happier. He would constantly think of using his resources to be happier than he has been. Sky is the limit, when it comes to seeking happiness.

We Love God without knowing

We categorize people based on religions, philosophies. Our perception towards them would be based on factors that are nonsensical; we are influenced by whether they are religious or atheists. When God Himself does not bother about such things, why should we? *In reality every living being loves God, whether they have faith in God or not, whether they know that it is God that they love the most or not.*

Every living being wants one thing in common—happiness. Every single thing that we do is for happiness. The reason why each one of us wants to be happy is because of our origin. Our origin is "infinite bliss". The true definition of God is "*sat-chit-ananda swarupaya*"; sat—true and eternal; chit-omniscient; Ananda swarupaya—of the nature of unending infinite bliss.

Being a potency of that divine bliss, we seek that happiness constantly. That divine joy—unlimited, everlasting and ever growing divine joy has eluded us forever till now, because we have been seeking happiness in this world and this world cannot give us the 'bliss' we want. The so called joy that we have experienced here is limited, temporary and diminishing.

Many a times, we end up experiencing pain and grief, while our attempt was to seek happiness.

We can be religious or atheists—everyone loves God equally. There is no living being who does not love God. If it is happiness that we love; we naturally love God. We may not want to accept God as the basis for happiness. It is implied that we seek God as we are a potency originating from Him. ***In reality, there are no atheists, though they do not accept existence of God, which is a choice they make. When they seek happiness; unknowingly they seek the same God they don't realize exists.*** *God does not stop us if we choose to deny His existence. He exists even in that denial. Azhwar declares—*

**"uLnenil uLan aranuruvam ivvuruvugaL,
uLanalan-enil avanaruvam ivvaruvugaL)**

He exists visibly in most beautiful forms and he exists invisibly as well; He is present even in the non-form which we cannot perceive.

The happiness a soul experiences is different in different bodies. The happiness of humans is more than that of the other species such as animals, birds etc. Even amongst animals, it varies from species to species based on the potential of their respective bodies. Plants and trees do not experience pleasure and pain, joy or grief. Happiness reduces relatively for the species with bodies of less functionality. Relatively, the happiness of the gods is much greater than that of the humans, and Brahma's bliss is more than the bliss of the gods of heaven. Yet all of us, including Brahma belong to this changing, mortal universe and all of us including Brahma have not experienced the divine bliss of the immortal world.

Similarly, even the pain, hurt, suffering and emotions vary from humans to animals. Humans are most vulnerable to emotions. We could die of heart attack, out of extreme shock or even extreme joy.

Chadogyopanishad—7-23-1 explains the true nature of divine bliss thus

> *"yo vai bhUmA tat sukham. nAlpE sukhamasti . . ."*

"He who experiences plentitude is infinite bliss,
there is no happiness in the little",

bhuma alone or that which has the quality of plentitude is happiness, bhuma alone is to be known and realized"

The quality of bliss expressed as 'bhuma' means plentitude; one that is complete, wholesome, unlimited, everlasting, and ever growing. Bhuma means plentitude but not in numbers, which means it is infinite. It is the opposite of 'alpa' or little or limited.

No one can think of God when hungry and starving.

Self realization, inclination to knowing about God is possible only for those who do not have to bother about their next meal. For the have-nots, who have to constantly worry about finding their next meal, it would not be practical to think of self realization or God. Their only referral to God would be to find their next meal. So it is all the more important for those who have surplus resources, to help others in need, so that they too can recover from their state of poverty and possibly think about higher knowledge. This would be our greatest service to God.

Our effort to realizing God would be possible only when we can free our mind from other issues relating to this world, sense gratification, material acquisitions, and obsession about relationships etc. We have to liberate the self from attachment to the body, wealth and this world.

Each one of us understands God based on the need of the situation. Our basic instinct is to survive and find happiness by any means and to protect our body. Even a doctor becomes our god if he saves our life. A man dressed in colored robe is made into a god when he succeeds in conniving to possessing special powers, though he might have duped us with cheap magic. We fall for such men because of our unhappy state and expectations from life. Smarter people would not fall for such gimmicks; for they would know that it is our good deeds that can bring us good results and not anything else.

Anything that supports our survival is God for us. We look for God in different forms. Those to whom money and wealth means everything, wealth is God for them; we see Divine Mother in several forms—goddess of wealth, 'valor' and 'knowledge', and 'annalakshmi' in the form of food. We have 'ashta lakshmi' or eight lakshmi's representing 8 types of wealth or attributes.

Science of Ramanuja.

Prior to Sri Ramanuja, the sacred knowledge was passed on from an authentic Acharya to a disciple, one to one basis. Every disciple would have to go through the rigors of extreme tests and earn to be worthy of receiving the most valued knowledge of the Srivaishnava heritage.

It was Ramanuja, who changed the tradition with a revolutionary view that anyone with true love and devotion for God is entitled to know the sacred knowledge that would enable him to practice that knowledge to reaching the eternal world.

Sri Manavala Mamuni in his prabandham 'upadesa rattinamAlai' sums up this aspect of Ramanuja thus—

"orANvazhiyAy upadEsittAr munnor, ErAr etirAjar innaruLAl,
pArulagil Asai-udayorkkellAm AriyargAL kUrumennu
pEsivarambaruttAr pin"

This glorious science of Ramanuja was an expression of his unconditional love and benevolent grace for the mankind. Ramanuja highlighted to the world that all humans are same in status in relation to God. He established a social order that all are equal irrespective of their background. He was easily the greatest social reformer when the whole nation was obsessed with the ridiculous caste system. There was a time when in some parts of North India, sati (widows would jump into the pyre of their dead husbands' funeral fire to immolate themselves) was practiced. This was easily the cruelest of them all. As we can see, sati was practiced only during the recent centuries, because we know that even during Treta yuga, when Dasaratha died, his three wives, Kausalya, Kaikeyi and Sumitra lived their full lifetime after his death. It is evident from this that even some 1.2 million years ago, civilizations were advanced, dharmic, kind and compassionate. Things have deteriorated during the last 2000 years or so. However, Ramanuja's philosophy was all about utmost kindness and compassion inclusive to all, without exception. His goal was to enable all humans to reach the highest state of existence.

Sri Ramanuja was the disciple of 5 acharyas. Ramanuja prayed to Tirukkotiyur Nambi, one of his Acharyas, to impart 'rahasyartha'—knowledge of secret mantras. The Acharya did not reveal the meanings straight away but informed Ramanuja that he had to be tested and if he qualifies to be worthy of this sacred knowledge, he would choose to reveal the meanings. Ramanuja had to visit Tirukkottiyur 18 times from Srirangam.

He was asked to confirm his understanding if he and his body were one and same; he should return to the Acharya after realizing that he was the atma and his body was non sentient matter and is different from him; and so on. (dehAtmAbhimAnam tulaindu vArum),

Finally he acknowledges to Ramanuja that he has reached the state, being worthy of knowing the sacred knowledge but under solemn oath that he would not reveal the same to anyone else. Ramanuja pledges that he would abide by the oath; the Acharya then reveals the secret knowledge to Ramanuja. He asks his Acharya as to what would happen if he reveals this to others. The Acharya tells him that he would suffer in hell and those who learn the mantra would attain eternal abode of the Lord. The Acharya's contention was—these mantras shall not be revealed without proper tests ensuring that the recipient is worthy of this knowledge.

Ramanuja sends out the message to all corners that he has the ultimate knowledge and would reveal it to all those who are desirous of knowing it, practicing which can lead them to God's abode. Thousands from all classes, caste, religion and background from different villages assembled in the space in front of the temple. Ramanuja then reveals the knowledge to all those present there, from atop the tower of the temple.

His Acharya was upset and sad as well, about what he did and questions his reasoning for breaking his oath. Ramanuja promptly replies—while hundreds of thousands could reach the highest state of existence with God, he was merely a sole atma that would perish in hell for going against the will of his acharya. It was important to reveal this knowledge to all those desirous of reaching God's abode, as many of them would never get the opportunity in several lifetimes to know this knowledge. *To do ones bit for the eternal benefit of others is indeed the purpose of human life and that in fact is the true service to God.* He also apologizes to his acharya for betraying his trust and asks to be forgiven for going back on his word.

The Acharya then realizes that indeed there can be no one like Ramanuja—one who wishes well for all the living beings and is the only one who would even be prepared to suffer himself, if in the bargain it would benefit others. The Acharya fondly calls him *"emberumAnAr"* (one who brings fame and glory to those associated with him). *Ramanuja's philosophy is pure science of kindness, compassion and total dharma;* that would please the Lord Himself. His science of God is inclusive, accepts one and all, irrespective of caste, creed, religion, or even gender. This is beyond all religions and philosophies; it breaks all barriers that were set prior to Ramanuja. He was able to see only the Atma in everyone and what's more, he was able to see God residing in every soul as the Antaryami.

To Ramanuja, all are 'bhagavatas'—(belonging to God, of God). He did not consider their birth as a criterion, but identified each one as a soul, originating from that supreme God, and equally dear to God. This was famously declared as *"empberumAnAr darisanam"* (philosophy of Emberumanar elevating others to attaining immortality).

Sri Thiruvarangattamudanar sums it up in one sentence in his Sri Ramanuja nUtrandadi—verse 25—thus

"kArEy karuNai-eRamAnuja, ikkadalidattil ArE aribavar ninnaruLin tanmai . . . ."

"Lord Ramanuja, there is no limit to your kindness, who on this mortal world could possibly comprehend your limitless grace?"

We have to understand that either God or the great mahatma's (azhwars, acharyas, saints, gurus, and such) have no desires. They are infinitely happy and fulfilled. Hence, they did not have to undertake any duties. Yet they would take birth in the world from time to time so that they could be of service to others; elevate everyone that wishes to be elevated to their level of existence. They do so in service to God, to help God. There is a big difference between God helping a devotee and an Acharya helping a devotee. We as humans recognize our own types better, as are able to co-relate better, but there is only one God and amusingly a Loner at that. He has no one equal to Him or above Him. When he tries to come to our help; we are unable to connect with Him due to our limitations. When an acharya who is just like us, guides us, we are able to connect better with him, for he knows our needs better; he does everything in a way we can understand and we feel comfortable following him.

We cannot say enough to praise the glory of Ramanuja. The least we could do is to practice as guided by him and derive the benefits which would please the Lord the most.

There are some of us who are convinced that by merely uttering "adiyen ramanuja dasan" or "emberumanar thiruvadigale saranam" we would be guaranteed of a place in the eternal world. The question is—would we say "adiyen ramanuja dasan" if it would not take us to 'parama padam' or even worse, if it would lead us to eternal hell? I am sure most of us would not.

So, our motive is reaching parama padam so that we can be well off there. And we use Emberumanar merely as an agent who can get us our desired goal. We have no need for him if not for attaining our goal. What we should seek instead is (thiruvadi sambhandam) relationship with Ramanuja's lotus feet and service to Ramanuja through his devotees, and not any other gain from that relationship; not even parama padam. Sri Madurakavi azhwar demonstrates to us leading by example. "tEvu mattariyEn kurugUr nambi, pAvi ninnisai pAdi tirivanE". He declares that he does not know of any god other than Nammazhwar. If we can even aspire to practice a minuscule of such devotion to the Acharya, we could use our "echil vai" (impure speech) to utter the divine name of Ramanuja, not otherwise.

Koorathazhwan was probably one of the few exceptions—he rejected the permission to see Lord Ranganatha when the Chozha king had declared that anyone associated with Sri Ramanuja shall not be permitted into the Temple. The gate keepers, however, would permit Azhwan, who was popularly known as a great person, to go into the temple. To Azhwan, his being a disciple of Ramanuja was the only state of existence he sought. If Ramanuja was not to be allowed to see the Lord, Azhwan would not see the Lord as well. Everything about Azhwan had no equal.

Que—and what is the sacred knowledge Ramanuja revealed to everyone?

Ans—each one of us has to take refuge with an Acharya to gain this knowledge. Ramanuja himself acquired this supreme knowledge from his acharyas just to lead by example. Not everyone, who thinks he knows this knowledge, is authentic or authorized to reveal. There is logic for this restriction—primarily, one who is not an authentic teacher might misinterpret and come up with his own wrong perceptions. That could mislead many. It is like a person who is not a qualified doctor, practicing medicine. Ramanuja has also designated 74 simhasanadhipati's (lineage of acharyas) to carry on his legacy. Only the acharyas of their lineage are authorized to perform 'samAshryanam' as well as reveal the essence of the 'rahasya mantras'. All others like us, that are not authentic, are permitted to merely make a mention of what this sacred knowledge is. They are—

> Tirumantram
> Dwayam
> Charama slokam

However, Charama slokam—

"*sarva dharmAn parityajya mAm Ekam SaraNam vraja,*
aham tvA sarva pApEbhyo mokshaishyAmi mA suchah"

Is a declaration by Lord Krishna in Gita and Ramanuja has written commentaries for us to know the intrinsic meanings. But Tirumantram and Dwayam would have to be bestowed by an Acharya.

Que—what is the proof that knowing this knowledge would lead us to attaining immortality? It sounds too easy and simple.

Ans—merely knowing these mantras would not take us anywhere, let alone to immortality. Knowing this knowledge would prepare us to practice a life that would enable us to realize God's 'nirhetuka krupa' (unconditional grace) and become true devotees. Or if we choose not to practice in accordance with this knowledge, but know their meanings, it would not make us any different from those who have not known these mantras. Knowing the intrinsic values of these mantras would make it easy for us to follow the prescribed life. This knowledge gives us direction, practicing which we can develop unconditional devotion. We have to start with subservience to the Acharya.

Ramanuja dedicated his entire life to serving humanity, while also ensuring that they come out of their state of being served to becoming self sufficient and be able to serve others. That is the true essence of service. Service to humanity does not mean to keep the under privileged in that state permanently. While we help them to get out of their state, we must guide them to attain economic independence so that they are empowered to serve others as well.

Simply gaining any knowledge is of no use, unless we implement what has been learnt. Knowing how to do business alone will not bring us money but actually doing would.

However, there are some mantras such as repeating the names of the Lord 'nama sankirtan' that are meant for chanting so that we cleanse our mind of polluting and lustful thoughts. When we chant 'Sri Vishnu Sahasra nama' (thousand names of the Lord) or *"hare rama hare rama, rama rama hare hare, hare krishna hare krishna, krishna krishna hare hare"*—we keep thinking of the Lord, also communicating with Him of our devotion. Here chanting alone is the purpose and nothing more need be done. There are psalms by the Azhwars and Acharyas praising the glory of the Lord which are meant for chanting. But Thirumantram, dwayam and charama slokam are mantras of *superior knowledge* which would have to be learnt from an Acharya and practiced for a lifetime, for them to be effective.

We see many learned scholars and spiritual leaders that are very knowledgeable, bestowed with excellent communication skills, being able to articulate and elucidate the concepts well, but do not practice what they preach. A lot of us would lose faith when we realize that the preachers themselves do not practice the doctrines. They would advise the prospective devotees to treat everyone as equals, without discrimination. They would advise us to help the needy at every possible opportunity if we are in a position to help. But we may witness their double standards when we notice that they themselves would ill-treat people based on their caste, religion, financial status etc. The preachers could be wealthy but would not give a cent to anyone, instead would accept money even from a poor man. We lose respect for them when we learn that they are merely doing what they know as a job, to make money. But there are some good ones as well, who truly practice what they know. We can see the difference between those who preach but do not practice and those who practice what they preach.

Whatever Krishna preached in Gita, He practiced as Rama, in His earlier incarnation. Hence it is all the more important for the preachers and persons of knowledge to set a standard in life, leading by example, for everyone to follow.

Gita 3/21—
  "yadyadAcharati sreshtastah tadEvEtaro janaha . . ."

"whatever a great person does, others also do,
whichever standard he sets, the world follows it"

Gita 3-22—
  "na me pArthasti kartavyam trishu lokEshu kinchana . . ."

"for me, there is nothing in all three worlds which ought to be done, nor is there anything unaccomplished that ought to be accomplished. Yet I keep working".

Gita 3/36
  "na budhibhedam janayEdajnAnAm karmasanginAm . . ."

"the great person should not bewilder the mind of the ignorant who are attached to work (doership), rather he should perform work with devotion, for others to follow suit"

The 5 things to be known

It is important to know the 'artha panchakam' the meaningful five, as clearly explained by Sri Pillai Lokacharyar, to attaining our goal. It sets the basis for us to pursue our goal. We can apply these five to everything we do.

a> 'sva swarUpa' (knowing the nature of the self) or who am I? Knowing about the self gives us the realization of our eternal relationship with the Lord.

b> 'para swarUpa' (knowing the nature and divine attributes of the supreme Lord) or who the Lord is? Or what is my destination? Knowing the Lord would establish that He is the cause and source for all the entities and worlds and that He is our eternal Father.

c> 'purushArtha swarUpa' (knowing what we should be doing on attaining our goal). Or what do I want? Only on knowing our goal, would we even decide whether to attempt to attain the goal or not. Realizing that we can attain the supreme goal, triggers the desire to reaching the goal.

d> 'upAya swarUpa' (knowing the means to attain our goal) or what we have to do in order to get there.

e> 'virodhi swarUpa' (knowing what prevented our attaining the goal thus far)—karma.

Reality of life in the mortal world.

Gita 2/27—
"jAtasya hi dhruvo mrutyurdhruvam janma mrutyuscha . . ."

"For, death is certain for the born, and re-birth is certain for the dead, Therefore, you should not grieve about what is inevitable" . . .

The moment we take birth, we journey towards death, as though death is our destination. In between, we are on the run morning to night. We have no time to think as to why we are running about the way we do, without the realization of our goal.

Sri Thondar-adi-podi azhwar in his prabhandam TirumAlai sums up a full life time of the humans in one song—

'vEda nUl pirAyam nUru manisar tAm puguvarElum,
pAdiyum urangippogum ninnadil padinaiyAndu;
pEdai, pAlakan, adAum, piNi pasi, mUppu, tunbam;
AdalAl piravi vEndEn arangamA nagar uLAnE"

"As prescribed in the scriptures, the humans are born to survive around 100 years. (some live less and some a bit more than 100 years, based on their karma). In that, half the life is spent sleeping, and in the balance 50, we fail to realize our relationship with the Lord—during infancy, childhood, teenage, (here Azhwar is afraid to even utter the word 'teenage' and hence he mentions ''adAgum' or 'that state'); ailments, hunger, old age and grief . . . Hence do not wish to be born at all in this world.

There is hardly any time for realizing the purpose of this life when a whole life is wasted away without being able to know our relationship with the Lord.

As infants, we would lie in our own excretion and someone else would have to clean us up, we would be totally dependent for everything. This is so because the Atma has to use the body based on its potential; as a newborn and infant, our body is still developing its capabilities.

As we grew up to be a child all that we did was play. In this stage, we would have no questions arising in us about the self except for the guided souls such as a Prahlada or Dhruva.

Then comes the state of infatuation or teen age, this is the stage we should be on our guard going out of control, be it attraction to the other gender, drugs, smoking, alcohol—any addiction, as all that we would be interested in is to indulging in non-stop pleasure-activities, seeking enjoyment from every quarter, totally believing that our body has to be fed with all sorts pleasures and that it is meant for that very purpose. Most of us lose our reasoning in this phase of life; so, there is no scope for realizing the truth about the self in that age. A lucky few escape from the clutches of sense gratification, focusing on good education or pursuing sports activities or arts or music due to right parental guidance, family environment or association with people that would guide them in the right direction.

Once out of the state of infatuation, either due to failures in achieving what they sought or by mere physical exhaustion or ailments that would prevent them from doing what they have been after, some realize their misdeeds and try to recover. Some others get totally lost. Our relationships increase with marriage. All that we are interested in this stage of life is to acquire maximum material comforts, accumulate wealth, to provide ultimate comfort to the self and family, in pursuit of happiness.

We constantly keep setting up goals in our lives. As we attain a state closer to our goal, the goal keeps changing, ever increasing. Those who have attained a state of financial stability, are constantly in the fear of losing whatever they possess; and those have-nots are constantly worried about how to get out of poverty and become rich. Every way—either in pursuit of material acquisition or in fear of losing what has been acquired. The fear of losing is like getting caught up in a black hole, it keeps pulling us into it.

The reason for this is simple. We always want more; the more we get, we want much more. Constantly unhappy about what we don't have. If we manage to fulfill some wants, it still does not make us happy as there are more wants unfulfilled. *Wants and desires are like burning fire and fulfilling them would mean to feed them fuel. The more fuel we feed, the more they burn; seeking much more fuel and this would be un-ending.*

It is said in the Gita 2/62, 63—
> "*dhyAyato vishayAnpumsah sangastEshUpajAyatE . . .*
> *. . . buddhi nASAt praNaSyati*"

"to a person thinking of sense-objects, there arises attachment to them, from attachment arises desire, from desire anger (if we don't get what we want); from anger comes delusion; from delusion loss of memory, from loss of memory destruction of discrimination (losing the ability to distinguish between right and wrong) and with the destruction of discrimination such a person is totally lost"

the fire of desire

It is needless to mention that we live more or less around 100 earthly years in this body, if lucky enough to survive ailments / diseases, accidents, natural disasters, wars and acts of terrorism that may end our life sooner. *However, our inclination to enjoy lingers on till the last breath and we leave the body with so many more desires and wants unfulfilled. Will keep taking birth to die, will die to take birth again.*

We acquire relationships with our birth.

It is fascinating to know that we acquire all relationships with our birth, including our association with our own body and lose all relationships with death. Each of us can realize one thing for sure—that we have no control over our birth or death. In reality, we have no control even over events during our lifetime, except that we think we are the ones doing everything! All that is in our control is making choices, not the outcome of our action or even execution of our choice.

We have reasons to be afraid of our relatives and other humans for the physical or emotional hurt they can cause. God is the only one we don't have to be ever afraid of, for He cannot and does not cause any pain or suffering to anyone. He is our true Father, who loves us unconditionally. If anything, we should dread doing bad karma which would have to be nullified by suffering. To be precise, there isn't such a thing as fear of God. The only relationship between God and us is unconditional love and devotion.

Even the richest and most powerful personalities on earth would have to relinquish their body at death. In order for us to understand this reality, the supreme Lord ended his incarnations, though it was in His power to remain here eternally. All the gods including Brahma would have an end. Everyone and everything except the Supreme Lord and the immortal world will go through cycles of formation and dissolution. The great souls—acharyas, rishis, gurus, and saints—that took birth here, gave up their bodies. Why even the earth, sun, galaxies and this universe will be gone one day, to be reborn again.

Our bodies are not different from the worlds, except that we take so many bodies going through birth and death cycles within one birth-death cycle for the worlds.

If we can devote so much time, working so hard to make this temporary life comfortable, should we not give it some thought and effort to keep the eternal Soul happy, which has been longing for that elusive bliss. *After all it is the Soul that is seeking happiness either by using this body or by attaining immortality.* Finding how we can attain eternal bliss would also ensure that our momentary life here would be a great one as well. If good education and knowledge of the worldly needs can make us successful in this world, devotion can bring us the knowledge to transcend to a life beyond this mortal world.

If we want to know, every household would have a heart melting story to tell; how they struggled to succeed in life, eventually making it big. And they would think, they have achieved everything in life when they become wealthy. But then, becoming rich is not the only purpose of life. We have simply acquired more resources to take care of our bodies, but in the bargain totally neglecting to safeguard the interests of the 'atma' which also needs to become rich by attaining immortality.

Que—are we in total control of executing our choice?

Ans—Five entities are involved in the execution of every choice we make.
- The self (atma) who is the choice maker;
- God (antaryami)
- mind/senses/sensory organs/our body;
- nature/prakruti/gods;
- other people (atmas like us) and

This is true to every little thing that we do, including breathing which we do on auto mode. It is by the presence of the Lord in us that we are able to use our body and senses. That apart even the gods of nature have their role in keeping our bodies working. But we are never aware of the other four contributors' involvement in the things we are able to do. We have no realization that without even one of the other four entities, we would fail to execute our choice. We credit ourselves for every accomplishment. Even a simple task as to eating would not be possible with even one of the other 4 not co-operating.

Let's say that I make a choice to eat something. This is the simplest and easiest task we do every day in our life.

a> 'I' am the *Atma. My* co-operation is guaranteed as I make the choice.

b> *The supreme Lord* who is the antaryami abiding in the Atma, who empowers us to do karma, though does not interfere or intervene in either our choice making or our actions, His laws of karma are always in effect. Based on karma, I could die that moment, before I could eat the food.

c> *My body/senses/mind*—Supposing I get a stroke and am unable to use my hand, or suddenly my health fails for some reason, I cannot complete the task.

d> *Nature-prakruti-gods*—Just in case there is a fire alarm, earthquake or some natural disaster occurring at that instant, I still cannot eat, even my health permitting.

e> *Other people*—Let's say at that instant someone in the family falls sick, or the person who has to provide me food has not prepared the food or someone else calls me on phone to report some emergency or if someone announces that the food I am about to eat is poisoned, I still cannot eat the food,

Yet, we think we are always in control of every situation and everything we do and never in realization of this truth. So how are we successful in executing many of our choices going well? It works well based on laws of karma.

Que—how does God empower our functioning in the bodies?

Ans—God is the supreme power by whom the souls are able to use mind, senses and body. He is like the central power house from whom we draw our energy. If we are able to draw energy in our homes by switching on, it is because there is power supply. The moment that power supply is cut off, we get no power. Similarly God is the infinite source of power who empowers our functioning in every sort of body we acquire, including when we attain immortality.

Chapter Seven

Source of knowledge.

Vedas are the eternal source of knowledge. Vedas originated from the supreme Lord, but not authored by Him. Vedas are acclaimed to be the most ancient text the human race has known. Vedas are known as 'sruti' or 'knowledge in sound form' and are the original source of knowledge about the nature and origin of the 'Atma', and the Supreme Lord. We can see the relevance of sruti, in the sound form being the means of knowledge. Even today we learn from hearing; with that we are able to see, perceive and understand. If not for the sruti/Vedas, there is no way of knowing of the Atman or God.

We can realize that there is no expression without 'sabda' or 'sound'. The syllable 'Om' comprises of everything there is in this universe. Mandukya Upanishad declares that creation begins with the vibration of the primal energy, prakruti, which has 'Om' as its sound symbol. We also realize that no object can be thought of without the sound related to it. It is clear that 'sabda' (sound) and 'artha' (object) are inseparable. Thus 'Om" which is the most universal and all inclusive sound, represents the whole creation; visible and invisible. Universe is merely a manifest form of the Divine. Om is the sound symbol of the supreme Brahman. Om represents all that exists in all times.

Mandukya Upanishad—1
"om-iti-Etad-aksharam-idam sarvam"

"All this world is the syllable Om, Its further explanation is this—
the past, the present and the future—everything is just Om. And
whatever is beyond the three periods of time is also verily Om".

Whenever we think of a person, we think of his name and form.
All our expressions are in the form of sound which is what we call
'a language'. There is no expression or thought without sound or
language. Even those who are mute, still express through sign
language, but grasped by the eye instead of ears.

What cannot be seen or known, can only be realized through
knowledge. Scriptures confirm that only 'sabda' is the 'pramANa'
or means of knowledge through the sound of Vedas. Scientists
use this very method to look for habitable planets like our own;

they listen to cosmic sounds. They confirm that the movement/ expansion of the universe resonates through sounds which can be studied to know more about them. They even listen to the sounds of our sun to analyze and predict eruption of sun spots spewing tremendous energy that can potentially disrupt our electromagnetic field and electrical systems.

Vedanta, in the form of Upanishads is the essence of Vedas. Any knowledge, whether we learn from the scriptures or we formulate on our own, is coming from God dwelling in each one of us as the antaryami.

To be precise, human science can only know of non sentient objects, be it matter or energy. Science has no way of knowing about Atma or God. Why, science has problem even knowing all about the physical universe so far.

There is logic to why the supreme Lord cannot be known. I do not know about my father at my birth, I started knowing about him only at a stage when I could grasp whatever knowledge that was given to me either by my father or the other elders. Even then it is only to the extent they told me or to the extent I could grasp. In the case of the Lord, no one can know about Him because He is the origin for every being including the first created being Brahma. There was no one that existed before God. Everyone and everything originated from God.

Katopanishad 6-12—
naiva vAcha, na manasA prAptum sakyo na chakshushA, . . .

"He cannot be attained either by speech or by mind or by the eye. How else can it be realized except from the words of the Vedas that expresses that it is?"

Knowing Paramatman is not possible on account of His infinite nature. He is not like an object of this world of which can be seen; can be known by means of speech and by means of mind. He can be known only through Vedas, even that, only to an extent. However, we can know Him when He reveals Himself; even then, only to the extent we can know of Him.

The beauty of Vedas and Upanishads is that there is no suggestion anywhere to accept anything as it is. This knowledge triggers inquest in us to finding correct answers for ourselves, *for we cannot be shown, taught or explained God, but only guided to realize.* God can only be experienced and realized through guided thinking and practice of 'tapas' (penance) and devotion (upasana). Vedas reveal information based on which we can further inquire to realize the truth ourselves.

The term 'Veda' means 'true knowledge'; 'sacred knowledge'. But Vedas have knowledge that is applicable and sought by all types of people. Each person can understand the meaning of the same sruti differently depending upon his state, disposition and perception; more often coming up with wrong interpretation. Vedas are absolute knowledge for they originated from the supreme Lord and that might be the reason why Vedas are not easily comprehended. Though Vedas reveal knowledge about God, we understand them differently based on the influence of sattva, rajasa and tamasa gunas.

Vedas seem to say that the Sun is the Paramatma, or the Agni is the Paramatma or even Brahma is the Paramatma. It would seem to suggest that even 'atma' is the Paramatma, or even the air we breathe (prANa) as Brahman; literally suggesting that everything is Brahman. But the correct interpretation is that the Paramatman is the indweller of everyone and everything yet He is distinctly different from the souls or gods or the worlds.

In fact Nammazhwar addresses Krishna as *'muniyE, nAnmuganE, mukkaNNnappA'* (as azhwar was able to recognize the supreme God as the antaryami in every one of these—in a sage (muni), Lord Brahma (nanmugan) or Lord Shiva (mukkannappa). The Supreme Lord dwells in *every god, every soul and all the worlds, belonging to Him. At the same time we should not mistake all others as the supreme God.*

So, are the Vedas vague and confusing? No, but they are not easy to comprehend even for Brahma, let alone humans. We can say that Vedas seem to hide their meanings and hence are termed as 'marai' in Tamizh, which is why Azhwars, Acharyas and Ramanuja have given us, correct interpretations in several sacred scriptures.

To make it easy, shouldn't Vedas contain references only for nurturing devotion that would lead all of us to immortality? Not everyone is interested in devotion and attaining immortality. God being the kind father has to look after all types of children based on their interest. Just as we assume 8.4 million bodies based on our karma/choice and not all the souls acquire a human body, though that is considered better. Eventually, it is our happiness that He wants. Only after being born as humans do we realize that human life is better than that of other species. Just as a rich person would not want to return to a state of poverty ever again, a devotee who has tasted the joy of being devout would never seek to return to the ways of non devotees.

Vedavyasa has written commentaries which are again not easy to understand for our minds. Hence many great souls appeared on earth to pass on the knowledge in a way we can understand.

Gita 15-15—
> "*sarvasya chAham hrudi samnivishto . . .*"

"I am seated in the hearts of all beings; From Me are memory, knowledge and their removal as well. Indeed I alone am to be known from all the Vedas. I grant the fruition of the rituals of Vedas; I alone am the knower of the Vedas"

There is *karma kanda*, that prescribes desire oriented rituals (kamya-karma or actions for desire fulfillment) best suited to people seeking enjoyment in this world. Those desirous of attaining heaven, and other material benefits, which in the course of achieving, would bind the soul to repeated births and deaths in this world. 'Karma kanda' is for those who are not interested in moksha / liberation from the cycle of birth and death in the mortal bodies.

And 'upasana kanda' advocates devotion and worship that would lead us to God. It is important to know that devotion on its own cannot grant us moksha or get us out of this world. Only the supreme Lord can liberate us from this world and grant us immortality or moksha.

Upanishads have everything we need to know about the Lord.—'upa' means—nearness or going near. 'Upanishad' also means to 'sit at the feet of'—bringing us closer to God. And then we have Bhagavad Gita which is the essence of Upanishads given to us by the Lord Himself, and there is Sri Ramayana and some relevant sattvika puranas (sanctimonious scriptures) that contain everything for nurturing devotion and understanding the nature of the Supreme Lord. Above all, we have the 'divya prabandhams' in Tamizh by the Azhwars, vividly expressing their close experiences with the Lord.

Vedas provide knowledge for all concerned based on their respective goals.

Krishna confirms in Gita about four types of devotees seeking His grace for different goals.

Gita 7-16
"chatur vidA bhajantE mAm janAha sukrutinorjuna . . ."

'Four types of men of good deeds worship Me, these are the distressed, the seekers of knowledge, the wealth seekers and the men of knowledge'.

Here Krishna is referring to all good men, but due to their conditioning and state, they seek different goals such as dharma, artha, kama and moksha.

Those engaged in *artha* and *kama* are seeking to obtain the objects of sense gratification under Vedic injunction. Persons desirous of *mukti* or *moksha* are seeking to detach with the other two, also under Vedic injunction. For the first two types of men, the truth about the Lord, His *infinite virtues and capabilities;* realizing the self (*atma*), and the transcendental relationship with the Lord, remains unrealized. This is because they are involved with the duality of *raga* and *dwesha* using their sense impressions which create a layer of ignorance between them and Brahman. But if they sincerely follow the guidelines of the upasana kanda (path of devotion), they would be lead out of ignorance into '*para-vidya*', *superior transcendental knowledge,* by the supreme Lord.

Even with modern science, scientists first formulate theories before transforming their invention into products. After it has been tried and tested by them, they are released for the benefit of the society. We then use the products without question. We do not doubt them for they do it in the larger interest of the mankind as also for a monetary benefit. Similarly, Vedas and all other sources of knowledge are given to the mankind by our Father-God, out of benign grace, for our benefit. We need to have faith in the knowledge which has been tried and tested by many divine souls and mahatmas who have added their own understanding and experiences for us to realize as well. We must trust our elders who trusted their elders for generations. Our elders would not pass on something to us without knowing the benefits. They filter and select the best for us, for our happy existence.

We have total faith in our doctor, we follow his prescription blindly. Sometimes, if the doctor is wrong, we suffer. Yet we continue to trust him. Similarly, we must have faith in the sacred scriptures and the message of the Azhwars, Acharyas and other divine souls who have left behind an ocean of knowledge for our benefit. When we follow their guidelines, we would not have to suffer like in the case of a doctor going wrong. With the doctor, we remain ignorant or blindly follow the doctor's directions. But with the scriptures and knowledge given by the divine souls, we become learned, enlightened and aware. There is no question of blind belief. We show faith, attain knowledge, apply and practice as prescribed and we can see tangible, real benefits soon enough. If we don't see any change for the better, surely it would be due to our deficient understanding and practice. However, there would be no harm done. There are no negative impacts. Even if we fail to attain the desired goal totally, we would still have made some progress towards the goal with zero harm.

Some of us are confounded seeing so many people engaged in wrong practices in the name of devotion and religion. Many people follow foolish practices such as injuring the body, piercing on their faces, walking on fire, breaking coconuts on heads, offering sacrifices of animals; imagining to please the gods—are all acts of foolish people, done in utter ignorance. One thing would be common with all of them. They would all be either uneducated people or follow these blind beliefs out of fear. They follow everything blindly in fear because they have desires to fulfill and they are made to believe they could drive away all their problems doing such things. They do not know what is right and wrong nor do they care. They would spend a whole lifetime wastefully, doing these things without realization. If these practices can protect them or benefit them in any way, they should have already, after doing the very first time. They do everything on the pretext that their acts would please a certain deity (even that is a wild imagination) and that they would prosper and resolve all their problems in life by doing these things. Hence we should not be guided by these acts into judging the true essence of religion or devotion.

People also question the concept of Hindu religion where many gods and goddesses are worshipped. They don't realize that God is personal to each and every person. As a matter of fact, each one of us has the supreme God dwelling in us. When we don't realize this truth, we go in search of gods. It is not different from fans following football teams or cricket teams. If the captain is the supreme God, and other players are lesser gods, not every follower of the game would be supporting the captain. There would be followers for every player based on the way each player plays the game. Or there are many football clubs in the world, but only one team is the champion in a year. Not every fan supports the champion team. Even the losing teams have millions of followers. Similarly, people follow different gods based on how they like their god. There is total freedom in Hindu religion to follow any god; each one can create his own god or goddess.

True devotion is of great knowledge, scientific understanding and clarity in perception, without an iota of blind belief. There is no place for fear when it concerns God; love and affection is the only emotion. Foolish practices involving physical or mental harm, either to the self or to others are neither devotion nor religion. Common sense would tell us that any practice that has no practical benefit cannot be termed as religion or devotion. And truly, God is not involved in any of such practices nor would He dissociate if we refrain from such practices. We are fooling ourselves in the name of gods. True devotion involves rites and rituals of scientific significance, resonating joy and bliss to all involved, devoid of any pain or suffering of any kind to any being. True devotional rituals bring all classes of the society converging as one people. Devotion is not for gaining any material benefit. Devotion is a state in which we seek nothing except to serve with love and affection.

We hear people being told that if a person visits a temple once, he must visit the temple at least for 18 years, if not; he would acquire the wrath of the deity and would suffer in life. We must realize that if a god can stoop to the extent of punishing us for not visiting his temple so many times, he is worse off than humans and not a god. A smart person would know that all these are bluffs by some people in trying to make easy money and nothing more or beyond.

We also see animals being abused, killing them in the pretext of sacrifice to a deity, which again is done in blind belief or out of fear. They do such killings wishing for their wants and desires fulfilled. If they don't accomplish what they sought, they assume the deity is angry or they should sacrifice more animals.

And there are some sports involving animals, causing them pain and injury, giving it different dimensions, such as, entertainment or display of human strength or bravery in controlling these animals. It is utter ignorance or reckless attitude without realization of the pain and suffering we cause to them. We see bull fights organized every year. The bulls go through real hell until the event ends and they end up in the slaughter house after being rendered physically damaged. How can causing injury and inflicting pain to an animal be a sport or display of strength and bravery? Imagine someone superior, doing the same to humans knowing well that we are no match to them.

That's why true knowledge of the Atma, and God is essential so that we understand the extent of suffering we cause to other humans or animals out of ignorance or arrogance.

If not for the Azhwars, we would have remained ever deprived of knowing our true relationship with the Lord. Even if the psalms of Azhwars are not easy to comprehend, we have commentaries by the great Acharyas, explicitly revealing every nuance of the intrinsic, devotional experiences of the Azhwars, for each one of us to understand God and His love for us.

Nammazhwar goes out of his way to impress upon souls like us
thus *"sonnAl virodamidu, Agilum solluvan kENmin"*—

"Though we might antagonize the Azhwar or dislike him for
mentioning what he would, he would still tell us what is good for
us and asks us to pay heed to his advice"

There are two ways to dealing with people in any situation. One
way is to establish what is considered "hitam" for the recipient.
'Hita' literally means "for the benefit of the one who follows the
suggested course of action" and the other way is 'priyam' to
express what is liked by the recipient, what pleases the person;
but may be harmful if followed.

Here, Azhwar is giving us the knowledge, following which we
would benefit immensely, though we may not like the suggestions
at the face value, which is Hitam or for our good. Priyam—is
an easy way, likeable way. We often say things to please
people, even if it is not the truth. We may do so in order to gain
their confidence or try to please them assuming they may be
potentially useful to us. We do not care if it is beneficial to them
or not, all that we focus on is to gain their favour by uttering
words that would please them, saying what they would like to
hear. But Azhwar does not know our ways; he cannot pretend.
He knows only one way and that is to speak the truth, for our
benefit.

Even at home, we can see the effect of hitam and priyam. If the
child wants expense money in excess of his known needs, for
commuting or food, we have to think twice before giving the child
any money, for it could lead him or her into wrong and harmful
ways. He could go astray and would become impossible to rein
in after a certain stage. We shall not worry if denying the child
what he likes would displease him. We have to do what is good
for the child. In this case, we have to firmly set the standards so
that the child shall not go out of precincts. We have to draw a

line when it comes to doing what is right and what we like to do. Hitam is that conscience that reminds us to doing what is right, what is good and beneficial as well. Priyam, though is what is mostly sought, as that gives us momentary desire fulfillment, the effects would be undesirable.

Que—who authored the Vedas?

Ans—it is said that the Vedas are 'a-paurusheyam'—meaning not authored by any person. *Vedas originated from God just as the worlds and souls have their origin in God. They are also said to be eternal and timeless.* **It is only natural that the source for this infinite universe and the countless jivatmas has to be the source for all the knowledge as well**. Vedas that we know today are perhaps not the total version of what was original. What we have today is a shortened version that may have also gone through additions and omissions. It is also said that during the 1200 years of foreign invasion, a lot of our original texts were destroyed by the invaders. If there are any differential perceptions in what we have today, anything arguable and questionable, would be because of changes incorporated by humans of this age to suit their preferences.

Vedavyasa gave us the Vedas and also wrote commentaries in Vedanta sutras. Vedavyasa is one of God's part-incarnations. Vedas were first passed on to Brahma by the supreme Lord and unto us through Vedavyasa.

Que—is there a specific language for God? Why are the Vedas, Upanishads, Gita and other scriptures in Sanskrit?

Ans—languages are for us. God knows all the languages we know and He also knows Sanskrit. Languages are a way for us

to communicate, without which we are constrained to express.
God understands the language of the mind, the thought. We
can express in any language, even if we don't understand that
language. There is no restriction that we should know a particular
language.

A person who does not understand English would ask the same
question—why should we communicate in English and why are
most of the modern day scripts in English? The answer is simple,
because people of this era understand and use English language
more than any other. Similarly, the Vedas and sacred scriptures
were passed on orally in Sanskrit from time to time. And Sanskrit
is a complete language, most scientific and expresses better
than any other language which is why it is considered the
'devanagari script' or 'the language of the gods'. Sanskrit is the
first language. As a parallel we also have arulicheyal and other
prabandhams in Tamizh. We should not have a problem with
Sanskrit as a language. If we don't know the language, we can
still express our devotion to the Lord in any other language we
know. Vedas and Upanishads contain knowledge about God.
Sanskrit was the spoken language of the first three yugas and
even early part of kali yuga and hence all the Vedas, Upanishads
and Gita are in Sanskrit. However, we have evolved so many
languages in the present day societies, based on our regional
preference and understanding. Even in that we have different
dialects and accents for the same language.

Que—we chant hymns and verses in Sanskrit and
other languages which many of us don't understand
the meanings of? Is it not a waste of time to simply
chant something we don't even understand?

Ans—First of all, we need to understand the purpose of chanting.
We chant the hymns and verses, be it in Sanskrit or any other

language, which are expressions singing the infinite glories of the Lord. These are not composed by us nor are we capable of such expressions. These are the sacred compositions by divine souls, Azhwars and Acharyas. It would be nicer if we try and understand their meanings for our own benefit, as we can enjoy much more, singing these hymns. Even otherwise, when we chant these hymns, they are meant for the Lord, who understands very well what we are doing or saying. We may even chant them wrongly, or miss-pronounce some of the words due to lack of knowledge. God still understands our intentions and accepts our effort even if deficient, even if we don't understand what we are chanting. When we chant simple names of the Lord such as "hare rama hare rama, rama rama hare hare; hare krishna hare krishna, krishna krishna hare hare . . ." We think we are simply repeating the name of Rama and Krishna which is only partly true. The name 'rama' comes from the root 'ramayati iti ramah"—meaning that the sound 'rama' brings immense joy to everyone who utters or hears that name; He who brings bliss to everyone. It is quoted in PadmapurANa that the word 'rAma' stands for the supreme Brahman. Similarly the name Krishna also defines "Akarshayati iti krishnah" one who attracts, one who is most beautiful and magnificent, which again refers to the supreme Brahman.

Similarly there is 'vishnu sahasra namam' listing the thousand names of the Lord, each name signifying the Lord's auspicious virtues and attributes. We need not know the meanings of all the names, but when we chant, the Lord knows that we are chanting His glories and that is the purpose. We can know the meanings if we truly want to know. It is up to us.

Let us say, I don't know English. I ask a friend to teach me few sentences and he teaches me bad sentences, but I am neither aware of their real meanings nor that they are bad. But he explains their meanings to me which is what I understand when I speak those words.

Let's say he teaches me thus:

> ➤ To invite a close friend or visitor, "you idiot, why have you come". I would be under the impression that I am extending a warm welcome to the visitor.
>
> ➤ To ask them to be seated and comfortable, and if they wish to have a drink—"you lazy man, don't you have any work, what do you want?
>
> ➤ When someone takes leave, to say that it was wonderful having them and to come again—"never come back, I don't want to see you again"

Whether I know the language or not, the person who knows English, would know that I am saying bad things, even though I think I am saying good things. Similarly, when we chant suprabhatam or thiruvaimozhi for the Lord, though we may not know their meanings, the Lord does and that is more important. All that we know is that these hymns are sung praising the Lord's inexpressible virtues. Surely, they are not composed by a friend who teaches bad words in a false sense of humour. And all those divine souls who composed these sacred prabandhams, expounding their knowledge about the Lord, would please the Lord when chanted by anyone, whether he knows the meaning or not.

Thondaradippodi azhwar declares "*iLayapun kavidaiyElum empirArkkiniyavArE*" "even if my expressions for Him are nothing more than an infant's utterances (imperfect, deficient) He loves them sweetly, out of kindness"; for we are capable of only so much. He is our own; He is magnanimous, bestowing kindness by virtue of his nature, who accepts even our shortcomings, crediting us the honour of doing great deeds.

A devotee does not seek anything from the Lord including immortality. Whether the Lord keeps the devotee in the mortal world or takes him to the eternal world, it would not make a difference to him. His nature is devotion to the Lord, doing what pleases the Lord. A devotee would not change his perception even if the Lord ignores the devotee, even if the Lord does not respond sooner. If the Lord is not responding, it is to test the extremes of his devotion and as a means to exhaust his residual karma, to see if he can surpass everyone else thus far. The Lord has no extent and is infinite in every aspect, and the soul being His potency, is also capable of surpassing limits. True devotion is more powerful; in that even the Lord submits to the devotion of a Prahlada or the Gopikas.

Que—Why did God create this universe and beings?

Ans—there has been no beginning as such; all the three main entities—the Jivatmas (individual souls), the universe and the Paramatma (Supreme Lord)—have no beginning or end. God is unborn in the literal sense. Jivatmas and universe are born from God. God has been there even before this universe manifested from Him. Just that they were merged into God prior to manifestation. God has no other origin for Himself but is the origin for all the worlds and souls. It is not easy to comprehend this reality. So, to make it simple—First there was God who was *unborn and always existing* and the souls and the worlds were born from Him.

Gita 9/4—
   mayA tatamidam sarvam jagadavyakta mUrtinA . . ."

"This entire universe is pervaded by Me in an unmanifest or invisible form (avyakta murtina), all beings abide in Me, but I do not abide in them visibly"

Gita 9/7—
   "sarva bhutAni kaunteya prakrutim yAnti mAmikAm . . ."

"all beings enter into My prakruti at the end of a cycle of time (pralaya or dissolution), again I send them forth at the beginning of a cycle of time" (srishti or manifestation or creation).

A close comparison to explain this would be to think of each atma as a drop of water, each one with its distinct identity (karma-DNA). When each drop merges into the ocean it cannot function. It would be static, in a state of suspended animation. When it is released from the ocean (evaporates) it goes into the created world taking a body based on its potential (karma).

This would be when the worlds are forming, similarly when the clouds cool down, they become rain drops and fall into the ocean (they also fall on land and other places, imagine if there was no land, if everything was ocean then all the rain drops would fall into the ocean. We are trying to use this analogy in order to understand how each soul originates from God in formation stage of the universe and how it merges into Him during annihilation. It is important to realize that the drops of water have not made the ocean. The ocean exists always, and the drops are made from the ocean. The drops of water do not exist without the ocean for they originate from the ocean and merge into the ocean again. In all states, every drop depends on the ocean for its existence. Its release, functioning and merger—are all governed by the ocean—The ocean is God and the water drops are individual souls.

What we seek as salvation from this mortal world is not merging into God during dissolution. We seek to attain God's eternal world getting a divine immortal body that is not bound by the process of manifestation and dissolution but remains beyond this mortal world.

God created this world for our sake, because we sought to experience an independent existence, away from Him. All that He has done is to give us what we sought.

God created because it came to Him naturally, by mere sankalpa (thought/will); without so much as blinking the eye; was done effortlessly. One of His divine virtues being "satya sankalpah" (what He wills becomes reality) illustrates that merely by His will alone, everything is caused into existence, including the release of the souls and manifestation of the universe.

Creation, sustenance and withdrawal of the worlds is like play for Him.

We do realize that one of the natures of the souls is to express. They experience great joy in every form of expression. They can express only in a functional body. When we express in the form of art or music or dance or sport—we not only enjoy expressing but also enjoy much more when the others appreciate our expression. It is the same with God. If you adore and appreciate the magnificence of the Tirumala hills or Grand Canyon and relate it to the beauty of God's expression, He is pleased. Admire the natural wonders, thinking of Him as the source of all, He is elated. Realize that the billions of stars in our galaxy and billions of such galaxies as part of this infinite universe being His infinitely sublime expression, He would be praised; which is why He made us sentient beings, in order to appreciate His infinite powers.

In reality, we know only to a certain extent about our universe, let alone God. All that we can do is wonder about God's omnipotence and admire everything about Him and His creation and feel proud to be His children. And this adulation is devotion. After all, He is our eternal Father, relative and friend; He is truly everything to us. Without the expressions or emotions, we would be like the non-sentient matter or machines.

Asking the question as to why God created this world is like asking a genius artist (a **Raja Ravi Varma**, a **Picasso** or a Leonardo Da Vinci) as to why they created master pieces of art; or a scientist, why he invented; or a child that plays with a ball even though it comes across a ball for the first time, why? They all do so because it is natural to them; they have pure joy in doing what they do. And it is in their power to express. We can ask, why the birds fly and the fish swim. Because they are naturally made that way and they have the capability. And the same with God, He created the worlds for the souls to explore His world evolving in bodies of their choice; as though like a play.

Gita 9/5—
"na cha mat sthAni bhUtAni, pasya mE yogamaiswaram . . ."

"Yet beings do not abide in me (visibly), behold My divine yoga. I am the upholder of all beings and yet I am not in them in a manifest form"—

This explains that God does not support beings like a vessel that supports water contained in it, he supports them by will, which is His divine yoga power, and yet He derives no help for Himself by anyone or anything. He projects, sustains and controls all beings merely by His will, but without directly involving or interfering in the cause and effect process of each soul. The laws of prakruti (His Maya) would be the governing force for all the souls in the mortal worlds, which works under His control. The Lord dwells in everything yet He remains invisible.

We understand that in order to create, produce or make something we need three things—a **maker**, tools/equipments/ **machinery** and **raw material**—let's take making of a clay pot for instance, as that is what is often quoted as an analogy for creation—we need clay and water (raw material), the pot making wheel that spins and a potter, who uses the clay/water and the wheel to make pots of different shapes / sizes. But in the case of manifestation of the worlds, God is Himself all these things—He is the raw material for He did not use anything outside of Him to will this world into existence, He used no machinery as His will (sankalpa) was the machinery and He is also the Maker from whom the worlds came into being. We cannot see this thing work anywhere else.

We cannot create anything out of nothing. After so many trial and error methods, when we see a resultant outcome or product; we claim to have made an invention. *All the scientific inventions and technological breakthroughs have been possible by understanding the potential energies and properties of this universe and earth.*

There is a joy in all our relationships. Relationship from marriage results in a baby or manifestation or creation. This is something we can all understand. It is important to know that the process of intent might be for sense gratification though; the resultant baby is pure joy. When a living being produces, it is an expression of joy; this is true even to animals, though they do not have the human intelligence. Why, we even feel happy when we produce products. A car well crafted gives all those involved, a sense of joy. A music well composed gives immense happiness to the composer and to the listeners. A scientific breakthrough or invention gives overwhelming joy to all involved in the project. However a robot though programmed to do certain activities, does not feel anything, for it is a lifeless machine without human emotions. This is exactly why the Supreme Lord's prime nature is "infinite bliss', as stated by the Upanishads. However, there is no intent of karma by God; He is detached from this universe.

The Lord has the joy while doing the job and after the job is done because He is not attached in the process. However, we feel happy when a job is well done. We become sad when we don't get the desired result. This is because we are attached to our actions and outcomes. What we experience is pleasure and pain. But what we seek is divine bliss, attaining which, it would not be lost.

Creation or manifestation of the worlds and beings has no first beginning. So, the differentiation of karma, jivatma and Paramatma even before creation of the universe has to be understood. Only in the creative cycle, the differentiation becomes evident, but in the dissolved state it remains latent and unmanifest. In both states—of created universe or the dissolved unmanifest universe, all the three entities exist. And paramatma is the common factor in all, at all times, in all states.

Entities and worlds

Mainly there are three entities and 26 in all.

Gita 13/5—
   mahAbhUtAnyahankAro budhir-avyaktamEva cha . . ."

"The great elements, the ahankara, the budhi, the avyakta, the ten senses and the one, as well as the five objects of the senses"

chith—sentient, chetana (jivatma),

achith (non-sentient, achetana, representing this universe as **matter/energy**) are 24 entities,
  - the **five great elements** (akAsa, vAyu, agni, Apa, bhUmi—ether, air, fire, water, earth),
  - **ahankara** (ego—primeval element),
  - **buddhi** (intellect),
  - **avyakta** (prakruti/maya)
  - **ten—comprises of—five sense organs and five motor organs and the one is the mind**—the five sensorial organs (ear, skin, eye, tongue, nose), and the five motor organs—speech, hands, feet, organs of excretion and reproduction. And the 'one' being the manas (mind), and
  - **the 'five objects of senses'** (sabda, sparsha, rupa, rasa, gandha—sound, touch, form, taste and smell), and

Paramatma (God).

To sum up—24 non sentient entities, 25th is the Atma and 26th is the Paramatma, who is the origin and indweller of both sentient and non sentient of the universe.

Our five senses are connected with the five elements of nature—sabdha to akasha (sound to ether), sparsa to vayu (touch to air), rupa to agni (sight to fire), rasa to Apa (taste to water) and gandha to prithvi (smell to earth).

Nature of the Souls is knowledge. The Soul knows himself and also knows other things he comes across. Soul is like a light which is self revealing and reveals other objects as well. You do not need a second source of light to reveal the first light. This essentially means that the 'atma' is knower of the self and as well as other things owing to his natural knowledge.

Everything we see with our eyes is part of this universe, including our body, and is non-sentient matter. They are created in support of our existence. Atma, once in this world, is under the influence of prakruti (creation). Souls are infinite in numbers and the universe is infinite as well.

God's virtues, powers are infinite. According to scriptures, Even God has not tested His capabilities completely. *His capabilities are unlimited with infinite possibilities.* He can keep coming up with ever new worlds, species, and beings as and when He wills. This is why possibly the dinosaurs and many other species might have become extinct and also new ones may evolve *due to the effect of karma.*

There are two worlds—one is the Lila vibhuthi—'the play world'—our universe, which is ever changing, manifests into cosmic (macro) form as we see it (sthula sthithi) at the beginning of the cycle of time and merges into God in micro form (sukshma sthithi) at the end of the cycle of time. It goes through the cycle of manifestation and annihilation, repeatedly, endlessly.

Gita 13/19—
"prakrutim purusham chaiva vidhyanAdl ubhAvapi . . ."

"both prakruti (universe/our bodies) and the soul (purusha) are without beginning; all modifications and the attributes are born of prakruti"

And then there is the Nitya vibhuthi—the Divine, imperishable world which is God's abode (parama padam—meaning—the highest state, beyond all worlds, but nothing else beyond it). The divine world is the eternal abode of God and the nitya suris and muktatmas.

Svetasvataropanishad 3-15—
"purusha EvEdam sarvam yadbhUtam yachcha bhavyayam . . ."

The essence of this sruti is that the supreme Lord has His supreme abode (paramapadam) which does not flourish on account of food". 'amrutatva' signifies the non material abode; paramapadam having 'aprAkruta bhogya bhogopakaraNa, which does not flourish on account of 'anna' It is affirmed that He is the Lord of both the VibhUtis—*nitya vibhUti* (eternal world) and *LeelavibhUti* (mortal world)

Atma is eternal and un-changing as well but cannot be seen due to its **unmanifest form** and it is always in the sukshma sthithi—'**aNu-matra**' (subtle state). There are mainly three categories of atmas—nitya suris, muktatmas and badhatmas; in addition there are kaivalyarthis and mumukshus

a> nitya suris—(***tad vishnoh paramam padam, sadA pasyanti sUrayah***) are the divine souls in the parama padam, ever in service of God, experiencing divine, unending joy. These souls would incarnate in the changing world in order to help God redeem souls that have been caught up in the cycle of birth and death eternally. Soon on completing their mission they would return to their eternal abode. They have no karma.

b> Muktatmas—(liberated souls)—souls that have taken birth in the changing worlds due to their choice and karma and later on by unconditional devotion through an Acharya, attained the eternal abode. The Lord accepts them to His abode and grants them similarity with Himself. They too would have no karma after attaining the eternal abode.

It is to be noted that the atma would have to relinquish all karma before the Lord accepts him to the immortal world. Both virtue and sin would have to be exhausted before he can attain immortality.

Badhatmas—(funnily enough, when spelt in English—you can see that we are "bad-atmas" by virtue of our choice and deeds)—we are the souls caught up in the cycle of birth and death in the changing worlds, eternally thus far. Some realize their deprived state at some stage and may become muktatmas, as and when they surrender to an Acharya, who would elevate them to the level of acceptance by the Lord to His world. And countless number of other souls may experience birth and death in this world till they realize their origin and wish to go back to God's kingdom. We belong to this group.

kaivalyArthis—are the souls that attain the eternal world but choose to experience the bliss within the Self and remain ever in that state. They have chosen not to engage in subservience to the supreme Lord. This is a state from which there is no return and considered the most wasted state. They cannot experience the ever growing bliss of the Lord.

Mumukshus—are the badhatmas in the mortal world, desirous of attaining the immortal world; taking refuge with the Acharya, following the devotional path. Badhatmas become mumukshus by choice.

Chapter Eight

Consciousness of soul and God.

Que—does the soul pervade entirely in the body?

Ans—No, the soul does not pervade everywhere in the body. The soul is seated in the heart—

Prasnopanishad 6—
> *"hrudi hyesha atma"*—"the jivatman is in the heart".

And as confirmed in Gita 18-61—
> *"Iswarah sarva bhUtAnAm hrud dEsE tishtati"*—

> "the Lord abides in the heart of every being",

God dwells in the atma who is seated in the heart. The power (consciousness) of the soul pervades the whole body, though he is seated in the heart. Like a lamp though placed in one place, the light of which spreads all around. That is the reason you can perceive sense of touch from head to toe, though the soul is not in the head or the toe.

Que—is it the same with God, when you say He is all pervading, is He not present everywhere?

Ans—No, it is not the same with God. He is present everywhere, God resides in every particle of this universe in **unmanifest form**. He is also present in every soul.

Sun and its rays—is a good analogy to understand the difference between God and individual souls. If sun is God, the countless rays of the sun are individual souls. The rays are formed out of the sun; the rays cannot exist without the sun. The rays exist by the power of the Sun. The sun however is not directly the rays and yet is present in the rays. The Sun is distinctly different than the rays though the rays originate from the sun and have some inherent characteristics that are similar to the Sun. The rays are the potency of the Sun. Sun does not depend on the rays for his existence but the rays have no existence without the sun. Similarly, souls are not God, but God resides in souls; the souls are potency of the Lord.

Que—there is dirt and filth as well in this world, when you say God is all pervading, does that mean He is in dirt as well? Is He also in the food we eat?

Ans—dirt and filth are what they are for our bodies. Not for God or the Souls. Dirt and filth are created by embodied beings. Otherwise, there is no dirt or filth in nature. In that case even our body is filth, made of blood, flesh and bones, smelling foul. For that matter even the Soul is not stained by the dirt and filth as he is always in subtle, unmanifest form.

Dirt and filth cannot touch God's divinity or sanctity. He is in everything and yet untouched by the whole universe! He is the subtlemost and hence remains blemishless and undefiled. He is not tainted by dirt.

By the same token, He is also there in the soul of the sun, does it mean it would burn Him. Neither God nor the soul of the sun is burnt by the tremendously burning body of the sun. Souls are present in food, sperm, in every cell of the human body. During the state of conception till it is born, it spends close to 9 months in a mother's womb. We don't seem to have any problem with that except the suffering for being confined for such a long time.

The Lord is in every particle, including food, but in unmanifest form. Souls are also in food we eat and fluids we drink. That is how we have made our bodies. The souls are subtle and the Lord is subtlemost.

If you want to know whether we eat up God along with food, you can stop worrying. God is not touched by anything, and same is true for the souls

What came first—egg or hen or bird, seed or plant?

Ans—you can see that both egg and chicken are bodies. This changing world has a natural built in mechanism to evolve, when life acquires potential matter to form a functional body. Our doubt is if humans came into this world first as new born babies or as adults (parents)? Let's understand how the souls acquire different types of bodies. *The evolution of birth and growing into adulthood is not the same for every species.*

Our universe is called 'brahmAnda' ('brahma' means creator, 'anda' means egg)—meaning 'cosmic egg created by brahma'.

In the literal sense, the cluster of galaxies, stars, and planets—earth and all its mobile and immobile beings are formed from the matter of this very cosmic egg. There is nothing more or beyond this cosmic egg in this created universe. The cosmic egg manifests by the prakruti of the supreme God. In that sense, He is the only source for everything that exists.

To understand how an atma acquires a body—if we keep a bowl full of milk or yogurt un-refrigerated for longer than a week or so, we can see that the micro organisms in the milk/yogurt would form into thousands of worms. (I have seen this). It shows that life and matter always exist and when they come together under the right conditions for the atma to acquire a functional body, they form a species. In this, there are no parents (mother and father) to give birth to the off-spring. For milk turning into worms, no scientist has cloned them to acquiring a body. There are many ways for an atma to acquire a body.

There is also life without functional body, such as bacteria, micro organisms, viruses etc.

Chandogya Upanishad 6-3-1—
   "tEshAm khalvEshAm bhUtAnAm trINyEva bIjAni . . ."

"There are only three origins for all beings other than Sat (Brahman/Paramatma who is unborn). They are born of eggs, born of creatures (wombs) or born of seeds (plants)".

Birds, serpents, fish and such are born of eggs, animals and humans (mammals) are born of creatures (wombs). Plants and trees are born of seeds. This clarifies that it was egg first for birds, snakes, fish and such, it was adults first for humans and animals (mammals) and seeds first for plants and trees.

It is surprising that there is a doubt only about the egg or hen, seed or plant. You can apply this question to every species; 8.4

million of them. Origin of all the 8.4 million bodies (species) did not come from the first life form.

The three main entities—God, jivatma (life/souls) and worlds (matter)—always existed.

We can wonder as to who put the fish into water. Obviously, fish would not survive without water. The formation of the world occurred in a sequence but that does not mean something was first and the others were later. They all existed and formed from one to the other.

Taittiriyopanishad explains the sequence of formation in "brahmakArya janmakrama"

 "tasmAdva yEtasmAdAtmana AkAsaha sambhUtah . . ."

"From the Paramatman, the atman of this nature, ether was produced, from ether was air born. Fire was born from air and from fire was water produced. From water came the earth. From earth were herbs produced. From herbs was food produced and from food was the body produced".

This verse clarifies the infinite nature of Brahman from whom everything was born and He is the cause for all.

Must understand that a body by itself cannot function or evolve, it needs a soul. A soul cannot function without a body either. *The souls can get into different bodies in different ways. Not all bodies need parents for them to be born and grow into adulthood;* especially, the plants and vegetation. Earth was formed with different seeds included, to grow into trees and other varieties of vegetation. There are hundreds of thousands of different plant species. Not everything came from one type of plant or seed. They were all formed as intended. We know for sure, we did not create any life or body here. We found plants and seeds when we appeared on earth.

Earth was formed with seeds and all the ingredients needed for plants and trees; and they borne more seeds of their kind to multiply.

Gita 14/4—

"sarva yonishu kauntEya mUrtayah sambhavanti yAh . . ."

"Whatever forms are produced in any womb, the prakruti is their great womb and I am the sowing father"

Every entity—gods, humans, animals, beasts, birds, reptiles—generated in whatever forms, prakruti of Brahman is the 'great womb" or cause. The conscient selves (atmas) are imbedded by God in the prakruti based on their karma and hence He is the sowing father

We do know that there are several types of plant life. There are plants that have no seeds; there are plants without fruits or flowers (sandalwood). We can cut off a branch of a plant and replant it on ground and it will start growing, seed is not needed here. We know there are fruits with or without seeds. This is God's way to show that when He wills, everything works, in different ways; some without seeds and some with seeds.

Two thirds of earth is covered by water. Life also acquired different forms in water as different species. Fish did not need parents to evolve. We have so many oceans and water bodies. We have same species of fish in all of them and in addition we also have some different species specific to those locations as well. Many fish species lay eggs separately without the male partners who drop their sperm on the eggs to fertilize them to become live eggs and hatch into fish. The eggs of the fish by themselves will not become fish; they are nothing but litter of the female fish. There are also mammals in water, such as the dolphins, whales that are born like humans and need parental care and protection to survive into adulthood.

Most fish are either a prey or a predator. A prey and predator could not be coming together to cross breed. Smaller fish is food for larger ones; larger ones are food for the much larger ones such as whales.

Even on land—most birds, animals and wild beasts are carnivorous. Most of them are food for the other—each one is either prey or predator, so there is no question of one species evolving into another.

Some species are formed without the help of parents. Some species are born pregnant, so they don't need male partners. In fact the mother snake goes away after guarding its eggs for weeks just before they are ready to hatch for the fear of eating them up, as snakes can feed on their own species. The young snakes have to survive on their own without the parental protection. So, in the case of snakes, souls acquired the potential to form eggs first and then they hatched as they don't need the adults. There are many species like the snakes that don't need parental care to see adulthood

Brahma was not born as a child who then grew up, nor was there a mother for him. He was caused directly by the supreme Lord by the power of His prakruti, granting him all powers and capabilities to carry out creation work. Many gods and goddesses, the 'sapta rishis' (seven sages) and forces of nature were caused into being with powers to perform their duties; many of them have no parents like we have. First beings were caused by the power of God. To us, it is a problem to comprehend what we cannot see.

We also know from the story of Viswamitra, who prior to becoming a brahma rishi, created a parallel heaven 'trisankhu swarga' which is testimony to the powers of great rishis and gods. If a Viswamitra can create a parallel heaven merely by the power of his penance, there is no limit to what the supreme God can create.

The first humans of each cycle of creation were willed into existence as adults. Same is true with the animals that would require adult parents to survive. Not just one or two but many sets of parents were caused and from them more were born in a way we can see today. Obviously the 7.00 billion people on earth today did not come from one set of first parents.

According to scriptures, there were more than 500000 people in Brindavan alone during Krishna's incarnation. Bhagavata purana mentions that there were 9.9 million people in Dwaraka; most of them perished before the deluge. We know that most of the people from 'dwapara yuga' did not survive to see 'kali yuga', which began 5113 years ago. New generation of humans evolved in kaliyuga.

Gita 10/39—

"yaccchApi sarva bhUtanAm bhIjam tadahamarjuna . . ."

"I am also that which is the seed of all beings, nothing that moves or does not move, exists without Me"

Why, we do not even know everything about our universe. If we think properly for a moment, one adult would not be able to give birth. As humans, it would have taken at least two—a man and woman. Even then, where did the first couple come from? Then, there was no guarantee that there would be a combination of male/female off-springs. What if the first couple could not give birth to young ones at all? What if they gave birth only to female or only male offspring? So there had to be many pairs of adult couple who gave birth to young ones and thus the generations evolved.

Even today, it is not in our control deciding to have a girl baby or boy baby. All that we can do is find out after formation of the body parts to know if the baby inside the mother is a girl or boy. Obviously, this would not have been humanly possible. It had to be the will of the supreme creator of this universe who also caused all the species to evolve by suitably enabling them to multiply.

In short, all the species were caused based on their potential to survive and multiply.

a> Egg or bird—Egg first

b> All first humans were adults. many first pairs of humans were caused and not just one set of parents

c> Seeds or plants—seeds first, as they were formed along with the formation of earth.

d> Fish in water—like seeds, many of the fish species formed eggs first. Not all eggs became the same type of fish, we see hundreds of thousands of species in water, each distinctly different. However the mammals in water were first adults that gave birth to young ones.

The concept of evolution as we understand—first life form (micro organism) becoming everything we have today—is an imagination. If they knew how to become a particular species, we would have had the world full of just one second species. If man evolved from apes, all apes should know how to become humans for we know it is better to be humans than apes. The other flaw in the evolution theory is that there is only one way direction for species to evolve into another. Ape can become a human, but a human cannot become an ape? It should be possible to evolve in both directions to make it logical. Or why should there be 8.4 million species if everything evolved from first life form?

Evolution theory can be logical and scientific if we realize that the supreme Lord is the only source for every world, every being, and every species that exists anywhere.

Evolution theory as we know it has a basic flaw—for most of the animals, fish, and birds are carnivorous and they cannot evolve into another species as each one is food for the other.

Katopanishad—5-7—

"yonimanyE prapadyantE sarIratvAya dEhinaha . . ."

"Some souls enter wombs for getting bodies; and some others take up the form of immovables (plants) according to their karma. it is to be noted that this brahmAnda is itself an egg and is capable of causing various types of bodies of movables (humans, animals, birds, fish etc) and immovables—plants, trees, vegetation.

Similarities between atma and God

There are few similarities as well as many dis-similarities. Just as God is divine, so are the Souls. Atma is divine by being His 'amsh'—being a potency of His 'para' or superior power. And the divine Mother is that 'para' power and hence is also a jivatma.

Gita 15/7—

mamaivAmso jIvalokE jIvabhutah sanAtanah . . ."

"an everlasting part of Myself (jivatma being an eternal amsh of the supreme Lord) having come to bind the self in the world of life, attracts the senses of which the mind is the sixth, and which abide in prakruti"

Though the jivatma is an eternal part (amsh) of the Lord, binds the individual self in the world of life owing to karma.

Jivatma's main similarities and dissimilarities with God are—

Atma is 'chEtana'—sentient; 'alpajna' knowledgeable, and intelligent and so is God or you can say He is 'parama chetana' and 'sarvajna' omniscient. Souls derive chetanatva by the presence of the Lord in them as the antaryami (chEtanschEtanAnAm) and Atma is eternal and unchanging and so is God (nityo nityAnAm)

Souls are endowed with a subtle invisible body comprising of intellect, mind, senses and a visible functional body, all of which belong to prakruti. However, the mind, intellect, senses and body of the Lord are ever divine; which is exclusive to Him. He is not different from His body.

When a soul acquires a body, the soul is always different from its body, be it in this world or in the eternal world. However, God and His body are one and the same. *There is no difference between the Paramatma and His mind, body and senses,* whether in the eternal world or when He incarnates in the mortal world.

> God is all pervasive, the atma can be at one place, God is 'omnipotent' (infinitely powerful) and the soul has limited powers. God is the Origin for all and the atma has its origin in God. God is both nirakar and sakar (unmanifest and manifest) but the atma is nirakar (unmanifest). God and souls are inseparable.

> God is the 'sEshi' master and Father, atma is 'sesha' the natural subservient, being the child.

> God is the governor and controller of prakruti/maya, and the laws of creation; and atma is bound by these laws when in the manifest world.

> Souls take birth in the changing world due to karma, but God incarnates out of His will. God is beyond karma.

> God decides the form, duration and place of His incarnation; but the atma has no control over what body it acquires or the duration of life in that body.

➤ The soul is divine in nature but acquires a material perishable body in this world; God's body is as divine even when He incarnates in this world. God's body cannot be slain, but the material body a soul assumes, can be slain.

➤ God is the controller of the laws of cause and effect (karma) and the soul has no control over the cause and effect, it is bound by the laws. Choice alone is in its control.

➤ God is the **atma** for all the souls and all souls are body for Him.

➤ On the funny side, God being "satya sankalpah" (one of His virtues) He can cause everything into existence by mere will or thought, the souls also have this virtue. We can will, **make a choice**; but it becomes 'karma' for us.

➤ God possesses only infinite auspicious qualities free of defilement; however atma taking birth in the mortal world acquires defiling qualities due to association with the bodies obtained from this prakruti inherent with the three gunas.

➤ God is not touched by 'avidya' or lack of knowledge or ignorance in any form, even when He incarnates in the mortal world. The embodied Atma acquires ignorance born of this prakruti which has to be dispelled by the knowledge of the self and the Lord.

Svetasvataropanishad 1-9—

> "*jnAjnau dvAvajAvIsanIsau ajA hyEkA*
> *bhoktubhogArthayuktA . . .*"

"of the two, one (paramatma) is omniscient and so the master of all, The other (jivatman) is sentient and never the master.

Both of them are unborn. *The other one, the unborn prakruti is associated with the enjoyer (jivatman) for the purpose of his experience (this is evident why God created this universe; it is for the sake of the souls who sought to experience this universe).* The Paramatman who has the universe as His body is yet infinite and a non-doer (he is not involved in the activities of the jivatma who is the enjoyer) When one realizes the distinct nature of these three clearly, he becomes freed (attains immortality).

Here the distinctive characteristics of *jivatman*, *Paramatman* and the *matter* are stated. Though jivatman and paramatman are unborn, the Paramatman is omniscient and the master. Matter (universe) is for the purpose of enjoyment of the souls. It is not the object of enjoyment for the Paramatman who has everything else as His body, for He is not engaged in action for gaining the fruits of karma like the jivatman. He is the Lord of karma, so karma cannot dominate Him. He is infinite with infinite auspicious attributes and the over Lord of all.

Que—And what about the many gods and goddesses, are they also the same supreme God or Paramatma?

Ans—No, the other gods and goddesses are not the Paramatma, There is only one supreme God. All other gods and goddesses are children of the supreme God. They are souls like you and me. The other gods—such as indra, kubera, agni, vayu, surya, yama, brahma and many more (it is said that there are some 330 million gods and goddesses in all, in this created universe, including Brahma, the architect of creation), get designated powers and suitable divine bodies to assist God in the functioning of the manifest worlds. They are who they are based on their choice backed by entitlement; in wishing to hold these positions, which comes with independence (it is this independence that is against the true nature of the soul which is the reason, a true devotee would never wish to be a god/goddess). One of us can become a god if we have the entitlement and choice. There is a problem with it though. You would have to necessarily complete your term as a god and that may take a long time. Have to be born again as humans and practice total surrender with devotion to the supreme God if we aspire to be with God in His eternal abode.

All except the Supreme God are jivatmas. Even the divine consorts of the supreme God—Divine Mother Mahalakshmi or Peria piratti (para power) and bhumi piratti (apara power) are jivatmas.

All the gods, goddesses have finite powers and are able to use their powers by the power of the supreme God.

Devotion to any god reaches the supreme God.

Gita 9/23 confirms that prayers and devotion to other gods would eventually reach the supreme God, for He is the antar-atma in all gods and souls.

"*Epyanya dEvata bhaktA yejantE shradhayAnvitAha . . .*"

"even those who are devoted to other divinities with faith in their hearts, worship Me alone, **though not as prescribed.(avidhi purvakam)**

Poigai azhwar in his mudal thiruvanthadi explains this phenomenon about the supreme God with so much clarity—

"*tamar ugandadevvuruvam—avvuruvam tAnE,*
tamar ugandadeppEr—mattappEr;
tamar ugandu evvaNNam sindittimayAdiruapparE,
avvaNNam AzhiyAnAm"

"Every form you desire for Him, God takes that form, every name you desire to address Him as, He becomes that name. God becomes all that you wish Him to be.

Here, the Azhwar talks about the supreme God and not the other gods. Azhwar is suggesting that you can think of the supreme God in any name or form and you can perceive Him based on your wish. However, it is not the name or the form that determines His supremacy, but His infinite auspicious qualities.

There is also a line from Bhagavata—"**AkASAt patitam toyam yathA gacchati sAgaram, sarva dEva namaskAram sri kEsavam prati gacchati**"—which re-confirms that prayers and devotion to all gods proceed towards the supreme God, Kesava. When you realize this truth, you might as well deal with the supreme God, as you are directly related to Him.

Que—Do the gods marry?

Ans—Human comprehension is limited to what we do. So it is a little hard for us to think beyond a level. It is important to know that all souls are feminine in nature including that of Brahma. God is the Only Purusha (Man).

Nammazhwar declares that we cannot determine or perceive God as anyone we know, for we have limited understanding. Tiruvaimozhi 2-5-10
> "**ANallan, peNNallan, allA aliyumallan, kANalumAgAn, uLnallan illaiyallan** . . . .

Azhwar explains that the Lord is the only Purusha, in this masculine expression, in every identity—ANallan—He is not a man we know of; peNNallan—He is not a woman we know of, Azhwar does not say she is not a woman we know of; in a normal expression it should have been 'peNNallaL'. By stating 'peNNaLLan' refers as 'HE'—He is not the woman we can perceive a woman as. 'alla aliyumallan'—He is not a neuter, here again masculine expression is used instead of 'It is not a neuter'. In explaining that the Lord is the only Purusha (Man) Azhwar has used masculine gender in mentioning that He is not a man, He is not woman nor is He a neuter. He is the only Purusha.

Azhwar declares that the Lord is not a man we think of Him as a man we know, for we know a man based on our own understanding of a man, but God is not that man we know. Similarly He is not the woman we know of, nor is He genderless based on what we know. He cannot be seen, He is neither non-existent nor does He exist in the way deem Him to be. In short, He is beyond our comprehension.

Svetasvataropanishad 5-10 declares the nature of the Atma thus

"naiva stri na pumAnEshah, na chaivayam napumsakah . . ."

This jivatman is neither a woman nor a man. However, is he a neuter? Whatever body he assumes, he will be associated with such and such.

Here it is clarified that there is no gender for the soul. The genders are for the body. However, it is declared that the jivatman is feminine in nature in relation to the Paramatman and Paramatman alone is the lone Purusha.

Our comprehension is based on our perception and understanding of this world. God does not need to be married like us. Yet we are all eternally married to Him. Marriage means being in union with one another, this does not imply physical union. God resides in every soul and all the souls are naturally married to the Lord, except that we don't realize it. Every time we take birth, we are married to our own body, if we are separated from the body, the body is dead, and the soul cannot function without a body either. When we realize the marriage with God, we can end our suffering in mortal bodies attaining Him in His eternal world.

Even the other gods and goddesses have no need for marital relationship like us. They have the powers to perform their designated duties, yet they function in companionship. They can create beings with their mind power as they are endowed with divine powers by the supreme Lord.

If you see in the SriVaishnava temples—God is accompanied by two Thayars (consorts)—one on the right side of God is the divine Mother of all the jivatmas—Para or Akshara power of God, 'Peria Piratti' and on the left side of God—representing the whole creation is the "Mother of all creation"—Bhumi piratti—representing His 'apara/yoga maya' power. We can see that earth is merely a planet but we call her mother earth. Both Periapiratti (para) and Bhumi piratti (apara) are equally divine as the Supreme Lord. They are eternal powers of the Lord and reside in Him, eternally. While the other gods including brahma end their tenure in the bodies they acquire and new souls can take up their position; *Para and Apara remain unchanging in their divine nature and position. They stand on the same pedestal as the Lord.*

Sri Pillai Lokacharya declares in Mumukshuppadi—45—'**Aga pirittu nilai illai".** *The Lord, Peria Piratti and Bhumi Piratti are inseparable, they remain eternally together.*

The Acharya confirms that our subservience or seshatavam (natural relationship) is indeed to the Divine Mother, Peria Piratti, which would enable God's acceptance.

All planets, sun, stars also have a presiding soul in them and God as antaryami dwells in all the souls. Proof that stars have a soul can be inferred from Dhruva's life story. After his meeting with the Lord and completing his lifetime, he becomes a star named after him "dhruva nakshatra or the pole star in the north".

The supreme Lord with 'ubhaya nachimargal'—God with two consorts—is true representation of the 3 main tattvas (entities)— Paramatma with jivatma and creation—they are inseparable. And there is no second like Him with His qualities and powers. This is precisely the glorious science of Ramanuja—"visishtAdvwaita".

Chapter Nine

Vedic philosophies . . .

We have three Vedic philosophies—adwaita first by Sankaracharya, visishtadwaita by Ramanujacharya and dwaita by Madhvacharya, in that order. It is important to realize that all three philosophies are based on the Vedas, Upanishads and sacred Vedic scriptures. All the three philosophies delve in to the same aspects of knowing the supreme Lord. In that all of them understand and confirm that Narayana or VAsudeva or Kesava or Hari is the supreme Lord or Paramatman or Brahman and there is only one of Him.

➢ **Adwaita**—as understood by many, this concept suggests that God is the only truth and the universe and creation are an illusion or a mirage; "**brahma satyam, jagan mithya jIvo brahmaiva nAparah**" meaning "God is truth and the worlds are a lie, jiva is no different from Brahman" a line from the Vedas, seems to have been *taken out of context and in isolation*. Sri Adi Sankara who is the author of adwaita philosophy, is a divine soul, and would not have meant what we understand this philosophy as; that everything except God is a lie or illusory. Its contention is that the Lord manifests as the worlds and beings due to 'avidya' or ignorance and soon as God who is now the soul in a manifest body realizes its state of ignorance and regains knowledge, becomes God again. *Paramatman and jivatman are one and the same*. God has no form, names, qualities, attributes, powers, and capabilities.

Yet, He manifests this universe and as infinite souls?

'Chandogya Upanishad' 3-14-1—'sarvam khalvidam brahma, meaning "all this is verily brahman'

Adwaita contends that everything is Brahman or God, but the *correct meaning is that everything is pervaded by Brahman and Brahman is the cause for everything.*

Chandogya Upanishad 6-8-7—'tat tvamasi' "you are that"— Adwaita contends that atma and Paramatma are one and the same, but the *correct understanding is "You have God as your atman (antaryami)"*

Bruhadaranyaka Upanishad—1-4-10—Aham brahmasmi—"I am Brahman" is the meaning according to Advaita. But the *correct knowledge of this sruti is "I realize Brahman in me", because I am different and Brahman is different. If I am myself Brahman, why am I caught up helplessly under the realm of karma and prakruti and why am I going through suffering and grief? And why are there infinite numbers of me?*

Adwaitins assume that the image in a mirror is a non-truth as it is only an image and not the real object. If there is no object, there would be no image. Reality as we know it, is that, if the object is true so is the image. That's why we rightly call it the 'image', and not as the 'object'. We are not imagining the image without the object.

A-dwaita—literally means 'no second' or non-dual, implying that there is only one and that is God and everything else is an illusion or a lie. Even our existence is a lie for we are a product of avidya (ignorance).

We cannot deny that humans have a form, all the species with a functional body have a form; this universe has a form. If everything is God, and everything has a form as we see them, obviously God has form as well!

What is amusing is that only an intelligent living entity of the nature of omniscience or supreme knowledge can cause, create, manifest and make-function, what God has created. The same God would not be able to create or manifest when in ignorance. *Upanishads establish that God is of the nature of '***satyam, jnanam, anantam, anandam***' which is unchanging and eternal state. Adwaita does not explain why and how God acquires ignorance?* Science and logic tells us that ignorance cannot prevail where there is eternal knowledge which is what God is. To think that this infinite creation with all the galaxies and worlds and beings can be caused by someone whose eternal nature is knowledge but somehow becomes ignorant to manifest as worlds and beings is not logical. If He can create this infinite universe when He acquires ignorance, then we have to call his ignorance as 'super knowledge' or super intelligence.

According to adwaita, when the Supreme Lord is of the nature of 'jnanamaya' which is an unchanging, eternal state, he behaves like an ignorant, doing nothing (nirgun, nirakar, nirvisesh). When the same God becomes ignorant, He creates, manifests, endowed with infinite auspicious virtues and capabilities and He himself dwells in everything sentient and non sentient of this universe!

When we cannot cause or produce even a small thing in ignorance, how can an ignorant god manifest and form infinitely functioning, infinite universe with infinite beings, everything working absolutely perfectly?

However, what the Upanishads say is different—

Mundakopanishad 2-2-7 confirms
"yah sarvajnah . . . *divyE brahmapurE* hyEsha vyomanyAtma pratishtitah"

The Paramatman who is omniscient (attribute/quality) . . . .
This Paramatman is established in the Supreme space in the **luminous city of Brahman**" the term 'divyE vyomani" signifies the "**tripAdvibhUti**" or the non material or—aprakrutik divine abode of the Lord, the city of Brahman is the 'Paramapadam'

Mundakopanishad 2-2-10—
  "hiraNmayE pare koSE virajam brahma nishkalam . . ."

"In the supreme abode of Paramapada is Brahman. It is without rajas (transcending sattva, rajasa, tamasa), without parts, pure and is the light of lights. It is which the knowers of the atman realize"

Mundakopanishad—3-1-7
  "bruhaccha taddivyamachintyarUpam sUkshmAccha . . ."

"It is great and is in the supreme ether; *its form is so beautiful that it is not accessible to speech or thought*. It is shining subtler than the subtle. It is farther away than the far off. It is also near at hand. It is stationed here alone in this body within the cave of the heart amongst the seers of Brahman"

He is great by nature, by **attributes** and **qualities**. **His auspicious, beautiful form is beyond speech and thought**. He is subtler than the subtle Jivatman, who is capable of entering into the non-sentient. He is beyond even prakruti. He is realized by the seers within the heart of the body, here itself.

Svetasvataropanishad 4-6
  "dwa suparNa sayujA sakhAyA samAnam
  vruksham parishasvajAtE . . ."

"Two birds (jivatman and Paramatman) of similar qualities and moving together cling to the same tree (body). Of these two, the one eats the fruit of karma that is ripe and the other shines out even without eating"—

Emphatically two entities, jivatma and paramatma are mentioned here, distinctly different from each other, and the tree is the non sentient body with which the atma is associated and engaged in activities accruing karma. The body is the third entity which the jivatma obtains from this prakruti. The Lord who is the antaryami dwelling in the atma is an observer without participation in the activities of the atma/body. This sruti confirms all the three entities as affirmed by Ramanuja.

Mundakopanishad 3-1-3—
"yadA paSyah paSyatE rukmavarNam
kartAramISam purusham . . ."

"when the seer of Brahman see the Supreme Self, the ruler of this universe, **having an effulgent auspicious divine body,** the creator of the universe and the cause of the unmanifested, then that knower of Brahman shaking off virtue and sin, being freed from the taint of matter (body), attains supreme similarity"

The body of the supreme Lord is described as 'aditya varnah' which refers to His having a non-material divine body.

Gita 15-6 Krishna declares that there is that imperishable world

"na tadbhAsayatE sUryo . . . "tad dhAma paramam mama"

"That supreme abode (paramapadam) of Mine, attaining which they (the souls) do not return anymore. The sun does not illumine it, nor moon nor the fire"

The sun, moon and fire are needed to illumine the material world here; the Paramapadam is divinely self luminous. The contention of adwaita that the existence of worlds is an illusion is disproved by the fact that there is another world which is eternal, imperishable and non transient unlike this material world which is changing. However, both are real and true. Here Krishna has ascertained the existence of His abode attaining which the atma does not return to this mortal world. Even if adwaita took shelter under the premise that this world disappears and merges into the Lord at dissolution of this universe, there is no such premise to dispute the existence of the eternal world, and cannot be termed as an illusion.

the true essence of 'brahma satyam, jagan mitya' is that—don't be under the illusion that this world will give you that divine bliss you are seeking, if you pursue seeking divine bliss with this changing, perishable world, you are going after a lie for this world though real, is non-sentient, devoid of knowledge. The only person who can give you that divine, ever growing bliss is the supreme Lord, and you should pursue knowing Him who is the unchanging, unborn and immutable Truth. He is the only ultimate truth you have to know, who alone can grant immortality. In that sense, this world is a mirage or 'maya', when we assume this world is where there is divine bliss.

There is a sukti in Sri Azhagiyamanavala Perumal Nayanar's Acharya hrudayam, 1-23, end part "**pagal viLakkum, minminiyumAkkum**'—pagal viLakku represents the 'sun' and minmini is an insect that glows in the night. Fireflies produce the chemical 'luciferin' a pigment emitting light and this is termed 'bioluminescence'.

If we assume that an insect which emits a feeble light in the night due to the presence of certain chemicals in its body would give us the light of the sun, which only the sun is capable of, we are illusioned to imagine the 'minmini insect' as the sun, which it is not. In this context we are going after a lie, thinking it can give the light we want, but in reality, the truth is that only the sun can give us the light we are seeking.

There are hundreds of thousands of other statements in the Upanishads vividly declaring that the Lord has most beautiful form which cannot be described as an expression; He has infinite auspicious attributes which are beyond our comprehension; He is the most lovable person and our eternal Father. Yet adwaita chose to go by just few srutis, disregarding everything else. Even in that, they have not understood the real essence of these statements.

Contention of Adwaita is, "I" (the Atman, who is Brahman) of the nature of 'knowledge' or 'jnanam', somehow became overcome by 'avidya' (ignorance) creating diversity in my mind. When "I" negate all such diversity, "I" realize that the universe does not really exist, and thus "I" attain oneness—my Self alone, becoming the Brahman. That is liberation. However Upanishads vividly declare that liberation is granted only by the supreme Lord and the atma cannot 'self grant' salvation to itself. There is still a hitch here. Even if I become Brahman by attaining knowledge; what about the infinite other beings, gods and worlds? Would they all vanish, soon as one Soul (I) becomes the Brahman?

The only plausible explanation for adwaitins' incorrect assumption could be inferred based on the fact that God is the origin for everything. God is not caused by anyone while He is the cause for everything and everyone. He has been there even before the souls were released and the universe manifested from Him. Since everything is born out of God and that He pervades everywhere; He supports everything; the souls and the universe depend on Him for existence and hence He is the truth in everything (*which implies that souls and universe are also true because He dwells in them and is all pervading*). The individual souls and universe is body for God. And Sri Sankara might have considered the **transient** nature of the created world as a reason to call it an illusion.

There is a divine eternal world (tripAdvibhUti) as well, as confirmed by all the Vedic scriptures, Azhwars and Acharyas. Upanishad, Purushasuktam declares "*pAdosya visvA bhUtAni, tripAdasyAmrutam divi"* affirming that there is the imperishable, eternal world Paramapadam, with countless nitya suris experiencing infinitely growing divine bliss of the supreme Lord (*tad vishnoh paramam padam, sada pasaynti sUrayah*). And the atmas of this world can attain immortality if they know their nature and relation with the supreme Paramatman. *However, knowing Brahman alone will not liberate us. Brahman is the only one who can liberate us from this world out of His nirhetuka krupa—benign grace, when we seek Him with unconditional devotion.*

In reality, even this universe is eternal, except that it goes through changes. What is transient for the universe is more than eternal in our perception, if we consider the age of a Brahma who is the architect for a part (anda tatAka) of the whole universe and his lifespan is 309.173 trillion earthly years. *If this is transient, imagine the permanent!*

We know that everything is real and true—God, souls and the universe. And each one is distinctly different from one another. Souls have certain similarities and dissimilarities with the Lord. Even if the universe is changing, it is true in its changing state. In short, God is the common factor present in every soul and pervading everywhere in the universe.

There is a humorous story about this concept—a scholar who followed adwaita philosophy—was once traveling with several disciples to reach another town. On the way, they had to pass by a forest in which wild tigers were on the prowl. It so happened, that a tiger spotted the group and started chasing them. Luckily for them they managed to escape unharmed. After they reached a safe place outside the forest area, one of the disciples asked his teacher, gasping for breath, as to why they had to run away from the tiger if the adwaita concept was true, that all that is happening in this world is an illusion or lie. If so the tiger chasing them would be a lie as well and why should they have to run like that. The teacher answered in the affirmative that everything was a lie, the tiger chasing them was a lie and their running away in fear to save their lives was also a lie, including the disciple asking him that question and his answering him. Everything was a lie.

Then, why, when and how God gets ignorance (avidya) and who or what causes him to be ignorant? When God is Himself jnanamaya (omniscient) which is an eternal state, how can he acquire avidya/ignorance? In reality, ignorance is lack of knowledge and not a negative phenomenon. If knowledge acquires ignorance, how it can revert back to knowledge? *If ignorance has overpowered and changed eternal knowledge into itself, there is no way for ignorance to become knowledge again, for it can convert all knowledge into ignorance eternally. When that happens, ignorance alone exists and nothing else.* If the entire universe and all its beings become ignorant, who else is there to dispel ignorance and how to acquire knowledge? There can be no one else, because it is God who has become all these beings out of ignorance. In such a situation, there has to be another entity, who is of the nature of knowledge to drive away ignorance and instill knowledge. In that case—adwaita (non dualism or no second entity) gets defeated.

Why should he manifest in the world as souls because of this ignorance? He could have remained nirgun, nirakar, nirvisesh— ignorant Brahman eternally, instead of manifesting the universe and releasing the souls into this universe. There are several flaws in this understanding. If God becomes so many souls in so many bodies, will all of these souls/bodies/worlds vanish and become God again, all at the same time? After all if god became so many (infinite) souls, does it mean He acquired ignorance infinite times, which would mean that he would be eternally ignorant and in that case there can be no change in that state. Will all of the souls become god again even if one of the souls gets the knowledge and realization or should each one wait for all of them to get the realization? If the original god is continuously ignorant, where is the scope for change from that state? There are just too many questions without a logical answer with this concept. If all this is true, then it cannot be termed as a-dwaitha, since we are talking about ignorance, knowledge, manifestation, God in his original nature of 'knowledge'.

Let us look at it in another way. If God manifests when He gets ignorance, then why is he taking births in so many bodies—as humans, animals, birds, fish, insects, plants (trees) etc. Why does he manifest into so many worlds and so many elements (forces) of nature and so many gods and goddesses with respective powers? Does he take birth as humans due to certain degree of ignorance and then as animals due to greater degree of ignorance and as gods due to better quality of ignorance? Does he acquire different and varied degree of ignorance to form into so many worlds and so many species (some 8.4 million species) and even more incredible is why does the forming of the worlds, their functioning and destruction happen cyclically, endlessly? Does it mean he becomes ignorant repetitively at exactly the same time as there is a specified time for each cycle of formation and annihilation? *So does it mean that God has self programmed himself into acquiring infinite ignorance, varying degree of ignorance and repetitive ignorance at exactly the same time, every time, to take different bodies in different worlds, time and again repeatedly, nonstop.* We are not trying to ridicule this concept or trying to belittle the greatness of this philosophy. We ask so many questions in order to understand what prompted for such a concept of nothingness except God, when the same God who is true, becomes the illusion himself as beings and worlds. *It is important to understand what is correct, as wrong knowledge can lead to dangerous perceptions. A killer, following this philosophy can call his act of killing an illusion!*

Why then do we have karma which has different effects for different causes? If God is causing all this to himself when he becomes ignorant, which is merely one cause, then why should there be so many different consequences. Then there is so much pain, suffering in this world, why is god self inflicting pain on himself? If He is Anandamaya why does he suffer grief? Scientifically, or even logically, Anandamaya and suffering cannot co-exist.

Why should there be varying degree of pain for one cause—ignorance, as we know that each one of us goes through different situations and we have differential perception as well. And everything is relative to each one with so many probabilities in the way we live life. And what about the differences in every human being, every animal, at a physical level? Each one of us has our own individual DNA, each one looking distinctly different from one another, every person behaving differently to the same situation at different times. How can adwaita explain the gender part—why are we born as men and women? Then why should there be children out of marriages? If God can manifest due to ignorance, why is there a need for marriages? Then we see so many children dying during birth, so many children die of diseases and starvation, there are so many natural calamities such as earth quakes, tsunami etc. Then we have different life times for different species. Humans can live around 100 years, but yet we see more than 90% dyeing earlier. What explains the difference in longevity for different animals? Some of the souls do not even have a functional body—like micro organisms. And then there are plants and vegetation that are living as well without the sense perception of pleasure and pain. What sort of ignorance does cause god to go through life in plants and trees?

We have people with so many skin colors, some tall, some short. Some more skilled than the others, some rich and some poor—why is god going through all these effects? And then why are we doing harmful things to each other, why should there be wars and fighting amongst people. There is so much violence in the animal kingdom as well. Even humans have so many disturbing qualities that can destroy other humans. We are intolerant based on religion, skin color and economic status. If it is the same god manifesting as so many why is he fighting against himself?

Then we should realize that the God who can create / manifest an infinite universe, with infinite souls acquiring bodies here, cannot be the same as the ones he created (just as my children are not me).

We can see that the Atma is superior in nature than the bodies it acquires or the universe, due to its unchanging, eternal and sentient nature. And God from whom the worlds and souls are born must be distinctly much superior to these two. What they go through cannot be the same for Him.

Then it is said that Sri Sankara is the composer of 'bhaja govindam'—if everything we see here is illusion, who is worshipping whom? If the Lord has no form, no senses and mind, and no attributes, who is Sri Sankara praising? If God cannot hear what is the purpose of this 'bhajan and sankirtan'.

Adi Sankara was a great devotee of Krishna as well. And he knew that Krishna was none other than the supreme Brahman, who incarnated here with His infinite powers, in the most beautiful form. If God is taking birth here already as humans, where was the need for His incarnations which is confirmed as His divine Self and not the mortal beings. Obviously Krishna is not a jivatma like the rest of the others. If He was real, it is testimony that the others were not paramatma and hence jivatma and paramatma are not one and the same. There were several incarnations by the supreme Lord as Rama and others. When Krishna killed Kamsa, Sisupala, Dantavakra and some other ogres, were they all Krishna the paramatma, killing himself?

And there are souls taking birth here due to 'karma' and few others due to 'karana' (for a reason) and we know they are not Paramatma. If God had no auspicious attributes and beautiful form why Sri Sankara would worship Him or is it God worshipping himself? But then some of us are not devotees, there are some atheists who do not accept God's existence as real at all. How are all these explained? *And there are souls in the bodies of plants, vegetation, micro organisms and animals—which can never attain knowledge or realization of the self in these bodies, so does it mean they are ruined eternally?*

We know that Adi Shankara was a divine soul incarnating to bestow knowledge and considered most knowledgeable. In that case it would be hard to understand that he acquired knowledge just when he ended his incarnation; according to him a soul becomes God when he regains knowledge. But he was knowledgeable many years before he ended his incarnation. Or if he passed away exactly only when he attained knowledge, did he preach all his concepts without attaining complete knowledge? If so, such knowledge cannot be flawless?

If knowledge is true so is ignorance. If god manifests, it also implies that he exists in the manifest form, so that is a reason enough that his manifest form is also true.

And how do we explain each one of us making different choices? If it is one God who became infinite jivatmas—why does he make different choices in different bodies? Each person has a behaviour pattern and would do the same thing repeatedly, most times. If it is one person who has become so many, all of them should do the same thing, think alike, and make choices alike?

We can think of many more questions but the truth is Sri Sankara incarnated here at a time when most people were mislead and lost in their way of life by the propagation of other groups, who claimed that there was no god, nor were they following the Vedas as the basis. If that state prevailed, scores of people would have lost their way in realizing their nature and relationship with God and hence Sri Sankara came up with his philosophy of adwaita to make people realize that every one (individual atma) is god and God is the only truth and everything else is transient and hence an illusion. He propagated this concept so that souls would be motivated to becoming God, by being devoted to the Lord and living a kind and compassionate life. His school of thought guided people into devotion and to following the Vedic knowledge. There is a subtle difference between Adi Shankara's philosophy in relation to Sri Ramanuja's. But even that little difference can take us away from reality, if not understood properly.

> **Dwaitha**—dualism (meaning two) by Sri Madhvacharya—it talks about God being the supreme power, creation of the worlds is a play for Him. God and souls exist independently of each other. Souls can reach the abode of God by devotion to Him. There is also gradation of souls by divinity from the divine Mother Mahalakshmi to other gods and goddesses to humans and animals. This concept is based on pancha-bedha (five differences) between God, soul and matter (universe)

The distinction between one atma to another atma (jeeva-jeeva), between the atma and matter (jeeva-jada), between one piece of matter and another (jada-jada), between matter and souls of other gods (Jada-Deva), between the Supreme Being and the individual soul (Paramatman-Jeeva)

In that case, there should have been three—God, souls and matter and not dwaita (two). For, God is different from souls and souls are different from non-sentient matter. The reality is that the universe and souls cannot exist without God. He dwells in both these entities. So too, our bodies cannot exist without the souls in them. Souls and universe are body for God and the three are inseparable—either during manifestation or in the merged into God state. Sri Madhvacharya probably thought that God being the Supreme Lord is distinctly different and superior to the souls and matter and hence categorized them in two—God as one and the souls as the other. The universe / matter being non sentient, is probably not counted. That is the only plausible explanation for this concept of Two (dwaitha)

> **VisishtAdvwaita**—explains that there is **only one God, without a second like Him**, with divine qualities, in most beautiful form. It reveals a holistic essence of the Upanishads. It explains that there is no second Brahman or Paramatman like Him who is the master of His universe and souls, both belonging to Him. Chit, achit and Iswara—tattva, establishes the fact that He is the sariri (atma) dwelling in the souls and pervading the universe. He is the supreme God who is the origin for this universe (achit) and jivatmas (souls—chit). *He is true, His created worlds are true and the souls are true.* And most importantly, these three are inseparable. When the worlds manifest they are visible and when they are withdrawn they merge into God. *The worlds and souls do not exist independently of God; He is always in them in any state. And when they merge into God they still exist inside Him, outwardly, He alone exists.*

Svetasvataropanishad 1-12 vividly establishes—*"Etat jnEyam nityamEvAtmasamstham nAtah vEditavyam hi kinchit . . ."*

"This Brahman should be known as the antarAtma dwelling eternally in the jivatman. There is nothing else to be known beyond this. This Brahman is the innerself of the 'bhokta' (bhokta is the jivatman who is the enjoyer), who is the innerself of the object of enjoyment (bhogyam is the body obtained from this prakruti) empowered by the 'prErita' (paramatman). All this of three kinds has been said. This is Brahman."

In essence, there are just the three entities and nothing more. The Paramatman is the 'antaratma' and controller of both the 'bhokta' the jivatman who is the enjoyer of the 'bhogya vastu' the prakruti.

This establishes that the atman should know the 'prErita' as different and distinct from 'bhogya' the object of enjoyment and the 'bhokta' the atman, the enjoyer, and this is all there is to know. There is nothing beyond the three existing. The 'prErita', the supreme Brahman is the 'antaratma' indweller of the bhokta and pervading the bhogya and the controller of both bhokta and bhogya. The three way knowledge of—a) reality of the existence of the atma' or chit; matter the achit; and the Isvara the supreme Lord; b) the means of the form of devotion or upasana and c) the result that would be attained from devotion. 'brahmamEtat' explains 'all this is Brahman as the innerself of the other two'— bhokta (jivatman) and 'bhogya' prakruti/maya.

The Upanishads, Gita and all the authentic scriptures mention three entities—God, sentient and non sentient. It does not say that sentient and non sentient entities are God. If they were, there was no need to mention the three different entities of totally different nature, characteristics and capabilities. It is confirmed that God is neither of the other two and is different and infinitely superior to both and there is only one such God

A lot has been said about visishtAdvwaita in analyzing the flaws of adwaita concept above, so we do not have to repeat all of it again in explaining visishtAdvwaita concept which in effect is the **true science of God**.

There is both **bheda and abedha**—dis-similarity and similarity between the three—God, jivatman and universe.

    a> **sa-jatiya bheda**—different entities having similarities— God and souls—are both knowledgeable. God is (sarvajna) omniscient; and jivatma (souls) are finitely knowing (alpajna). 'jnAtrutva' is a similarity both God and souls have. Both God and jivatma are sentient, possessing 'chetanatva'. Both God and Souls are eternal, unchanging and immutable (nityatva).

b> **vi-jatiya bedha**—(vibhinna jati) different entities with no similarities—god and souls are totally dis-similar to matter which is non-sentient (achith) devoid of knowledge. Matter is perishable and changing while the Lord and souls are imperishable, immutable, and unchanging.

c> **sva-gata bedha**—different within—we can see that a tree is different from its flowers, fruits, and leaves. We can understand that hand or parts of human body are different from his body as a whole. Here we can relate to the 'achith (worlds)' and chith (jivatma) originated from the same God, though they are different in nature, they are from the same source. In that, neither the physical worlds nor the souls are God, but both belong to God and cannot independently exist or function without the support of the Supreme Lord.

The Upanishads state that Brahman is both *savisesha*-with auspicious qualities; and *nirvisesha*—without defiling qualities. The word *bheda* (difference) is said in four different Vedanta sutras to stress that the souls are not the Supreme Lord: *bheda-vyapadesat cha* (*V-s* 1-1-7), *bheda vyapadesat anyah* (*V-s* 1-1-21), *bheda vyapadesa* (*V-s* 1-3-5), and *bheda-sruteh* (*V-s* 2-4-18). Yet the Lord and the souls share the transcendental nature of eternality *"nityo nityAnAm";* and sentient awareness *"chetanas chetanAnAm"*.

The jivatma is *karta*, doer of activities, possessing knowledge, senses and mind: 'esha hi drashta, sprashta, Srota, ghrata, rasayita, manta, boddha, karta, vijnanatma, purushah sa parE akshara atmani sampratishthate. "The jivatma is verily the seer, toucher, smeller, taster, thinker, knower, doer, the individual purusha who is of the nature of pure knowledge; he becomes established in the transcendental divine nature of the Supreme Self (Paramatman)

Chandogya 6-3-2 says—*"anEna jIvEnAtmanA anupravisya nAma rUpE vyAkaravaNI iti"*: "Brahman enters into creation *along with the jivatma* in order to manifest as material names and forms. "The word *anupravisya* indicates that Brahman associates with matter and the individual souls as their controller, but remains ever untouched by both the universe and souls.

The principle of sarira—sariri (body/atma) confirms one-ness and distinction and difference from one another. Paramatma pervades this universe and the souls as antaryami—yet He is distinctly different from the other two (atma / matter), sentient and non sentient.

Sarva vastu samAnAdhikaraNam and sarva vastu vilakshaNatvam. This implies that the body/soul relationship is spiritual union and not a physiological principle. Atma in the body are considered one when taken together, yet there is distinct difference between the atma and body. Similarly, Paramatma is different from souls and universe.

Ramanuja philosophy emphasizes that we have to interpret the mention of 'nirguna' and 'abheda' in the holistic view taking into account the innumerable other statements in the Upanishads. The nirgunatvam indicates that the Lord is devoid of and beyond all dosha (defilement) of any sort, which the souls possess due to association with this prakruti and qualities arising out of raga-dwesha. The Lord possesses only sa-gunatvam or infinite glorious virtues which is not the case with the souls. And 'abheda' indicates similarity of 'jnatrutvam' being of the nature of knowledge and nityatvam—being the eternality, for both the jivatman and Paramatman.

And there are certain statements—**yassarvajnah; sarva vit, apahatapApma—vijaro vimrutyuhu; . . . satyakAmah, satya sankalpah**—enlisting infinite auspicious qualities alone, devoid of any defilement. While certain phrases say '*sarvam khalvidam* *brahma tajjalAn iti; aitadAtmyam idam sarvam*, "**aham brahmAsmi**" illustrate this universe of different forms caused by Brahman, is one with Brahman, yet Brahman being distinctly different from the others.

Just as the Vedas hide their intrinsic meanings and many a times misinterpreted, adwaita is a similar case of wrongly interpreting the statements of Upanishads, in saying that only Brahman is the truth and the worlds are a mirage. True meaning on these statements is that without the 'sariri sarira' *(atma/body)* realization, we are lost in the illusion of this world. When we realize that the Paramatman is the sariri (antaryami), residing in every atma and the universe, ascends to reach Paramatma. "aham brahmasmi" does not really state the atma deeming the self as paramatma, but a declaration that I have realized the presence of the Paramatma in me as the sariri (antaryamin) and with that realization he also realizes that the Paramatman is distinctly different than the self and the nature of the self being subservience to Paramatma. Thus confirming *"antah pravishtah sAsta janAnAm sarvAtmA; ya Atmani tishtan Atmanontarah yasya Atma sarIram"*

All these affirm 'no-second' stature to such a Brahman.

Taittiriyopanishad—*"Brahman is described as that from which everything is born, in which everything is residing and that into which everything merges in the end".*

Importantly, it confirms that the sentient and non-sentient entities are real. However the difference between these entities and the supreme Brahman is also real. Each atma (sentient being) experiences this supreme bliss (ananda) on attaining this supreme Brahman

Swetasvataropanishad further declares the three realities— bhoktha (jivatman), bhogya (world) and prErita (Paramatman).

The adwaita relied on total abheda (total dissimilarity) in its concept. If it accepts similarity then the idea of 'no-second' entity would be defied. However, Sri Ramanuja also confirms that there is '**no second Brahman, with such qualities**'. The qualities, attributes, glorious virtues of the supreme brahman distinguishes Him from His both sentient and non sentient—jivatma and matter respectively and establishes that both matter and jivatma are body for Him.

The dis-similarity can also be seen between the atma and body. They are inseparable when alive yet, the atma is distinctly different from the non-sentient body. There is this Paramatman inside the jivatman which has to be realized for the jivatman to attain divine bliss.

Sri Ramanuja picks out seven basic flaws in the Adwaita philosophy based on '*avidya*' theory:

1. *Nature of Avidya*—Avidya must be either real or unreal; no intermediary possibility exists. Based on Adwaita, neither of these is possible. If Avidya is real, non-dualism is disproved into dualism. If it is unreal, it self-contradicts.

2. *The position of avidya*—which gives rise to the illusory impression of the reality of the perceived world? There can be two ways; it could be due to Brahman's Avidya (lacking knowledge) or the individual soul's. Neither is a possibility. Brahman is pure knowledge; Avidya cannot co-exist as an attribute with jnanam. Nor can the individual soul be the place of Avidya, because the individual soul exists due to Avidya; this would lead to going round in a circle without end.

3. *The inexpressibility of Avidya*—Adwaita thinks that Avidya is neither real nor unreal but indescribable or '*anirvachaniya*'. Knowledge has to be either of the real or the unreal, there is no in-between.

4. *The basis of knowledge of Avidya*—No proof can establish Avidya in the sense adwaita contemplates (as unexplainable). Adwaita philosophy presents avidya not as a mere lack of knowledge, but something purely negative, as a layer covering Brahman and is dispelled by true Brahma-vidya or brahma-jnana. Avidya is lack of knowledge and not mere ignorance. Ramanuja contends that positive ignorance is established neither by awareness, nor by presumption, nor by scriptural statements. On the contrary, Ramanuja contends that all knowledge has to be of the real and not of the unreal.

5. *Avidya's negation of the nature of Brahman*—Adwaita would like us to believe that the true nature of Brahman is somehow covered by Avidya. Ramanuja thinks this is absurd. If Brahman is pure consciousness, concealing it would mean either preventing the nature which is an impossibility since Brahman is eternal, unchanging and infinite; or the destruction of its nature—equally meaningless.

6. *Dispelling of Avidya by Brahma-vidya*—Adwaita claims that Avidya has no beginning, but it is dispelled by Brahma-vidya, the knowledge of the reality that Brahman is pure consciousness. But Ramanuja denies of the possibility of a nirguna Brahman, arguing Brahman has infinite auspicious attributes. *Liberation is a matter of His nirhetuka krupa alone (divine Grace) and no amount of devotion and knowledge will deliver a soul from this world.*

7. *The elimination of Avidya*—Based on adwaita, the bondage in which we are caught up before attaining Moksha, is caused by Maya and Avidya; and knowledge of reality (Brahma-vidya) releases us. Ramanuja, however, asserts that bondage is true and real. *No knowledge can remove what is real. On the contrary,*

knowledge reveals the real; it does not remove it. Exactly what knowledge would deliver us from bondage of Maya? If it is real then non-duality becomes duality; if it is unreal, then we are faced with absurdity.

We understand that we have to be granted visa by the embassy of a foreign country, if we have to visit that country. Does not matter whether we think that we have met all the requirements or not, it is the prerogative of the visa issuing country to grant visa and it cannot be questioned. It is also important to realize that they don't grant visa arbitrarily to someone who does not deserve or deny someone who deserves. If God were to grant visa, He being the omniscient, would know the entitlement of the devotee. We cannot self declare or grant visa for ourselves for being entitled to visiting that country. Likewise, we cannot grant liberation, mukti or immortality to ourself. It can only be granted by the Lord. It is not in our power to go beyond this prakruti. The Supreme Lord alone has the power over the prakruti/maya and He alone can take us beyond this created universe.

Essence of all religions

We have many religions in the world today—Christianity, Jewish religion, Budhism, Jainism, Sikhism, Islam, Hinduism, and a few more. All that can be said is *that all philosophies are holy and sacred*; by following them a devotee would reach his God. Every philosophy preaches high values and virtues to their respective devotees. All philosophies including Hindu philosophy talk about dos and don'ts and right and wrong so that followers can lead a moral and happy life while in this world. The righteous life they lead here can guide them to reach their God after this life.

What we are discussing here is not any religion, not even Hindu religion. We are trying to understand God as Science; *you can call it 'science of God' and 'science of life'*—a way of life not restricted to any one person from any one religion or caste. The science of God is inclusive to all. We are not talking about God in a particular form or name.

As humans, we cannot relate to things that we cannot see, experience, realize and perceive, and it is hard to be devoted to an invisible God. It is like the scientists who say that there is dark energy present everywhere but they don't know anything about it. So it is very evident that we cannot experience or realize God in His invisible form.

Even in other religions where they do not follow idol worship, they still have a designated holy place or structure to signify a place for God. *We cannot focus on empty space to visualize God or think of God in nothingness. If we can use form, place and structure to signify nothingness, why not create a proper form, idol and temples. If we can assign a place to worship a formless God, why should we not give him a form we love, when all the scriptures affirm that He has the most beautiful form? The entire universe is His body which in itself is evident enough that He has form and this universe is one of His forms.* Though the souls are invisible they take bodies with form, *if our bodies have a form, God being our source, surely has form.*

We are not habituated to look inward towards the antaryami who is present in all of us. Azhwar declares that He is there even in the place we refer to as 'nowhere". He has the most beautiful form with all His auspicious attributes even in His formless form, except that He remains invisible to us.

We use form in everything. As a loving son, I look at the picture of my father who is no more. If I can retain his form in my mind, I still have to recall the form to think of him. Even in real life, when I wish to call my son or anyone for that matter, I think of him in my mind first. A young married couple, when not together, would hold each other's photograph in their hands to imagine each other's presence. Or recall moments they spent together. We need some form or the other to express our emotions.

We have numbers as a form for mathematical expressions. We depict in paintings to express our creativity and imagination. I can't show someone empty space and ask him to look at an imaginary work of art. We have a need for form in everything we do, we have alphabets as form for our languages, sounds to express and communicate. We are made with our eyes because 93% of our sense perception of this world comes from the eyes alone. If there was no form, we would not need the eyes. Everything in a way has form which is why it is logical that God has a form as well. *Though God can be both in visible or invisible form, we would not be able to relate to Him if He is formless.*

If I think of my father, looking at his photo, he would not know of my thoughts, nor does he exist in the picture. However, if I make a form for the Lord in my mind or look at his idol or picture, thinking of Him, He would know of my thoughts for He is there right inside me and in my thoughts. He also exists in the photo or idol for He is all pervading.

Most importantly, true devotion for the Lord can be tested only when we relate to Him in these forms—saligramams, idols, photos etc; for He remains invisible as also would not perceivably respond. If we can serve Him unconditionally, in these forms; if we are able to express love for Him even when He remains dependant on us, without visibly reciprocating, that is unconditional devotion. Going one step further, we should worship Him even if He is useless, even if He is not the supreme Lord, even if He is powerless, even if it brings us problems, losses, even if it would lead us to hell instead of immortality. *We worship Him not for any benefits but because of our imperishable, eternal relationship alone.*

Would we serve our father even if he is useless? We should, because of the relationship. Similarly, we should be devoted to the supreme Lord, because He is our eternal Father. We protect our children and take care of all their needs without expectations which is true love and all that we have to do is extend the same love towards God.

What is the purpose of such worship when the Lord does not respond nor favours us in any manner? The benefit would be immense; the Lord would know soon as we convey our unconditional love for Him. The effect of our worship is unmistakable for we would feel the bliss in our heart, coming from the Lord dwelling in us. We cannot feel that bliss in anything else. He is the one who gives us that joy when we worship.

People, who visit temples such as Srirangam and Tirumala and Kanchi Varadaraja and several other divyadesams, have confessed that they feel the real energy of the Lord in the Deities of these temples. Several friends have confided that when they stand before the Lord in Tirumala, they feel the divinity and supreme bliss which they don't experience outside the temple. And they are never satisfied seeing the Lord any number of times, which is why they visit such temples as many times as possible. What they feel is true, because the Lord is invoked by chanting the divine psalms, praying Him to energize the idol, which He gracefully does for our sake. One of my friends has even mentioned that He is able to feel the Lord in the deity. Most people would go to Tirumala temple with a list of things they should seek from the Lord. However, the moment they stand before the Lord, they forget everything and their mind is devoid of all other thoughts. Instead, Lord fills their heart. There is that inexpressible feeling and experience which cannot be explained but only felt.

We belong to Him and He to us. Sri Andal confirms our relationship with God thus "*undannoduravEl namkkingu*

ozhikka ozhiyAdu" and in the next verse she affirms
"*ethaikkum EzhEzhu piravikkum, undannoduthome yAvom
unakkE nAmAtcheyvom*", she declares that our relationship
with Him is imperishable, and cannot be obliterated, and Sri
Andal pledges our allegiance of subservience only to the
supreme God and none else, for the simple reason that we are
related only to Him.

Parasara Bhattar once mentions that—Namberumal with His
abhaya hastam—right hand—held in place—to reassure His
devotees that "He is there to protect them and not to fear"—
establishes that He is the only protector. Even if Namberumal
openly declares that He would not protect Bhattar, Bhattar would
still remain at His Lotus Feet and not seek refuge with anyone
else, even though they may offer protection.

It does not matter if He does not protect us due to our sins; our
relationship with God is irrevocable. It is eternal. There is no one
else who can protect even if He does not. He would not interfere
in our karma. *But then we don't seek Him because He can take
care of us, but because of the inherent relationship with Him
and Him alone and the same goes with Him. He seeks us for
the same relationship. Except that we have forgotten this reality
while He does not, ever.*

Chapter Ten

Souls are body for God!

At least, we leave our bodies at death, but God has never left us for a moment. *We Souls are an eternal body for Him* and hence there is that imperishable relationship. We use our bodies for our purpose. The body itself does not want anything as it is non-sentient matter. Similarly, we as the bodies for God should become useful to Him for His purpose. Except that our bodies are matter and do not make a choice by themselves and hence we are able to control and use our bodies as we deem fit. But God does not use the souls for His purpose, unless they make that choice to want to be serving Him.

Kulasekara azhwar expresses beautifully in his PerumAL thirumozhi—4-9 last line "**padiyAy kidanthu un pavazha vAi kANbEnE**". 4-10 last line "**emberumAn ponmalaimEl EdEnumAvene**"—let me be anything, assuming any sort of body; would like to be in your proximity, all that I seek is to be serving you in a way that makes you happy and my only purpose is to see your divine smiling face, doing what you wish me to do.

The beauty is that our material bodies do fulfill this requirement that Azhwar has sought for the souls. There is a difference when we use our body for seeking pleasures. We feel the pleasure but not the body or senses or mind, as they are non-sentient. *But when the soul is serving God, not only does God reveal His happiness, but the soul would also experience the divine bliss of being in service to God.*

Then, does God love only His devotees and not the others?
It is not so. God loves everyone equally. But only a devotee
seeks God's love and hence he gets to experience His grace.
Other's don't seek His grace and hence are deprived. God
does not force His will on any one.

Krishna serves Arjuna and the Pandavas throughout their lifetime
because they were righteous and devout. They did not serve
Krishna in any way.

One other weakness in God when it comes to His devotees is
that He is never satisfied with whatever He does for them. He
seems to forget the extent of grace He bestows on them and
wants to continuously engage in their service, without limit, without
end. Before ending His incarnation, Krishna proclaims that He
was going away without doing anything for 'Draupati' and the
Pandavas. Krishna did more than they could have asked for, yet
He is not satisfied with anything He does for His devotees. As a
matter of fact, Pandavas did nothing for Krishna, He was the one
constantly working tirelessly His full lifetime for the benefit of the
Pandavas and yet He feels He did not do anything. In comparison,
as a contrast, we do very little and claim to have done more. We
don't show true devotion, yet claim we are great devotees.

Indeed this might be the only weakness that God might have, if
we consider this as a weakness that He gives in to His devotees,
like a true father. One of His virtues is "Ashrita vatsalyaika
jaladhe' (the only infinite ocean of love and affection to those
seeking Him).

Varnas are not the caste system we practice today.

The terms 'Hinduism' / 'Hindu religion' or 'Hindustan' are
recent ones. India was originally known as 'bhArata desa" after
"Bharata, son of dushyanta" and earlier 'Jada Bharata', who was

a great mahatma after whom it was named as well. The term 'religion' was not the intent before, original title for the way of life that civilizations adapted was based on 'righteousness' and it was titled 'sanAtana dharma" meaning, it is so ancient that it is beginning-less and the primeval philosophy based on dharma (definition of dharma is 'being righteous'—in simple terms "caring and doing good for others' well being). What is referred to as Hindu religion today has undergone lots of changes made by the people in the last few thousand years to suit their conveniences from time to time. All other religions are recent ones.

Mainly, concerning the Hindu religion, certain people have misrepresented and misinterpreted these religious doctrines in such a way that they could take advantage to suit their ulterior motives. For instance the caste system that is prevalent today was not intended that way.

Que—why then does Gita refer to the four varnas? Is it not the caste system?

Ans—what Gita refers to in 4/13
"chAtur varNyam mayA srushtyA, guNa karma vibhAgasaha"—

"I have defined people in four stations (types) based on their nature, qualities and deeds".

There is no mention of the caste system we follow today. There is no mention of birth here. It is vividly declared that people are identified by their guna (qualities/nature) and karma (deeds)

Birth alone does not decide who we are. Every person would be recognized based on his deeds in that life. We develop qualities influenced by the gunas which are born of this prakruti from which we have obtained our bodies.

Gita 18-40—

"na tadasti prithivyAm vA divi dEvEshu vA punah . . ."

"There is no creature, either on earth or again among the gods in heaven, that is free from these three gunas born of prakruti"

Krishna has also mentioned how we can excel and transcend these gunas to attain immortality. We should be more focused on achieving the state of immortality than debating on the varnas. Being born as a brahmana, also binds us to repeated birth-death cycles. We need to go beyond the three gunas, renouncing action and fruits of action in devotion to the Lord to attain His world. The best birth here, even that of Brahma does not bring us immortality.

Gita 14-5

"sattvam, rajastama iti guNAh prakrutisambhavAh . . ."

"Sattva, rajas and tamas are the gunas arising from prakruti, bind the atma in the body"

The 14th chapter explains the nature of these gunas further—

> ➤ Nature of sattva being without impurity, is luminous and free from morbidity. **Even sattva binds by attachment to pleasure and to knowledge**.
> ➤ Nature of rajas is of passion arising from thirst and attachment. It binds the atma with attachment to action.
> ➤ Tamas is of false knowledge and delusion, it binds the atma with negligence, indolence and sleep
> ➤ **Sattva** prevails on knowledge that illumines the senses; greed, longing enable **rajas** to prevail; and inactivity, negligence and delusion make **tamas** to prevail
> ➤ Fruit of good deed is pure, of the nature of sattva; pain is the fruit of rajas; and ignorance is the fruit of tamas.

> One who realizes that the gunas are the agent of action and **one who transcends beyond all three gunas attains the Lord**. The traits of such a person are: he hates not illumination, nor activity nor delusion when these prevail; nor longs for them when they cease. He would be unconcerned, undisturbed by the gunas. Who remains same in pleasure and pain, dear and hateful; blame and praise.

Gita chapter 16 enlists qualities we should nurture in order to excel beyond the three gunas for the Lord to recognize our entitlement to grant us the state of divine existence.

> Qualities of a person seeking divine destiny—based on which he attains an existence beyond this mortal world—fearlessness, purity of mind, devotion to knowledge of the self, philanthropy, self control, worship, study of scriptures, austerity, uprightness, non-violence, truth, freedom from anger, renunciation, tranquility, non-insulting others, compassion to all beings, freedom from desire, gentleness, sense of shame for wrong doing, freedom from fickleness, grandeur, patience, fortitude, purity, freedom from hatred and false pride. One who possesses these qualities irrespective of his birth would be considered a person of divinity which is what each one should aspire for.

> Qualities of demoniac person: pompousness, arrogance, self-conceit, wrath, rudeness and ignorance. Knows not either action or renunciation, they do not know cleanliness nor right conduct. Who think this universe is without truth, without foundation or a Lord. They know only lust, doing cruel deeds. They seek insatiable desires; acquiring wealth unjustly through delusion, aiming for enjoyment of desires as the highest goal and deciding that this is all there is to life. They strive unjustly to acquire wealth for desire gratification assuming "I have acquired this, I shall

fulfill this desire, and this wealth is mine and shall remain so hereafter. I shall slay this enemy and other as well for I am the lord, I am the enjoyer, I have the power and strength and hence successful; who is equal to me? I can do what I wish—people of these qualities perish in hell and low births of animals, insects etc.

After taking birth in families that match with our nature and qualities, we have to perform again in that birth to earn our standing. Birth alone does not entitle us to a status of who we are. *We got this birth based on who we were, and now in this birth, our actions will determine who we are*.

The Gunas—sattva, rajasa, tamasa (nature) applies to the entire creation—to all the beings in the universe—beginning with Brahma up to a cluster of grass. Any soul taking birth here cannot escape the influence of the three gunas, without devotion.

As humans, we can discuss about the evils of caste system, but the same soul also acquires bodies of animals. We can see different breeds of dogs, horses, cats and cows.

Though we question our taking birth in different families according to our qualities, we accept the disparity and discrimination practiced in the corporate world and in governments. Everyone is given a rating based on hierarchy. They have created chain of command of people who are made to feel the distinction based on their status in the organization, from the lower level to the higher levels, regardless of their qualification or virtues. This is also a type of caste system that is practiced everywhere in the world today, to which we don't seem to either have problem accepting or interested in finding a level playing field for all the people, treating everyone as equals. At least the varna system gives us our birth, based on our nature and quality, but the business world has no such logic either.

Even in the corporate world, some people are given statuses based on their qualification. Ones that are more qualified are given better positions and better emoluments. Likewise, lesser qualified people get lower positions and lower salaries. We don't complain about it, though it is similar to a caste system of giving people a rating based on quality and capabilities or guna and karma. However, an attendant or the president should be respected equally for being humans, and not distinguished on their position and the pay scale, just as we must treat people from all the varnas as equals.

We also buy products based on their quality; willing to pay more for products rated better in quality. We look for quality and attributes even in inanimate objects. However, when it comes to humans, we seem to have a problem in accepting that people are defined on their inherent nature and quality and yet everyone should be respected equally.

In the varna system, nowhere it is stated that any of these stations are untouchables or one of them is superior or inferior to the others. Nor any of these stations stand qualified or disqualified to reaching God based on their birth. All these branches are merely an indication of each ones nature. Sattva being a nicer quality than rajas, and rajas nicer than tamas.

These gunas are applicable to the bodies we take and not the atma.

Viswamitra was born as a kshatriya, a rajarishi and by virtue of his guna and karma in that life, became a brahma-rishi (brahmana).

Krishna chose Arjuna, a kshatriya, to bestow upon him the knowledge of Gita. There were many brahmanas there but Arjuna was the most entitled to receive this knowledge. So there is no caste discrimination by God to bestow His grace.

Krishna declined to eat at Bhishma or krupacharya's place but opted to visit Vidura's home instead, though Vidura was a sudra. However Vidura was titled 'mahatma vidurah". He was an embodiment of dharma. So birth in a particular varna has no relation to what one can achieve in that life. Vidura practiced a life better than that of a brahmana, endowed with pure sattva guna which surpasses the blend of three gunas—sattva/rajasa/tamasa. Developing suddha sattva is what is essential and not birth. Anyone who practices sattva guna would be considered a brahmana. But our focus should be to transcend even sattva guna, which also binds us to this mortal world.

Rama ate fruits bitten by a hunter lady 'Sabari' who bit into each fruit before giving them to Rama. Sabari had transcended all gunas. She was a divine soul by virtue of her pure devotion.

Krishna incarnated though as the 8th child of Devaki/Vasudava, grew up in the family of the chief of cowherds, Nanda gopa—is said to be a vaisya by virtue of his duties. Krishna took birth though in His divine form, unlike us, lived a childhood as a cowherd and later on became the king of Dwaraka (assumed the role of a kshatriya by His functionality).

God's incarnation as Kalki at the end of this millennium (kali yuga) would be as a sudra. *These 4 stations merely represent the guna and karma based on inherent nature. Our endeavour should be to elevate everyone to becoming righteous, pious and noble which are the qualities beyond any of these stations, that of a pure devotee.*

What's more amazing is that God incarnated even in the form of fish, tortoise, boar, in the combination of man's body/lions head (Narasimha); *to God all the creatures of His creation are equal and same, none superior or inferior. Does not matter what form they take. It is the soul that can reach God and not this material body.*

If you score 40% marks in the 10th class exams, you would be promoted to 11th class with a grade 'D', those who do relatively better, would all be promoted but with relatively better grades of C, B and A. Student obtaining A grade would have to start all over again in the 11th class and he would not be assessed based on his 10th marks alone. If he fails in the 11th, he has to fall behind, while the 'D' grade student who performs better in 11th would be elevated to 12th class.

If a Brahmana belies his nature by not performing his duties, would not be considered a brahmana. A Sudra, who practices qualities of a brahmana, would be considered a brahmana by virtue of his nobility. However, both of them cannot attain immortality. The only way to attaining the Lord, would be going beyond the nature of these 4 varnas, by becoming true devotees of the Lord, like a Vidura, who was a Sudra though, became a 'mahatma' by his devotion. Practicing the varna— asrama dharma would not take us to God. Only devotion would.

Now let us look at natural qualities of each station—Gita 18/41

We don't stand on a special pedestal based on varna dharma or ashrama dharma

> Brahmana—the qualities and duties of a brahmana—gita 18/42—"*Samo damastapah, Soucham, kshAntir Arjavam Evacha, jnAnam, vijnAnamAstikyam brahma karma svabhAvajam*"—control of the senses and the mind, austerity, purity, forbearance, uprightness, knowledge and faith—all these constitute the **duty** of brahmana born of his inherent nature. *Anyone who has these qualities irrespective of which station he is born, is a brahmana by virtue of his deeds*. But failing to do his prescribed duties will disqualify him to be a brahmana. The same applies to other stations.

> Kshatriya—*"Souryam, tEjo dhrutirdAkshyam, yudhE chApyapalAyanam, dAnamIswara bhAvascha kshatram karma swabhAvajam"*—"valour, invincibility, steadiness, adroitness and courage to face situations, generosity and lordliness are the duties of a kshatriya born of his inherent nature.

> Vaisya—*"krushi, gorakshya, vANijyam vaisya karma swabhAvajam, paricharyAtmakam karma sudrasyApi swabhAvajam"* . . . "agriculture, animal/environmental protection, trade/business are the duties of the vaisya born of his nature and the duty of a sudra is one of service born of his nature.

The varna system is not different from the Olympic races. Let's take the 100 meters race. 4 of the fastest from each preliminary races would qualify for the next round. Winners from all the preliminary races would qualify to run in the finals. Their reaching the final is not an entitlement to winning. No runner can claim for a medal because he ran faster than everyone else in the qualifying rounds. They have to perform again in the finals to be declared as winners. There is only one winner and others stand 2nd and 3rd in the race conducted by humans. Rest of the runners don't get any prize. In God's race, each one can be a winner for there is no pre-qualification to make a fresh start. God even accepts the last loser for merely trying to run. Winning is not important but the intent to run, righteously and devotedly is what is essential. We don't have a problem declaring fastest runners as winners. Being a brahmana or sudra is the same which is based on performance in last life and qualifying to getting a human life is similar to reaching the finals. Brahmana to sudra—all of them have to perform again if they want to reach God. All of them stand entitled to perform and all of them can be winners, unlike the running race where only the top three runners are declared winners. It is also true that a person who outran all others in preliminaries has the potential to win for he has been running faster throughout. This is similar to the effect of 'karma vasanas' from past births. A good natured person, in several of his past births has a better chance to be a good person in this life as well.

What makes a person great and respectful are his deeds, righteous conduct and respect for the others and how much he cares and works for other's well being, here and now in this life. We do not know if a person was great in his last birth and hence cannot assume his virtues based on birth alone. *What define a person are his deeds and not his birth.*

Nambaduvan

Nambaduvan, one of the greatest devotees of Lord Varaha, was born as a chandala (a so called untouchable) due to his past karma. The story of Nambaduvan is evident enough that all that God considers from a devotee are his virtues, qualities and unconditional love for God and his fellow beings and nothing else.

Nambaduvan was a singer from pANar kulam. He sings for Lord VarAha every morning before sunrise. On a particular dwadasi (12th day) he was on his way to the temple when a brahma rakshasa (a soul acquiring an ogre's body due to a curse) waylays him. He was a brahmana named Soma Sharma in his earlier life and was cursed for his misconduct. The brahma rakshasa proclaims that he was indeed lucky to find his meal early in the morning, and would devour him. Nambaduvan requests the rakshasa to let him go and he would return in a couple of hours after singing for Lord Varaha. The rakshasa suggests that he knows Nambaduvan was a chandala, and based on his nature, why should he trust him to return? Even a brahmana would not hesitate to lie if it came to protecting his own life and he being a chandala, it would not matter to him to be a liar. Nambaduvan gives him several assurances declaring that he would attain great sins if he failed to return. But the rakshasa would not trust him. Finally he states that if Vasudeva was indeed the supreme God and was indeed the sole cause for all gods, souls and the worlds; and if there is no other god or entity that can be **equated** with Him; he should allow him to go and surely he would return. On this assurance, the rakshasa lets him go, as Nambaduvan revealed the awareness of *'highest knowledge'* about the supreme God. Someone with such a profound knowledge must be a true devotee and hence cannot be a liar.

Nambaduvan promptly performs his singing for the Lord and returns to the rakshasa who was surprised to see him come back. He admits to Nambaduvan that he was truly impressed with his truthfulness and that he must be a true devotee of the supreme Lord. He then suggests to Nambaduvan granting him the 'punya' or good effects of his singing for the Lord and he would let him go. Nambaduvan declines the offer and asks him to consume his body instead. The rakshasa comes down to begging Nambaduvan to give him at least, the benefit of one line from his song and in return he would let him go. Nambaduvan then explains to the brahma-rakshasa that he was unable to give him the credits of even a syllable for he was not singing the praise of his Lord for any benefit in return. It was an unconditional service to the Lord as he was capable of doing only so much for His Lord. It was indeed God's kindness that He accepted his singing which in itself was his goal. It was then that the rakshasa relates how he was a noble brahmana in his earlier life but due to a curse he has acquired the ogre's body and he can be relieved of his curse if Nambaduvan can grant him the divine effects of his devotion. Nambaduvan then reaffirms that he had no power to grant him the benefits of his singing but he would pray to the Lord for his salvation and it would be **God's grace alone** and not the effects of deeds or devotion that can lead to a higher state. It was then that Sri Varaha relieves brahma rakshasa from his curse and also endows Nambaduvan with the blanket power to grant anyone the salvation /moksham (parama padam). Nambaduvan being a true devotee, attains the eternal world.

The essence of true devotion is to show kindness and affection to every person (bhAgavatas).We cannot give God anything, for He is complete and infinite in all respects and does not need anything from anyone. What can you give God when everything already belongs to Him?

Service is the true nature of a sudra who is best suited to be devoted to God. Merely being born as a sudra does not give a person the special status of a devotee. Same is true for all other varnas as well. However, a brahmana having the pride of knowledge, and kshatriya having the pride of power, stand to lose if they do not control their pride and ego. It is purity of mind, righteous deeds and humility that are foremost qualities that can nurture devotion.

All the Azhwars and Acharyas confirm that there are just the souls and the Lord. There is no other caste. Sri Azhagiyamanavala perumal Nayanar goes to the extent of disapproving some of the interpretations of Manu-sastra, declaring that it should be discarded as an extreme view, if it does not match with what is said by Nammazhwar. Acharyahrudayam 1-64—

> ". . . . Ivar (nammazhwar's) uraigoLin mozhikondu
> SAstrArttangaL nirNayikka vEndugaiyAlE valankonda
> idukku chErAdavai "manu viparltangaL polE"—

A lot of the sastras have been deliberately altered and misinterpreted by some, which is pointed out in this sukti. Sastras are always correct and mean good for humanity, but it is the misinterpretations that are the root cause for all the discriminations we see today.

Krishna suggests to Arjuna who is a kshatriya (but this is applicable to all varnas) about the three gunas that sets the nature in us for our deeds and in turn that influence our birth in a particular station—Gita 2/45—

"thryguNyavishayA vedAnisthriguNyo bhavArjuna . . ."

"The Vedas have the three gunas as their field; you must become free from the three gunas and the pairs of opposites. Abide in pure sattva alone, never care to acquire things and to protect what has been acquired, but be established in the self".

Krishna suggests overcoming the effects of "duals" to develop pure sattva guna and to remain equipoised, un-affected in all situations—duals such as—sukha / dukha (pleasure and grief), mAna / apamAna, (honour and dishonour) kIrti / akIrti, (fame and defame) lAbha /alAbha, (gain and loss) jaya-apajaya (victory and defeat) and such.

Here, Krishna is advocating developing pure sattva guna which is superior in nature than the blend of sattva/rajasa/tamasa gunas.

We can practically see how these three gunas prevail in each one of us, every day of our life, does not matter what station we are born in and what we practice now. We see people behaving inconsistently to the same situation, at different times, each time differently.

The easiest way to overcome the blend of three gunas is to realize that the self (atma) is divine and pure and is not touched by these gunas. It is due to our association with the body which inherently has these gunas that influences the Atma. So whenever I am angry, I must think for a moment to realize that my nature is not anger, but the rajasik guna is affecting my nature making me angry. This is the consciousness that reminds us of our actions. When I am deluded, unable to control my emotions, causing distress and pain to others, I must realize that the tamasa guna is affecting my behaviour.

Developing devotion to God would bring about a noticeable consistency in our behaviour remaining pure-sattvik, in all situations. Every time we pray and worship, thinking of God or doing something to help others—invariably, we would be sattvik in nature, peaceful in mind, content and happy. Pure Sattva also keeps us undisturbed to situations.

The Soul is beyond this prakruti but is imprisoned in this prakruti due to karma and hence acquires different bodies. However, the effects of the gunas and karma bind the Soul to this world, as the soul is the user of the body and also beneficiary of the karma effects.

It is also known that 8 of the 10 Azhwars were not born as brahmanas. This is evident enough that kula (varna) is not the criteria to attain greatness; for, the greatest of them all—Sri Nammazhwar, was not a brahmana. Krishna appears before Nammazhwar just before it was time for Azhwar to end his incarnation—Krishna was in deep love with Azhwar and suggests taking Azhwar with Him to paramapadam with his human body.

Azhwar reminds Krishna that He should not break any rules due to His boundless affection for him and that he shall relinquish his mortal body here. Azhwar had to correct the Lord from doing something unprecedented as He was all powerful (omnipotent) and could do anything He wished. It is perhaps His only weakness that He forgets who He is when He is overwhelmed by the devotion of His devotees. Krishna accedes to Azhwar's advice and accompanies Azhwar's divine Atma personally to His abode.

Azhwar confirms thus in 3-7-9

"*kulamthAngu sAthigal nAlilum keezhizhindu,*
ettanai nalanthAnilAda sandALa sandALargaLAgilum,
valanthAngu sakkarattaNNal maNivaNNarkAL ennuL
kalanthAr, adiyAr tam adiyAr emmadigale."

"Even those born much below the 4 stations or varnas (such as a chandala due to their past karma), if they are devotees of the Lord, they merge into me and they and their followers are our masters"

Having obtained a PhD, if a person fails to perform at his level or even the levels of high school learning, he has to go back to elementary learning, but those who are in the high school and under-grad school would eventually go beyond the PhD levels due to the path they choose. Just as those who are born as brahmanas develop tamasa and rajasa gunas, fall to the lower levels, those who are born in other varnas may develop sattva guna reaching great heights in this life.

Basis for our nature

Whether we brand us as engineers or doctors or kshatriya or sudra—we naturally come under one of these 4 stations based on our guna and karma. I don't feel bad if someone calls me an electrician, a teacher, an agriculturist, a driver, a pilot, an astronaut, a scientist or technician, a mechanic, a designer, an architect, a politician, a soldier, a sportsman, a beautician, an artist, a dancer, an actor, hair dresser, maker of shoes—watches— dresses, etc.. We could be born in any of the varnas, pursuing any profession, if we remain righteous, nurturing sattva guna, we would be considered a Brahmana by virtue of our conduct.

Krishna dispels all doubts about who can attain the Lord; He declares that even sinners can become great devotees irrespective of their birth or past.

Gita 9/32
   "Mam hi pArtha vyapASritya yE'pi syuh pApayonayah . . ."

"By taking refuge in Me, even men of evil birth, women, vaisyas and sudras attain the supreme state"

Gita 9/33

> *"kim punar brAhmanAh puNyA bhaktA*
> *rajarshayah tathA . . ."*

"How much more then the brahmanas and royal sages *who are pure and are My devotees,* (they too will reach Me). So, having obtained this transient, joyless world, worship Me".

Interestingly enough, every soul, irrespective of his birth station, truly devoted to God, is expected to show keenness to doing service.

All are equal

Pillai Lokacharyar declares that—everyone is entitled to surrender to God, there is no restriction about who they are— caste, status, gender, place, time, method. The only requisite is our unconditional devotion.

"prapattikku dEsha niyamamum, kAla niyamamum, prakAra niyamamum, adhikAri niyamamum, phala niyamamum illai, vishaya niyamamE uLLadu"

A true religious philosophy would always accept everyone **"emmathamum sammathame"**—"all religions are sacred and equal"; accepted and revered.

Nothing establishes equality more than this real life incidence of Sri Ramanuja. Ramanuja comes to Thirunarayanapuram (Melkote near Mysore in Karnataka). While he was here, God asks Ramanuja in his dreams, to go to Delhi to bring back His idol that was taken away by Ghajni Mohammed. The Melkote temple was without the presiding utsavar deity "Chella pillai", as he was fondly called by His devotees.

Ramanuja goes to Delhi, Ghajni was long dead and his son was in power. He was not such a cruel and intolerant person. Ramanuja mentions to the mohammaden king about god's message and asks permission to bring back the idol. The king mentions that there were thousands of idols from different temples lying dumped in a yard and he could take back his idol if he was able to find Him. Ramanuja goes to the spot where the idols were lying around. In one glance he determines that his Chella pillai was not in that lot. He mentions so to the king and the king responds saying his religion does not permit idol worship and he considers it a bad omen to be in possession of an idol of a Hindu god. That it couldn't possibly be in his place, if he couldn't find it in the lot.

Ramanuja then suggests to the king that the idol was in his palace and this is based on the signs he has received from his God. The king becomes nervous and denies that there was such a possibility, as it was forbidden for him or his family to be in possession of an idol. If Ramanuja was sure it was in the palace, he could take it back with him. Ramanuja was allowed into the palace. He goes straight into the chambers of the king's young daughter, who was found to be in possession of the idol. Ramanuja was overwhelmed with joy to find his Lord very well cared for by the muslim girl and that God seemed to enjoy being with the girl as well. Ramanuja relates the whole story to the girl. He requests the girl to give him the idol to be taken back, as that would be a great service to the devotees who were craving to have their 'Chella pillai' back in the Melkote temple, where he belongs. She responds saying that she couldn't possibly survive without Him and that He was everything to her and the very purpose of her life. Ramanuja reasons with her, knowing full well how much devoted she was, to part with the Idol, even though it would be impossible for her to be without Him, considering the fact that so many devotees like her deserve this God as much as she.

Ramanuja explains to her that God's kindness has no limits; that she has proved to God and to the world that she is no less than the greatest of them all. To God, the Greatest Jagadacharya, the nitya suri Ramanuja—and a muslim girl, the daughter of a muslim king whose dynasty has killed millions of Hindus and destroyed idols and temples—are same and equal.

Ramanuja enlightens her that the Idol was not wanted in her place, for her father considers possessing the idol as a bad omen. The Idol would be discarded and abandoned after her life. She obliges at once and hands over the Idol to Ramanuja. Ramanuja thanks the king and starts walking towards the palace gates, when he hears voices asking him to stop and he turns around to see the girl being rushed to him in a palanquin by her maids. She gets down, holds on to the idol and gives up life. The King thought she was punished for worshipping the Idol and Ramanuja was allowed to take away the Idol. He promptly establishes the Idol in the Melkote temple. Ramanuja establishes a small idol for the muslim girl at the feet of the Lord and is considered equal to the consorts of the Lord and she was titled as "tulukku nachiyar". Even today, almost thousand years later, we worship this muslim girl along with the Lord Chella pillai in Melkote. The fun part is that His consorts have separate idols but this girl is embedded into His own idol to represent how dearly she was to Him.

Love of God for his devotees has no bounds, it is infinite, which we cannot comprehend, while our love for Him has both limits and limitations and He gracefully accepts our devotion even with deficiencies. In this Ramanuja philosophy God does not belong to any religion, caste, gender, color, nor do His devotees. He is for everyone. On one hand there is God and on the other hand every person belonging to one community—atma/soul. There is not even the gender consideration.

Uttanga rishi's obsession to untouchability

Uttanga rishi does penance and Lord Krishna appears before him. The Lord says that He was pleased with his devotion and asked if he wanted something? The Rishi who said he had no desires, does not ask for anything. When Krishna wished to grant him something, he asks for water to be made available in the desert, wherever he goes. Krishna mentions to him that it would be improper to change the nature and eco system of the desert just for his wish, however, he could think of Him whenever he needed water and it would be provided.

Soon after, on a hot day, the Rishi was thirsty and he thinks of Krishna, who summons Indra, the god of heavens asking him to bring nectar to the muni. Indra hesitates as nectar is not meant to be given to humans. Krishna realizes his thoughts and asks him to take nectar to the rishi in the guise of a chandala. Indra turns himself into an ugly looking chandala (so called untouchable) dressed in dirty rags and animal leather and a dog accompanying him. He comes to the muni with leather sacks hanging on shoulders and enquires if he was looking for water. The muni looks at the chandala in disgust and asks him to stay away. The chandala mentions to the muni that he does not mind his reaction to his appearance and he has sweet water and was willing to give him if he didn't mind his being a chandala. The muni refuses, insulting him further that he would rather die than drink water touched by him. The chandala disappears in a flash which intrigues Uttanga rishi. He realizes that it was not an ordinary person and he had erred in his conduct by disrespecting the chandala who was also a human being and the same God dwells in him.

Krishna appears before him. He then confesses to Krishna of his blunder. Krishna mentions to him that it was Indra who brought the divine nectar from the heavens but he missed out on the opportunity owing to his discrimination in people.

He then accepts that merely having all the knowledge does not make one a great person, but practicing a life in accordance with the knowledge was indeed what one has to follow for developing true devotion. Merely knowing that God resides in every one does not fulfill one's status of being a devotee but practicing it in real life and treating everyone with respect and dignity, is what is essential.

We surrender at God's Feet

Now, if God appears before us, (obviously it would happen only if we have earned that entitlement of being able to see God), and the first thing a devotee would naturally do is fall at His Feet. The most important part of God for a true devotee is His Lotus Feet. Even in temples we prostrate in front of the deity, with the soul/ mind and body surrendering at the Feet of the Lord. We don't surrender at God's face or shoulders. Now, according to purusha suktham (Upanishad / taitriaranyakam) it states "**padbhyAm sUdro ajayatha**" meaning the sudras originate from the Lotus feet of the Lord. And it is only at God's Feet that a devotee can surrender and only His feet can redeem us from this world.

Thondaradippodi azhwar (who never reveals his name or identity—who was named by his parents as 'vipra narayana') names himself as the dust from the feet of the devotees.

The true essence of our surrender, prostrating before God or Acharya, signifies that we have nowhere else to go and He is our only refuge. when we join our palms together, it signifies that we have nothing to give, indicating that we are subservient in nature.

Chapter Eleven

Migration of souls in different bodies

Que—how is a soul born in different bodies?

A soul when not in a body is floating around in space. He does not experience any pain or pleasure when not in a body, but would be in a state of suspended animation due to his inability to express and does not like this experience. The rain drop brings him down to earth. Many get into food grains; many remain on earth and may end up becoming grass, plants and other insects; species originating from earth. Some of them may drop down in water and ocean, entering the bodies of the fish and their reproductive system. When we (and other species) eat food, many of the souls get into the reproductive system of humans and other animals *as seeds of life*. When a man and woman come together in a marital relationship millions of these life seeds (sperm) are sent forth into the woman but only one gets a body in a mother, rarely more than one as twins or very rarely more than two (this happens due to correlative karma of the twins). Rest of the sperms are rejected and thrown out of the human body, and they go through the process again to get their turn, in accordance with their karma. Many of the souls can become life cells in our bodies, micro organisms in water, air, everywhere. Will keep changing their state of existence based on karma they exhaust. Souls in plants, sperm, as cells in our bodies, micro organisms, bacteria, virus, food, seeds, water and air have no feelings.

Que—what happens to the soul at death of each body? How does it find another body?

Ans—the soul is always in a sukshma sarira (subtle body) when it leaves a body at death. Even in this state it remains invisible. The subtle body is a package of consciousness, ego, intellect, mind and the five senses. Of course, God is always there inside the soul as Antaryami. The soul exits with the subtle invisible body. It has to follow the process of getting into any food and into a man's body and acquire the next body from a mother. It is the same with most species. That apart, there are viruses, micro organisms and life cells that can multiply without the above process. We are primarily concerned about humans because true realization of the self is possible only for humans.

Que—Is there any suffering during the process of acquiring a body? Does every soul get into a new body immediately after death?

Ans—Even in the state of conception in a mother's womb, the soul goes through a lot of suffering. That may be the reason why babies cry soon after birth, as though to express the untold misery and grief they experienced being imprisoned in the womb of the mother for such a long time.

Sri Kulasekara azhwar suggests how we don't have to suffer being caught up in a womb again—mukundamala—26, lines 3 & 4

"hA nah pUrvam vAkpravruttA na tasmin,tEna prAptam garbhavAsAdi duhkham"—

"Had I not missed being devoted to the Lord (chanting his names) in the last life, I would not have had to suffer spending time in the womb, this birth"

Having lost the opportunity to be devoted to the Lord in the last life has resulted in this life; at least we should not miss this time. When trapped in the womb, the soul, whose nature is to experience boundless freedom, is literally imprisoned. And the duration of conception varies from species to species. Everything happens scientifically. Nothing is arbitrary or random. Sometimes a soul will have to hover around for a long time before getting a body. There are souls in space, souls getting thrown out of bodies, and they have to go through the cycle till they get their chance again; all based on their individual karma. Many souls are trapped in a state of suspended animation without a functional body, for longer duration of time.

Que—when did karma start for us, did all the souls come to this world as humans first?

Ans—karma originated from souls. Souls when inside God also had the ability to making choice. Karma has no beginning, however for our understanding; we can say that karma started when we made our choices. No, not all of us would have taken first birth here as humans. We do not know what our choices were based on which we could have gotten a life of an animal, bird, insect, fish, plant, etc. Gradually, based on spending the effect of our karma we would have been elevated to a human life getting which we get full potential to realize our nature, and our relationship with God. Once we acquire a human body, we should not miss the opportunity to attain God's world. If we continue to get entwined in this material world, we will continue in the cycle of getting in and out of the bodies of 8.4 million species, based on our karma. And this can go on and on for eternity till at some point in time we realize our true potential in a human body again. We would have acquired human bodies countless number of times.

Que—what about a person who is bad all his life, will he continue to be bad in the next life as well?

Ans—God seems somewhat partial to those with bad karma, though He truly is impartial. If we die being bad, God allows us to start a new life in the next birth, as we will not have the memory from past life. He is doing us a favour by not giving us the memory of past lives; if not, we would continue to be bad. Without the memory, we get a fresh start. However, we would still have to bear the outcome of our bad deeds from past lives. We would have the vasanas (impressions) from past lives, but we can overcome that by conscious effort to being good people in this life and progress towards becoming a devotee within a life. The impressions from past lives are not as intense as the memory we possess within the same life. If I am a liar or thief, it is hard for me to change. If I am a drug addict in this life, it is almost impossible to break that habit. However, if I lose memory in an accident, it is possible for me to change within this life. We can break the impressions by our conscious effort but it is hard to change if we have the memories. In any case, when a person consciously chooses to be a good person, God would enable his success.

Que—we see many bad people having a great life, being very rich. Likewise, we see good people, but suffering. How do you explain this?

Ans—A person is born in a rich family, due to some of his past good karma. Obviously he is entitled to the effects of his good deeds and hence gets a good start. If he chooses to be a righteous person in this life, he would progress towards having better lives in the future. If he chooses to be a bad person causing harm to others, situation might change and he would have to suffer the consequences of his bad deeds. We must remember that he has no memory of whether he was a good or bad person in his last life, except he would have the vasanas (impressions) of karma and he can choose to change now and not abide by the vasanas. If he gets a good start in a good family, it is surely due to his good karma from past lives. But that does not guarantee that he will remain a good man even now, for we are influenced by the association of the people we are with. He can choose to do bad things now but we cannot take away the good he has done in the past. He will continue to be rich and powerful till a relevant portion of his past good karma is spent. But it may seem outwardly that though he is a bad person, he is still enjoying a good life. But that can end very soon, within a life. Sometimes we see many swinging fortunes in a person's life. A great man loses everything, regains everything and may lose it again. We have seen a Madoff who robbed many people for many years and successfully evaded the law, till he ran out of the good effect. Eventually ended up losing everything and is spending his last days in prison. We know that Saddam Hussein ruled for many years though he was cruel, but his life ended miserably. A Hitler met with a bad end. We know of many military dictators who rule countries by force but meeting with dreadful deaths or having to hide in another country to save their life. Bad people cannot have long runs for ever. It has to end sooner than later. Nor can they escape the effects of their bad deeds as they will have to take several lives in suffering the consequences of what they caused.

A good person might face difficulties due to some of his past karma, soon as he exhausts relevant bad karma, his situation will change for the better. If he lives a righteous life now, he would endure the suffering with less pain and may become a better person still. *What is important is to remain a good person throughout this life, as life does not end with the death of this body.* **Karma and its effects are much more complex than we can set them into a definitive programming**. Because we do most things without being conscious and as a result, we have no awareness of our actions.

A person might live a whole life spending merely a part of his bad karma and then he may have many good lives and vice versa. But we must not miss out being good people when we get a human life. Be it good or bad—we have to keep taking lives to spend our karma.

Que—what defines good and bad?

Ans—karma is defined in three ways—

Good karma or bad karma is not what we do for ourselves. For instance, *I cannot claim to have performed 'anna dAnam' (feeding the poor) by treating myself and family to a delicious and sumptuous meal either for a day or for a lifetime. It becomes 'anna danam' only if we feed the needy, not related to us. I* cannot donate a million rupees to my son and claim that I am philanthropic.

Good karma is what we do to help others. If we do the same, renouncing the fruits of karma, we will not accrue the effects.

Bad karma is what we do harming others. We cannot renounce the effects of bad karma. We would have to necessarily exhaust by experiencing the consequences.

Neutral karma is what we do in taking care of the self and our dependents in fulfilling our obligatory duties. If we do neutral karma for the sake of the self, it will bind us in repeated birth-death cycle. **If we do all karma—good and neutral in offering to God, we would not accrue effects. However we cannot do bad karma in offering to God.**

There is no tit-for-tat in karma. For instance, if I cheat someone of thousand rupees, I may lose ten thousand rupees as a consequence, to someone else. If I had killed someone in my last life, he need not kill me in this life as a consequence. I might die suffering in this life from chronic illness or disability. Karma—cause and effect is somewhat like the Newton's third law of motion—"every action has an equal and opposite reaction"—if we can understand this law, it would not be hard to realize the effects of karma. *We have to realize that we are ourselves the cause for all that is happening to us—good or bad. **It is like pre-ordering the effects that will meet us at anytime from the time of the deed**.*

Que—Do we acquire karma even when we perform our righteous duties?

Ans—Gita 18-17—yasya nAhamkruto bhAvo budhir yasya na lipyatE;

"He who is free from the notion "I am the doer" and whose understanding is not tainted, slays not, though he slays all these men, nor is he bound"

Here, the state of a righteous person who does his dharmic duties renouncing karma and results is explained.

This verse is often misquoted and misinterpreted. This does not mean that a person who considers himself as a non-doer can do anything and get away. This verse refers to a true devotee who has renounced ownership to karma or the fruits. Such a person would surely not engage in wrong-doing nor would he slay people. This verse refers to the state of a person who would do only 'dharma' or righteous duties without ownership to even the good deeds, for he has no desire for enjoying the fruits of his good deeds. He would anyways do good things for the benefit of the society while carrying out his duties. Such a person would not kill. If he has to kill, it would be in doing his righteous duty. A soldier who kills enemy forces will not accrue the effects of killing for he is doing his dharma he has undertaken to perform. It is to be noted that the soldier has no personal enmity with the opponents. He is merely doing his duties in protecting the countrymen. In the bargain, he might even end up sacrificing his own life. Either way, he would not accrue bad karma.

When a doctor, doing his duties, in an effort to save life, though does the job correctly, is unable to save the life of the patient, is not held responsible for the death of the patient. When a father, in trying to rescue his child from perils of death, ends up failing, resulting in the death of the child is not the killer of his own child. The intentions, actions of the devotee, a soldier, a doctor or a father—are honest, selfless, without desire for self benefit. They all perform their righteous duties and outcome is truly not in any of their hands. Hence, even if they fail in achieving the desired result, they are not to be blamed or held responsible for the outcome. That is what Krishna implies in the verse above when he tells Arjuna that while doing his rightful duty in protecting dharma, if he ends up killing the enemies in the war or even if he dies in their hands, he is not stained by such actions.

That is why, it is essential that we must choose to do our natural duties and not undertake something that is not in our nature. If a person who is not fit to be a Prime minister, accepts that position for attaining power, fame, will cause more damage to the country than good, even though he is not a bad person. His being incompetent for the post is enough to bring down the economy. Similarly, if you appoint an incompetent person as the CEO of a multinational company, though he is honest, he would still render the company into bankruptcy.

Que—is there karma for animals?

Ans—No, there is no karma for animals and other species, because they are not attached to their actions and outcomes like humans. They exhaust certain karma and will go on to get next birth based on residual karma. It is important to realize that we do karma based on our attachment, influenced by likes and dislikes. Our karma and longing will get us what we seek. However there are some exceptions. If someone takes birth as an animal due to a curse, would regain his original birth after exhausting the effects of curse. Normally, there is no karma for animals.

As we know, all animals act on instinct that is natural to them. They have no disappointment. They would continue to work based on the potential of their body in accordance with their nature. Some have no ears, some have no head or brain, some are cold blooded etc. We acquire animal bodies in order to exhaust karma accrued during human lives. In each human life we accrue so much karma, that we might have to take millions of lives in other bodies to exhaust even part of our karma.

We know that lifespan of different animals, birds and insects are varying, some only few days, some few years and some 80 years, such as an elephant and tortoise has a lifespan of around 160-180 years. Effectively, we accrue and spend majority of karma only as a human being. In all other bodies and in heaven or hell—we take bodies to exhaust karma.

Que—what is the basis for us to acquire animal bodies and such . . .

Ans—if deeds and choices are not well matched, one is not entitled to his choice. If one has lots of good karma, then he is entitled to fulfilling his choice/wish. Otherwise, he would have to accept whatever consequences come his way purely determined by his karma.

If I like eating a lot of meat and am never satisfied with the amount of meat I eat in this life, I could take birth as a lion or a beast in the forest that can potentially eat a lot of meat. This would happen because I am going down the ladder from being a human to an animal, and my desire for meat eating will work even if I do not have great deal of good karma in accrual. Similarly, if I enjoy pestering every one, I could take birth as a pest. Or if I have done lots of good things in this life, towards the last moments of this life, my thoughts are wishing to be a rich man; I could take birth in a rich man's family. By the same token, if we wish to be rich in this life, even that is possible, if we have the backing of good karma. Or if I am attached to the dog that was very dear to me, I could take birth as a dog. But every cause and effect is so scientific, because God resides right inside the soul and He knows every karma, by every soul, eternally. He would let us go through the consequences based on our karma and choices we make. If we do bad deeds and wish to have a glorious life, it will not happen. We have to suffer the consequences as an animal or bird or anything based on what we have done.

Let's say I am a silk producer. We know how silk is produced these days. The silk worms feed on the mulberry leaves. They spin a web of silk thread around them and just before they emerge out of the silky shell making a hole to fly out, they are boiled in hot water so that the silk thread is one continuous long string. If they are allowed to escape by making a hole, there would be many joints due to the hole made by the worm. For such karma, one would have to go through millions of life cycles being born as a silk worm (at least once) and as several other insects that can go through similar experience that he caused to millions of silk worms. (it takes some 50000 worms to produce one sari)

In the earlier days, they would allow the silk worms to make a hole and get out. They would patiently make joints at broken spots. And that was the proper way to do if one cared not to cause pain to these beings. There are still some silk producers who do not kill the worms which is the right way to go about ones livelihood.

Similarly leather business is another trade where people kill animals just for the sake of leather. Earlier days, they would use the leather after natural death of the animal. We can go on finding many things we do, without concern for pain caused to humans or animals—just for monetary gains. Obviously, all these acts would accrue into our bad karma account and we will have to repay by experiencing pain we cause. Not everyone kills animals for leather, and that is the right way to do leather business.

We may ask—what happens when we kill so many insects and ants when we walk but are not aware of it or we could kill insects in the dark as we cannot see. We do not kill them intentionally for our benefit and hence it is considered beyond our control. Imagine, if we drop our own infant by accident and the baby gets hurt, we did not do it on purpose. It was something beyond our control. We may kill people in an accident, which is not intentional, or if the accident occurs due to the other person's mistake, which is why even human law does not punish a person for accidental killing; however, he would be punished for negligence or any other reason, if proven.

God knows if it was deliberate or unintentional as He is right inside us. If we step on an insect intentionally to kill it, then it would tantamount to killing.

We do not realize the suffering we cause to others

Imagine if we were one of those who produce and sell alcoholic drinks, which is a highly profitable business. It also causes untold misery to many of those who become addicted, and would not stop for anything. Many bread earners of a family, on whom the whole family depends for survival, die or develop chronic ailments, consuming alcohol. They even go to the extent of indulging in illegal activities to be able to buy alcohol. Eventually many of them and their families suffer total destruction. Most of them are poor but develop this habit because it is made available to them. They lose control over their senses and hence are addicted to the habit. Everyone including the persons who produce and sell alcohol knows full well that the consequences for those who get addicted would be disastrous.

People argue that they are not responsible for the addiction, because they don't force anyone to drink. If someone can ill afford to buy drinks, they should be strong enough to show restraint and control.

All those who drink cannot produce these themselves. If someone makes his own alcoholic drink and gets ruined as result of his own doing, no one else is at fault for what he has done. Many would be first timers who would otherwise have had no opportunity to these addictions; they fall for it only because it is made available.

Though the alcohol producers and the society consider producing alcohol legal, law of God does not consider this a legal business. All the suffering and pain that every drinker goes through, will have to be borne by the provider, either partly in this life or in several future lives. And for the extent and number of people he has caused this suffering to, will take the alcohol provider thousands or millions of lives to exhaust consequences.

Que—when natural calamities occur, the untold suffering and pain that it causes, is hard to digest. Can God not avoid calamities and protect living beings?

Ans—**natural calamities are an effect of collective karma.** We are affected only when we happen to be in the vicinity, not otherwise. It is important to understand that when we suffer due to ailments, chronic diseases, or die in an accident or lose our limbs surviving with disability from any natural calamities or suffer due to poverty—this is solely our own doing that puts us in such a situation. Large number of people may suffer the same consequence which is due to the effect of their common karma, why they experience the same effect. As a matter of fact, whatever suffering due to survival or death is much less of a consequence than what we would have done in the past. We would have caused much greater pain and suffering to so many living beings, the effect of which we suffer. Imagine, what sort of suffering would compensate for the killing of millions of Hindus by the Moghul invaders? But we do not have the knowledge of our wrong doing. All that we remember is the suffering that we undergo, as it hurts when we suffer. When we face painful situations, it is a lesson for us not to commit sins again; and prepare to face and exhaust the effects of what we had done. Suffering brings us more wisdom; it becomes a deterrent for us to be sinful ever again. And none of this suffering is caused by God for He does not directly involve in punishing us, born of karma. When He incarnates, it is to protect the devotees who don't deserve suffering, karmically.

However, we must realize that whatever atrocities we commit on women or when people engage in illegal activities or crime—it is not due to the past karma of the offenders and the victims. It is not pre-decided that the offender does what he did or the victim goes through the suffering caused to him or her. It is a fresh act of bad karma. If I kill someone, I am doing a new karma. The person I killed would have died differently, by himself.

We also notice that while so many suffer the effects of disasters, a few may escape unhurt. This is again due to their good karma and not God's involvement in saving them. We have a hundred people dying in an air crash, while one or two surviving. It is because they didn't deserve to suffer, owing to their good karma.

Que—is everyone's death and the way they die pre-decided?

Ans—no, we have to understand that a consequence is due to a cause. If I cause suffering and death to many, I also deserve the consequence which will come back at me, some during the same life and many in future lives. If I am responsible for the death of hundreds of people by being a drug supplier, I cannot die hundreds of times in one life, so it will be spread out to hundreds or thousands of life as I cannot exhaust all the bad karma in one life. If Hitler was responsible for the genocide involving millions, he would have to be born at least millions of times to suffer the consequences. I may not have to be a human in future lives to exhaust some consequences. In fact what body I will take will be determined by my deeds during this human life. If I have to suffer untimely death, suffering pain as a consequence of what I caused earlier, it can come to me either in an accident, earth quake, or any natural disaster, or chronic ailment. It is not pre-decided what causes my death or how I suffer pain. *What happens to us is our own doing and it can come in any form or anytime without the involvement of another person causing it to us.* If someone hits me, it is not due to past karma. It is a new karma he is causing. This suffering is not pre-decided. If I fall down to get hurt, it is due to my past karma and not caused by anyone else. That's why it is important that we do not harm or hurt anyone in any manner as that becomes a new karma which will have to be suffered by us anytime in future.

It is also true that many of us cause our own death without completing our full life term. If I am a smoker or drinker or drug addict, I am curtailing my longevity which is not pre-determined by karma from earlier births. Karma does not decide that I should become an addict in this life. If not for the addictions, surely I would be living longer till I die naturally.

We know that we are able to do most things on a daily basis, throughout our life without hindrance. We are able to execute many of our intended tasks without any bother. However, only at certain times we fail to execute our actions, which is due to the effect of past karma.

If there are no terrorist activities, no killers, no bad people, then would all those who get killed in these incidents get away from their karma consequence? No, they would still have to meet their end experiencing natural disasters or epidemics, diseases and ailments or heart attack. The consequence for our bad karma is not exactly pre-destined to happen in such a way in the hands of such a person. If I am a terrorist who would want to kill so many people, it is not pre-destined. I am engaging in a new act of karma of my own choice. I have the choice to do it or not to do it. Those who would get killed due to my act would have found their end some other natural way, some other time, if not for me. So, I do not have to accrue bad karma by doing bad things to others.

Que—how do we know what events are due to our past karma?

Ans—*If something happens to us without our doing anything, it is the effect of past karma.* Effect of karma is always from the past, whether from previous lives or this life. *We have to be able to differentiate between a consequence of past karma and the karma that we do afresh.* We generate a thought, make a choice and execute it as a deed—this is the process every time we do a new karma. We know that we do most things as intended everyday in life. A student goes to school most days. A working person is able to go to office every day. There is no one or no karma preventing us to doing what we wish. This is proof enough that we do all our karma based on our choice. Only once in a while things go out of control, even though we would have done the routine things, normally. When something happens beyond our control, it is due to past karma. What is in our control is the choice, not the execution part as we are only 1 of 5 contributors to all our actions. When things go as expected, it means that we are able to execute our choice in the present without past karma interfering in the present. We eat and take care of our body needs. All these cannot be a consequence of past karma.

To elaborate it a little more—suppose I am standing on the roof of my house, talking on mobile phone, if something falls on my head (say a lightning strikes or some object hits me falling from the sky) causing my death or injury, it is surely due to the effect of past karma. Alternatively, if I decide to jump from the roof, it is a new karma, as I made the choice to jump to kill myself. You can call it an effort to commit suicide. I may die or I may survive with injuries and disabilities which is not in my control. If I succeed in committing suicide, that is the last karma before death, the consequence of which I shall bear in any of the future lives, depending upon the amount of karma accrued.

It is also essential to know that we are not alone in this world and our karma is interlinked with many people; which is why we take birth to parents who have karma connectivity with us. We may become victims of a consequence caused by others due to our past karma. We can apply this to every event, if we can consciously peruse over the event, it would not be hard to realize if the consequence was an effect of past karma or new karma we have just done. *Hence it is important to remain conscious of every thought, speech and action.*

Sometimes, whatever we wish comes true without our doing anything. It is not by magic or miracle that a wish comes through, it is a scientific phenomenon of cause and effect, for which we were responsible earlier. I am in a restaurant and get injured due to a fire accident or stampede; is again due to past karma. But in this case no one else is causing this to me specifically. It is the effect of collective karma of many others present in the same restaurant, many of whom would suffer injury for the same reason. Or if I am poor and someone comes in search of me and makes me the legal heir to his multibillion dollar inheritance, it surely is due to past karma. If something happens without our effort, has to be due to past karma and same goes for things going wrong. We do everything correctly, put in the right effort and yet things don't work out as desired.

We can keep relating to every event in our life—maximum of about 40% could be due to past karma and balance 60% would be new karma. Sometimes we may exhaust only a small portion of past karma in a life due to the enormity of karma backlog. We can be sure that there is no interference by God in anything that happens to us as a karmic effect, but of course, we must know that everything happens because of the laws of karma set by God but without His involvement. We should take ownership for everything that happens to us, good or bad, as everything that happens to us is caused by us either in the past life or in the present life. Sometimes we may see the consequence of our action immediately. If I pushed someone with an intention to hurt him and he gets injured as a result of my action, he may hit me immediately and break my nose. Or he may just walk away, and I may fall down on my own getting injured. Only the net result is decided by our actions and not the exact way it shall happen. Unless, there is a curse involved.

Embodied Atma is responsible for karma and not God

Often people say that the jivatma is powerless and cannot do anything by himself and hence everything we do is influenced and controlled by God or past karma (vidhi) or prArabdha karma and we are merely a tool in His hands; helpless and unable to take control of our lives. In that case how can we hold people responsible for what they do or what happens to them? Is it not

God's doing which is the reason for everything happening to everyone?

Often people quote from scriptures such as—Tiruvaimozhi 3-5-10 "*karumamum karuma palanum Agiya kAraNan tannai*". (Lord is the cause for karma as also for the consequences of karma). If this is true, then, even if I want to change, becoming a better person, I would not be able to change because, all along I have been a bad person, which must have been either due to God's doing or past karma.

God is relevant to us only when we renounce karma and seek Him, realizing our nature and relationship with Him. If God was the reason for everything that everyone does, even a killer would claim he is not responsible for the killing and it was God's doing or he killed because of prarabdha karma.

Krishna explicitly declares in Gita "karmanyevAdhikaraste, mA phalEshu kadAchana . . ." "*humans have the right to doing karma alone and not to results*", which emphasizes that we are the doers of karma out of our own will and God is neither involved in our choice making nor in our actions. However, what happens as a result of our action cannot be controlled by us, as results would be commensurate with the laws of karma.

God is our Father who loves us unconditionally. He would not do anything that makes us unhappy. Controlling us would certainly make us unhappy. If God wants to do everything, He can do everything by mere will, He does not have to use us as a tool. He is not different than good human fathers. We don't control our children nor use them as a tool. The fact that He created this world because we sought to experience independent existence shows that He does not control us in any way.

We cannot involve God to becoming an accomplice in our karma and consequence, blaming Him for both good and bad that we do or the consequences of our actions.

When Arjuna refuses to fight due to delusion, refraining from doing his dharmic duties, Krishna preaches him Gita and eventually mentions to Arjuna that he was free to act according to his wish. If Arjuna had no choice, there was no need for Krishna to preach him the whole of Gita and also declaring to him that he was free to do as he chooses.

Often we confuse everything as a consequence of sanchita karma (karma from past lives). We should realize that there is sanchita karma because we chose to do karma in the first place. However, there is also what is called 'prarabdha karma'—karma that we do during this life. It can be a blend of both. Only 40% of what happens to us in this life could be from prarabdha or sanchita karma and balance 60% is new karma that we are adding in this life.

It is also true that we have accumulated 'vasanas' or impressions from countless number of lives which also influence our behaviour. However, we can break the impressions with our effort to become better people.

You don't decide when to spend past karma or when to accumulate new karma. While exhausting past karma, we also accrue new karma, as we keep making choices non-stop and this is unending process. You cannot choose to do new karma for six months and then choose the next six months to spend accrued karma. *Past karma comes without our control and new karma is done with our choice*.

God is merely empowering us to doing our karma, or He empowers us even if choose to renounce karma, becoming His devotees.

"*Aduvum avanadinnaruLE*" refers to Lord's benign grace for the souls, and His unconditional love for them. He grants us His world, giving us similarity with Himself. '*innaruIE*' confirms that He can only do good things for us; He is never involved in anything harmful to us. It is an affirmation of the fact that the jivatma on his own, regardless of his devotion or sadhana or tapasya, cannot attain 'salvation' or mukti or 'moksha prapti'. It is not in our power to grant immortality to ourselves. And this kindness of the Lord, granting us similarity with Him is nothing but His 'innaruL' (unconditional grace) and not something we have earned.

Que—what if we have done more good karma?

Ans—you continue to enjoy the benefits of your good karma. It is like earning a lot of money and keeping it in a bank. You can spend it for any purpose, till there is balance in the account. While you spend, you will also keep earning, increasing your bank balance. If you desire for greater pleasure and enjoyment you will take birth in heaven. The degree of enjoyment would be several times more than what we can experience here on earth. Soon as you exhaust your good karma, you have to take birth again on earth. A lifetime in heaven is like total holidaying, having enough bank balance after long years of hard working. Once your bank balance is exhausted, you cannot withdraw money anymore; so you have to go back to earning. Heaven is only for experiencing good karma. You do not cause new karma in heaven. If you wish to have good births on earth you will continue to be born in good families, rich and wealthy. Krishna confirms in Gita 9/20 . .

> "*. . . . tE puNyamAsAdhya surEndralokamaSnanti divyAn divi dEvabhogAn*"

"Based on your good karma and prayers seeking a good life in heaven—you will reach the realm of Indra in heaven, to enjoy celestial pleasure of gods".

Gita 9/21—

> *te tam bhuktva svargalokam visAlam,*
> *kshine punye martya lokam viSanti . . .*

"After enjoying in the world of heaven, they return to the world of mortals (earth) when they exhaust all merits (good karma), thus driven by desire they perform good karma, come and go".

Que—what if we do more bad karma?

Ans—like heaven, there is a world 'hell' where you will get a body just to experience pain. Normal pain on earth would feel manifold more unbearable in hell. Soon as you exhaust certain portion of bad karma, you will take birth on earth again. Not all bad karma will have to be accounted for in hell, bad deeds of lesser magnitude will have to be experienced here.

Thirumangai azhwar gives us a hint of what a grave sin is and what would be a relative punishment in hell for that kind of a sin

Peria Thirumozhi 1-6-4

> "*vambulAn-kUndal manaiviyai-tturandu, pirarporuL*
> *tAramennu ivattai, nambinA-rirandAl namantamar patri*
> *Etrivaittu, 'eriyezhuginna, sembinAl-iyanna pAvaiyai-ppAvI*
> *tazhuvu' ena mozhivadar-kkanji, nambanE vandun tiruvadi*
> *adaindEn naimisAraNiyattuLendAi*"

Briefly, the Azhwar suggests that we would attain hell if we seek extra marital relations or illicit relations with another woman giving up our wedded wife or acquire others wealth and property deceitfully. The relative punishment for illicit relationship with another woman is depicted that we would be made to embrace the red hot woman figure made of copper.

Azhwar prays to the Lord "In order to keep away from doing such sins, out of fear for such punishments, I come to you my Lord, seeking refuge at your Lotus Feet, for only You can save me, though am unworthy"

If we take refuge at Lord's feet, surrendering through an Acharya, we would be insulated from committing such sins. Lord chose to become Thirumangai Azhwar's Acharya, which is a special case.

Isavasyopanishad 3—
asuryA nAma tE lokE andhEna tamasAvrutAha,

"Those worlds known as 'asura' are covered by blinding darkness. People who are soul-slayers go to those worlds after death"—quite frightening even to think of.

Que—can animals, birds and other species also reach God's world without another birth . .

Ans—they could like a Gajendra or a Jatayu did, if that is the last life they get as a consequence of exhausting a curse or karma. Mostly, they would be re-born as humans; as the best opportunity to reach God is for humans. Jada bharata, in his previous life was said have taken birth as a deer due to his attachment to a deer he saved. But he regained human birth and attained immortality as 'jada bharata'

Gita 8-5
"antakAlE cha mAmEva smaranmuktvA kalEvaram;

"He who, at the last moment, while leaving the body, departs, thinking of Me alone, attains Me, of this there is no doubt"

Remembering the Lord all the time would enable one to think of the Lord even at the last moments. It is not possible to think of the Lord exactly at the last moments. Only a true devotee would be a habitual thinker of the Lord.

Que—Do the non living things like buildings, rocks, stones, manmade things such as machines have souls in them?

Ans—No, there are no souls in the non living things. The term 'non-living' signifies that—there is no life in the object nor do they possess knowledge or consciousness. There can be exceptions though. Ahalya—became a stone due to a curse and by the touch of Rama's feet, she was released from her curse. This does not mean all stones have life or there is a soul in them. Rama touched many stones, but they did not become anything else. Ahalya becoming a stone due to a curse was an exception.

Living beings can be classified in two groups—chara (mobile) and achara (immobile). Humans, all animals, birds, insects, fish etc are 'chara'; plants of all kinds are 'achara'. All the non living things including atoms have no soul in them, though they have sub-atomic particles present in them, though the electrons are constantly moving around the nucleus of the atom and further there are quarks as well and now the god-particle. However, there is God in every particle and sub-atomic particles; He is present in them in un-manifest form. For that matter even energy in the universe is non living and non sentient.

Que—what about rituals—yajna, yaga and fasting etc . . . Are they meaningful practices?

Ans—absolutely. Rituals are practices to gain knowledge and to remain steadfast in being righteous. Rituals give us the scope to keep improving in doing our actions. Without rituals even devotion would not be possible. Rituals are the basis for knowing anything. In simple terms rituals are like 'practical' classes. In the Vedic philosophy nothing is asked to be taken for granted. We have to follow the rituals, learn from the process and realize for ourselves.

Yajna or yaga are rituals performed as a sacrifice using the non-living materials for the benefit of the society. It is a way of offering oblations to the supreme God, as well as the gods and forces of nature to whom we are indebted and the purpose is for the general well being of the people. Performing yajna or yaga provides material and financial support to many sections of the people. After performing yajna, gifts are given away to people who seek support. Yajna is never complete without philanthropy. Everything is done as a sacrifice, as an offering to the Lord, in devotion.

Fasting is a scientific practice. For one, it not only helps regulate our body and digestive system and to remain healthy, but also nurtures care and compassion for the needy and deprived people of the society. By fasting we would realize the state of those who go hungry. Fasting makes us better people for it gives us the realization to share our resources with the have-nots. Otherwise, we would never know what hunger is or understand the suffering of those going without food. When we undertake fasting as a ritual, it also nurtures self control.

Human body is in itself a temple for it houses the Lord as the indweller of the soul. That's why, sacred scriptures and Azhwars and Acharyas prescribe 'purity of mind, heart' (**ullam tUyarAi**) or 'antahkaraNa suddhi' to nurture devotion for the Lord.

Que—why should we perform 'shrAdh' or tiruvadhyayanam to our forefathers? Would they know?

Ans—We take birth with obligations even though we are born due to our past karma, we come with certain indebtedness in every human birth, in three ways—

- ➤ to our parents and forefathers,
- ➤ to the rishis, saints, gurus, acharyas,
- ➤ to the nature, devatas (gods)

When parents pass away; we perform rituals (tiruvadhyayanam) repaying our debt to them. Since they are no more, we cannot serve them or take care of them. So we perform a ritual, inviting persons from society and request them to accept our offerings—a feast, dress, money. One who has no father or mother or both, shall do this till he is alive, once every year on the day of their death, as a token of clearing his debt towards them. If parents were alive, we would have taken care of them. *This is merely to pay back to the society in their name.*

To my father who is no more, I am not his son from the moment he has left his body. It was his body that I consider as my father and the body is no more. The atma who was my father could be in the eternal abode of God and would have nothing to do with me the moment he relinquished his body. However, I am duty bound to performing my obligatory duties for him, till I am alive.

If one does his obligatory duties properly, he does not acquire any credit for that. If I have not committed any crime for so many years, no one would give me an award for being a law abiding person. However, if I commit a first crime, I am liable to be punished. So doing one's duties does not entitle one to special credits. But each and every time he fails in his obligatory duties he would accrue consequences of bad karma. If we want to accrue credits for good karma, we have to do good things for others.

Que—we see people worshipping machines, new motor vehicles. What is the sense behind such worship?

Ans—to understand the significance of these rituals and practices, let us look at even the societies of the west. Christians pray before eating food served on their plates. They thank God for providing them food, because they realize food is God given.

To those who do not understand the true sense, may wonder why you should pray or thank God before eating. In reality, man works for procuring food, preparing food and to bring it to the table. But those who realize that everything in this world is God given; by His grace alone we are able to obtain food on our plates; praying God or thanking God makes perfect sense, but not for those who cannot understand.

Similarly, in the Hindu tradition, we do 'sandhya vandanam' (nitya karma) a daily prescribed karma, thrice a day, praying the supreme Lord, to give us the power to be righteous in our functioning, without causing any harm to any one either by mind or by speech or by deed. We pray the supreme Lord dwelling in the sun god because, we cannot see God in this world, but are aware of His presence in the sun, whose light is pervading all over our world. We seek the light of knowledge to dispel the darkness of ignorance. We seek the Lord's empowerment to be righteous in all our actions. It is also a reminder to the self to remain conscious in being righteous, refraining from committing sins.

We celebrate 'ayudha puja' by cleaning up all the machines and equipments, including the motor vehicles and pray the Lord for His benevolence in enabling us to use these machines. In these pujas, we worship the Lord and not the machines. Likewise, once a year, we worship the Lord thanking Him for the knowledge He has bestowed upon us. Symbolically, we use the books to represent the source of knowledge. Same is true with the new vehicles that we buy; we dedicate them to God before using them as god-given. Everything has a meaningful significance and nothing is nonsensical. It makes sense when we understand and seems foolish when we don't.

Our problem is misinterpreting everything. When we say God is in everything, we assume everything as God, which is wrong. It is like saying there is electrical energy in the bulb which is why it is glowing; but the bulb is not the electricity.

Que—What is astrology and how is it relevant in our lives?

Ans—Astrology is one of the six 'angams' or branches of the Vedas. It is used to schedule daily time tables and programmes in conducting worship.

Astrology is a science of planetary and star systems, their position in realtion to our birth. We know that the Sun is the life sustaining source for every being on earth. Even the Moon influences life on earth. Similarly, our birth in relation to the position of the planets and the stars gives us an indication about the nature of the person, as the planets and stars have their characteristics which can relate to our behaviour. Their position in relation to our birth is indicative of our karma impressions from past lives. However, our life is determined by the karma we do in this life and not by the influence of the stars and planets. Astrology can be useful in understanding a person's basic nature and to know of any relevance about the past and not be sought to predict future events. Though our karma vasanas or past impressions influence our thinking and behaviour, we have the power to choose to go against our past pattern and not be dictated by past impressions.

Astrologers are sweet talkers; they are professionals in gaining information from the clients and use the same to impress them. They would tell us some of the past events which we already know. That is enough for us to accept all their predictions about the future. They would tell us things we like to hear.

Either when we have problems and are anxious to find relief, or even when things are going well, out of fear of the unknown, we go to an astrologer. There is a story about an astrologer, who really knows nothing about astrology. He poses as a specialist who can foretell the gender of the unborn baby. He would confuse the parents mentioning that they would either have a son or daughter. While declaring to them, he would write down in his book the opposite of what he tells them. If he tells them they would have a boy, he would write in his book as 'girl', but they would not read what he is writing. Now, if they have a boy baby as declared by the astrologer, they would be very happy and come back to thank him and shower money and gifts. From then on, he would rule their minds for the rest of their life. If they have girl child, they would go back to the astrologer to tell him that he was wrong in his prediction. The astrologer would tell them that he had written in front of them and show them his book, in which he would have written as 'girl'. Then, they would be convinced that they mistook or were confused and still feel happy about whatever he predicted.

This is how unmindful we are about our own lives, that we need someone else to tell us about our life; someone who knows nothing about us or about the future would be able to solve all our problems. And we believe them more than reality, which in any case, cannot be altered.

We cannot cleanse our sins by taking bath in holy rivers.

People often say that taking bath in Ganga or other sacred rivers would wash away our sins? The physical aspect of merely bathing in these rivers does nothing more than our having had another bath. In reality no sin can be washed away by taking a bath.

Sins originate in our mind and the only way to insulate ourselves from committing more sins is by cleansing the mind, keeping it pure. Taking a physical dip in a river does not do any such thing. Taking bath in Ganga gives us the realization that we have sinned in the past and must make an effort to become righteous from that point on in life.

Purity of mind is the primary requisite to be a righteous person, driving away all the despicable qualities. Sins committed thus far, cannot be undone, except by exhausting them, by suffering consequences.

To see how sins cannot be cleansed by taking a physical bath, fill a bottle with dirty water, tighten the cap to ensure water does not leak from the bottle. Drift it on the river (it would float). After few minutes, check if the water inside the bottle has been purified. It is a silly notion to think it would have become purified. Similarly, if we keep our heart and mind filled with impure and sinful thoughts, taking a physical bath would not cleanse our mind.

If we want to cleanse our mind of impure thoughts, we have to develop devotion to the Lord.

Chapter Twelve

$\sim\!\!\sim\!\!\mathbf{\mathfrak{P}}\!\!\sim\!\!\sim$

Acharya

Que—Is our devotion to Acharya only for the purpose of attaining the Lord?

Ans—Devotion to Acharya is considered greater by the Lord, than the devotion shown to Him. We can see the delight of Lord Venkateswara from this incidence.

The forest areas of the Tirumala hills were home to many wild beasts and no one dared go there to attend to the daily rituals of the Lord. Sri Ramanuja desired to nurture a flower garden on the hills so that there would be daily floral adornments for the Lord. He expresses his wish to his disciples and suggests that he would like some of them to undertake this 'pushpa kainkaryam' (adorning the Lord with fresh floral garland). No one came forward to accept this dangerous mission of passing through the forests of the seven hills and to living there, to fulfill this mission. The excuse they gave Ramanuja though, was that they could not bear his separation and hence preferred to remain with him, serving him. It was then, that a young Srivaishnava in his late teens volunteered to do the pushpa kainkaryam as desired by the Acharya. Ramanuja was pleasantly surprised that it was Ananthazhwan, who had the courage to go there while no one among the disciples was willing. Ramanuja proclaims that he was truly the 'man' amongst them.

Ananthazhwan, accompanied by his wife, goes up the hills and starts working on the flower garden. They were totally devoted to the task on hand. An incidence occurred while they were busy clearing the ground to make it cultivable. The Lord comes to them as a young boy and offers to help. Ananthazhwan declines to accept his help mentioning that he had no authority to share his work with anyone, unless directed by his Acharya and sends him away. He then finds out that it was none other than the Lord who came to test him. There is also a mention that Ananthazhwan hits the boy with the crow-bar as the boy repeatedly bothered him offering to help, **which cannot be true**. For, a true devotee, that too a srivaishnava and a disciple of Ramanuja, cannot hurt even a wild beast, even in thought, let alone physically hit a boy. These might be stories to enhance Ananthazhwan's 'acharya vakya paripalanam' (unconditional devotion in carrying out the wish of the acharya). The reason why a srivaishnava cannot cause hurt or harm to any one either by thought, speech or action can be perceived by this next incidence.

While working in the garden, a poisonous snake bites Ananthazhwan, he suffers the effects of the bite but does not harm the snake that bit him, and lets it go. The temple associate suggests that Ananthazhwan should have anti venom administered, to save his life. Ananthazhwan contends that if his body was powerful enough to counter the effects of the venom, he would serve the Acharya here in this world, if the snake's poison was more powerful, he would still serve his Acharya in the eternal world. Either way, his nature is subservience to the Acharya, be it here in the mortal world or in the divine world—parama padam. Such was the state of their mind, that they could not hurt even a poisonous snake. How can they hit or hurt someone with a crow bar? According to the story, if he claims that he has no authority to share the work with anyone, how can he take the authority to deny someone to doing work or worse, hit a person? Neither God, nor the divine mahatmas can do anything to hurt, harm or injure any living being, let alone a human being; even if they come to be harmed by that person.

Ananthazhwan survives the snake bite and continues to work on the flower garden, making beautiful garlands for the Lord, from frangrant and colorful flowers.

One day, the priest comes up to Ananthazhwan to inform him that "the deity has commanded his audience in the temple at once". Ananthazhwan requests the priest to pray to the Lord that he was half way through completing the garland and he would be there soon on finishing the garland, for it would bloom if delayed. It was important to adorn the Lord with un-bloomed flowers so that they can blossom and flourish from the effect of contact with the divine touch of Lord's Tirumeni (divine body).

The priest returns saying that the Lord wants him to stop his work and come at once. Ananthazhwan asks to pray to the Lord that he was doing as commanded by his Acharya and he cannot overrule his acharya's wishes and hence he would come soon enough; the garland would be completed very soon. The priest returns again with a message from the Lord that Ananthazhwan should understand that his Acharya has sent him here for the kainkaryam (subservience) to the Lord and He was the purpose why Ananthazhwan was here and if he disobeys His command, the Lord would not accept the garland, so how does he intend serving the Lord if that was the wish of his Acharya. That he was about to fail in his mission, if he does not come at once to the Lord and that he could complete his garland after seeing the Lord. Ananthazhwan contends that his mission was to follow the wishes of his Acharya and not the Lord's. Though the Lord was the purpose why he was there, but he was there by the command of his Acharya. If the Lord refuses to accept the garland he prepares, it would not make a difference to him, for he would hang it on the NAIL on the wall nearby. The Lord is Supreme and is truly the ultimate in every sense and He can choose to do anything, but Ananthazhwan is bound by the subservience to his Acharya and he could not overlook that to shift his subservience to the Lord now. His subservience is totally for his Acharya and based on his true nature, he has no independence to change that. To him, the NAIL or the deity who is accepting the garland every day, are one and the same.

Obviously, Ananthazhwan would not be considering a nail and the deity as one and the same. To our understanding, the deity is the Lord and a nail is a piece of iron fixed on the wall to hang things. How could he say that he would hang the garland on the piece of nail if the Lord does not accept the garland?

The truth is Ananthazhwan is a nitya suri (divine soul) from the eternal world who has taken birth here to show us the way to serving the Acharya. He finds the Lord even in the Nail just as He is in the Deity. God is all pervading. To us, with our incomplete knowledge and inadequate comprehension, we are able to see the Lord only in the deity but the divine Azhwars and Acharyas were able to see the Lord in everything.

Everything is not God though, He is in everything. Ananthazhwan was able to see the Lord everywhere, in everything and hence he would still be accomplishing his kainkaryam to the Lord even if he hangs the garland on the Nail instead of the Deity. God knows that Ananthazhwan understands this; Ananthazhwan knows that God understands this about him. Just that we are unable to see the truth. And the same is true with the individual jivatmas. The Lord dwells as the antaryami in every jivatma. If we can feel the Lord in a deity, we should also realize that the same Lord is also the indweller in all living beings. And yet, the jivatmas are not God.

Confirming the Lord's pervasiveness Sri Nammazhwar declares in Thiruvaimozhi 1-1-10—

"pranthataN paravaiyuL nIrtorum paranthuLan,
parantha andamithena nilavisumbozhivara,
karantha silidanthorum idantigazh porudorum,
karanthengum paranthuLan ivai unda karanE"

In essence—the Lord pervades everything; he is hidden in everything of this universe, in unmanifest form, as also everything merges into Him after dissolution.

Que—why should we surrender to God or do thiruvaradhanam only through an Acharya. Are we not God's children or will God not accept us directly?

Ans—You can surrender to God directly but your surrender might be deficient and incomplete and hence might not work. If God accepts you with deficiencies, then he might as well accept everyone with or without surrender. Even a Dhruva or Prahlada had a Narada as their Acharya who guided them to attaining the supreme state. The only way we can surrender directly to the Lord is when He comes seeking our discipleship, like He came in search of Tirumangai azhwar, bestowing upon him the Thirumantram, thus becoming his Acharya.

We have no problem going to a doctor for our healthcare. We do not ask a question there, "why should I go to the doctor?", "why can't I treat my own ailment? Would I not be cured if I took medication myself?" We would be cured if we took the right medication, but we do not know the right medication ourselves; nor are we sure of the diagnosis.

Our health is too precious and hence we do not want to take a chance. A doctor is a qualified, authentic person who knows the cause as well as the cure. He is a specialist for the job. He knows much more than we can possibly know, even if we learn a little bit of this and that about medicine. Even a doctor would consult another doctor if he has health problems. And the doctor exists for that very purpose. At least, the doctor is treating patients for a cost, as he does that for his livelihood and not as service. But the Acharya does not charge anything at all, though he provides eternal solutions.

An Acharya is a qualified, authentic person who is complete in his knowledge about the nature of the soul, and God. And an Acharya takes birth for the very purpose of guiding people like us and enlightening us about the prescribed ways of devotion. He is the kindest person there can be, for he wants nothing in return from us. His reward is when we attain God's abode, seeing God happy to find a soul coming home. God looks up to an Acharya to help Him in guiding souls like us to the ultimate state of existence. He is doing free service and yet we question why we should be guided by him? It is our ego that is preventing us from surrendering to an Acharya. An Acharya is a total care taker, providing complete solution to attaining the Lord that is beyond compare with anything else we have in this world.

Sri Manavalamamuni sums up an acharya's invaluable grace to his disciples.

> *"AchAryan sichan Aruyirai pENumavan, tEsArum sichan avan sIr vadivai asaiyudan nokkumavanennum . . ."*

That his only focus and goal is sishaya's 'atmojjIvanam', to attaining immortality and all that a disciple has to do is take care of the 'tirumEni' (good health) of the Acharya; to enable the Acharya succeeding in his pursuit.

As a matter of fact, an Acharya surrenders to his Acharya and considers himself as a disciple of his Acharya. He looks at his disciples as disciples of his Acharya; bestowing them similarity with himself.

It is the Acharya who performs "samAsrayaNam" to a disciple, giving him the status at par with himself or perhaps preparing the disciple to attaining elevation to the levels similar to that of the Lord. He also performs the 'pancha samskara' giving us the purity of body and mind, in 5 steps

- ➢ Imprinting the divine chakra and shankha—disc and conch (**tApam**) on top of the arms at right and left shoulder joints.
- ➢ adorning the 12 namams (**Urdhva pundram**) at 12 designated spots of the body, each one signifying the five senses, five sense organs, mind and intellect, denoting the 12 names of the Lord—kesava, narayana, madhava, govinda, vishnu, madhusudana, trivikrama, vamana, sridhara, hrishikesa, padmanabha, damodara
- ➢ giving us Acharya's own identity—**dasya namam** (we lose our identity and will be identified as the disciple of our Acharya—tiruvadi sambandam
- ➢ preaching the sacred mantras (**thirumantrartham**)
- ➢ the procedure for performing thiru-aradhanam (**thiru-aradhana kramam**)

This should answer the question why we should do thiru-aradhanam through an Acharya. For one, he taught us how to perform, and it is a gesture of gratitude to the Acharya for his benevolence and giving due credit to what is his. We can do directly, but it would not be authentic, as we are neither entitled nor pure. By the mental process of invoking the Acharya to perform thiru-aradhanam, we become sanitized and pure. It cleanses our mind and heart. It drives away our ego, which is a destroyer.

We can see that right from our birth, at every stage in our lives, we have had a guru guiding us, helping us, protecting us, and teaching us from time to time. Our parents are our first gurus; then the other elders in the family, friends and well wishers in our society. We have the teachers at school, who impart knowledge of this world so that we learn enough to becoming competent to earn a livelihood. If we need so many people to guide us at every stage, just to be able to take care of this body, how can we possibly be successful in attaining the highest goal of reaching God without an Acharya?

But the Acharya who guides us to God is the one that has no equal. God is equated to a 'priceless precious diamond' and an Acharya is the one who gets us that diamond. In this case, would we feel grateful to the diamond or the person who gives us the diamond? Obviously, we would thank the person and not the diamond.

It is said that if a person fails in his devotion to his Acharya, though would fall short of the Acharya, he would still reach God, as the Acharya stands beyond God. *If we succeed in our devotion to Acharya, God comes to the Acharya, in search of us, seeking us.*

God is more pleased if we surrender **to** the Acharya than merely using the Acharya to reaching God. Sri Pillai Lokacharyar confirms—

"AchAryAbhimAnamE uddhArakam" and

"bhaktiyil asaktanukku prapatti;
prapattiyil asaktanukku, idu".

"One, who is inept in devotion, can still succeed by surrender and he who is incompetent even in surrender, has the Acharya coming to his rescue. Even if we fail in devotion, or surrender, we can still succeed in attaining the goal by the benevolent grace of acharya.

The ultimate state of subservience to the Acharya is revealed by Madhurakavi azhwar, who declares—"**tEvu mattariyEn kurugUr nimbi, pAvininnisai pAdittirivanE**", "I do not know of any other God other than you, 'kurugur nambi', (Nammazhwar).

Madhurakavi Azhwar also reveals a secret *"payanannAgilum, pAngallarAgilum, seyal nannAga tirutti paNigoLvAn"*

When we take refuge with the Acharya, even if we have proven to be useless and inept, he would still nurture and mould us to attaining the state, being worthy of acceptance by the Lord.

If we can make an effort to understand the virtue and glory of an Acharya, we could not be but overwhelmed by the extreme kindness he bestows, sacrifices he makes.

Krishna categorically declares that He is indebted to all acharyas for their selfless service in making devotees worthy and in leading them to God. He tells Udhava that He considers them as Himself.

Sri Manavalamamuni reveals—

> *"jnAnamanushtAnamivai nannAgave udayanAna,*
> *guruvai adaindakkAl,* and

> *"uyyaninaivundAgil unkurukkaL tampadattE vaiyum,*
> *anbutannai indamAnilattir,*

All that we have to do, if we wish to attain Vaigundam, is seek refuge with an authentic Acharya, and reaching God's abode is a given.

We cannot give God anything; everything is already His, for He is the source for everything, including us. He is "avApta samasta kAmah" "one who is fulfilled and has nothing to attain" or even if He wishes for something, it comes true by a mere will or 'sankalpa'. Thus, the only way we can serve Him is by doing Thiruvaradhanam or daily worship. Even in that, we end up benefitting experiencing bliss more than serving Him.

Thiru-aradhanam (daily worship) is nothing but a simple ritual that the Lord accepts every day. There is no **greater joy** than experiencing the Lord delightfully going through the process of thiruvaradhanam. It is very real, for the Lord inside us would give us that bliss, which is unmistakable. The ritual part is very essential, engaging mind, speech and deed.

It is important to know that our body is impure due to various sinful activities committed using the body and the filthy thoughts vilifying our mind; our mouth filled with dirty speech, hence we can do thiru-aradhanam only through our acharya; praying him to lend his divine hands and speech so that we become worthy to worship God.

God's simplicity is such that He accepts even a non-act of this thiruvaradhanam as a great service. To Him there is nothing equal or better than the daily worship done by a devotee. You literally treat him like your child. In this state, He is referred to as "archaka parAdhIna"—one who abides as conducted by the devotee"

It is a simple procedure of waking up the Lord; wetting his hands and washing up His Lotus feet and giving Him water to sip (argyam, padyam, achamaniyam), drying up with a piece of pure cloth filled with fog of divine fragrance, giving Him a celestial bath in the water invoked from the divine 'viraja river" from paramapadam, adding fragrance of clove, cardamom and saffron, doing all this while chanting the divine verses such as 'purusha suktam' and 'nirattam', then use the fragrant towel exclusively prepared for Him, to dry Him after shower. Apply sandal paste, adorn Him with fresh, fragrant flowers. If we do idol worship, adorn Him with colourful dresses, jewelry. Then pray to Him to accept the food especially prepared for Him and then offer dessert and also request Him to enjoy the rendering of 'arulicheyal' (divine psalms of Azhwars) that attempts to express His infinite glories and auspicious attributes, then pray to Him to forgive us for any discomfort caused to Him while making Him undergo thiruvaradhanam and put Him to sleep till the next session of worship. We must thank our Acharya (mentally) for graciously enabling us to experience the process.

It is said that the epitome of Thirumantram is indeed in His 'archAvataram' in which He pervades with completeness, in the form of idols in the temples and homes.

By their nature, souls are dependents. We are dependent on our bodies and this world for our functioning; we depend on so many people for our daily activities, right from birth. We are all inter-dependent for everything till we die and even after death, to take care of last rites of our mortal remains. Yet we want to believe that each one of us is independent and can take care of ourselves. It surely must be ego that is preventing us from accepting our dependent nature; be it to others or to an Acharya or even to God. Dependence is such a beautiful state; if we truly realize its value. There is a sense of unconditional belonging to each other, without expectations. We can remain totally fearless, worriless, for there is someone taking care of us, just as we would do the same to them.

Valmiki

Story of Valmiki would inspire most of us to realize that we too can become true devotees of the Lord if we faithfully follow as prescribed by the Acharya, leading to devotion and God's grace.

There is a mystery about the early life of Valmiki. Some sources reveal that he was the son of Sage Prachetasa. He was named Ratnakara. At a young age when he went into the forest, lost his way and was raised by a hunter and his wife. Soon he developed skills of a hunter and as he attained adulthood, was married to a beautiful girl from a hunter family.

Soon Ratnakara shouldered the responsibility of taking care of his foster parents who had grown old, and his own family with a few children. He found it hard to feed the large family and soon took to robbing people passing by.

One day, devarishi Narada was passing by the forest and was promptly waylaid by Ratnakara. Narada was playing his divine Veena, singing praises of the Lord which had a positive impact on Ratnakara, feeling the peace within, contrary to the turmoil he was constantly experiencing in the effort to bring home the resources to feeding his family. Ratnakara however, asked Narada to handover everything in his possession. Narada asks him why he had chosen a sinful life and if he realizes that he would have to take terrible life forms to undergo consequences for what he is doing now. Valmiki explains that he was compelled to rob people to provide for his family's needs.

Narada asks him if his family would partake in his sins for whose sake he is robbing others. This triggered a thought process in Ratnakara. He ties up Narada to a tree and goes home to find the answer. His parents and his wife tell him that it was his duty to provide for their needs and they cannot stake a claim to share his sins. He then realizes that all relationships are merely selfish till their purpose is served, including that of parents, wife or children. He runs back to Narada, unties him and falls at his feet to save him from ruin.

Narada tells him to chant the sacred name of "Rama", till he returned; assuring him that if he chants this name he would develop true devotion and the Lord would redeem Him from destruction. And only the Lord is selfless, loves every one unconditionally and is the eternal relative, who alone wishes well for His people; and no one else is like the Lord. Valmiki had difficulty even in pronouncing 'Rama' and instead he was able to say 'mara'. Narada asks him to continue repeating 'ma—ra'—ma—ra . . . and eventually it would be the same as chanting 'ra—ma—ra—ma'. Narada leaves him, who had started chanting with great sincerity. His undivided devotion lead him into deep rooted penance for many years that an anthill developed around him and he was unmindful of even that. That was how he came to be known as 'Valmiki' (one surrounded by ant-hill). Narada returns as promised and bestows him with the title of Brahmarishi and the new name 'Valmiki'. Thus a robber transformed into a great adi-kavi, who gave us the treasure of Ramayana which stands testimony to Valmiki's greatness even today.

Chapter Thirteen

———◦◦◦———

Supreme Lord is Absolute!

Que—you say that nothing exists without someone causing it, and that cause is supreme God. By the same token who is the cause for the supreme Lord?

Ans—We can see the logic why the Supreme Lord is the only one who is unborn and has no cause for Himself but is the cause for everyone and everything in the universe.

God or a person cannot be the sole cause or Absolute, if—there can be more than one person the cause for some things or if he can cause something now and not later on, or if he can cause some things and not everything.

If a bmw can make cars, they are not the only ones who make cars. There are others as well. Now even if bmw is the only one who made cars, they did not make watches or other products. They may not make cars sometime in the future. When we are not the only ones the cause for everything and always, it eliminates the possibility of our being the absolute cause. And also such a being would not be the one who is not caused. God is the only one who fulfills all the criteria. *For anyone to be the cause for everything and not having a cause for himself, He must be eternal, unchanging and the only one of his kind, without a second.* We, the souls are eternal and unchanging though, we are infinite in numbers; and we know that we have not caused either ourselves or anything else. So it has to be someone distinctly more superior, without a second, who can be the true cause for everything. Even the other gods and goddesses are souls like ourselves but in godly bodies possessing greater powers and capabilities.

Nature of Brahman is described in the Vedas as 'satyam, jnanam, anantam, anandam. 'Anantam' denotes the nature of being without limitation of place, time or substance. His infiniteness applies to both nature and attributes. Anantam signifies that it is not limited spatially, temporally or with reference to substance. Brahman is free from all the limitations such as 'desha parichcheda' (this is here and not elsewhere), 'kala parichcheda' (this is now and not any other time) and 'vastu parichcheda' (this is not this). Brahman is without any limitation related to substance. This non-limited nature would mean infinite auspicious qualities by which it has no equal or a superior and hence Brahman is the absolute in all respects.

The reason why the universe is said to be caused is because it is non sentient matter, changing and perishable. Even scientifically, anything that has a beginning must end and anything that has beginning has been caused purely due to its transient nature. Something that has a beginning cannot cause itself. Either it is unborn, not caused and hence will have no end. Or it is born, and naturally will have an end and hence has been caused. And God is the only one who fulfills all this. Though the souls are divine, being the potency of the Lord and unborn and unchanging, they are subject to obtaining a body in order to function and depend on the Lord who is the antar-atma of every soul, empowering them to function. It is also not applicable to the material universe which is transient, going through stages of formation and dissolution. It is similar to the birth and death of our bodies. Hence, God is said to be that power without a cause for Himself.

Que—it is said that ignorance cannot prevail where there is knowledge. Then, how is that the jivatmas become ignorant when their nature is knowledge? And how the same ignorance can not affect God while He is also stated to be of the nature of 'knowledge'?

Ans—Knowledge cannot become ignorance for knowledge dispels ignorance. Ignorance cannot prevail where there is knowledge, nor can we seek knowledge from ignorance. Similarly Light cannot cause darkness, for light removes darkness. We cannot seek light from darkness. Darkness cannot exist where there is light. We, the souls have knowledge as our nature. This world and all the non sentient matter have no knowledge or intelligence.

Atma acquires ignorance due to attachment to his body which will be dispelled the moment he realizes the nature of the self. Jivatma may be affected by avidya or lack of knowledge but jivatma himself can never become avidya or ignorance. Atma is eternal and unchanging and immutable; so his nature cannot change either. There isn't such a thing as ignorant jivatma.

Ignorance can affect the jivatma only when in a mortal body, due to his delusion, *identifying the self with his body*. Jivatma is also 'alpajna' and not 'sarvajna' and hence there is big difference between the extent of knowledge of jivatma and knowledge of Paramatma, who is omniscient. Avidya or ajnana in simple terms is a state of mistaken identity, thinking that I am my body. Even the gods, including Brahma are affected by this prakruti/maya and its gunas—sattva, rajasa, and tamasa.

When the atma associates with the ignorant world from which he obtains mortal bodies, he is engulfed or enveloped by ignorance. The moment he realizes that he is not his body, and his true relation is with that supreme Lord who dwells in him, his ignorance is dispelled.

On the other hand, the Lord can never be affected by ignorance or avidya even in the material universe, for He is divine and infinite in all respects, eternally. He is untouched by the material universe even though He is all pervading. Krishna confirms in Gita 9/9-

"na cha mAm tAni karmANi nibadhnanti dhananjaya,

"Actions do not bind Me, for I remain ever detached from them like one unconcerned".

Gita 7-25—
"nAham prakASah sarvasya yogamAyAsamAvrutah;"

"Obscured by My maya, I am not manifest to all. This deluded world does not recognize Me as the unborn and immutable"

Gita 7-26
"vEdAham samatItAni vartamAnAni chArjuna;

"I know all beings; past, present and those to come; but no one knows Me"

So there are distinct differences between God and the souls in many aspects. The same souls in the divine world would not be affected by ignorance or avidya, for avidya cannot exist in the divine world. Avidya or ignorance is confined to the mortal worlds alone.

When we are ignorant of our ignorance, we cannot overcome ignorance; however, when we realize we are ignorant, we can dispel ignorance by the knowledge of the self.

Que—can we fool God by thinking something in our minds and doing something else in our actions, for He is said to be noting our karma from mind alone?

Ans—Some spiritual leaders contend that the Lord, who dwells in the atma as the antaryami, notes our karma based on our thoughts originating in the mind alone and not our actions. But it cannot be true. We have known many people, including ourselves; we think of something in the mind, speak another, and do a totally different thing, without connecting it to what we originally thought or said. Does it mean that we can fool the antaryami by thinking good things in our mind but doing bad things outwardly, deceitfully, without thinking of what we do?

We know of terrorists, some of whom are brain washed to believe that they are doing larger good by killing innocent people. Many of them are trained to chant the name of God while shooting people, so does it mean they have pure thoughts in mind while they kill; and can gain good karma because they are thinking of God?

Many of us act in reflex, without actually thinking of what we want to do. If I hit someone without the intention to hurt seriously, end up killing the person in one blow, I am still responsible for his death even though, honestly, I had no thoughts or intentions of killing him.

Every time I see an earthquake or tsunami or any natural calamity, I decide in my mind that I want to help by contributing some money, because I have some extra money to spare. But never really translate that thought into action. The truth is that I never realize that I have failed in executing my good thought, so the negative thought of not helping does not ever occur to me. Will the Lord dwelling in me give me credit for good karma for such good thoughts, I never really executed?

I have seen people promising to help for medical treatment or for a marriage in a poor family or for some other good cause. Many of them conveniently forget that they had made such a commitment.

I know of my own near ones, and few friends who often talk so much about helping and wanting to help. Many of them have even committed to help some charities but did not send a cent to them. They talk and lecture about how we should help at every opportunity. When they convey their intentions, they may be honest. They don't fail because they have no money. Just that they never really give it a serious thought of executing.

That's why, if we truly want to help someone, we must just do it; without even thinking about it or mentioning about it.

It is not merely our thoughts that matter as karma, it is also our speech, and actions. Tri-karaNa (three-mode); thought, speech and action determines our karma. Kindness merely in mind or words is of no use to anyone.

So everything will be noted by the Lord, our thought, speech and actions. Because the Lord is not just dwelling in us, He is everywhere and also in every one. When I commit to help, the Lord in that person would have noted the recipients thought to my commitment and if not executed it goes against my good karma.

Que—how can we perceive God's all pervasiveness?

Ans—This is a story of an atheist king, who did not accept existence of God as the truth and also did not lose an opportunity to insult the Hindu philosophies whenever he came across spiritual leaders who preached the knowledge of atman and Paramatman and their eternal relationship. They would explain the all pervasive nature of the Lord in this universe in unmanifest form and hence He is invisible.

The king would mock at people for worshipping idols in the temples and the photos of God. He would claim that existence of God in the idols or the photographs was unscientific for they were merely man made things. Perceiving God in these objects was foolish. He showed scant respect for the idols or the photos. To him, if God was all pervasive, He should be visible in these idols and pictures. Since we cannot see God in these objects, nor does God come personally to prove His existence, it is obvious that He does not exist. He would ask everyone to prove God's existence by tangible evidence.

In other words, if a person is alive, can he reveal himself? We cannot see his soul, though he can assure us that he is alive in his body. Or when someone is dead, why is that body not functioning like a body of a person alive? What keeps someone alive?

Once, the king was celebrating his ancestors' dynastic rule. He organized a display of portraits of all his forefathers with grandeur. A learned scholar who was an invitee, who wanted to dispel the wrong notions of this king about the existence of God, picked up the portrait of his ancestors and placed it on the floor. The king noticed his ancestral picture lying on the floor and was furious. He picked up a sword and was enquiring with uncontrolled rage as to who dared put his family portrait on the floor? He considered it a great insult to his dead forefathers, which was an unforgivable offence and punishable by death.

The learned yogi approached the king admitting it was he who did that unpardonable act. The king then questions his rationale behind doing such an act knowing full well that he would be given a death sentence for insulting his forefathers. The king went on to explain that they were most sacred belongings of his inheritance and was pure royalty, sanctity of which shall not be slighted. The scholar starts to explain that it was wrong for the king to think that by placing the picture of his forefathers on the floor, he has insulted them in any way, for they don't exist in that portrait. They were long dead and could not be possibly present in the portrait.

The king then realizes that when he insulted those who worshipped God in idols and photos, he had offended the sensibilities of so many devotees and this wise man was explaining to him if God cannot exist in the idols and photos which He does, how his ancestors can exist in these pictures, which indeed, they don't.

The scholar then explains to the king that in reality, his forefathers don't exist in the pictures because they are not all pervading. However God truly is present everywhere, in every particle of this universe and hence He is present in the idols and pictures His devotees worship, except that God cannot be seen by our material eyes or grasped by our material senses, because He is divine in all respects.

Though we don't exist in the pictures, we hold these pictures in reverence and even worship the photos of our ancestors. However, the Lord truly exists everywhere and it is scientific to realize this truth of God's all pervasiveness.

Que—we often hear stories of people who claim to have memories of their past life. How true is this?

Ans—these are merely expressions from the minds of people who believe it is the memory of their past life. It cannot be real memories from the past life for the simple reason that they have to use the brain in this body to recall memory, and the brain now can only retain memories of events from the new life in this new body. We know that we have no memories about our conception in the mother's womb—of our birth or even the couple of years as an infant. Then, how possibly can we have memories of past life? It is possible for spirits and ghosts to retain impressions of the past life for they have not obtained a new body. However, even spirits or ghosts would lose such memories the moment they acquire a functional body. What they narrate as memories is merely their impression of some thoughts and visuals they have acquired in the present life, which they believe are from the past. It is like recalling a dream. We dream of situations and people we have never met in real life. Even when we narrate our dream from memory, we do make some changes and adjustments in the way we express our dream. It may not be accurately as dreamt. Sometimes, what they portray of people and places based on the past impressions may coincide, however, not everything would match. We cannot make a connection merely because one or two things match with the impressions they relate.

It is to be noted that every atma carries impressions from countless number of lives which is referred to as 'karma vasana'. We take every birth based on our past karma and accrue karma vasana from every life. This is not memory of the past but the impressions acquired over several lives influenced by guna and karma from past lives. We call this impression as the nature of a person or guna of a person based on which he acquires his next birth. When we see children showing different preferences, revealing different probability amplitude to the same situation, we call that their nature, which in reality is the influence of 'karma vasana' from several earlier lives. These impressions can change with our conscious effort now in this life. If I was a bad person last life, I can change in this life to become a good person, which is God's kindness that we don't have to carry memory of our past bad karma which would prompt us to going the same way in this life as well. We can break the trend by conscious 'effort' and 'practice'.

Gita 4-5—Krishna explains to Arjuna that only He knows everything from everyone's life, a jivatma cannot know his past life.

"bahUni mE vyatItAni janmAni tava chArjuna . . . ;

"Many births of Mine have gone by; and so is it with you as well; I know them all, but you do not know them"

It is evident from this verse that atmas born of karma, cannot know things from their past lives, unless, it is intended by some divine intervention.

Some people have a flair for music right from childhood, some for painting. Every person has a distinct nature which influences likes and dislikes. Without any reason, we like something which may be disliked by our brothers and sisters, though growing up in the same environment. You can give 10 children from the same family the same input, but each one might have different output due to his 'guna' or vasanas or impressions from past life. Vasanas can be changed or broken by 'abhyasa' or conscious practice. We can choose to either improve and progress in this life or can continue and pursue the same behavior influenced by our impressions from past lives.

Chapter Fourteen

---∿❦∿---

Sequence of events for the soul

Que—why did God send us to this world, I would much prefer to be a nitya suri or mukthatma, living with God.

Ans—God did not send us to this world. We came here on our own accord, due to the choice we made, seeking to experience the changing world, being on our own. We chose to come here when we were given the choice of either staying with God in the immortal world under His care or coming to the changing world, being on our own. Just as a loving father would offer his children the option to choose what they wish to be, God gave us the options. Had we chosen '*Abhimukhyatvam*' or being '*sanmukh*' to the Lord, we would have been one of the nitya suris, but we opted to being '*vimukh*' or '*turning away*' from Him. As a result, we came to this world.

It is pretty much like our opting to try something unknown, then deciding it was not a good idea to have chosen to do so, and then realize we should have chosen the other option. For some who like the wrong option based on their instinct, may say they are happy with what they are and may not want a change. They continue to feel this way, till they start experiencing the struggle, pain and suffering.

Even if we choose now to be with God in His abode, it is still possible. All that we have to do is surrender through an Acharya.

You, I and many more like us, now feel that we should have been in God's world for whatever reason. Some of us may feel so because we have had a glorious, wonderful life; yet may feel disenchanted of it all, as it is pretty much repetitive, transient and superfluous. We do know some famous, rich and successful personalities in our times that tried to take their own life or would get addicted to drugs as they would not be able to sleep like normal people. They would have everything anyone could ask for. Yet, they may not be happy or they may find the repetitive nature of life too boring, even if that is what is considered happy living by the rest of the world. They may want to end their life (Elvis Presley—not so lucky; Boris Becker—survived in his attempts to take his own life; recently Michael Jackson who died of drug over dosage, though he had no intention of dyeing). *It is true that we do nothing more than using our 5 senses and body to seek constant pleasures and if that is the purpose of life, it is meaningless. The same senses and mind can be used for attaining our Lord.*

It is paradoxical that some of us have everything, yet we are not happy and ever in search of happiness; while we also see some poor people not so unhappy. Their prime concern is to acquire resources to fulfill their needs for survival. Some of those who struggle to meet their basic needs would want an end to this life as there is mainly sorrow and grief in life. The reason for both the groups feeling disillusioned with either their good life or those suffering, are different. The rich are fed up because they expect more from life but this material world does not have what they seek. The poor are suffering because they want to get out of poverty. Once they come out of that state, they too would develop attachment to life. Both types of people are disenchanted with life because they are seeking that elusive happiness.

Those blessed few who manage to realize their true nature, remaining ever in equilibrium with the emotional duals, would find a purpose to this life, while enjoying every moment of life.

In this world, we can never over achieve anything. Though we are inclined to over enjoying; never satisfied with what we have; more often we end up suffering pain when our attempt is to seek pleasure. If we enjoy eating more than anything else, we suffer due to over eating. This shows that we get grief when our attempt is to become happy, even when we are successful doing what we intended.

How can we ever be unhappy with the realization that we possess the Supreme Lord dwelling in us? What can be greater than having the Lord of all the worlds reside in us?

Purandaradasa expresses in one of his compositions thus—

> *"nAnEke badavanu, nAnEke paradEsi,*
> *Srinidhe hari yenage neeniruva tanaka"*.

"How am I poor and how am I a stranger?

when I have Hari, the abode of Sri (divine Mother), with me eternally"

Though the Lord is not involved in our activities, we can involve Him if we make that choice. If we are hungry, we should include the antaryami and eat for His sake. If we are sleepy, put the antaryami to sleep as well, while we go to sleep. Include the Lord in everything. With practice, we would not forget the Lord even in our subconscious state. This way a devotee would never seek outward happiness for he would have realized the presence of infinite bliss residing in him. Even the physical pleasures would be experienced involving the Lord within.

The added benefit of including the Lord in everything we do is that we would never do anything bad, when we realize He is watching, and that He does not like us doing bad things, then we would do what pleases the Lord. Lord is pleased when we are righteous. Koorathazhwan re-defines the essence of dharma in declaring that *"what pleases the Lord is dharma"*.

We thought change is interesting and permanence can be boring and opted for this world. *The only thing permanent about this world is change,* and so do all good things end as well as bad. For some, good may be lasting a bit longer than bad for others. But we do not realize that all good and bad are caused by our own selves. We seek good things for ourselves but are willing to do bad things to others.

Que—Obviously there was a time when we made our choices, what were we before we came to the stage of choosing between this changing world and God's immortal world?

Ans—We have to go to the time before creation when the worlds had not manifested. It has to be understood that the Lord and His divine immortal world were always there. Only the changing world manifests from the Lord and dissolves into Him periodically.

We have to visualize this reality—let us understand that God gave us the knowledge of both the eternal world and the changing world. Had we chosen the option of being 'sanmukh' or seeking to be with the Lord eternally, we would have attained His immortal world. We chose to become 'vimukh' choosing the 'maya / prkaruti' and to experiencing independent existence in the changing world, being on our own. Our choice would be a factor to decide where we go, and we were free to choose what we wished. Based on the choice of each soul, they acquired different bodies. The reason why all the souls did not end up taking birth as humans solely depended on what their choices were. *We can relate to the fact that the probability amplitude is infinite when it comes to the choices each soul can make. Probably, our thoughts fell into the collective group of 8.4 million; which is why we came here taking some 8.4 million bodies, each one based on his choice. God being the antaryami would have known our choices and we went into bodies and worlds based on that.*

Even today, many of us like this life here and not seeking to go to the eternal world, because we seem to be happy with what we are. However, the problem would start when we start experiencing pain and suffering.

I have to tell you the story of a noble king, here. The king ruled wisely, constantly caring for the welfare of his people. He was a devotee as well. The royal guru tells the king that he has just one more life before he might be accepted to the eternal world by God. He would be born as a pig soon after his death. Lifespan for pigs is around 12-15 years, and as he would leave the body of the pig, he would then be entitled to go to the eternal world, *if he chooses to.*

Hearing this, the king was delighted, he was looking forward to the day and time he can end this suffering of taking birth and dying repeatedly since eternity. Towards the end, he feels tired and was bed ridden. He then calls out for his ministers and family to stay beside him during his last hours—and relates to them about what his guru had mentioned of his next birth as a pig. He tells them that what he was about to advice them was very important and that they should assure to fulfill his wish. He would be dead anytime soon and gives them the description to identify him in his next birth and location where he will be born as a piglet. And that he would like them to kill him in the body of the piglet so that he does not have to spend some years as a pig before going to the eternal world and this would be a great favour for him. They agree to fulfill his wish.

He dies; they complete his last rites, then go to the location as directed by him and find the new born piglet with description and identity marks he had narrated. They pick up the piglet and prepare to kill it. To their dismay, the piggy starts communicating to them. It requests them not to kill it, that it does not want to end its life as a piggy, though as a human he thought he would prefer to end his life as a pig, but has a change of mind and would not like to be killed and he would like to complete full life term. In fact he feels very grateful to be a pig and loves being who he was and is happy with the family and association he has obtained with his new birth.

From this story, we have to realize that when in a human body our perceptions are totally different. As a devout human we may be determined in our goal to reach the eternal abode of the Lord. But the same soul in the body of other species will not have such realization. So we have no understanding as to what choices or thoughts occur to us and why? That is the reason why so many souls have come to this world, going through life in different bodies.

Krishna confirms in Gita 8-6—
   "yam yam vApi smaran bhAvamtyajatyantE kalEvaram . . ."

"Remembering whatsoever thoughts one leaves the body at death, to that alone he goes, ever in that thought thereof"

Whatever we think of at the time of death is what we desire to acquire and end up taking such a birth based on our wish, backed by karma.

Gita 9-25—
   "yAnti dEvavratA dEvan pitrUn yanti pitruvratAh . . ."

"Devotees of the gods attain gods, worshippers of the manes (ancestors) attain their state, and the seekers of bhutas go to them. And those who worship Me come to Me.

The above verse confirms that we attain what we seek backed by our karma. If we worship the gods of the heaven suitably, we attain heaven. If we are devoted to our forefathers, we attain their state. If they were bad people and based on their karma they have taken lower births of animals, we will get the same birth as they, due to our attachment to them. However, if they were true devotees of the Lord and have attained immortal world, we would also attain their state in the eternal world. Those who worship bhutas and piSachas of demonic nature will attain their state and those who are devoted to the supreme Lord will attain Him.

But Azhwars and Acharyas have categorically declared that any devotee who takes refuge with an Acharya, who is endowed with 'samaSrayaNam' by the Acharya, would not have to follow the above norm. The Lord would be thinking of such a devotee and it does not matter if the devotee thinks of the Lord at the time of death or not. A person devoted to Acharya is an exception to this rule.

Different states in our life

In the total duration of our life as humans, our body goes through three states—
   a) Awakened state,
   b) Dreaming state and
   c) Deep sleep state (without dreams).

However, we have found another state while being in the awakened state—intoxicated state—when either we are drunk or under the effects of drugs.

Of all the activities we do, we find that a good sleep is the most enjoyable experience, though we are not in a state of total consciousness during our sleep. We do nothing during deep sleep state and yet that brings us the greatest joy. The reason for this is that we get close to the Lord in this state but without consciousness. This in itself is evident that we do not have to do anything to remain happy or we are more joyful even when we don't indulge in sense gratification. When we wake up, we claim, "oh that was a good sleep and I feel great". However, we were neither conscious during sleep; nor aware of anything. It is also said that humans are harmless when sleeping, as we cannot hurt anyone during our sleep; unless we are sleep walkers who would transform dreams into reality. *In fact deep sleep is the greatest joy that all living beings experience in a body. It is evident from this that we experience true bliss only with the Lord; from the Lord.*

We also realize that all our problems, worries, suffering, pain and grief are experienced only in the awakened state. Every person does everything to experience happiness in the awakened state. Be it a religious person, a devotee, a commoner, an atheist—everyone, whether working or relaxing, active or lazing, playing or idle—is done seeking happiness, peace, bliss, joy or anandam. While our attempt is to find happiness in everything we do, we also end up suffering pain and grief. This is when we are awake. And the moment we go into deep sleep, nothing can bother us. We could have experienced greatest calamity and grief, moments ago, but the moment we go into deep sleep, we do not feel any grief; at least not until we wake up. And the moment we wake up, we come to face all our problems again.

When we are in grief, we seek happiness. However, when we are happy, we do not experience grief. This shows that grief and happiness do not co-exist; when we attain happiness; automatically happiness drives away grief. But getting rid of grief does not automatically bring us happiness. Similarly, when we are in pain, we want relief from pain. Having been relieved of pain in itself does not give us pleasure. When in pleasure, obviously there is no pain.

Prasnopanishad chapter 4-5 declares that—in the dream state the jivatman experiences greater forms of same things he experiences in waking state. Whatever he has seen, heard and perceived in the waking state, he experiences again and again in the dream state assuming all forms. He experiences even things not experienced before; such as death of his own body. This is so true and an amazing experience as well.

I have dreamt of experiencing my own death and have watched over witnessing many of the dear ones crying over my dead body; in this there are three of me—one that is sleeping, one that is dead in the dream and one that is watching over the dead body in the dream. I have also experienced one stage more in this; while I see my relatives expressing grief over my death in the dream; I also realize that I am not dead and am alive by the realization that one of me is witnessing the event in the dream. So this makes it four of me. I have also dreamt of others telling me in the dream of my own death. There is a movie named 'inception' that talks about how we can go into several layers of dream state and how we can influence others in their dreams to turn the outcome of events to our advantage, in reality. This shows that there are no limits or extent to what we can do in dreams. Many a times I felt that I was dreaming exactly as I wanted to dream, though situation and events in dream have no relation to what I have experienced in waking state. Sometimes, as the dream is ending, we would remember the dream as we wake up momentarily in the middle of night and then we go back to sleep. When we wake up in the morning, we cannot remember the same dream, even if we try to recall.

We also do remember some dreams totally and some of them partly. And I also felt that I was changing the course of the dream intentionally, as desired. And some other times, I would be dreaming in the dream and if I was killed in the second dream, I was still aware that I am alive in the first dream and that the killing in the second dream is not real. Have also experienced a second level of dream in a dream with the awareness that it was a dream and hence not real and would continue dreaming in the first level. Flying, being invincible, not dying even after being killed, fending off stronger people when attacked, experiencing being a superhuman with super powers; even seeing God and having a conversation with God with the realization of His supreme nature, experiencing that divine bliss in the dream while being in the company of God and many other impossibilities in real life are possible in the dream.

Even if the karmendriyas (sense organs) do not function in the dream state, the jivatman becomes the seer, doer and experiencer through the subtle body and indriyas he obtains (enabled by the antaryamin) just as everything else we do in awakened state is God-enabled.

Prasnopanishad 4-6—In the dreamless, deep sleep state—the jivatman is fully embraced by the Paramatman and experiences happiness. It is to be noted that jivatman experiences this happiness only when in a body. Body alone is the cause of worldly happiness. Desirable and undesirable do not affect one without a body.

Mandookya Upanishad—expounds all the aspects in different states. Omkara, comprising of 'akAra' ukAra, makAra and ardhamAtrAtmaka—thus having four parts, correspond to the four aspects of Brahman—viSva, taijasa, prAjna and turlya. All this universe of sentients and non sentients is omkara, expounding the modes of guna, vibhuti and upasana. PraNava (Om) is the form of Brahman. Everything, either limited by time or not limited by time, are omkara alone.

The Paramatman who is the innerself of the jivatman is never tainted with any defect in the—waking state, dream state and dreamless state. Though, in the dreamless state, the jivatman experiences the presence of the Lord, but it would be without realization. The only outcome is happiness. This is unmistakably true for I have always enjoyed watching infants sleeping. I wonder if all the infants must be going into deep sleep more often than the adults. And we cannot miss that blissful smile on their face. And they smile often, when they are sleeping. You can see that there is a noticeable difference in their smile while sleeping and the smile while they are awake and playing. The smile during sleep is one of total bliss and tranquility and the whole face smiles in delight.

a> the waking state—(vysvAnara—ordainer of waking state) in this state the consciousness of the atma relates to things external, the atma uses all his body parts, senses, mind, intellect, ego and antahkaraNa (inner heart)—enjoys and experiences the gross objects—enabled by the Paramatman who is the innerself. In the waking state, if I play music or play sports, it is also experienced by others. More persons can participate doing the same activity.

b> Dream state—(taijasa) consciousness is internal and the atma experiences all that he does in the waking state but he enjoys subtle objects which is exclusive to the atma who is in the dream state. His external organs are shut. Others cannot experience what the dreaming atma experiences.

c> Deep-sleep state—(prAjna) in this state the atma does not desire any enjoyment nor sees any dreams. Oneness is attained with the Paramatman who causes the atman to experience bliss of deep sleep. Atma is not involved in any activities except experiencing the 'bliss'. He would not remember anything from this state for he has not experienced anything in a conscious state.

d> Turiya—The fourth state cannot be perceived by the atma for it describes the supreme Lord 'Vasudeva' who cannot be grasped by the mind as 'this much' for infinite cannot be known in its totality; while He is instrumental in the atman experiencing the other three states.

We make choices based on our thoughts and forget about them, but God would not, being a kind father, who is always interested in our happiness, let's us have what we want. And we have become what we wanted based on our choice backed by karma.

Taittitiyopanishad reveals in 'AnandamImAmsA': that the joy experienced by humans and other superior celestial beings varies manifold.

> ➤ joy of man—suppose, one who owns all the wealth in the world, who is in prime youth, wise, well educated and learned, most expeditious, strong in body and mind—is considered one measure of human joy. Remember, there is only one person like this in the whole world and the joy of all others is much less than his.

> ➤ The joy of 'manushya-gandharvas' is at least a hundred fold more than human joy, for they are not affected by desire and are established in Brahman

> ➤ The joy of deva-gandharvas is hundred times more than 'manushya gandharva's joy, they too are established in Brahman and unaffected by desire

> ➤ The joy of 'AjAnajAnA' gods is hundred fold more than that of deva gandharva, for they are fixed in Brahman and untouched by desire.

> ➤ The joy of 'karmadEva gods' is hundred fold more, for they are steadfast in Brahman, having Vedic rites and unaffected by desires

> ➤ The joy of 'gods' is hundred times more than the karmadeva gods

> ➤ The joy of 'indra' is hundred times more than the gods' joy

> ➤ The joy of 'brihaspati' is hundred times more than Indra's

> ➤ The joy of 'prajapati (brahma) is hundred times more than that of brihaspati's.

Yet, the manifold joy experienced by every celestial being, though much better than the best man's joy on earth, is still a joy of this changing world. It is bound by the 'prakruti/maya' and is transient in nature. None of these superior beings have ever experienced the 'divine bliss' or the 'premanandam' of the supreme Lord, which is the highest bliss the souls seek to experience. These gods are not satisfied with what they are, constantly seeking a better state of existence.

God does not force His will on us

Que—why does not God control the functioning of this world in a perfect way so that there is no pain or suffering anywhere?

Ans—God is a perfect and loving Father. He does not force his will on the souls who are all his children. His main purpose is that souls should feel good out of their own choice; choosing what they want to do; He gives them the right to action and enjoyment. He does not interfere either in our choice making or in our actions nor would he intervene when we have to face consequences for our actions. Souls are conscient beings, they like to choose for themselves. *If He controlled our thoughts and actions he might have a perfectly functioning world but it would be like having infinitely programmed robots without happiness or emotions, because they are not allowed to choose or act on their own accord.* There can be no happiness when controlled.

In a controlled world, there would be no relationships. Imagine if you have 100 children and you decide every choice and action for them, their full life time; they would tell you that you might as well build robots instead of having human children. However, God has not left us helpless or out of His reach totally. He has given us everything we need to be happy. Can you imagine infinite numbers of robots functioning by pre-programs? They would all be doing the same things, exactly the same way. Then next question would be, why have such machines, if not for the emotions and relationships. After all He created this universe because we wanted to experience such an existence. If he had robots, they would be like the rest of the non sentient worlds, not the souls with joy, or feelings and devotion. Souls are of the nature of knowledge, who make their own choices and act accordingly; either to be devoted or doing things for themselves. *If they are devoted, they are under His care, if they want to be on*

their own, they have to take care of themselves. If their actions and choices are good, their life here would be good as well.

We control our body, as our bodies are non sentient matter, devoid of knowledge and hence they can be controlled. Souls who are sentient and knowledgeable; would not like to be controlled and hence the Lord does not control them to making choices or have them function against their will.

To the question as to why god does not have a perfectly functioning world without pain and suffering—the answer is *'the immortal world'* where every soul is in a divine immortal body, where everyone is experiencing unlimited, unending, ever-growing bliss. *That is the perfect world.* God gives us that choice as well. Had we chosen the perfect world in the first place, we would not be asking this question. If we choose to go there now, it is still possible, but we have to back it up with our actions. *We wanted to experience this imperfect, changing world and hence are here*.

When we want to own anything in this world, we have to work for it and if successful, we get what we want, but the world is longer lasting than the bodies we obtain from it. However, when we want to be with God in His world, all that we have to do is seek Him and we don't have to do anything. God works for us, giving Himself and His world to us. **This world is changing and so is our bodies, but we and God's world are of the same nature— both are immortal, eternal, and unchanging**.

If He controls the whole world, then there would be so many unhappy souls and God being the kindest father, cannot bear to see us unhappy. He has set the laws in place and has given us the knowledge and provided with adequate support to act in accordance with our free will and choice. Any other way would not work with sentient beings. This is evident from Gita 18-63— after preaching all that there is to tell, Krishna mentions to Arjuna:

"ithi te jnAnamakhyAtam . . . yathEchasi tathA kuru"

"I have declared to you the knowledge which is the mystery of mysteries, reflecting on it completely, do as you wish (as you desire)". He did not tell Arjuna—"well, I have imparted such great knowledge purely out of kindness, and it is now binding on you to do exactly as the knowledge conferred upon you". Krishna could have insisted so and even Arjuna would have agreed to follow Krishna's directions. It is up to each soul to reflect upon the knowledge he has bestowed upon us. If we choose the right course of action, the outcome would also be good, as well as it would please God; and He is happy when we do well. If God controlled everything and every soul's functioning, we would all be looking the same, doing the same things, all at the same time—if one of us is a cricketer, all of us would be cricketers too. Even in that there could be a potential problem, for everyone wants to be a batsman, in which case, we cannot play cricket. You also need bowlers, wicket keeper, fielders and umpires and spectators watching us play. If so, even such cricket would be too boring for us as well as God!! Thank God He did not think of something like this, of controlling every soul to doing things against his will.

Or if He controlled us to doing different set of things in different groups, so too, we would be upset, for we would complain that we would prefer to be doing something else or taking part in the other groups. Anywhichway we look at it, controlling someone against his will would simply not work.

Alternatively, God could not have given us the half option—allowing us to choose some and control some—even that would not work. We would complain even then that He should have let us do what we wanted in all aspects.

Each one of us, doing the right thing, choosing rightly and yet we would all be doing different things rightly, either for our sake or in devotion of God. Either way, the outcome would be joyous. *It is the nature of the soul to be so different from one another; the options are unlimited when it comes to making choices.*

God would not involve in this karmic world. It is similar to getting into a school. The teacher is there to teach us, but we as students have to study well to do well in the exam. We cannot ask the teacher to write the exams, nor can we ask the teacher to help us with questions to which we do not know the answers. God has given us this world because we asked for it. He has given us the knowledge and ingredients to live here happily. He will not involve in our actions or consequences. If we so decide that we don't want to continue in this world, we have the option of seeking Him and only then would He get involved.

If we truly want God's involvement, even in this karmic world, all that we need to do is totally surrender to Him through an Acharya. Even then God would guide us, instead of controlling.

Que—why does God have to incarnate in this world to protect us when He can will for everything to happen from where He is?

Ans—God is not an outsider; this is His world and *He is our only permanent relative*. He is already with us, always.

In this world, we all know who our father is and about our father as well, though we share this relationship with him only in this life. However, when it comes to our eternal Father God, we seem to have no knowledge of His being our Father nor do we know about Him.

If you are a father and your children need your help in a serious situation—will you go there personally or control the situation from where you are through other people? Based on the gravity of the situation, you would much prefer to reach out to your children and save them from danger. Similarly, God, due to His only weakness that He loves His devotees beyond our comprehension, likes to come personally to take charge of the situation and protect His devotees. It is natural for Him. He came personally several times to rescue Prahlada every time he was being attempted to be killed. Prahlada did not ask the Lord to save Him from death.

Also as devotees, we have to realize His hand in protecting us, which is possible only when He is personally involved. He is a super sensitive father. He cannot bear it if His devotees were to complain that He didn't come to their rescue when they needed Him most. Being personally involved or using His powers are not the same. We as human fathers feel bad when our children question us as to why we could not go to see them off if they were leaving town or come to receive them at the train station or airport when they arrive—even in simple situations, the father is expected to be present. When it comes to grave situations, there is no alternative but to go personally. *Above all He incarnates only to re-assure devotees that He loves them so much.* He loves being with us, to experience our love for Him, to share our expressions and experiences with Him. He misses us so much for we have stayed away from Him for eternity.

By the same token, He would not remain here eternally when He incarnates, for that would not serve the purpose of this karmic world, which is sought by souls for experiencing and enjoying karma without interference.

Sri Pillailokacharyar in his SrivachanabhushaNam—sukti 384 reveals the secret of God's incarnations.

"tripAd vibhUtiyilE paripUrNanubhavam nadavAnirka,
adu undadu urukkAttAdE, desAntaragatanAna putran pakkalilE
pitruhrudayam   kidakkumApolE,   samsArigaL   pakkalilE
tiruvuLLam kudipoy, ivargaLaippirindAl AttramAttadE . . . ."

Brief essence of it is: "Though He is totally fulfilled in the divine world in the company of nitya suris and muktatmas, the plight of our Lord, owing to His affection for us, who have come away to this mortal world, compels Him to come to us to this world. Like a father who would worry about his son who has gone away leaving home, would have his heart and mind longing for him; would go after him to facilitate him with all his requirements and doing everything to enable his return home.

There is a story to show how God is our only permanent relation. A sage and his son live together in the forest. The son is very powerful owing to His penance. The son has great affection for his father and literally takes care of all his needs. His father grows old and dies a natural death. The son finds the separation hard to bear. Using his yogic powers, he goes to the god of death (Yama) who on seeing the son, extends extreme courtesies to him and enquires as to how he could be of service to him. Yama recognizes his special yogic powers and does not dare to negate anything he would ask. The son comes straight to the point and expresses his desire to have his father back, as he finds it hard to be without him. Yama agrees to return his father but before he could do that, he requests the son to close his eyes and connect with him mentally, as he wishes to reveal to him his past. The son then gets the memory of his past 100 lives, as to who were his parents in each birth and what he was in every life. He could see that he was not a human in a few lives; he had even donkeys as his parents. He was also a human in many lives and had many fathers of greater virtue. His only connection with the father, who just passed away, was that the same soul had once murdered him in one of his earlier lives, and was not related to him in any of his other earlier births. Now he is the son of a person who had killed him in an earlier life. In fact it is the son who loves his father so much in this life but on the same scale his father's love for the son is nominal and nothing special. His fathers from earlier births were in fact much greater in virtue and loved him most as well. In comparison, this father was not even close.

Yama asks him to wake up. He then asks the son "which father would he like to have back", "the one who just died in this life or the better ones from earlier life?" The son then realizes that what he recognized as his father was a body, related to him only temporarily in a life, and he acquired this relationship with his birth and soon as he dies, all his relationships would be gone as well. He has had so many good fathers and was confused which one was better of them all, and for a moment he was bewildered about his attachment to his father now. Yama then explains to him that his only true Father is God, who is also the Father for eternity, who is unchanging, as He is not going to cease to exist ever and He has always been with us except that we have forgotten our true identity and our eternal relationship with our true Father, whose love for each one of us cannot be understood by a soul nor can be equated to any of the love and affection we have experienced as humans. The son then realizes that it was his attachment and obsession that was the cause for disillusionment.

And as a true father, God comes to us personally whenever He needs to come here, to rescue us from grave situations, which we do not deserve to suffer due to any past or present karma, but are made to suffer due to fresh acts of crime by some evil doers. When noble and wise souls cannot survive the onslaught of a tyrant, then God comes to save them, personally.

Sri Pillai Lokacharyar confirms that God is our eternal relative, related to us in every conceivable way. He confirms in his '**nava vida sambhandam**"—

   "*pitA cha rakshakassEshi bhartA jnEyo ramApatihi,
   swAmyAdhAro mamAtmA cha bhoktA chadyamanuditaha*"

He establishes all the relationships between the Paramatma and jivatma rooted in the 'Thirumantram'

1. **pita**—putra sambhandam (Father-son).
2. **rakshaka**—rakshya sambandham (protector-protected)
3. **seshi**-sesha sambandham (master-subservient)
4. **bhartru**-bhAryA sambandham (husband-wife, Lord being the antaryami, the souls are eternally married to Him)
5. **Jneya**—jnatru sambandham (the omniscient, and one deriving knowledge from that omniscient, who is to be known)
6. **swAmy**—sva sambandham (owner, owned)
7. **adhara**—adheya sambandham (supporter, supported)
8. **atma**-sarira sambandham (antar-atma, atma)
9. **bhoktru**—bhogya sambandham (enjoyer, enjoyed)

Incarnation of Lord Narasimha:

It is wonderful to know how the Lord incarnates as Nara-simha. He did not

pre-decide the form and place. After several attempts, when Hiranyakashipu could not have his son killed, he asks his son, as to who was protecting him every time. Prahlada confides it was the supreme Lord. He then suggests to Prahlada that his Lord was protecting out of fear of him who was the most powerful in all the worlds and if Prahlada, his son died, he would be enraged and could destroy all the worlds including his Lord. And Prahlada should recognize this truth that he is the son of the most powerful person in all the worlds, who is also immortal, for there is no one that can end his life, including Brahma, who granted him the boons.

He enquires where his Lord resides. Prahlada declares that the Lord is everywhere without exception. He is in every one and pervades everywhere in the universe eternally, but is invisible. He then questions why He was hiding if He was everywhere. If he was so sure He is everywhere, he pointed to one of the pillars in the palace and asks if the Lord was also in that pillar? *Hiranyakashipu was so sure that the Lord could not be in that pillar which he had himself overseen while building his palace.* Prahlada confirms that He is everywhere and He would reveal Himself whenever He chooses to.

Thiruvaimozhi 2-8-9—Azhwar says—

> **"engumuLan kaNNan enna maganaikkAindu,**
> **ingillaiyAl enru iraNiyan tUN pudaippa,**
> **angappozhudE avan vIyattonniya,**
> **en singappirAn perumai yArAyum sIrmaittE?**

"When Prahlada affirms that the Lord is everywhere, Hiranyakashipu questions if He was not there (in the pillar) and breaks the pillar (he was wishing God might not be there), to his dismay the Lord appeared that very moment from the pillar! Who can comprehend or perceive the glory of the Lord!"

It was then that Hiranyakashipu takes an aggressive stance and declares to his son that he was going to break that pillar and if his Lord was not found in that pillar, he would kill Prahlada like a lion would maul a baby elephant, and strikes on the pillar with his mace. The pillar breaks into pieces. Then and there emerges from the pillar Lord Narasimha in a form of a man with a lion's head.

The Lord had not decided the form till that moment. He determines to take this form only on hearing Hiranyakashipu's declaration that he would kill his son like a lion would kill a baby elephant. He could have taken any form to counter Hiranyakashipu's boons which grants him immunity from death either by a man or a god or an animal, either by a living or non living weapon, either in day or night, either on land or in space. Just to be doubly sure he also gets Brahma's assurance that no one created by Brahma be able to cause his death. He was convinced that he had covered all possibilities to defy death and that he was an immortal.

Hiranyakashipu was bewildered seeing this bizarrely aggressive form coming at him and yet regains his courage to thank his son for showing his Lord and now he could kill Him, who has been evading him. Narasimha does not waste even a moment; he picks up Hinayakashipu effortlessly, who struggles to strike blows at the Lord but remains ineffective; Narasimha walks across to the entrance step, lays his body on His lap and rips open his heart with his nails. He ensures to fulfill all the conditions of the boon granted by Brahma, for he was neither a man, nor an animal nor a god; it was dusk, so neither day nor night; He lays him on his lap, so neither on land nor in space, he uses nails which is neither living nor non-living weapon. And above all, He was not created by Brahma. On the contrary Brahma was created by the Lord.

A true devotee is one who cares and worries for his Lord's well being, always. Hiranya kashipu, Prahlada's father tries to have him killed many a times but fails in all his attempts. In one of his efforts to have Prahlada killed, they drop him off the top of the hill cliff. While falling, Prahlada holds his heart with both hands to protect the Lord who is ever dwelling in his heart. He was not worried he would die or get hurt, but was constantly conscious of protecting his Lord who would also roll over as his body flips and flops while falling down. And that is true love for the well being of the Lord.

Que—why does God kill bad people when He takes incarnations here? If all are His children and dear to Him, is it proper for Him to kill?

Ans—*God does not kill; He cures illness to protect good health of the society.* Imagine yourself to be the god controlling your body. In fact, literally, you are the lord of your body. Let us for a moment forget about the antaryami in you. Let us say your body acquires some disease, say cancer for instance. What would you do? You do chemotherapy or some such treatment, which would destroy the cancer causing cells, so that you can arrest the spread of cancer to the rest of the body. When you destroy cancerous cells, you also end up killing many good cells. Aren't these cells part of your body? Then, is it right to destroy them? What if your hand or leg gets infected causing gangrene and has to be amputated? Don't we do so?

Exactly for the same reason, when a society gets infected with some bad people that are incorrigible, who in turn would want to destroy dharma, harmony and peace in the society or would make it impossible for others to survive or not allow others to go about their life righteously, God has to incarnate on earth to eliminate such bad elements. If not, existence for the whole population would become impossible. Either all the people would become bad in which case they would end up destroying each other due to their nature or the bad people would destroy the good ones. If the good people of the society are able to defend themselves from the onslaught of the bad elements, then God would not venture incarnating. He would incarnate only when the bad elements become overpowering. He incarnates only when the noble souls need to be protected; for, karmically they don't deserve to suffer in the hands of the evil forces.

Just as the master of a human body is its atma, who in order to protect his body from the cancer cells or viruses and bacterial infection, destroys them and expels them from the body, God owns this world and this society.

Our bodies have a natural immune system, fighting many infections, regularly. We need the help of medication or treatment only when our immune system is overpowered. Similarly, God comes here in some form to protect His children, when they are unable to defend themselves. He would intervene only when it is imperative for Him to come here personally. He would not involve in every incident just as we don't need medication or treatment for minor illnesses which can be cured by our immune system, many of which we are not even aware of. This whole universe is in fact God's body. He has to do whatever it takes to protect his good children from being destroyed by bad elements and He does so, as and when needed. In doing so, He also helps those whom He kills. If not they would accumulate so much bad karma, it would become impossible for them to exhaust consequences. By killing them, he ends their bad deeds in that body so that they can start a new life in a new body. *However, only God can put an end to some one's life. We shall not. We cannot intentionally kill someone and claim that we are doing what God does. We have no right to kill either ourselves or anyone else.*

Soldiers and others involved in their dharma to protect the country, do their righteous duties when they defend the nation or fighting a war. It is not the same as killing someone for personal reasons. They are protecting us; they are fighting for us and not for themselves. In the bargain, they put their own lives in danger to save ours.

Though God is everywhere, we as ordinary humans, cannot see Him or experience Him. So the only option is for Him to come in person and show that He has come for us. That's exactly what Rama or Krishna did when they took birth in this world.

Krishna declares in Gita—4-7
*"yada yada hi dharmasya . . . tadatmanam srujamyaham . . .
paritranaya sadhunam . . . sambhavami yuge yuge".*

"whenever there is a decline of Dharma and uprising of adharma; to protect the noble ones and to punish the evil doers, I incarnate time after time"

This is evident from what happened at the end of dwarpara yuga. Krishna incarnated to put an end to the atrocities of Kamsa who imprisoned his own father. He was an evil person who would have destroyed all the goodness in the society.

Duryodhana who was the leader of the Kauravas was an evil man who had no concept of right and wrong and would commit any atrocity, because it was in his power to do so as the ruler. If he and his associates (some of them were good people, but they chose to support him for their own personal reasons) were not checked and destroyed, his evil would have spread to the entire population and no good man could survive in that kind of a society. *And then, what is the purpose if all the people become bad? There is no need for such a society to exist; just as a totally sick man would see no reason to live with incurable ailments.* Duryodhana schemed to have Pandavas killed several times. He took away their kingdom by tricking them in a gambling game and refused to give them even 5 villages, though he should have returned their kingdom after fulfilling the conditions of the wager.

On a humorous note, Krishna would have been fascinated by the claims of Duryodhana that he would not give any land to Pandavas. As a matter of fact, the whole universe is God's property and belongs to Him alone and here was someone who was claiming he would not give some land that never belonged to him in the first place. Why alone the universe, even all the souls and beings belong to the Lord. We are all His property and He supports us to function in our bodies by being the indweller of each one of us.

Que—In that case, is it wrong to own lands and properties?

Ans—We don't really own anything here. Everything is literally God-owned. Evidently, this world and materials of this world are longer lasting than our bodies. So, the sense of owning something, including the self or our body is purely imaginary. Whatever we claim to own here is merely in our possession, legally, righteously, for our use. By the same token, each one has to realize that every one of us has this need for shelter, food, clothing, education, healthcare etc, equally.

It is wrong to forcefully acquire land belonging to others by power. Using land or building homes or even growing food crops is the purpose why the Lord created this world for us. When we buy a piece of land legally, paying monetary consideration either to the government or to the society or to a person who is willing to sell it, is not wrong. However, grabbing land from others or forcing poor people to sell their land, using our powerful position and wealth is wrong. We cannot deprive others of their livelihood. When we buy a piece of land and build homes, it is wrong to think that we own them. We are simply in possession of these properties for our use. We will be gone.

None of us own anything in this world. **If we truly want to claim to anything, it is only to the eternal relationship with the Lord, for we come from Him and belong to Him and it is natural to claim rightful relationship to our own source.**

Dharma (well being of people) is above all else.

For God establishing righteousness (dharma) is the most important purpose of his incarnation. At least that is what He says; but all the Azhwars and Acharyas feel that He comes here to be with us for He cannot stay away from us. We are dearer to Him than the infinite numbers of divine immortals in the eternal world.

On knowing that Krishna would not use a weapon or fight the war, Bhishma vows that he would compel Him to wield a weapon. Krishna comes to know of this new oath by Bhishma.

Arjuna was disillusioned at the start of the war and refuses to fight, out of grief that he could not kill his own kith and kin. Krishna then preaches him the knowledge of the Gita and Arjuna starts fighting. However it was nearly 11 days and yet Arjuna was not fighting with integrity against Bhishma who was his grandfather, whom he loved more, though Bhishma was fighting with all his might directing his arrows against Arjuna, wounding him several times. It was then that Krishna had to remind Arjuna that he was not fighting sincerely and that if he continued in his method, Bhishma would wipe out the entire Pandava army. Even after a while there was no change in Arjuna. It was then that Krishna jumps out of the chariot, wielding a wheel, declaring that He would have to kill Bhishma and all of the kaurva army by Himself as Arjuna proves to be a timid and insipid person and unfit to be a kshatriya warrior who was supposed fight with all his might to protect dharma.

Krishna holds up a wheel and advances towards Bhishma who was taking advantage of Arjuna's weakness (kindness). Seeing Krishna holding up the wheel, Bhishma drops out of the chariot, surrenders at the feet of the Lord with tears in his eyes. He asks Krishna to kill him with His own hands. What can be a greater glory and honor than being killed by the supreme Lord Himself? He also asks Krishna if He broke His own pledge in order for Bhishma to uphold his oath—"that he would force Krishna to wield a weapon".

Krishna then explains to Bhishma that it was not important that one is successful in keeping his word, if that meant to harm the whole society. For Krishna, protecting dharma (righteousness) was more important than keeping his word. If He failed in His word by protecting dharma, He would be happy to accept a personal blame for failing to keep his word but would not tolerate the whole population getting ruined due to the reign of the evil rulers. He would rather be a liar than allow His people being harmed by the wicked kauravas. He also explains to

Bhishma that *it was more important to do what was right in accordance with dharma than being supportive to evil rulers in the pretext of honoring ones oath* which was what Bhishma was doing. Krishna demonstrated to Bhishma and others that it was important for dharma to prevail and not His vow. It was their ego that was driving them to protect their oath. In the bargain, they were supporting and allowing the society to rot and evil powers to permeate into all levels which was not the purpose of all the knowledge and devotion some of them like Bhishma possessed.

Que—why did Krishna choose Arjuna to preach Gita? Was he the most deserving?

Ans—Yes, Arjuna was the only one amongst all of the Pandavas & kauravas who was entitled to the knowledge of Gita from the Lord. Sri Pillai Lokacharyar clarifies in his Srivachanabhushanam—

"jitEndriyaril talaivanAi, AstikAgrEsaranAi, 'kEsavasyAtmA' enru krishnanukku dhArakanAy-irukkira arjunanukku . . ."

Arjuna was kind and compassionate to all; even to those who considered him and the Pandavas as their enemies. Most importantly he had conquered his senses; had total control over them. Having complete control over senses was hard even for the sages and rishis. Even the great Viswamitra was found wanting when it came to controlling his senses. He fell for Menaka from the heavens, who was sent to earth to seduce him. Viswamitra who had undertaken to do penance, was attracted to her during his penance. It is understandable if someone falters when intoxicated. But he had his mind and senses totally focused on penance, yet he fell for the attraction of her beauty.

In comparison, Arjuna stands tall, along with a very few, when it comes to controlling senses. Pandavas, having lost the game of gambling the second time, had to spend 12 years in the forest and one year in anonymity to regain their kingdom. Towards the end of the 12th year in the forest, Krishna advised Arjuna to prepare for the war and to acquire the divine astras from Lord Shiva and his heavenly father Indra. Lord Shiva tests Arjuna and was pleased to bestow his divine 'pASupatAstra'. Then, he was invited by Indra to visit him in heaven—Arjuna was born to Pandu and Kunti by the power of Indra. When Arjuna arrived in heaven, seeing Arjuna's lustrous personality, Urvasi was attracted to him.

Urvasi is considered the most beautiful woman of the heaven. Indra, the king of heaven has always been in the habit of spoiling anyone doing penance. The supreme Lord incarnating in Badrikasrama was sitting in divine yoga. Indra mistook him to be in penance for acquiring his throne and sent all of his most beautiful ladies from heaven to distract his penance. Obviously, the Lord could not be distracted. Eventually, having failed in his attempt which had brought him success in all his previous attempts, Indra comes in person to find out the reason for his penance and realizes that it was the supreme Lord. Indra prostrates asking to be forgiven for his low behaviour and stands before the Lord in shame. The Lord then creates a most beautiful woman who comes to life from his thigh (Uru in Sanskrit means 'thigh'). The Lord then asks Indra if he wished for something. Having seen the beauty of Urvasi, he asks the Lord for Urvasi, as he does not have anyone so beautiful in heaven and the Lord mentions to him that she was created for that very purpose.

Arjuna did not waver even for a moment at seeing the most beautiful Urvasi, who had even the Indra falling for her looks. Such was the greatness of Arjuna's control over his senses.

Urvasi expresses her desire to marry Arjuna, which he declines. She tries to trick him by asking for a boon—that she wishes to have a son from him. Arjuna falls at her feet and asks her to accept him as her son. He also talks sense to her that he really was her son as he was the son of Indra. She is his mother as she belongs to Indra and the heavenly world. He could not possibly marry anyone from the heaven. Though she is the most beautiful woman, he can only look at her as his mother. She tried hard to persuade Arjuna but he was so steadfast in his sense control that he could not be tempted despite her heavenly efforts to seduce him. When she realized he was not going to budge, she curses him to become a 'eunuch' for a year and he returns to earth after obtaining divine astras from Indra.

This curse helps him during ajnatavasa (remaining anonymous) as they could not recognize him as Arjuna. He spends the 12 months of ajnatavasa as 'Brihannala' a dance-teacher in the palace of King Virata and so do the other Pandavas and Draupati, spending the year in disguise, in the same palace.

It is rare for one person to have all these qualities. Even great sages and rishis faltered at times, but not Arjuna. Hence he was the most deserving candidate for being the rightful recipient of Gita.

Arjuna was aware of his ability to control his senses, yet even he could not control the mind. When Krishna suggests to him of ways to control and train the mind:

Arjuna asks—6/34—*"chanchalam hi manah Krishna pramAthibalavaddhrudham;*

"Mind is fickle, impetuous, powerful and stubborn; restraint (control) of mind is as difficult as that of the wind"

We can see that Arjuna had not only conquered the senses, but was also truthful and honest in accepting that he who had won over the senses, was unable to rein in his mind, as mind cannot be firmly fixed easily. Controlling the mind is against its fickle nature. This shows that he was not a hypocrite or one who pretends to be what he is not.

And Krishna accepts Arjuna's plight and suggests 6/35—

"asamSayam mahA bAho mano durnigraham chalam;

"No doubt, the mind is fickle and hard to subdue, but by practice and by the exercise of dispassion, it can be brought under control"

Krishna agrees that mind control does not come easy, even if it does; it comes only by continuous practice. However, it is possible only for those who have kept their senses under control. For those who have no sense control, cannot achieve mind control, even with practice and dispassion.

Now you can ask a question—why can't God merely wish the bad elements to disappear from the face of the earth just as He willed this creation into existence merely by a thought? Simply because it would be against the laws of karma that He has set in to work. If He eliminated all the bad people, they would never be able to complete their karma effects. The only way they can fulfill their obligation to their accrued karma is to experience the good or bad effects in so many lives. So, He cannot interfere directly; yet protect those who deserve His help, without interfering with His laws of karma. If I am in trouble due to my past sins, I do not deserve any help from God. If I am a righteous person, a devotee of God, then God would create situations to help me within the karmic framework. Or, if the whole society is in trouble and cannot follow righteous life due to some evil rulers preventing them, He would then have to incarnate to protect the righteous.

God would not use His divine powers on His children to kill them. Krishna killed mainly three persons—Kamsa, Sisupala and Dantavakra, all of whom were born for a reason (karana janma). He also graced several demons as a child when Kamsa sent them to have Him killed. He did not actively participate in the war between Pandavas and Kauravas nor kill any one during the war, but guided them to fight protecting dharma. Those who did, had His support and those who did not, perished.

God gives everyone maximum chance to redeem

Most of the bad characters we know during God's incarnations, have taken birth as bad people for a reason and not due to karma. Hiranyaksha/hiranya kashipu, ravana/kumbhakarna and shishipala / dantavakra—and many others associated with God during His incarnations are considered "kAraNa janma".

Krishna did not kill Sisupala till he completed 100 sins. He gives everyone maximum opportunity to change, with a hope that one might change eventually, even at the last minute. Rama offered a hand of friendship to Ravana even when Ravana was defeated in their first days fight. Rama asks him to accept his offer of friendship to end the fight and to return Sita. He did not ask Ravana to surrender to Him; He treated Him as an equal. Yet Ravana did not choose to change and hence he opted for his own end.

Chapter Fifteen

True nature of souls

Ans—It was Sri Azhwan who established beyond doubt that seshatvam is the prime nature of the soul.

> **seshatvam**—soul's first and foremost nature is subservience to the Lord. Precisely, subservience defines our natural relationship with the Lord as our Father and we, as His children.
> **jnatrutvam**—is the knowledge that we are the pure souls and not the bodies, and an eternal undivided part of the Lord, who dwells in the souls. Atma is naturally knowledgeable, intelligent, and conscious, as endowed by the indwelling Lord.

As you can see, we have come away from both of our prime natures and qualities due to attachment to our material bodies and this world.

Azhwar advises in Thiruvaimozhi—3-3-1
> "*ozhivil kAlamellAm udanAi manni,*
> *vazhuvilA adimai seyya vEndum nAm*"

"We must engage in eternal kainkaryam (subservience)—serving the Lord in ways it pleases Him, without pause". Here, it is important to know that we derive infinite joy when in service to the Lord. Not that God needs to be served or He is lacking or wanting something. He does not need anything from anyone.

He is the giver to all and He is the source of everything. He is complete in all respects, with infinite glorious divine virtues. Yet He has given us this inherent virtue of serving Him, for our own benefit. Seshatvam defines our imperishable relationship with Him.

We love, adore and admire anything that is beautiful; we naturally like to serve anyone special, especially if they possess great skills and attributes. We become followers of all those who excel in their respective fields—a Roger Federer, a Pete Sampras, for their artistry in tennis; a Broadman, a Viv Richards or a Sachin who give us joy playing cricket, a movie star who can perform, a singer, or a Messi for his football skills. In fact we are willing to pay from our precious earnings to watch them play; we are willing to contribute materially and even serve them, to please them, because we are able to recognize some specialty in them and we value their qualities, admire everything they do, and we aspire to emulate them.

But none of these greats would even know us personally, nor reciprocate the affection we show for them. They just remain recipients of our service and appreciation, as they think they deserve all the accolades because they are better than the rest.

The extra special talents and skills that we see in humans which we adore are insignificant and temporary in nature. Federer has to retire soon as he gets old and others take his place as best tennis players and our loyalty would keep changing as well from one to the next. But the Lord is supreme in everything, eternally. His unparalleled love and care for us is not comparable to anything we have perceived. He would reciprocate infinite times more than us. *What's more, He grants us many of His supreme attributes, enabling us to feel similar to Him.*

When we realize and recognize the super divine qualities of our Lord, we naturally fall in love with Him; naturally because we are a natural part of Him. In order to love someone, we need two reasons. One, we have to know, of the special abilities in them; and two, when we realize that we are related to them as well. When we realize even a minuscule of Lord's magnificent qualities, not comparable to anything we have known, it would be hard for us not to fall in love with Him. If it is natural for us to admire and be in a—ever-willing-to-do-anything—state of mind for humans, the same would be manifold when we recognize God's supreme nature. And there is a big difference between the people we adore and the supreme Lord. The people we hold in awe are not even related to us nor do they know us personally, nor do they love us for who we are; it is one sided. But the supreme Lord is directly related to us. He is our Father, and we belong to Him. It is mutual; and hence it is very natural for us to be attracted to God. And He loves us more than we can imagine.

Here, we are reminded of the episode Sri Ramanuja had with Pillai urangavilli dasar.

DhanurdAsa (Pillai urangAvilli dAsar) and wife ponnAcchiyAr lived in Srirangam. Ponnacchiyar was a beautiful lady and even more beautiful were her eyes.

Dasar was a great admirer of his wife's beauty. He was so passionate about the beauty of her eyes, that he thought she had the most beautiful eyes ever. He was not shy of openly expressing his admiration of her beauty to the world. He would protect her from the rays of the sun, whenever she came out in the open, by holding his top robe over her head or if the ground was too hot, he would lay the fabric on ground for her to walk on. He did not care if anyone thought differently about openly exhibiting his devotion for his wife.

Sri Ramanuja happened to see them during the Chitra Festival of Lord Namberumal. It is to be noted that Dasar was not a brahmana by birth. Ramanuja calls out to Dasar and asks him if what he was doing so openly wasn't a bit too excessive and if he was not ashamed to behave in such a manner out in the open. Dasar responds promptly suggesting, 'what was there to be ashamed of? After all, his wife was the most beautiful person and especially she had the most beautiful eyes and what was wrong in adoring and protecting something so precious, which had no equal'. Ramanuja realizes his potential to becoming a great devotee of the Lord, for someone, who can admire true beauty, cannot miss to see the divine beauty of the Lord, whose beauty cannot be equated with anything we have known or seen. Ramanuja does not try preaching him anything philosophical, that this was a material, perishable body and all this beauty would only last for a few years and soon enough we have to give up this body and such. Instead he asks him "what if I showed you more beautiful eyes and greater beauty?" Dasar challenges that there could not be anything more beautiful and if there was, he would surrender to such a beauty.

Ramanuja then takes Dasar into the temple and prays to the Lord Ranganatha (Peria Perumal) to reveal His divine beautiful form to Dasar, who had the potential to be a true srivaishnava. And indeed, Dasar experiences the divine beauty of the Lord and was lost in the beauty he had never imagined existed. From that moment, he was an ardent disciple of Sri Ramanuja and spends rest of his life in subservience to Ramanuja, the Lord and other devotees.

Ramanuja's affection for Dasar was beyond compare that he would lean on Mudaliyandan, his nephew, before going for his bath; and on Dasar after bath.

There is no one equal to Sri Mudaliyandan either, when it comes to subservience to Ramanuja, his acharya. He had the added grace that he was also related to Ramanuja as his nephew. Sri

Mudaliyandan, who is also known as 'Dasarathi, is none other than Lord Rama.

The nature of the soul is often mistaken for slavery when it is said that we have to serve God or the Acharya. This is a joyful subservience and a voluntary choice. Acharyas are like our mothers who show us our father and lead us to him. Acharya and God do not expect service from us, but it is in our nature to want to serve them. What we can do for them is negligible when compared to what they do for us. *It is essential to know that a soul's subservience to God, who is his eternal Father, is natural and voluntary. It is not forced.*

The first nature of water is fluidity. Similarly, seshatvam is to practice our true nature which is subservience to our Lord. Jnatruvatvam is the state of knowing our nature; it does not translate our knowledge into practice automatically; and such knowledge is of no use.

Many contend that it was important to know first in order to practice. This can be true for all other things we learn in life from childhood that are not natural to us. This rule is not applicable to what is natural to us. Our nature can be practiced without knowing. For instance, soon as a baby is born it cries naturally, no one teaches it how to cry or what to cry for. The same is true for the new born baby feeding on mother's milk. We cannot apply this rule to other skills which can be acquired only by learning and knowing first. If I want to ride a cycle, I must learn first before riding, if I want to drive a car, I must learn and know driving techniques before actually driving.

Birds don't learn the art of flying; they just fly, for it is in their nature to fly. When they are able to fly, the knowledge of flying is inbuilt. Fish don't have to learn swimming technology to swim; to swim is in their nature, while they swim, the knowledge is an integral part of what they do.

Serving God the way He likes is important than serving Him the way we like

Azhagiya manavala perumal nayanar categorically declares in his 'acharya hrudayam' thus—"*sEshatva bhoktrutvangaL pol-annE pAratantrya bhogyataigaL*"—he states the important aspect of being in subservience to God; that it is essential to serve Him in a way He likes than serving Him in a way we like. Here Sri Nayanar quotes Bharata, Rama's brother as the epitome of subservience, for Bharata remained in Ayodhya as wished by Rama, taking care of the kingdom, though he wished to accompany Rama to the forest; unlike Lakshmana who served Rama in the forest which was what he liked.

Greater than serving the Lord is serving the 'bhagavatas' (His devotees), starting with one's own Acharya, which pleases the Lord more. In reality the only service we can do for the Lord is daily 'thiruvaradhanam' and 'sevakalam'—chanting the divine verses of the Azhwars and Acharyas in the temples and homes. Sri Andal in her Thiruppavai makes it easy for us to understand how we can serve God—"*tUyomAi vandu nAm*, *tUmalar tUvitozhudu, vAyinAl pAdi, manttinAl sindittu,*"—here purity is defined by our unconditional devotion for the Lord, without seeking anything from Him, expressing our exclusive devotion for Him; being pure of body, mind and heart, having no other thoughts or worldly desires. True worship is—thinking of His divine virtues, chanting His glories and adorning Him with flowers. We have to employ all the three modes we possess— thought (mind), speech (expression) and hand (deed) in His service. This is what is referred to as "tri-karanangal" we use in every aspect of functioning. When we bring all the three modes in focus in worshipping the Lord, is in itself 'bhakti' or devotion.

When we 'speak our mind and do what we say', it is the first step to acquiring other virtues. One who speaks his mind would always speak the truth, he would not be a hypocrite, and one who does what he says, is a person of great integrity and honour. These are basic traits of a good human being. Such a person would also be healthy, happy and would never be perturbed by events and consequences.

Much greater benefit of speaking our mind and doing what we say, would keep the mind pure and peaceful. Such a person would be ever relaxed and fearless. He would be able to sleep well at nights. More than any of these, he would slow down the ageing process of his body due to less wear and tear impacted on the body by a turbulent mind, thus increasing his longevity. There can be so many benefits with just being able to speak what's in our mind and doing what we say. And such a person would not have to contemplate as to what to say to each person, for he would simply speak the truth. Most of us prepare before speaking, we pre-decide and line up our thoughts and are always pre-occupied mentally. We end up saying different things to different people on the same issue.

Stress, anxiety, tension, anguish and distress have become common mind related problems for most of us. We have more psyche related—psychiatrists and psycho analysts today than ever before. Eventually the psyche experts would tell us that we need to learn to relax; free our mind from unwanted thoughts. We fill our minds with so much of unwanted information and data that many of us want to forget, but would struggle to rid us of those thoughts.

To forget unwanted thoughts, we cultivate addictions such as alcohol etc. It is indeed quite contrary to what knowledge is supposed to mean. Knowledge brings us joy and not stress.

Many of us have a problem when we see people around us prospering, doing well or sometimes as a coincidence, if one of them has made it big due to our contribution. If such a thing happens, we should feel good that we have been instrumental in their success. We should feel happier when we see all the people around us doing well. When others are more successful, it does not take away anything from us. If my neighbour builds a bigger house next to ours, it would enhance the value of our house as well for being his neighbour. We should truly wish for everyone to be well off—healthy, happy and prosperous and that is the ultimate prayer and worship to the Lord, which God would also be happy about. True devotees would always wish for the well being of all the people "lokAh samastah sukhino bhavantu"

Que—why is God established in the temples? If He is everywhere, why go to temples to offer prayers?

Ans—*As God is everywhere, He is also in the Temples.* We cannot perceive God in nothingness, though He is present even in nothingness. The idols of God are established in the temples and God is invoked in the prescribed Vedic chanting and He empowers the idols with His divinity which is the reason why we feel that supreme energy in the temples. An ambience is formed for devotees to connect their inner mind with the Lord and communicate with God in the idols. Many people even converse with God within their own minds. Rama and Krishna also incarnated on earth in the most beautiful human form. We could give Him any form but it is important to give a form we can relate to, so that we can feel His presence.

While the temples were built to nurture devotion, they also established a social order and benefited scores of sculptors, scholars, artists, architects and vendors, who were involved in the process of temple building. Building a temple today in the scale that was done by the kings is beyond our capabilities. Temples are a social institution in themselves. A lot of support structure and layer of people skilled in their respective fields were established in the functioning of the temple. Devotees visiting temples offer money, food, clothing, food grains etc based on their capacity. Their contribution would sustain the team of people who would totally devote themselves for the functioning of the temple. There is a system of timely prayers—daily, weekly, fortnightly, monthly and yearly program calendars for events to be conducted in temples. Scores of traders, vendors, and businesses would develop around the temple complex generating employment in the sidelines.

The feel good factor is undeniable when we go to the temple and take a glimpse at the deity. When the temple collects more resources than it needs for the daily functioning, it would employ such resources in the sustenance of the society, it would be used for the benefit of all the classes of people. They would set up free health care centers, free schools and colleges. They would also organize spiritual discourses, cultural events such as music and dance programs etc. The deities would be taken out in procession in the streets around the temple so that those who cannot visit the temple due to old age or physical disability could also see their God.

Every time people go to the temple, *they are developing a relationship with the Lord which is natural.* This they would understand after frequent visits to the temple, listening to the spiritual lectures, and by being associated with pious devotees.

We can also establish God privately in our homes and conduct all the events, but outsiders will have no access to such private facilities. It would be restricted to the families, their close relatives and friends. Hence there was need for setting up temples to promote togetherness in diversity and establish the high values based on which the entire society can co-exist peacefully, respectfully. Every devotee visiting the temple wants to give; everyone is filled with kindness and compassion. There would be no negative thoughts, no hate and enmity, no selfish desires and wants. Everyone would be deeply engrossed in the thought of Lord filling their hearts and minds, thus becoming pure of mind.

Temples were built in this Yuga (kali yuga). Especially, the Vaishnava temples were built by many kings, between 600 and 1200 AD. Ramanuja established an order in the functioning of the temples. It is open for all classes of people in the society. The beauty is that there is no caste system in the Vaishnava tradition, not even the gender difference as everyone is known as a Soul and a child of that supreme God.

Que—why should we not worship other gods?

Ans—It is a wrong question to ask; there is no such thing as we should not worship the other gods. Even the Vedas prescribe worship of other gods based on our state. When God does not stop us from doing what we wish, what's stopping us from worshipping any god? We have total freedom to create our own god if we feel comfortable that way. Devotion helps in developing righteousness and compassion for others.

However, there is difference between the supreme Lord and the other gods and goddesses. Only a CEO or chairman is the supreme authority in a company and all others are not. It does not mean we don't interact with the others based on our needs. When we deal with the CEO, who can fulfill all our needs, we don't have to deal with the others in the company. When we deal with the others, CEO does not get involved.

We even worship mahatmas, divine souls, and sages, acharyas who are better than us by virtue of their deeds, who guide us in the path of devotion.

Not worshipping the other gods should not be viewed as narrow mindedness either.

If you ask me why I call only my father the father, the answer is 'I am born to him', and I know who my father is by the grace of my mother. And no one else can be my father. All others can only be father-like figures. I also worship my mother, for showing me my father. In the same way, we seek the supreme God because He is our eternal Father and origin, as revealed by the saints, rishis, azhwars, acharyas, gurus, and our own elders and forefathers; who are like our mother in guiding us to the supreme Lord. If the whole population has one father, all the others would be children. I love and respect all the children of my father but I have only one father. I am related to all the children of my father, through my father.

Similarly, we can be devoted to the supreme God when we realize the nature of our relationship with Him. At the same time we show reverence and great respect for all the other gods for who they are. But we have nothing to seek from them. Those who are devoted to other divinities (gods) have probably not realized their relationship with the supreme Lord, once they do, they too would be devotees of the supreme Lord.

And the supreme God is seeking us much more than we seek Him. It is mutual. He needs you because you are His child; you seek His grace because He is your Father. *We do not have this relationship with anyone else other than the supreme God. The only other two people that stand equal to the supreme Lord are the divine Mother, who is the Chief of all souls, and the Acharya who selflessly strives in leading the Atma to attaining the Lord.*

Just to explain this a bit more—there are so many gods and goddesses; all are divine. For instance, Lord Shiva is the son of Brahma the creator. Many of us worship for various reasons. Most of us seek something or the other from every god or goddess we worship.

A devotee of the supreme God worships Lord Hanuman, who is said to be the amsavatara (part incarnation) of Lord Shiva. The difference is Hanuman, though Lord Shiva's incarnation, is a devotee of Rama, who is the Supreme God. Claiming to be independent is against the nature of the soul for it is the supreme Lord who empowers the soul, dwelling inside every atma. Vedas may seem to suggest that every god is the Paramatman. But the inherent message is that the Paramatman is the antar-atma in every god, and every god is an individual soul and not the Paramatman. A devotee of supreme God would worship other devotees, saints, swamys, acharyas, priests and gods if they guide the devotee to the supreme God. A devotee of supreme God would not worship other persons, gods and goddesses who claim independence and lead him away from the supreme God, simple. *Independence is detrimental to realizing our true nature and relationship with the supreme Lord.*

When we worship the supreme Lord, it includes all the gods and goddesses in the universe, for He dwells in all of them and also is the origin for them. It is like watering a plant. We don't need to water every leaf. When we water at the roots, it reaches every part of the plant.

Thirumazhisai Azhwar

The story of Thirumazhisai Azhwar would help us become open minded thinkers. This Azhwar was a devotee of a god who is not the Paramatma. He was eventually guided by Peyazhwar into realizing his goal. Peyazhwar found true potential in Thirumazhisai azhwar, who was seeking the infinite from the finite. Peyazhwar planted a Tulasi sapling upside down (the roots on top); he was then lifting water from a well in a pot that was full of holes. Each time he lifted up the pot, he would have no water in the pot due to the holes. He kept on doing this till Thirumazhisai azhwar couldn't watch this anymore; he came up to Peyazhwar and said "peyaro neer" (are you a ghost or spirit without the brains, are you not human). For only a brainless, senseless person would try to water a sapling planted upside down, that too with a pot having so many holes. Peyazhwar seizes this moment to reveal to him that he might even succeed in his effort to growing the plant but Thirumazhisai azhwar had no chance of attaining his goal. He explains to him that if he is seeking to attain his eternal Father in the parama padam, and salvation from this world without rebirth, he would have to be devoted to the supreme Lord for no one else other than the supreme Lord was in a position to grant him what he sought.

Thirumazhisai azhwar realizes the truth and becomes devoted to the Supreme Lord.

This azhwar is a nitya suri who incarnated here to guide us, if we are lost in pursuing a wrong course, in our attempt to attaining our goal of immortality.

Chapter Sixteen

—◦◦◦—

Worship supreme God seeking Him alone.

If I want a good life in this world, my good karma can take care of that. I don't need to go to anyone seeking benefits for my karma; it would come to me automatically. I don't have to worship even the supreme God for benefits of karma, as He does not interfere with my actions or consequences in this world. If I am happy with this state of existence, I can fend for myself.

Sri Pillai Lokacharya affirms thus in mumukshuppadi 175, 176—

"Kainkaryam tAn nityam';
"nityamAga prArtittE peravEndum"

"Subservience to the Lord is our eternal nature owing to our relationship with Him; and subservience has to be sought by prayer, seeking to be in His service, eternally".

We can attain and achieve every other glory in this world, but being in service to the Lord is the greatest state there can be in either of the worlds.

Once in a while, we may be fooled to believe that things have gone well due to God's involvement. But reality is that whatever happened did so due to our karma. God involves only with true devotees.

God cannot be arbitrary in choosing devotees or accepting them. It is purely by entitlement and that entitlement is true love for

Him, unconditional, undivided devotion for Him. *Unconditional devotion signifies that we seek nothing else from Him, other than Himself, to be in eternal subservience to Him, for His pleasure.* And undivided devotion signifies that our subservience is to Him alone and none else. Soon as we strive fulfilling the two conditions, we can feel the difference within us.

Que—who is the Paramatma? Does He have any specific identity?

Ans—*Taittiryopanishad*—Bhriguvalli—3-6 declares, **"anando brahmeti vyajanat:** "Brahman is bliss. "

Brihadaranyaka Upanisad 3. 9. 28, says **"vijnAnam Anandam brahma:** "knowledge/omniscience; bliss is Brahman. "

Upanishads also declare—**"Esha sarvabhUtAntarAtma apahatapApma divyo Eko narAyanah** " "He is the indwelling Self of all living entities. He is free of all sin. He is the divine One, Narayana. "

Brihadaranyaka Upanishad 3-7-19 declares—

> **"yah sarvEshu bhUtEshu tishtan**
> **sarvEbhyo bhutEbhyo'ntaro . . ."**

"He who dwells in all beings, who is within them; whom all these beings do not know; for whom all these beings are bodies, who empowers all beings from within, He is your atman, the inner ruler.

Vedanta-sutra 1-1—2. defines Brahman as **"janmAdy-asya-yathah"**, that from which everything originates.

Isavasyopanishad 5 states, "**tad antarasya sarvasya tad u sarvasyAsya bAhyatah**, "that Brahman is within everything and also outside of everything".

Taittiriyopanishad 2-7 vividly states : **raso vai saha**, "He is *rasa*. " **esha hy eva Anandayati**, "this verily bestows bliss. If *rasa* is *ananda*, and Brahman is rasa, then Brahman is the nature of bliss.

Taittiriyopanishad 3-1 says "**yato vA imAni bhUtAni jAyantE . . .**"— "*That from which all these beings are born, that by which they live and that unto which they enter when they depart this world; seek to perceive that, That is Brahman*".

This is a scientific phenomenon. All matter would naturally return to their original state. The universe of sentient (individual souls) and non-sentients (matter) originated from the supreme Lord of the nature of 'divine bliss'. The souls being sentient would naturally seek to attain that bliss alone. The

non sentient cannot experience bliss and hence it is formed for the experience and enjoyment of the sentient souls.

Chandogya Upanisad declares: "**esha mA atma antar-hrdaye**" He is the Self in me within the heart.

Svetasvatara Upanisad 3—17 & 18 explicitly declares: "**sarvasya prabhum IsAnam; vaSI sarvasya lokasya sthAvarasya charasya cha**": "Brahman is the Lord and ruler; He is the controller of all the mobile and immobile entities in the world."

Svetasvataropanishad 3-9 confirms—
      "**yasmAt param nAparamasti kinchit . . .**"

"all this is fully pervaded by that Purusha (paramatma), to whom there is no second entity more celebrated than Him; compared with whom there is no subtler or greater entity, one who stands in the eternal abode"

Sri Nammazhwar confirms vividly in his Thiruvaimozhi—4-10-1
"onnum tEvum ulagum uyirum mattum, yAdumilla anru,
nAnmugan tannodu, dEvarulagoduyir padaittan . . ."

In this expression of confirmed knowledge, Azhwar categorically declares to us the process of how creation happened and who is the Supreme Brahman.

"When there was nothing, no gods, no worlds and beings, along-with Brahma, gods and the celestial beings and their worlds; souls and worlds were caused by the Supreme Lord, who as 'AdippirAn' is standing in ArcharUpam (deity) at ThirukkurugUr for our sake.

Azhwar worries for us that we are wasting precious human life which is hard to get and it is possible only for humans to realize their nature and their relationship with the supreme Lord. Even though He, who is the cause for all the beings and all the worlds, is with us here; we haven't the realization that He alone is our Father and none else.

Prasnopanishad 8—
"visvarUpam hariNam jAtavEdasam parAyaNam . . ."

"the jivatman who is the body of the Lord, who is possessor of knowledge of multi things, who is prANa, the supporter of movable and immovable bodies, who is shining like the sun, arises at the time of creation in hundred forms in different bodies such of men, gods and others from the Paramatman, who has everything else as His body, from whom the Vedas came out, who is the resort for all, who is one non-second light illumining everything, who is radiating heat as gastric fire and who is the Lord Hari.

Mahanarayanopanishad 15
"vEnastatpasyan visvA bhuvanAni vidvAn . . ."

"The omniscient ParamAtman directly perceives all the worlds like the sun, all this universe becomes one, in Him. All this universe becomes united without the differentiation of names and forms, in Him, and also with the differentiation of names and forms, when the universe is formed. That all pervasive Lord is in all entities sentient and non-sentient".

Svetasvataropanishad 6-16
"sa viswakrut viswavidAtmayonihi,
jnah kAlakAlo guNI sarvavidyah"

"He is the all-creator and has gained everything. He is indweller in the souls, He is the omniscient, the ordainer of time, the repository of all auspicious virtues, the promulgator of all kinds of knowledge, master of matter and souls, the one who is perfect with the six qualities such as jnAna, sakti, bala, aiswarya, vIrya, tEja; the one who is the cause of release from samsAra (mortality) and bondage in samsAra.

This sruti confirms that the supreme Lord alone can get us release from this samsara and He is the cause for us to acquire bondage through obtaining bodies in this world based on our choice and karma.

Sri Parasara bhattar says in his ashtasloki—1 *"akArArtho vishNuh jagadudaya-rakshA-praLayakrut"* the syllable 'A' represents the supreme Lord who causes the release, sustenance and dissolution of the worlds"

He is the same God; but functions in 3 different ways—'paramatma, parabrahma, and bhagawan. It is important to know that all three are one and the same God.

➤ He as **paramatma** resides in every soul, noting every soul's karma, giving it the suitable effect as per the laws set by Him. The laws of this universe and karma were set by Him before creation and His power of maya/ prakruti works based on the laws. He does not interfere or influence the soul in any way. He is simply an observer without participation.

➤ as **parabrahman**—nirgun (without defiling qualities), nirakar—(invisible), nirvisesh—(without revealing His auspicious glories). Azhwars say that there is no such thing as nirgun, nirvesesh, nirakar Brahman; in the literal sense, even this state exhibits His omnipotence to remain invisible without revealing Himself and even this is one of His auspicious attributes. As parabrahma, He does not do any activities related to the creation, sustenance and annihilation of this universe. He remains in His essential nature of 'jnanam' and 'anandam'.

➤ He as **Bhagawan**—sagun—with infinite auspicious qualities; sakar—in His divine, most beautiful, magnificent and resplendent form, which cannot be seen by us from this world; savisesh—revealing His divine glorious attributes to His devotees, and nityatmas. He is always present in the eternal world bestowing unending bliss upon the divine nitya suris and muktatmas. (**tad vishnoh paramam padam, sadA pasyanti sUrayaha**). By a mere sankalpa (will alone) He forms, supports and withdraws the souls and worlds. Performs all activities in this state. He can take any form or shape. Upanishad / purushasUktam confirms thus "**ajAyamAnao bahudhAvijAyatE**'—*being of the nature of having no birth, He is born many-wise on account of His divine will*". Whatever form He takes, He remains divine. God's divinity is not comparable to the divinity of other gods like Brahma, Indra etc.

Gita 4-6—*ajopi sannavyayAtmA* . . ."though I am birthless and of immutable nature, though I am the Lord of all beings, yet by employing My own Nature (prakruti) I am born out of My own free will"

He came to earth as Rama and Krishna. He engages with us, trying to go out of His way to please His devotees. In this state, devotees can relate to Him, interact with Him, engage with Him— literally there is no extent or limit to the joy He can bestow on His devotees during incarnations.

The Divine souls from the eternal world, also take birth with Him in this world to enjoy His divine acts. To them there is no joy greater than experiencing God in every possible way and *it is in His Bhagavat swarupam that He gives the ultimate joy of serving Him and sharing His divine bliss with us.*

Que—can we see God?

Ans—No and Yes

God pervades this universe in invisible form so there is no question of seeing God here. We cannot see God because we are in a material body. Our intellect, mind, senses are all non-sentient and acquired from this world. Forget about seeing God, we cannot see even the material objects that are beyond the scope of our vision. We cannot even see bright light, and we close our eyes. All that we see is brightness of the light and not the light itself. We close our eyes looking at the sun from a distance of 90 million miles (144 million kilometers). Imagine seeing the sun from a close distance? We cannot even imagine. The brilliance of God is infinite times more than the sun!! We keep asking this question if we can see God. But we have not seen an 'atma' ever.

God is said to be "koti surya prakashakah". He is infinitely brighter than 10 million suns—here "koti or 10 million" is a mere expression for infinite brightness. Even if He appears before us in His divine form, we do not have the compatible vision to see Him.

brilliance of a million suns

However, God can see us and hear us. *So we don't have to worry about not being able to see Him or hear Him. He will know everything we want to say, every thought we have for Him.* He would respond only if we have reached a state of acceptance by Him.

Yes, we can see God and interact with Him only when He gives us His own divine senses. This is exactly what Krishna does when Arjuna expresses true desire to see Him in His divine cosmic form. Krishna grants him divine sight (***divyam dadAmi*** *tE chakshuhu pasya mE yogamaiswaram . . .*") Lord gave Prahlada His divine senses, Dhruva saw the supreme Lord. In other words, God is the only one who has His senses and capability, not even the other gods and goddesses with their differently divine senses, can see God.

Que—can we know God?

Ans—We cannot know Him on our own. We can know Him when He reveals Himself.

Katopanishad 2-23, mundaka Upanishad 3-2-3—
> *"nAyamAtmA pravachanEna labhyo*
> *na mEdhayA na bahunA srutEna . . ."*

"The supreme God is not attainable either by thinking or by meditation or hearing. *He is attainable by him whom the supreme God chooses and reveals His form to him, when he reaches the state deserving such"*

Isavasyopanishad—4
> *"anEjadEkam manaso javlyo nainad-devA Apnuvan . . ."*

"Paramatman is unmoving. He is the one without an equal, swifter than the mind; the gods have not attained Him who has already reached them. Remaining still He overtakes others that run ahead.

His powers are beyond anyone's comprehension. He is all pervasive and hence unmoving. He is swifter than the mind for mind has limited perceptibility and He is beyond the reach of the mind. Even gods have not attained Him though He is all pervasive, for their knowledge is impeded by the prakruti and their mind and intellect is a product of this prakruti and He is Aprakrutik (divine)

To understand God's infinite capabilities and unending extent—
let us compare Him to the sky, which has no extent. If we want
to reach Him, we cannot, for He has no extent. We can keep
going and going and yet we would not reach Him. Since He is
everywhere, He has reached us at every point, but due to our
limitations we are unable to see this truth, and without this
realization, we and the gods attempt to reach Him by running
around, thinking that we are ahead and would catch up with Him.
Because He has no extent and every extent is bound with in
Him, He cannot be attained on our own. If we realize His infinite
nature, we don't have to run around in trying to reach Him for
He is right there where we started. So there is no need to go in
search of Him as He is right inside us and right outside us on all
sides.

Kenopanishad 2—
   "nAham manye suvEdEti no na vEdEti vEda cha . . ."

"I do not think that "I know Brahman very well" nor do I think "I
do not know", but verily I know. He amongst us who understands
thus—not that I know well, not that I do not know" really knows
Him".

Brahman is not totally unknowable, just that He cannot be known
fully. Knowing thus is knowing Brahman.

Kenopanishad 3
   "yasyAmatam tasya matam matam yasya na vEda saha . . ."

"He knows who does not think of Brahman as limited, He who
thinks of Him as limited does not really know Him, He is unknown
to those who know Him as limited. He is known to those who do
not think of His finiteness.

If Brahman is not knowable at all, there was no point in all the
scriptures trying to reveal to us the essence of knowing God.

Thus confirming Brahman is knowable, but to a limited extent as He is infinite and infinite cannot be fully known.

Mundakopanishad 3-1-8—

> *"na chakchushA gruhyatE nApi vAchA nAnyairdEvaihi*
> *tapasA karmaNA vA . . ."*

"He is not comprehended through eye, or through speech, or through the sense organs or through austerity or karma. By meditating upon that indivisible Paramatman a person becomes purified in mind by the grace of Paramatman; can realize His nature through the knowledge bestowed by Him, assuming vivid perception"

Vedas declare that He is beyond speech or mind and intellect, not only for humans but also for the other gods, as everyone including Brahma are created beings like us—taittiriyopanishad *"yato vAcho nivartantE, aprApya manasA saha"* "speech and mind turn back (fail) without being able to reach Brahman, as Brahman is infinite"

Mundakopanishad 2-2-8—

> *"manomayah prANasarIranEtA pratishtito'nnE*
> *hrudayam sannidhAya . . ."*

"He is capable of being grasped by the pure mind; He is having prANa (life) as his body. He is the Lord of all. He is seated in the body, the result of food. Placing their mind in Him, the wise realize that Brahman which shines out in the form of Bliss and which is free from even the smell of samsara, through meditation of the form of vivid vision"

Paramatman is the cause for the soul to have prana and sarira (air and body); body is developed from food. Focused thinking about Him would give us the realization about Him.

Katopanishad—6-9—
"na sandrushe tishtati rupamasya na chakshusha.
pasyati kaschanainam . . ."

"His form does not stand for perceiving, no one can see Him with his eyes. He is attainable by the mind through devotion and steadfastness. Those who know Him thus, become immortal.

Following verses expound an honest teacher's perception to disciples about knowing God when the disciples seek the knowledge of Brahman.

Kenopanishad 1—3
"na tatra chakshurgacchati na vAggacchati no mano . . ."

"The eyes cannot reach there, nor the speech or the mind. We do not know Brahman fully as such; we are not aware how we can teach Brahman (for Brahman cannot be known by external or internal sense perception)

4—anyadEva tat viditAt atho aviditAt adhi . . .*"*

"That is distinct from what is very well known, and again it is distinct from what is totally unknown. We have learnt thus from the ancient teachers who taught this truth clearly"

This verse explains that Brahman is not the same as what we know based on our understanding nor is He unknown like many things that we do not know. It reveals that He is the only one of His kind, who is distinctly different from everyone or everything else. *He cannot be fully known, nor totally unknown.*

5—*"yadvAchAnabhyuditam yE na vAgabhyudyatE . . ."*

"That which is not illumined by speech but that which illumines speech, know that alone to be Brahman, it is not which is worshipped as fully known".

We are able to speak by the power of the Paramatma and yet that speech can not reveal Him to us.

1-6. *"yanmanasA na manutE yEnAhurmano matam . . ."*

"That which is not known by the mind but that by which the mind is known, know that alone as Brahman.

1—7. *yacchakshushA na pasyati yEna chakshUmshi pasyati* . . . .

That which is not seen by the eye, but that by which the eyes see, yet eyes cannot know Him as this.

1-8. *yacchrotrENa na shruNoti yEna shrotramidam shrutam* . . .

That which a person does not hear with his ear but that by which the ear hears . . .

1-9. *yatprANEna na prANiti yEna prANaha praNIyate* . . .

That which is not smelt by the nose but that by which the nose can smell . . .

All these verses above, confirm that it is the Paramatman who is the innerself of all beings, and who enables all our activities. We breathe, move our body, and use our intellect, mind and senses by the power of God dwelling in us. So there is no way these non sentient entities can perceive God.

Kenopanishad 2/1—
     yadi manyasE suvEdEti dabhramEvApi nUnam . . ."

This is a revelation by the teacher to the students—

"If you think that I know Brahman very well, then you know verily very little. The form which you have known Brahman in this world is very little. Similarly, the form of Brahman known among the gods is also very little. Hence, Brahman is still to be understood into by you.

This confirms that we know very little of the supreme God in any form. Though He pervades everywhere, we can never know fully about Him, *but we must continuously inquire about Him for we can never exhaust knowing Him.*

However, more importantly, God knows each one of us, individually. He can hear us and know our thoughts. We can communicate with Him, though it is a one way communiqué.

We should be encouraged from this verse which confirms that God can be known—Svetasvataropanishad 3-8—

> **"vEdAhamEtam purusham mahAntam**
> **AdityavarNam tamasah parastAt, ...**

"I know this great Purusha, who is of the brilliance of the sun and who is beyond matter. Knowing Him alone is the way to transcend death. For attaining that state there is no other way".

There is only one supreme God, we call Him different names.

Que—why should we consider Narayana and His incarnations—Rama and Krishna as supreme God?

Mahanarayanopanishad Verse 92—
> **"patim visvasyAtmEsvaragm sAsvatagm**
> **sivamachyutam . . ."**

"Narayana is the master of the universe; This Paramatman is the ruler of Himself. He is eternally auspicious and unchanging. This Narayana is the highest to be known. He is the innerself of all. He is the supreme goal for attainment."

Ans—Taittiriyopanishad—Anandavalli/anandamayavidya— expounds thus—

"*brahma vidApnoti param. TadEshAbhyuktA.*
Satyam jnAnam anantam brahma . . . ,

"The knower of Brahman attains the highest state. Brahman is true, conscious and infinite. He who knows Brahman residing in the cave of the heart of all beings, enjoys in the supreme abode, all the auspicious qualities of the Brahman along with the all-knowing Brahman"

The exclusive nature of supreme Brahman which is the cause of origination of this universe is expressed by the passage "satyam, jnanam, anantam brahma"

'Satyam' declares that Brahman possesses non-conditioned existence and is absolute. In this, non sentient matter that goes through changes and the sentient souls associated with the non-sentient are eliminated as both sentient souls and non sentient matter have conditioned existence.

'Jnanam' signifies eternally consistent consciousness without contraction. In this, the liberated souls, whose knowledge was once contracted, are eliminated. Does jnanam mean that Brahman is consciousness or having consciousness as an attribute? Jnanam signifies both, just as Brahman signifies greatness by nature, as also greatness by attributes. The supreme Brahman is therefore, known to be also of the nature of consciousness.

'Anantam' denotes the nature of being without limitation of place, time or substance. His infiniteness applies to both nature and attributes. Anantam signifies that it is not limited spatially, temporally or with reference to substance. Brahman is free from all the limitations such as 'desha parichcheda' (this is here and not elsewhere), 'kala parichcheda' (this is now and not any other time) and 'vastu parichcheda' (this is not this). Brahman is without any limitation, related to substance. This non-limited nature in respect of substances would mean infinite auspicious qualities by which it has no equal or a superior and Brahman is the absolute in all respects.

Satyam, jnanam, anantam—explains the term 'brahman' that which is dwelling in the heart, to signify 'vit'. The muktatmas have desire for nothing other than the subservience, experiencing auspicious qualities of the Paramatman due to dispassion to all other objects. The supreme Brahman is distinct from the nitya suris and muktatmas. He is the only one who is with infinite natural independent knowledge of all things, at all times.

Munkakopanishad 2-2-2—
"yadarchimadyadaNabhyo'Nu cha yasmimllokA
nihitA lokinascha . . ."

"That which is resplendent, which is subtler than the subtle and that on which are fixed all the worlds and the beings living in them, is this immutable Brahman. He alone is the self of prANa (life in all beings). He alone is the speech and the mind. This is the indestructible. It is immortal. Know that it is to be the known by the mind.

Vedas and all the scriptures have identified the supreme God based on His infinite capabilities. The root of the name 'narAyaNa' signifies—**'narANAm ayanah yasya saha'** *He who is in everything and everyone; and has everything and everyone in Him*—one who upholds and supports all that is there in the universe, including all the beings, gods, goddesses, while He is not supported by anyone else or anything else. If anyone possesses these capabilities, He is the supreme God. However, there can be only one of Him, without a second. The name 'Narayana' signifies this essence. 'Nara' signifies everything and everyone other than the supreme God and 'ayana' signifies the supreme God. Obviously there can be no competition to this position. One, who is not, would know that he is not the supreme God as all others except the supreme God are souls in different divine bodies or mortal bodies.

The Upanishads also confirm *"Ekohavai narAyaNa Aslt . . ."*— Narayana alone existed (prior to the creation or after the worlds merged into Him), neither Brahma nor Shiva, nor gods, nor the stars nor this earth, none of this creation existed.

"narayana param brahma tattvam narayanah parah . . ."

"Narayana is the Supreme Brahman. Narayana is the Supreme Reality. Narayana is the Supreme Light. Narayana is the Supreme Self"

Now you can ask how any other god is not the supreme God and why only Narayana is acclaimed as the supreme God. We may think that the name or word 'Narayana' is merely an expression and if we call another god as Narayana, that god would become the supreme God? I cannot name myself Narayana and think that I can become the supreme God. It is not merely a meaning of the name that can qualify anyone to be Him. His unlimited powers and capabilities are associated with Him. No one and nothing can exist or function without Him and He does not depend on anyone or anything for His existence and functioning. He alone is Absolute.

It is also substantiated in Gita as to why only the supreme God is supreme and no one else can take His place merely by changing their name; for they do not possess the infinite powers of the supreme Lord. Importantly, every other god is a created being and only supreme God is unborn, and the cause for all the gods, beings and worlds.

Gita—9/6—
> *"yathAkAsasthito nityam vAyuhsarvatrago mahAn,*

"Just as the powerful element air moving everywhere remain in the ether (sky), so too all beings abide in Me".

Gita 7/7—
> *"mattah parataram nAnyat kinchidasti dhananjaya,*

"**There is nothing higher than Myself**; all this is strung on me (all of the creation and beings) like rows of gems on a thread"

The Lord is absolutely superior to everyone in two ways—
  ➢ He is the cause of both the Prakrutis (chit and achit or Souls and matter) and He is also the controller.
  ➢ He is supreme to all in another sense as well—as the possessor of knowledge, power, strength, infinite auspicious virtues and omnipotence eternally. There is no entity other than the supreme Lord with such attributes of equal or superior nature.

Svetasvataropanishad 6-11—
> *"eko dEvah, sarvabhUtEshu gUdhah,*

"**The one God** who is hidden in all beings, who is all pervading, who is the innerself of all the souls, who is aware of all karmas, who resides in everyone, who is the witness and creator of all this universe *but yet who is detached, is free from defiling qualities*"

Gajendra

There is a story about the true identity of the supreme God. Gajendra the elephant—was king Indradyumna in his previous life; he was a noble king and a great devotee of the Lord Vishnu, but due to negligence in attending to rishi Agastya, became the victim of a curse by the rishi to be born as an elephant. Despite being a noble king and a devotee he had traces of 'ahankara' and arrogance. On apologizing and praying to be pardoned, the rishi mentions that he would be saved by the supreme Lord, but after suffering and realizing that the 'ego' is to be renounced and the 'self' surrendered to the Lord, and only such a state would be devoid of any ahamkara/arrogance.

The king elephant lived with his herd in the mountains of Trikuta. He had developed a practice of offering lotus flower from the lake to the Lord owing to the effect of his devotion from last birth. One day, when Gajendra walks into the lake, a gigantic crocodile grabs his leg and starts pulling him into the water. Elephant being a strong animal, tries his best to wriggle off the crocodile's hold. The other elephants tried helping him as well but could not match the strength of the crocodile which was much stronger being in water, which was its natural habitat. After a long struggle, the crocodile starts gaining strength and the elephant feels drained of strength; realizing it was losing out to the crocodile, the elephant thinks of the supreme God—He calls out to be rescued by the One who is the absolute cause for all the worlds, gods and beings, who has no cause for Himself. (he calls out for 'akhila jagatkaranaya', 'nishkaranaya', Adi moolamE).

Thirumangai azhwar in his 'siriya thirumadal' expresses divinely

"nArAyaNA O maNivaNNA nAgaNayAi, vArAy ennAridarai nIkkAi . . ." describes how the Elephant cries out for the supreme Lord's help and how the Lord relieves him from the crocodile"

Many gods including the creator Brahma hear the elephant's call but do not respond as they all realized that he was not addressing them, for they did not possess the attributes Gajendra mentioned. It was Narayana who comes to the rescue of the elephant. Both the crocodile and Gajendra the elephant get relieved of their curse due to which they were born.

The crocodile in its previous birth was a gandharva king. Sage Devala visits him. When both of them were taking bath in the river, the king pulled the sage's leg while the sage was offering prayers. The enraged sage cursed the king to become a crocodile in his next birth. The repentant king asked to be forgiven. The Sage proclaims that he cannot reverse the curse; however he would be liberated when the Lord graces him by ending his life as crocodile, upon invocation by a holy soul (Gajendra).

Now we should ask why the other gods did not come to rescue Gajendra. Not because they were not capable of saving him from the crocodile. All of these gods, merely by a wish, could have rescued the elephant from the crocodile as they were all divine and powerful.

The fact that Gajendra was seeking to be saved only by the supreme God by His identity—as the one who is the absolute cause for all and the one who has no cause for Himself—only Narayana was the one who possessed those qualities. The supreme God cannot be changed. He cannot become lesser nor can anyone else become Him or greater nor obtain His infinite capabilities.

If you don't want to call the supreme God as Narayana, it is not a problem. You can call him by any name, but that does not change His capabilities. He is the only supreme God. No one else named narayana can become the supreme Lord, because they would not possess His infinite powers.

It is not much different than Bill Gates being the richest man. He is considered the richest because of the wealth he owns and not because his name is Bill Gates. You can change his name to something else, but he would still remain the richest. Or by changing my name to Bill Gates I do not qualify for being the richest. Here we are comparing with a status that can change. If your worth is more than Bill Gates, you become the richest. But supreme God is unchanging. Hence it is not the name alone that identifies the supreme God but His capabilities and unchanging state that determines His Supremacy. **You can call Him God (like the Christians do), you can call Him Allah (like the Muslims do), you can call Him Narayana, Krishna or Shiva or Brahma, Indra, vayu etc. like the Hindus do or call Him what the Sikhs, Jains, Jews or from any other religion call their God or even think of Him as a non entity; but that does not change who He is. All the religions that have different names for their Gods are indeed talking about the same supreme God and there is only one supreme God. Names are different but He is the same.**

Sri Azhagiyamanavalaperumal nayanar gives an easy method to identify the supreme Lord "**sriyahpatiyAna sarveswaran**" Sriyahpati is the identity of the one who possesses the superior 'para' power and that 'para' power is the Divine Mother Peria Piratti. There is no other god who qualifies this status except Sriman Narayana.

All the Azhwars and Acharyas refer to the Supreme Lord as the one who has Peria Piratti residing in His heart. He acquires the status of being the supreme Lord solely on this ground. If not for Her, He would lose His status of being the supreme Lord.

'**agalagillEn iraiyum ennu, alarmElmangai uraimArba**' as declared by the Azhwar, gives the Lord His true status as the Supreme Brahman by having the Divine Peria Piratti in His Lotus Heart, ever. He and She are inseparable, eternally.

Que—if we can all be happy being who we are, why should we aspire to reaching God.

Ans—in a way yes and yet, no in another way.

Katopanishad 6-14—
"yadA sarvE pramuchyantE kAmA yEsya hrudisritAh,

"When all the desires attached to one's heart of the soul are removed, then mortal becomes immortal and enjoys the supreme Brahman here alone"

If you are a divine soul that has descended here on earth to serve the Lord, of such a person being in this world or being in the eternal world, does not make a difference. God is here for a reason and soon as the reason is achieved, He ends His incarnation.

This is exactly what Thondaradippodi azhwar tells Lord Ranganatha-
"icchuvai tavira yAn poi indira logam Alum,

"other than serving You here, I do not aspire even for the eternal parama padam, ruling over the heavens of Indra and such" and like sri Parashara Bhattar says to Lord Azhagiya Manavala— when Lord mentions to him that He has granted him the eternal world, Bhattar suggests to the Lord that if He does not get this divine transcendental experience in parama padam and if the Lord is not as glorious and beautiful as He is here, Bhattar would jump out of the eternal world and come back here.

There is a big difference between nitya suris taking birth here along with God during His incarnations and souls like us remaining here at the same time. We do not recognize Him as God nor can we understand His supreme nature, when He incarnates in the human form. Only true devotees would be able to recognize His divine nature. Krishna confirms this in Gita 9-11-

"avajAnanti mAm mUdhA mAnushlm tanumaSritam;

"The fools (non devotees) disregard me or cannot recognize Me when I dwell in a human form, not being able to see My higher nature, and know Me as the Supreme Lord of all beings".

I am sure we would have seen Rama and Krishna, yet we are here, still taking birth repeatedly. This is because of our attachment to this world, our bodies and relationships, why we fail to see God when He is in front of us.

We could say that God has an interest in taking incarnations, because we belong to Him and He loves us boundlessly. We and the universe are His property. The ultimate goal for God is our well being, being happy in everything we do. Whether we think of Him as the cause for us and the world or not, He still loves us and wishes well for us. Since He knows more than anyone else that this mortal world is a blend of pain/pleasure, suffering/joy— He has given us the ways to seek Him for attaining His immortal world. He is in a way selfish in taking care of us, as our Father.

Due to our obsession to pleasure and wealth, we look at everyone with suspicion. We assume that the great mahatmas who gave us the sacred scriptures have done so with some motives. We attribute everything to making money or profits. We do not do anything without 'self benefit' and when God or great mahatmas take birth here selflessly for our sake, we do not trust them, nor recognize their superior nature.

We do not impart knowledge without a fee. We attach a cost factor and price to all intelligence we share. Every breakthrough becomes an IPR so that every user would pay a charge. We do not do anything without "what's in it for me" answered. *If everyone thinks the same way, there would be nothing for anyone in the world. On the other hand, if we ask "what we can do for others" it would influence others to think similarly. If everyone thinks of being useful to others, this world would be overflowing with joy and happiness.*

If we are asked to try anything, we need immediate benefits. But the benefit with God will be wholesome and not in piecemeal, and to attain that stage, we have to get their 100%. Imagine, if we have to cross a well, it would have to be 100%. Even at 99.99%, we would fall in the well. If our devotion for God is not 100%, we will keep falling in this world taking repeated births.

For water to turn into ice, it would have to be at 0*C, even a fraction of a degree short, there would be no ice. If we can understand and accept that we have to achieve 100% to accomplish anything in the material world, and we are capable of doing so, it should not be a problem for us to practice total devotion. Devotion is easier than the effort it takes for us to succeed in the material world. Devotion is merely a state of pure mind and heart which does not require any physical effort or strain. What is the test to know if our devotion is total and pure? God's acceptance. How would we know if God has accepted our devotion? We will feel the difference; we will realize His grace with a difference, being able to realize that He is the indwelling power in us. If we do not feel His grace, we have to keep at it till we get there 100%. *It cannot be done merely by a momentary instinct just to test if He exists or not. God will know whether our intentions are sincere or a momentary impulse. If we possess true longing for God, it will work, if not it will have to wait till we reach that stage.*

The nitya suris who take birth here (Krishna's friends—gopalas and gopikas of Brindavan and the populace of Ayodhya during Rama's incarnation), for a good reason; either to experience the Lilas (super-human acts) of God during his incarnations or as Azhwars and Acharyas to bestow upon us the easy ways of devotion to attain the ultimate state of existence with God, which they have themselves experienced. This they do as service to God because when God incarnates, we are unable to perceive His supreme nature due to our ego and ignorance caused by the association with our bodies. We fail to recognize Him and continue to get deeply involved in our own activities.

It is important to understand that divine souls have no karma even when they assume human bodies.

Thiruvarangattamudanar explicitly conveys of Ramanuja's unequalled greatness in his Ramanuja nUtrandAdi—41 thus-

"maNmisai yonigaL torum pirandu,
engaL mAdavanE kaNNura nirkilum kAnagillA,
ulagorgaLellAm aNNal eRamAnusan vandu tonniya
appozhudE, naNNarum jnAnam talaikkondu,
nAraNarkkAyinarE"

"the souls are going through the eternal cycle of birth and death in all sorts of bodies; even as humans they failed to see the Supreme Nature of the Lord when He came to them as Rama and Krishna. However, the same people acquired knowledge and realized their true nature and relationship with the Lord, soon as our Ramanuja incarnated amongst us"

It is said that despite the Lord taking ten incarnations, He was able to convince only 18 people, and even in that not all of the 18 attained His abode. The Pandavas, among the 18, attained heaven. However, when Sri Ramanuja and azhwars and acharyas incarnated, millions attained the eternal world. In glory of the Azhwars and Acharyas taking birth here—Sri Pillai Lokacharyar defines in his Sri-vachana-bhushanam—about the difference between them and us.

Bhakti pAravasyattAle prapannargal azhwargal—Azhwars are the embodiment of infinite devotion. Their state is unchanging and eternal.

JnAnAdhikyattAle prapannargal acharyargal—Acharyas are personification of wholeness of knowledge. The transcendental knowledge of the Acharyas about the devotion of the Azhwars is an eternal state. Their knowledge about the Lord is unparalleled.

AjnAnattAle prapannargal asmadAdigal—souls like us are deep-rooted in ignorance; have become ignorant of our true nature, due to the association with the bodies obtained from this prakruti which is 'mayik' or non-sentient. We seem to be in a spree, feeding our body with non-stop sense gratification, seeking pleasures and perceiving this material world to be the object of our ultimate goal. The word 'prapannargal' defines that we are eternally drowned in ignorance due to our deep attachment to this samsara.

If you take the 7 billion plus humans on earth today, how many do you think are happy even momentarily? Probably only some, that too only relatively. The majority of the population experience a blend of pain, suffering and a little of happy moments. We think we are happy, because *we have no idea of what true happiness is*.

Having obtained a human body, smarter ones would find a way to attain immortality. When we fail to achieve this goal, it is not different than a man who goes through struggle all his life to become rich and after becoming rich, he continues to struggle, which he is not supposed to. We are like a beggar who wins lottery but continues to beg. Who is to be blamed for this but ourselves?

We are all the children of that supreme Lord with the potential to enjoy everything He has. The very purpose of getting a human life is to enable us to attain immortal state, but we continue to miss this opportunity and keep going back to birth/death cycles in millions of different mortal bodies. It could take millions of lives in all sorts of bodies before we get a human body again.

"iruppidam vaigundam vengadam"—*"the place we dwell can become similar to the Lord's Vengadam. Vengadam signifies "the place where there is no sin"*; as mentioned in Ramanuja nutranthadi. We can make this mortal world somewhat similar to the eternal world, vaigundam, if we learn to co-exist caring for each other, in devotion of the Lord.

Chapter Seventeen

Means to devotion

It is said that we develop devotion for the Lord in the following ways.

> Srotavyam (listening to God's glories, and His divine acts)

> Mantavyam (thinking of the Lord)

> Nidhidhyasitavyam (incessantly meditating upon the Lord and His glorious virtues)

> Drashtavyam (being able to feel Him in everyone with the realization that He is the indweller of everything and everyone)

> Kirtitavyam—singing His glories, chanting His divine names and divine psalms of the Azhwars.

When we become true devotees of the Lord, we express our devotion for Him broadly in five ways based on our own state, and He accepts every devotee's expression, unconditionally.

> **shAnta bhAvam**—in this 'pure' state of devotion, we serve the Lord without getting too close to Him. We keep at a distance with the awareness that He is the supreme Lord, being aware of His supreme nature. We look at Him as the protector.

- ➤ **dAsya bhAvam**—we look at Him as the master and seek to serve Him unconditionally. We don't seek anything except to serving Him. Even this state keeps a gap between us and the Lord. We don't allow Him to get close to us for we can only look at Him as our superior.

- ➤ **sakhya bhAvam**—showing our affection like we would to a dear friend, there is a certain level of intimacy that prevails between friends. While being friendly, the devotee is aware of the Lord being the supreme Brahman, still keeping a certain distance from the Lord.

- ➤ **vAtsalya bhAvam**—in this state, we would literally treat the Lord like our child, bestow unconditional affection and love for Him, taking total care of Him. This is the state of Mother Yasoda, who does not relate to Krishna as the supreme Brahman; but merely as a child who was everything to her.

- ➤ **mAdhurya bhAvam**—is considered to be the ultimate devotion. The gopikas and Sri Andal—were considered higher than all other devotees. In this state, there is no space between the Lord and the devotee to the extent that they are never separate from one another, eternally. The Lord remains in their hearts forever. This would be very hard for us to understand, for there are no rules here; there is no differentiation of God or atma here. They treat each other with great liberty without barriers. The Lord becomes overwhelmed by the extent of devotion from such devotees. There is no gender involved; there are no restrictions of any sort. This is also the state when the Lord shares His divine bliss (divya premanandam) with all his devotees and they remain in collective groups and never alone. They don't look at Him as the supreme Lord but the most-dearest person without whom they cannot exist. The Lord goes following such a devotee for He cannot bear their separation. They exist solely based on their inherent relationship with each other. The sole intent of the devotees is to engage in eternal subservience to the Lord and the Lord would be focused on bestowing every devotee with the ultimate bliss.

That apart, it would be surprising to know that even those who looked at God as their adversary also attained immortality, purely owing to their non-stop attachment to Him alone. Kamsa, out of fear, saw Krishna in everyone, and everywhere. He saw Krishna even in the food! He did not lose Krishna from his thoughts even for a moment, though in fear. He was attached to Krishna more than the self, constantly thinking, feeling and hearing about Krishna which is also devotion. He attained the Lord's world after death.

Same with Sisupala, whose detest for Krishna from childhood, transformed into 'virodi bhakti' or 'hostile devotion' for Krishna. Sisupala did not think of anything other than Krishna throughout his life and attained immortality after death. This shows God's unconditional love for us and He finds some pretext or the other to bestow His grace on us, granting us the highest state.

We have to remember that both Kamsa and Sisupala were born for a reason and not of karma and hence their life story is a testimony for us that even if we were bad for some time, our constant attachment to God in everything we do, would elevate us to the entitlement of God's grace. Attachment to God would inculcate detachment to the worldly matters.

Krishna confirms to Uddava that He is extremely fond of His devotees; that He loves feeling the dust from the feet of His devotees falling on Him; and that He is more often controlled by His devotees, though they think of Him as their master. He loves serving His devotees and enjoys their happiness.

God is Himself the means to reaching Him

Que—what are the prescribed ways to reaching God?

Ans—the scriptures, Upanishads and Gita—all of them prescribe three ways to be followed for our well being and to attaining the Lord. It is important to know that all the three are interconnected, one leading to the next. **Karma** *(doing our righteous duties),* **jnana** *(knowledge of the self; our relationship with the Lord)* and **bhakti** *(undivided, unconditional devotion to the Lord)* are the three modes that can elevate us to the state of being recognized by the Lord for granting immortality. Srivaishnava acharyas advocate 'prapatti' or SaraNAgati through an Acharya, as a means for those who are unable to practice 'devotion'. Pillailokacharya declares that if we fail even in our saranagati, acharya's 'nirhetuka krupa' (grace) would enable the Lord to accept us. Prapatti or saranagati does not require any practice. It is a total surrender.

We follow these means to communicate to God of our devotion and *eventually it is only God who is the means to reaching Him. Nothing we do can liberate us from this world or give us salvation or mukti. Liberation or mukti is not a self granted state* by attaining enlightenment or knowledge. Lord is the only '**upaya**' (means) and '**Upeya**' (goal). *He is the one who can take us to Him and He is also the goal we want to reach. This is also exclusive to God where the goal and the means to attaining it, are one and the same*.

Karma marga—We do karma by three modes; mind, speech and action. All our actions qualify for karma. Obviously, we are referring only to doing righteous karma and not sins. Karma can be either for the sake of the self or in devotion to the Lord. When karma is done in devotion to the Lord, it becomes 'kainkaryam' or subservience.

Krishna gives us an easy way to understand doing our duty.

Gita 2-47
"karmaNyEvAdhikAraste mA phalEshu kadAchana,

"To work alone you have the right, and not to the fruits. Do not be impelled by the fruits of work, nor have attachment to inaction".

If we follow this advice, we would be totally focused in doing our duties, without worrying about the results which are any way not in our control. We must realize that the result will be commensurate in accordance with the laws of karma and not as desired by us. We are anguished when we are attached to the cause and result. When we are detached, we would execute our actions much more efficiently, effectively and competently. Abstaining from duty is not an option. There is a danger if one says that 'I do not want to do my duty as I have no desire for any results'. I shall feed my children even if there is no benefit for me personally because it is my duty to take care of my children who are dependent on me for everything.

If we can practice to remain detached in our actions, the fruits will come to us anyways but we will remain unaffected by the results. You can see that even at work; we are much attached to our work. We start calculating the results for everything we do. If I am an employee of a company, I start evaluating the work I do in relation to the emoluments I am paid and would be impelled to doing only so much work in accordance with the benefits I derive. I would think I should not do more than what I get. In the bargain, I stall my own progress in the company by underperforming. Were I not attached to my karma, I would have performed to the best of my abilities and that would have resulted in my growth in the company.

When we say, we should be detached in doing our karma or to the results, it does not mean that we become indifferent in doing our duties or that we couldn't care less what happens. It is merely that we would perform to the best of our abilities without becoming attached to what we do or to the results. Obviously, a job well done will also yield good results. If we become attached to the job, we may ill perform due to our ill conceived notions of how much to perform based on the expected results. Doing social service and giving charity and helping others without expectations are good ways for us to develop the art of doing 'nishkama karma' or desireless action, as we do not expect anything in return, and still do the best we could to helping a cause.

We are engaged in doing karma the moment we acquire a body. *An embodied soul cannot refrain from karma, for there can be no state of inaction.*

Gita 3-4
"na karmaNAmanArambhAn naishkarmyam purusho'SnutE;

"No man experiences freedom from activity by abstaining from works; and no man ever attains success by mere renunciation of works"

Gita 3-5
"na hi kaschit kshaNamapi jAtu nishtatya karmakrut;

"no man can even for a moment, rest without doing karma; for everyone is caused to act, in spite of himself, by the gunAs born of nature"

Gita 3-8
"niyatam kuru karma tvam karma jyAyo hyakarmaNah;

"You must perform your obligatory karma; for action (karma yoga) is superior to non-action (jnana yoga). For a person following non action (jnana yoga) not even the sustenance of the body is possible"

Gita 3-9

"yajnArthAtkarmaNo'nyatra loko'yam karmabandhanah;

"This world is held in the bondage of work (karma), only when work is not performed as sacrifice; you must perform karma to this end, free from attachment".

In the verse above, it is emphasized that if we wish to be insulated from the effects of karma, we must do our duties without attachment. When we are attached, actions bind us to the results. When we do nishkama karma; doing all our actions as a sacrifice, without attachment to either the karma or the fruits of karma, we become relieved of the consequences and still derive the benefits.

With or without our involvement, the key factors are active in the functioning of our body. We cannot consider the self as an agent of fulfilling the vital functions of our body, such as hunger etc. we breathe even without our involvement. Everything works even when we are sleeping, without our active consciousness (due to the presence of God in us)

It is important to follow karma yoga as prescribed by the dharma-Sastra. If we succeed in being righteous, the result is heaven; for karma yoga cannot lead us to God on its own value. However, a karma yogi who performs 'nishkama karma' or 'desireless action', renouncing doership and fruits of action, is also devotion or bhakti.

Let us take for instance, performing a yajna (sacrifice) as prescribed in the scriptures. Doing yajna was considered a sacrifice as the intent of using materials (non living materials such as molten butter etc) would support the sustenance of so many people in the society.

We have to abide by the following 6 conditions in order to complete a yajna:

Karta—one who undertakes the yajna shall be qualified to perform the yajna;

Artha—shall procure all the materials and resources legally;

Desha, kAla—conduct the yajna at a right place and time;

Niyanta—engage authentic scholars to conduct the yajna;

Mantra—chant appropriate mantras, pronounced correctly; and above all

KAraNa—the intention of doing the yajna shall not be for causing harm to anyone.

Though it may sound simple to be a karma yogi, there can be no perfection to our actions. Even if we miss out in any of the six conditions, the yajna would not yield the desired result; instead we would be adding to our karma account. We can apply these conditions to everything we do.

-   Kartha—the person undertaking the work must be entitled to undertake such a task. (if I am not a pilot, I shall not fly an aircraft). He or she shall do only those actions that are within his/her realm and nature, to avoid any harm to self or others.

-   Desha / kala—He shall choose a proper place/time for his undertaking so as not to endanger others. If one chooses to practice target shooting in a crowded place or at a wrong time devoid of proper lighting, it could prove to be dangerous.

- Artha—the materials acquired for performing our duties shall be legally earned and not stolen or procured from ill gotten wealth or acquired by force.

- Niyanta—shall be directed by an authorized and authentic person. If I want to learn medicine, I shall join the course at a certified, authentic school of medicine.

- Mantra—and the procedures to be followed. If we perform the wrong way, the consequences could be disastrous. Imagine doing a chemical experiment or a nuclear experiment. If you follow incorrect procedures, will end up causing colossal damage.

- kAraNa (purpose)—the purpose of the whole exercise should not be with an intent to harm others, it should be for the common good of the self and others.

Even if we manage to do them perfectly, the result is a good life for the self and would attain heaven after death, for greater enjoyment.

Purpose of karma is for the well keeping of the body. It does not still lead us to the ultimate goal of reaching God. It does not exhaust past karma nor would our new karma be without consequences.

One might ask as to what is the difference between kamya karma (action for desire fulfillment) and nishkama karma (desireless action). If we think carefully, there is a big difference. Philanthropy for the purpose of gaining fame and popularity is a good deed but with a self interest to gaining glory. Doing the same thing as service to God; being fully aware that the self is neither the doer nor claiming ownership for the results, would insulate us from the consequences of karma.

Further, we are advocated to remain detached to our karma and results thereof, in three ways in order for karma to be an integral part of knowledge and devotion—

> ➤ kartrutva budhi tyagam—relinquishing the thought 'I am the doer'

> ➤ karma phala tyagam—relinquishing the fruit of action 'this result is because of my doing'

> ➤ Mamata tyagam—giving up the notion of ownership "it is mine, and it belongs to me'.

Jnana marga—the path of knowledge. This is a difficult mode to practice. If we realize that knowledge is part of every action, then we do not have to abstain from action. Even a person who has attained knowledge would still have to maintain his body. He has to work and do his prescribed duties to take care of his body. Knowledge in itself cannot sustain him.

Arjuna asks if doing karma yoga (natural duties) is better or jnana yoga (knowledge of our nature) was better. Krishna confirms that 'karma yoga', is superior. Jnana yoga, without the execution part, would not be of any use. All that is accomplished is attaining awareness.

Gita 18/47—Krishna emphatically confirms that 'doing ones natural duties / karma is the ultimate way to attaining glory.

"srEyAnsvadharmo viguNah, paradharmAtsvanushthitAt,

"Better is one's own natural duty, though not perfected, than the duty of another though well performed. When one does his natural duty, he incurs no stain" 'sva dharma' here points to 'karma yoga' or doing our natural duties and 'para dharma' refers to 'jnana yoga', which is not easily attained. jnana yoga is almost impossible for an embodied soul, for one has to attain total control over senses as a first step, considering one succeeds in that, it is difficult to control the mind, for even the great conqueror of senses, Arjuna, confesses that he could not control his mind.

Above all, even if one succeeds in jnana yoga, what is achieved is the knowledge of the self (atma jnAna) and that would not take us beyond this prakruti. Our goal is reaching the Lord or 'bhagavat prApti' and that is not possible by 'atma-jnAna' alone. A jnana yogi cannot forsake his karma or consequence. He would still have to be born repeatedly to exhaust karma. Jnana marga is not recommended as it will not get us the desired goal. Jnana yoga is only for those who would renounce the need for a body which is not a reality for an embodied soul.

Here Krishna is hinting that it is of no use running away from our duties in search of peace. We are of no use when we shun our duties, in an effort to finding peace for the self. Even if we attain knowledge and find bliss, we are merely selfish and not useful to others. This karmic world functions solely on karma. We can attain bliss in doing our duties righteously that would also benefit others.

Even those who renounce 'samsara' and undertake austerities as a 'sanyasi' becoming a saint, serve the society for the rest of their life. Even a 'tapasvi' who does penance to attain enlightenment, devotes his life for the benefit of the people. Anyone who shirks his duties would be causing self distress instead of attaining bliss.

However, knowledge of our nature and relationship with God, would nurture devotion. Merely knowing about our relationship with the Lord is not devotion. One must act in accordance with this knowledge; practicing subservience to the Lord and even that is karma. Knowledge without devotion has the potential to boost our ego which would be detrimental to our cause. ***Thus, only devotion is the answer if we truly want to reach God.***

Bhakthi marga (devotion)—devotion is the easiest and simplest way. Devotion would have to be 100%, not 99.9%. A simple definition of devotion is "a state of total care and love for the well being of the Lord". A devotee would be conscious of God 24x7 just as he is conscious of the self, all the time. Firstly, devotion should be unconditional, without seeking anything from God. The second condition is that our devotion should be undivided and exclusive. If we mix up devotion with anyone and everyone, it becomes adulterated, it loses purity and sanctity. Devotion for more than one god would end in failure. For the simple reason that there is only one Supreme God and everyone else is not Him. The soul belongs only to the Supreme God and not to others. A devotee can also extend his devotion to another devotee or the guru who guides him to the Lord, but not to others who are not the above two. There are devotees even amongst other gods—such as Hanuman.

Devotion would have karma and jnana as its integral part, for karma inherently has knowledge, leading to 'jnana' of the self and *jnana* would give us the realization that devotion is the essence of all knowledge. A devotee would be a karma yogi, doing his righteous duties renouncing karma; would also be a jnana yogi, pure of mind and heart, devoid of ego.

Krishna advocates the easiest way to be a devotee—to surrender unto Him, doing our righteous duties and He would take care of the rest. Gita 18/66—

"sarva dharmAn parityajya mAmEkam saraNam vraja, aham tvA sarva pApEbhyo mokshayishyAmi mA suchah"

"Relinquishing all dharmas completely, seek Me alone for refuge, I will release you from all sins (punya and papa karma), do not grieve".

Here the Lord affirms that He is the only means to attaining Him.

When we relinquish all karma, we also end up relinquishing all dharma because there is no dharma without karma. When it is said to relinquish all dharma, it is not suggested to refrain from doing our obligatory duties. We shall continue to do everything righteously, without the desire for the results. However, the Lord would bestow upon us all the good things even though we have no desire, for till we are in a functional body, it is imperative to take care of the needs of the self and dependants.

On one hand Krishna says "sarva dharmAn parityajya mAmEkam saraNam vraja", on the other hand the Lord says "aham tvA sarva pApEbhyo mokshayishyAmi". Give up all dharmas, surrender unto Me, I shall relieve you of all sins". There seems to be a contradiction in the statement above. If I have only dharma to give up, why is Krishna saying He would relieve me of all sins? Instead He should be saying "I will relieve you of all dharma and accept you".

As long as there is karma and dharma, we have to be taking repeated births. God can accept us to His eternal world only when we have no karma balance; punya karma or papa karma. We have to relinquish both punya karma (noble karma) and papa karma (sins). We cannot surrender to God being sinners. However, we can surrender even though we have sinned in the past, if we have realized our true nature and eternal relationship with Him; and from the moment we surrender, we would not sin again, and past sins would have to be exhausted by us. God would enable us to exhaust sins suitably after surrendering to Him. We don't have to exhaust punya karma as He would accept it as an offering. This is what Krishna means when He says, 'He would accept our surrender when we are righteous' (sarva dharmAn parityajya mAmEkam saraNam vraja'). Without surrendering to God, even our righteousness would bind us to repeated births. In that sense, a true devotee would consider even noble karma as sins as it would impede his progress to attaining the Lord. Thus even noble karma is equal to sins if we don't relinquish them surrendering to the Lord. (*Ivan puNyattai pApamennirukkum*—a devotee considers even punya karma as sins). Be it papa karma or punya karma, both are detrimental in attaining the Lord. However, punya karma can be renounced but papa karma would have to be exhausted. We would not accrue further karma after surrendering to God.

It is to be noted that Sri Pillai Lokacharya confirms unambiguously that Krishna is referring only to dharma and not adharma. 'Papa karma' or bad deeds here refers to our ineptness in executing our good karma and not sins. We are deficient even in executing noble deeds, which also needs to be nullified.

mumukshuppadi 205—

'*sarva dharmangalayum vittu*' enru sollugayale, silar '*adharmam pugurum*' enrArgal'—"some contend that 'sarva dharmAn'(righteousness) includes even 'adharmam' (sins)".

206—

> *adu kUdAdu, 'adharmngalaichchei' enru sollAmayAle'*. "no, that is forbidden (sinning). for the simple reason that it is not advocated to do sins"

207—

> '*tannadaye sollithagAdo? Ennil*'—"can we not assume that 'dharma' also includes adharma (sins)?"

208—

'AgAdu, dharma shabdam adharma nivruthiyaik kAttAmayAle'. "surely not, for the word 'righteousness' explicitly excludes unrighteousness, the word 'righteous' is not a state of relief from being sinful or the word dharma does not include anything related to adharma"

We don't need to look beyond Sri Pillailokacharyar, as he has incarnated to provide the ultimate knowledge for everyone to know and practice.

He confirms in SrivachanabhUshaNam thus—

280—**"puNyattukkanjugiravan pApattaippaNNAnirE"** (one who even fears the effects of noble deeds, would not do sins)

281—**"ivan puNyattai pApamennirukkum, avan pApattai puNyamennirukkum, avanukku adu kidayAdu, ivan adu seyyAn"** ('ivan' refers to a true devotee who would not sin, 'avan' refers to a sinner who expects good results for committing sins)

a devotee considers even his good karma as ignoble because he would have to take repeated births owing to his noble karma as well; and the sinner would consider even his evil deeds as puNya or noble, expecting good out of his bad deeds. The sinner is not interested in nobility and the devotee would not sin"

A devotee has no desire to experience pleasures as a reward for his good deeds, for he knows that the desire for fruits of action would entangle him in repeated life cycles; keeping him away from engaging in eternal service of the Lord. A devotee would not sin, for he would dread the effects of sins. Not because he would suffer for sinning, but because of the hurt/harm it would cause to others.

An intentional sinner would not realize his sins; would not repent or regret the harm he causes to others nor does he care to become noble.

I cannot claim to want to be a devotee on one hand, and continue doing sins on the other. God would accept even sinners as all are His children, but the sins would be detrimental to his surrender. Like a drug addict who wants to seek rehabilitation, must stop using drugs for the rehabilitation to be effective. By totally giving up usage of addictive drugs, a person may suffer the effects of withdrawal symptoms, which would be taken care of by the programme. Similarly, a sinner has to realize that he wants to change and make that effort to becoming a good person, only then he can be devout or even be able to surrender to God. Even then past karma would bother him now and then. But by becoming a devotee he would have the mental resolve to deal with the situation. This he can achieve by focusing his mind on the Lord instead of his past.

In order to reach the Lord, we have to exhaust all karma—good, neutral and bad. It is to be noted that we can give up the fruits of good and neutral karma. But we cannot renounce bad karma, for bad karma can only be exhausted by suffering the effects. Good karma is like owning wealth which can be given away in charity. However, 'papa karma' is like debts, which cannot be renounced or transferred to someone else, and has to be necessarily repaid.

Scriptures affirm that we cannot attain God without knowing Him, and we cannot know Him unless He reveals Himself. He would reveal Himself only when we seek Him with unconditional devotion. ***Thus it is decisive that devotion alone can prepare us for God's acceptance***.

For those who are incapable of practicing devotion, the easier option is to do 'saranagati' or 'prapatti' taking refuge in an

Acharya. Even if our surrender is not perfect, Lord would accept us due to our subservience to the Acharya.

All that the Lord is looking for is our love for Him, in everything we do. Gita 9-26

> *"patram, pushpam, phalam, toyam,*
> *yo mE bhaktyA prayacchati;*

"be it a leaf, a flower, a fruit or water, whoever offers to me with true devotion, I accept that offering by him who is pure of heart".

Here 'asnami' suggests that the Lord literally enjoys the essence of food offered to him. Most people consider that the food offered to God is merely a physical ritual as God does not really eat anything. That is because of our limited understanding, as we see food only as physical object, the quantity of which has to reduce if tasted or eaten. But when God eats, the quantity does not reduce. We have to understand that there is a big difference in the way we eat and God eats. We have a physical material body and we need physical material food to energize our body. Even in that we do not eat anything and everything. If someone gave me clay with lot of proteins and vitamins, I would not touch it, let alone eat it. We eat not only because we are hungry but also we enjoy the **taste, flavour**, the **feel** and **essence** of food and the experience of eating. We do not eat food tasting bad, smelling foul or if it is rock hard. When in a physical body, if we can experience the taste and flavour in food, why wouldn't God who is divine, not accept the taste, flavour and essence of food offered to Him. Surely He does, except that we are unable to understand it. Just as we cannot feel and recognize many physical realities, we are unable to realize a divine reality. It is not much different than asking why I cannot see God if He is everywhere?

God is not hungry nor does He need physical food like us. He is divine and by His will and kindness He would taste the food offered to Him and lets us enjoy that food as His prasadam. God tasting the food seems much more realistic than our eating as most times we are not even conscious or aware of what we are eating.

Similarly, God accepts when we adorn flowers on the deities and photos. We don't adorn deities with paper or plastic flowers. When we greet people on special occasions, we give them fresh flowers that are colourful, beautiful, pleasant looking, smelling nice etc. Even the women in our families adorn their hair with fragrant flowers. When we adorn God with flowers, God accepts the feel, beauty, colour and fragrance. And more than that, we enjoy seeing the adornment on idols and photos.

There are lots of incidents of true devotion by many great souls, who showed us the way to God's acceptance. Meera, Kabir, Tukaram, Kanakadasa, Purandaradasa, Tyagaraja, Tulasidas—and many more.

Azhwars and Acharyas were the epitome of bhakti. Only their devotion could be compared to their own devotion.

Each one of us can express our devotion to God in our own unique way. We do not have to know the psalms and learn scriptures. Devotion is a pure form of love and affection for God. Artistes can express their devotion with their talent—musicians, dancers, painters, sportsmen—each and every one can dedicate his skill to God in devotion. It is a fact that everything we do, every skill we have, is indeed God-enabled.

Gita—9-22
    "ananyASchintayanto mAm, yE jahAh paryupAsatE,

"Those who exclusively think of Me and worship Me, ***aspiring for eternal union with Me***, I look after their prosperity and welfare (yoga and kshema)".

Those that are devoted would be taken care of by the Lord while in this world and also would be granted the eternal world from where they would never have to return to this samsara. Prosperity here refers to attaining immortality and welfare refers to eternality in immortality. Yoga is acquiring something that we do not have (eternal world) and kshema is retaining what has been acquired—meaning when we attain the eternal world, it would not be lost, ever.

Krishna re-iterates to Arjuna in Gita 18-65—
  "manmanA bhava madbhakto madyAjl mAm namaskuru,

"Focus your mind on Me, be My devotee, be My worshipper, surrender in Me, you shall come to Me alone, I assure you, truly, for you are dear to Me"

Our devotion would work on two conditions:

nishkama bhakti—when our devotion is unconditional, without seeking anything from the Lord. If we seek anything, then devotion becomes a business deal. Pure devotion is an expression of our realization that He is our eternal Father and that we seek to serve Him, for His joy.

ananya bhakti—our devotion for Him must be undivided, exclusive, unadulterated and pure; because He is our only origin and none else.

With devotion Happiness becomes divine bliss.

Devotion is a state in which we remain blissful with the realization of God's presence in us.—Taittiriyopanishad 2-7 states—

  "yadAhy Evaisha tasmin adrusyE' nAtmyE'
  niruktE' nilayanE'bhayam . . ."

"*Whenever the devotee gets established* (through undivided, ceaseless remembrance) *in this*(Brahman who is)*unperceivable, invisible, inexpressible and boundless; gains fearlessness. With any break in his meditation* (thought) *about Brahman, fear grips him* (with the realization that he has lost a precious moment thinking of his Lord which in itself is the fear for him). *For a devotee who is not ceaselessly meditating (thinking of the Lord), that itself is fear for him"*

The fear is on two accounts—one, the lost opportunity even for a moment, of thinking of God, and two, when not remembering the Lord, the mind thinks of anything else, which leads to fear. To think of anything other than the Lord sends shivers in a devotee. This is not hard to understand, for every jivatma is directly related only to the Lord and none else. To think of anything unrelated and to forget thinking about the related is indeed a fearful state.

We can relate this state to every child, including us when we were children. If we have to pass through a dark space or go to the bathroom in the night (at home or outside), we need the presence of an adult with us. The moment we think that the guardian is not with us, fear grips us. The mother or father may merely stand at a distance while we go alone. We have in our mind the presence of the father, though he is not physically walking with us. Similarly, for a devotee who is literally like a child, totally relies on his Lord, constantly thinking of Him and when he forgets the Lord, even only for a brief moment, he is startled. Why should he be distressed for not remembering the Lord? When he forgets the Lord, he has to think of something other than God and the other thing is mortal relationships from this world and a devotee dreads attachment to this mortal world. We become attached to things or people we think of. There are only two things other than us. One is God and the other is the mortal world. Thinking of God brings to the devotee, bliss; and attachment to the world, grief.

Nammazhwar:

It is said that Nammazhwar would faint for six months when Krishna would disappear from his thoughts merely for a moment; it would be unbearable for the Azhwar to miss Lord's company even for a moment. Azhwar would be incessantly pleasing the Lord by his unmatched devotion, but it was a play for Krishna to disappear from Azhwar's mind and sight and that alone was enough for Azhwar to pass out.

Sri Azhagiyamanavalaperumal Nayanar describes Azhwar's unequalled state in his acharyahrudayam 1-58 thus

'*dharmaviryajnAnattale hrushtarAy teLindu mEIE mEIE toduppAraippolannE, aruLina bhaktiyAle uLkalangichogittu mUvArumAsam mohittu varundiyEngi tAzhnda sorkkaLAle nUrkkiravivar'*.

This sukti refers to Azhwar's fluid state in reference to other great souls such as Valmiki, who fears for Rama's safety in His fight with the rakshasas but does not become unconscious at that thought like Azhwar. Even the great souls were strong-hearted, in comparison to Azhwar who was feeble-hearted and sensitive when it concerns the welfare of the Lord.

No one is comparable to Nammazhwar—acharyahrudayam 1-77—

"krishNakrishNadwaipAyanotpattigaL polannE krishNatrishNatattva janmam"—

Even the great Vedavyasa is not an equal to Nammazhwar, while Vedavyasa is the author of great epics of devotion, has written commentaries on the Vedas, the Azhwar is the embodiment of Krishna-bhakti. Just as the Vedas declare the nature of Paramatman as "**rasovai saha**"—meaning the Lord is 'infinite bliss', similarly Nammazhwar's nature is '**Krishna-bhakti**". While other devotees have bhakti (devotion) for the Lord, Nammazhwar is himself Krishna-bhakti.

Azhwar reiterates his true nature in Thiruvaimozhi 6-7-1—

> *"uNNumsoru parugunIr tinnumvettilaiyumellAm kannan,*
> *emberumAn ennennE kaNgaL nIrmalgi . . . ."*

to him—food, water and after-meal delicacy—vetrilai (dessert) were all—Krishna.

He had the Lord filling every atom of his body from head to toe. He ate, drank and lived Krishna bhakti. In that all his senses competed to become engrossed in experiencing Krishna—eye, in addition to seeing the divinity of Krishna, did all the functions of other senses as well, of hearing, smelling, tasting and feeling the presence of Lord. Similarly, the sense of hearing and ears did the functions of all the five senses. His divine experiences of the Lord were at least five fold more than that of the other great devotees. The other devotees could only use the eye to see and other senses for their respective purposes. But each of Nammazhwar's senses functioned as the other senses as well. As an expression of his unequalled devotion, it is said that Azhwar wanted to send out his mind as a messenger seeking Krishna's audience. And was immediately worried that his mind might betray him and remain with the Lord without returning to him.

In contrast, we are devoted to the Lord for the sake of attaining comfortable state in life—getting our food and sense gratification, without hinder. We want everything from Him except Him.

Purandaradasa confesses the state of our devotion for the Lord thus *"udara vairAgyavidu, namma padumanabhnali lesa bhakuti illa"*. We pretend devotion to the Lord only for the sake of our desires for enjoyment and wealth acquisition fulfilled and not because we truly love Him. We show same tendency towards the Lord that we show amongst relationships here. I love all my relations because they are useful. All our relationships of this world are purely relative to the benefits we can get from one another. Our relationships here are like business deals. If there are no profits for the self, we don't want such relationships. But God loves us unconditionally; only similar love from us will lead us to His acceptance.

This incidence in Sri Ramayana explains the state of Lord Rama and Mother Sita. Hanuman finds Sita in the 'asoka-vana' and returns to 'kishkinda' where the Lord was waiting. Hanuman conveys to the Lord of Mother Sita's message that she would not be able to survive if He does not come to rescue her in 30 days. Then Rama reflects on this message and mentions that Sita was indeed strong-hearted that she could live for 30 days more without Him, while His own state was that He could not survive even for a moment without Her. This explains the extent of affection He has for her and she for Him. Rama was hinting that His affection for Her was infinitely greater than Hers for Him. The answer to this is quite contrary to what Rama contends. Sita's noble qualities were infinitely greater than Rama's which is the reason He cannot live without her, while it was possible to hold on to life without seeing Rama for a month, which makes Him so much less in comparison to Sita !!

Hanuman also confesses that before going to Lanka to find Sita, he was mystified at the manner in which Rama conducted Himself, expressing uncontrolled grief about missing His wife. Rama would wander about talking to the trees and plants in the forest; asking if they knew where Sita was. He would even ask Lakshmana who Lakshmana was and who He Himself was! He appeared as someone who had lost his mind. Hanuman had never seen anyone behave that way and wondered how someone can be so obsessed about his wife that he could not bear the separation; so much so, He seemed totally lost.

Then, after seeing the Mother at 'asoka-vana', Hanuman felt that he was so wrong about his perception about Rama's behaviour and now he felt that Rama was indeed stone hearted to have endured her separation. Such was Her kindness and grace for everyone that he felt speechless about Her benevolence in all aspects.

Sri Pillailokacharyar confirms Sita's greatness thus—
"itihAsa srEshtamAna sriramAyaNattAl
sirai-irundavaL Ettam sollugiradu"—

"Sri Ramayana is the superior virtuous epic and this epic speaks all about the greatness of the one who remained captive"—

This statement glorifies Mother Sita more than Rama, though the title of the epic is Ramayana—about Rama.

On one other occasion, after Ravana was killed, Hanuman goes up to Mother Sita in asoka-vana to inform her of Ravana's death and to escort her to Rama; he suggests to her that he should kill all the rakshasis including Trijata, all of whom troubled Sita during her captivity.

At that suggestion, Sita called Hanuman 'plavangama'; a 'monkey'; hinting that he was revealing the nature of a monkey. She explains to him that they were not at fault, for they were under the command and control of Ravana and did not deserve any punishment. It was then that he realized how there can be no one kinder than Mother Sita. True to Her nature, there really can be no one more kind; She is the origin for all the souls and hence only she can be kinder even than the Lord. All the Azhwars and Acharyas emphasize the fact that the devotees should take refuge with an Acharya, and seek the divine Mother's grace before reaching out to the Lord, for she is eternally partial in bestowing her benevolence on all the souls; that she would be oblivious to their mistakes like mothers would; she looks at every soul as a child. While the Lord is impartial, the divine Mother is totally partial to everyone, equally.

Sri Pillai Lokacharyar in his 'mumukshuppadi' grantham indicates states of different people and what is desirable and undesirable for them—

> *samsarigaLukku virodhi satrupldAdigaL, apEkshitam annapAnAdigaL* (for people attached to pleasures of this world—undesirable is impediment to what they seek and desirable is sense gratification and enjoyment)

> *mumukshukkaLukku virodhi samsara sambandham; apEkshitam paramapada prApti*—(for one desirous of immortality—undesirable is attachment to this world and desirable is attaining eternal world—paramapadam)

> *muktarkkum nityarkkum virodhi kainkaryahAni; apEkshitam kainkarya vruddhi*—(for the immortals and nityasuris—undesirable is losing even a moment of subservience to the Lord and desirable is continuous enhanced state of serving the Lord)

Nammazhwar gives us the simplest way to attaining devotion to the Lord—Tiruvaimozhi 10-5-1

> "*kannan kazhaliNai, naNNum manamudaylr, eNNum tirunAmam, tiNNam nAraNamE*"—

"Anyone wishing and desirous of attaining the Lotus feet of the Lord, think of (chant) His divine names"

Sri Thiruppanazhwar declares in his 'amalanadipiran'—5 thus

> "*pAramAya pazha vinai pattaruttu, ennaittan vAramAkki vaittAn, vaittadanni ennuL pugundAn, koramA tavam seidanangol ariyEn . . .*"

"the Lord has accepted my past karma, relieving me of all effects (this Azhwar is a nitya suri from the eternal world and has no karma, however, it is suggested here for our sake that the Lord accepts our renunciation of past good karma which also has to be nullified), made me His own, enabling subservience, and above all, the Lord entered my heart; though I have not done any austerities or penance to deserve such unconditional grace by the Lord", yet He bestows His 'nirhetuka krupa' on us.

Devotion is the most wonderful feeling there is. All of us have a natural sense of adventure in wanting to try the unknown. But devotion is the most blissful experience devoid of any ill effects. We should worry if someone asks us to try something dangerous, or if it is unaffordable. If someone invites us to a divinely delicious feast, we would go on a feasting spree like there is no tomorrow. Devotion is also something like tasting the most delicious delicacies, for free. We must do it like there is no tomorrow. Once we get the taste of it, we would not let go. Instead of costing something, it would prove to be beneficial; materially, emotionally, and in every conceivable way.

In devotion, we remain the same, God remains the same but the experiences keep changing. It can happen only with God. Experiencing the divine bliss of the Lord is ever different and ever growing, every moment; like with the flowing water in the river; you would never have the same water. Every day we look for new experiences. We cannot change our senses or the self, but we seek different experiences using the same set of seekers. This is true with all the things we experience in this world. But amazingly, when it comes to God, the same God would give us different experiences every time.

Even a localite would not visit a popular monument in his place every day. However, those who would have experienced even little bit of devotion would visit their place of worship often and feel good every time they pray. Those who are in the habit of performing their prayers at home, would do so, everyday and do not feel monotonous about it. Everyone's common response to the question 'why they pray or visit their place of worship'—would be that they feel good, happy, blessed, joyous, peaceful, fulfilled, blissful etc—they all mean the same thing. They feel so because of the presence of the Lord in them and the time they spend thinking of Him brings them that bliss.

Thirumangai azhwar in his Peria Tirumozhi 1:3 :2/4/5/6 pleads with us to seek the Lord with devotion before we attain old age; before our body becomes weak; before our legs become shaky; before our mind fails. Devotion flourishes best at a young age, when the body and mind are perfectly ordained to propitiate and nurture devotion, and to establish the Lord in our hearts. Azhwar advises not to lose time till we become old and frail when it would be too late, for our body and senses would not co-operate at old age.

When we are devoted to the world and people, eventually it would result in grief. The reason is logical. All our relationships and associations, either with our body or with family that we are so attached to, are temporary and perishable. We or the people we love will be gone, ending in grief for the survivor. Any which way we look at it, Lord is the only one we are eternally related to.

This verse from Bhagavata gives us a simple way to attaining release from the mortal world. "*mana Eva manushyANAm kAraNam bandha mokshayoh*" mind is the sole reason for humans, to either binding them to this world or getting release from it.

If we are attached to this world, we keep going round in birth-death cycles in this world, if we attach our mind to the Lord, we attain Him.

There is a big difference between attachment and affection. When we are attached, it is for self benefit, either for the pleasure, or for material gains. Affection, however, is devoid of self benefit and can be unconditional. We can be attached only to those who are useful to us. However affection can be shown towards everyone. Attachment binds us, affection releases us from bondage.

We false praise people in this world to gain some benefits from them. But any praise we express for God is totally true or merely an under-statement of His virtues because we can only say so much in words while His divine qualities are infinitely glorious but there is no equivalent expression to sing His true glories. He is beyond words and expressions. Yet, even if we understate His glory, He loves us for our effort and affection for Him.

A Farmer is a greater devotee than Narada.

Once, Narada was in conversation with the Lord. Narada is known for his devotion, and keeps chanting Lord's name all the time. Narada who also has the ability to appear anywhere in the world in that instant, mentions to God that after seeing so many devotees in so many worlds, he is of the opinion that he is the only one who chants His name always. No one else seems to be thinking of Him constantly except him. God smiled at him, agrees that Narada seems to chant His name frequently but there ends the comparison; and there are many devotees who may seem extraneous and simple, but in reality, only He knows them as greatest of devotees. Among devotees there is no comparison as to being the most devoted or the best devotee. Each and every devotee is unique and equally dearer to Him. Narada feels a little discouraged with this opinion from God and questions if God was including Narada in the comparison with His other devotees and God confirms affirmatively. God then brings Narada to earth, both of them disguised, go to a poor farmer's hut in a village. The farmer shows extreme delight on seeing them and speaks to them with kind words and invites them into his hut and expresses his gratitude to God for having them as his guests. While he was busy attending to them, he was constantly praising his God for being able to serve the two visitors. He is not a scholar who has mastered the scriptures; he is someone who works hard every day in the field to feed his small family. He washes their feet, feeds them with whatever food his wife had made for their family. After they finish eating, he yet again praises the Lord and thanks Him for the wonderful opportunity to have been of service to the visitors. He literally treats the guests as the Lord Himself. He then gets his bulls ready to go to the field and the two visitors express their desire to go with him. They watch him work hard all day. At every opportune moment he would pause to praise God and continue working. They return to the hut by evening, the farmer gives his bulls a wash and feeds them, and the cows. Then he invites them to have dinner. Narada did not miss to notice that once again they were eating up his family's share and he, his wife and their son went to bed eating the leftovers, but happily without any complaint. Instead the farmer seemed happier and praises his God again and again. Next morning God in the guise of the guest mentions to the farmer that they want to go to the fields again with him as he needs him to do a small task for him which the farmer accepts gladly.

He explains to both of them—farmer and Narada—that they should carry a pot full of oil, up to a certain distance and return without spilling a drop of it. The path they would have to walk was not paved, there were uneven surfaces and one would have to watch every step to avoid tripping. He adds, one who does not spill the oil would be considered victorious. He first asks Narada to do the act and Narada returns without spilling the oil. He was very careful, placing each step on smooth ground to ensure that he does not fall nor the imbalance of the uneven surface causes spillage. God tells Narada that He was impressed with his focus on the job. It was the farmer's turn to accomplish the challenge. The farmer walks up and down, he was not being as careful as

Narada in sure-footing every step. To Narada it seemed that the farmer was not taking his job sincerely. God rewards the farmer even though he spilled oil.

They had both noticed that the farmer was not focused on his job but was focused on uttering praises to his God and seemed totally filled with thoughts of his Lord; hence his attention was not on the pot of oil. While Narada was successful in not spilling the oil, he did not think of the Lord even once during the mission. God did not have to explain to Narada, who seemed to understand that though the farmer had spilled oil, he was constantly thinking of God. Not spilling the oil did not seem important to him. Narada bows down as a gesture of recognizing the true devotion of the farmer.

Gopikas are the greatest devotees.

Devotion is like madness but without claiming rights about the person you are devoted to. You don't claim any rights or ownership over him. There are few types of devotions and varying devotions at that. The unconditional devotion of Gopikas is considered the highest state in devotion.

Nammazhwar depicts the state of extreme devotion in Thiruvaimozhi 3-5-8 thus

> *"vArpunal andaNNaruvi vadatiruvEngadattendai,*
> *pErpala sollippidatti pittarennE pirar kUra . . ."*

This verse explains the state of a true devotee who is deeply immersed in the ocean of Lord's auspicious qualities, who is ever singing praises for the Lord, uttering His names. But the others think of him as bizarre or peculiar, for he is oblivious to his surroundings and totally engrossed in the divinities of the Lord, and he keeps going from one town to another, chanting the glories of the Lord. Even the divine souls of the eternal world worship such a devotee, while he would seem different to us, who do not understand devotion.

Perumal tirumozhi 3-8
"pEyarE enakku yAvarum; yAnumor pEyanE evarkkum idu pEsiyen; AyyanE ! arangA ! ennazhaikkinnEn; pEyAnAyozhindEn empirAnukkE"

KulasekarAzhwAr expresses similarly that a devotee is looked at as a weird person by others for they do not understand his state and the devotee wonders why the others are peculiar; in that they are not devoted to the Lord. A devotee is able to experience the supreme joy and wonders how others cannot seek to experience such joy, for even the devotee would have seen the state of ordinary men when he was not a devotee.

No one surpasses the gopikas when it comes to devotion. Their devotion for Krishna is acclaimed to be of the highest state. Gopikas are the divine souls from the eternal world who took birth on earth to experience Krishna's incarnation. Krishna leaves Brindavan as a seven year child and does not return ever. He had promised his gopika friends that he would come back soon. They waited for Him in eternity. Krishna was everything to them. They existed for Krishna's sake. They did everything for His sake, without an iota of self benefit. Their happiness came from seeing their beloved God happy. They would accept even extreme suffering or eternal hell if doing something would keep their Lord safe and protected. They realize that He is the supreme Lord and no harm can come to Him but their love for Him was so overwhelming that they would not look at Him as the supreme Lord; instead, they look at Him as a person they love the most and want nothing from Him except His well being. They don't even seek immortality; they have just one goal, and that is to serve their Lord in a way it pleases Him.

Sri Andal explains true state of a devotee thus—(as a 5 year old kid) in her 'nachiyar tirumozhi'—

> *9-6—nArunarumpozhil mAlirumsolai nambikku,*
> *nAn nUru tadAvil vennai vAi nErnthu parAvi vaittEn,*

> *9-7—"Innu vandu ittanaiyum amuthu seithidapperil,*
> *nAn onnu nUrAyiramAgak—koduttu pinnum ALum*
> *seivan,*

The significance is in the latter part ((9-7) of the dialogue Andal had with God. She says I would like you to accept 100 mega bowls of butter and 100 mega bowls of delicacy 'akkara-adisal" (a dessert made with rice-milk-sweet) and Lord asks her what would she want in return, she says 'make me do this 100s of 1000s of times, to keep serving you as that makes you happy, that's what I would want in return. So worshipping God, praising, singing His glories is for His pleasure and not for any favours He can grant us.

Narada learns true devotion from Gopikas

Once, Narada visits Krishna and offers obeisance to the Lord. After a while, Krishna suddenly fakes having acute stomach pain and head ache. Narada was alarmed seeing Krishna in pain. Narada was confused and asks Krishna as to how He can be in pain for he knows that He is the Paramatma, the Supreme God and His body was divine-most. Narada suggests he would fetch the royal doctor who could probably find a potion to relieve His pain. Krishna negates that suggestion, assures Narada that there was no need for the royal doctor and He knows the remedy Himself. Krishna mentions to him that sri pada duli (dust from the feet of His devotees) and sri pada tirttam (water taken from washing the feet of His devotees) was the right medicine. He would apply the dust on to His forehead for the head ache and drink the water to cure his stomach pain. He then points at Narada "who can be better than you for this; you are my dearest devotee". Narada shivers in fear at this suggestion. He folds his hands together and addresses Krishna "oh the supreme Lord of all the gods and all the worlds, what type of play is this and how can you ask me to stoop to commit a sin that is un-equaled. And how can I commit such un-pardonable sin. Please forgive me; I shall not buy into your trick to commit such a grave sin".

Krishna suggests to Narada, to approaching his 16108 wives for this medicine. Incidentally when we are on the subject of 16108 wives that Krishna married during His incarnation—shows the extent of His unequivocal, unsurpassed kindness and esteem for His devotees and the barriers He will break to save them from disgrace. He would break all precedence as only He could, not for Himself, but for the sake of his devotees. Krishna marries Rukmini first, then Satyabhama, Jambavanti, Nagnajiti, Kalindi, Madra, Mitravinda, Bhadra—eight of the divine souls from eternal world (incidentally Rukmini is none other than the Mahalakshmi, the Para power of the Lord) who takes birth on earth just to be associated with Him. His other 16100 wives were the women that Narakasura abducted and imprisoned, forcing them to be his wives. They were imprisoned because they refused to marry him. Krishna graces Narakasura with his death and then these 16100 women who were devotees of Krishna, mention to Him that they have been vilified by their abduction and they have no social standing nor would they be accepted in their homes by their own relatives. To save their honor all that was left for them was to take their own lives as they had nowhere to go. Though they remain pure in soul and body, others would not know of it nor would they be magnanimous enough to accept their sanctity. Since birth they were devoted only to Krishna and now He was their savior. If He does not accept them they would have no option but to end their lives. Krishna marries all of them, giving them the status of being His queens!

The relevance of this is brought up at a much later stage. Ashwathama uses brahmastra to wipe out future generation of Pandavas. Parikshit the unborn baby of Abhimanyu and Uthara becomes lifeless in his mother's womb, due to the effect of brahmastra. Krishna then declares thus—which epitomizes His incarnation—that the dead baby shall come alive if He had lived the life of a **chaste bachelor** all His incarnation as Krishna and if He had only spoken the truth all His life—and Parikshit comes alive from dead. Krishna did not use His divine powers to bring Parikshit back to life. Similarly, Rama grants Jatayu His eternal world, merely by the power of His virtue and righteousness. Jatayu had lost his wings in fight against Ravana while the latter was abducting Mother Sita. Rama did not use His powers as God. Rama declares that he was a human and son of dasaratha ('AtmAnam mAnusham manyE rAmam dasaratAtmajam'), when Brahma reminds the Lord that He was the Supreme Lord and should return to His eternal abode now that He has accomplished the mission of his incarnation by putting an end to Ravana's atrocities. Not only God, even great sages, yogis and devotees had so much power out of their righteousness and virtuousness that they could simply wish for something to happen and it would come true.

Narada approaches the queens—starting with Rukmini—they explain that they know that Krishna was the supreme God and they would be committing unpardonable sin if they subscribed to Krishna's suggestion. Even otherwise, He is there Pati (Husband) and Lord, and in accordance with their subservient nature to Him they cannot yield to His suggestion.

Narada promptly reports to Krishna his failure to obtain the dust and water from them. Then Krishna suggests that Narada should go to Brindavan and try with the gopikas who are also His greatest devotees. Narada comes to Brindavan and mentions to them that he has a message from Krishna. On seeing him, the gopikas show extreme happiness and start pouring in questions asking about Krishna's well being. They express gratitude for bringing news from their Lord and offer him all courtesies. Narada then relates the episode of Krishna's head ache and stomach ache. He also mentions that the remedy would be to apply the dust from their feet to the head and drink the water washing the feet of His devotees. He mentions that neither he nor the queens of Krishna obliged doing this as they considered it an unforgivable sin, for they were aware that He was the Supreme Lord.

On hearing that Krishna was in pain, they literally experienced deep anguish and were unable to bear the news that their Lord was in pain. Without even answering Narada, they started dusting their feet and collected the dust in a piece of cloth and also washed their feet and collected the water in a bowl. They handed them to Narada and asked him to rush back to Krishna as quickly as possible so that he feels relieved from pain. Narada questions them if they knew what they were doing, did they know that He is the supreme God of all the worlds and to give him what he was asking would be committing untold sin and that they would acquire hell for such a sin which no one dared commit till then. Narada was shocked when they said that they were fully aware as to who Krishna was and they also realized that is was a grave sin. But that did not matter; they would be glad to suffer eternal hell if that could relieve their Lord from pain. It was important for them that He had no pain and nothing else mattered. They would do anything for His well being. They sought nothing from the Lord, for themselves. They sought to remain with His Person so that they could remain in His service.

Chapter Eighteen

Age of our world!

Que—Is there age for worlds and creation? Is there specific time limit for the universe to form and annihilate?

Ans—Yes, there is age for the worlds just as there is age for different bodies we obtain from these worlds. The created world is governed by the power of God's prakruti; it manifests and unmanifests in a cycle of time as determined by God. No one else other than God has the power to control, surpass or change the functioning of prakruti. Not even the divine powers designated to controlling the nature can alter their purpose, for these gods function by the power of the Supreme God.

Yes, there is a specific time for earth, sun, stars, galaxies, in this universe. A Brahma, nominated to supervise the formation of a cluster of galaxies has a time limit for his life as well. His day or night is not the same as our earthly day and night. It goes like this—

Formation of the worlds happens during his day and annihilation during his night.

- There are 4 millenniums (yugas)—kruta, treta, dwapara, kali—one cycle of 4 yugas is called a 'tama'. 71 tama's make a 'manvantara' and 14 manvantaras make a 'kalpa' or 994 tama's make a kalpa which constitutes a day for

Brahma and a similar period for his night as well. Two kalpa's make up his day/night or one day. He lives for his prescribed 100 years, comprising 360 days a year. This calculation of Brahma's age is based on earthly years and would differ if it is seen from the satya loka, the abode of Brahma. The time zones are different and with varying duration for each world, we are concerned with what is relevant to us, from earth.

- kali yuga lasts for 432000 years, 'dwapara' 864000 years, 'treta' 1296000 years and 'kruta' 1728000 years—adding up to 4,320,000 years, which is a 'tama'.

- 4.32 million years times 994 tama = 4.294 billion years or a day for Brahma and 4.294 billion years—his night. His day and night would be 8.58816 billion years for us.

- His 100 years—100 x 360 x 8.58816 billion years, is his lifetime—make up to 309.173 trillion earthly years.

At the end of 309.173 trillion earthly years, there would be a maha pralaya (total annihilation of a brahmanda) and a new Brahma comes into being, and thus, time and creation goes on endlessly.

According to scriptures we are in the 28th tama of the 994 tama's of Brahma's day, we have some 966 tama's to go before our Brahma's night begins—966 x 4.32 million years = 4.173 billion years to go before our sun and solar system would be annihilated. It is said in the scriptures that 3 of the Brahma's worlds—bhUh, bhuvah and suvah—the worlds of human, the worlds of demigods and the world of Indra or heaven would be dissolved during every night of brahma and new ones would be formed at the beginning of his day. And our Brahma has completed 50 years since and we are in the 2nd half of his lifetime (dwitEyE parArdhE, Sri SwEta varAha kalpE, vaivasvata manvantarE, ashtAvimSati tamE, kali yugE)

Not many are interested in attaining immortality.

We should know that the souls are infinite in number. And not many are interested in relinquishing their attachment to this world and life here. In other words, not everyone is seeking to attain God's world.

Krishna declares in Gita—7-3
"manushyANAm sahasrEshu kaschidyatati siddhayE;

Amongst thousands of men, someone strives for perfection; even among them; someone only knows Me; and among those who know Me, someone only knows Me in properly"

Gita 7-19
"bahUnAm janmanAm antE jnAnavAn mAm prapadyatE,

"At the end of many births, the man of knowledge finds refuge in Me, realizing that "Vasudava is everything and all".

Imagine if it is hard for God to find a soul that can become entitled to His world, not many souls really leave this world. *This is not a discouragement to scare people that it would be difficult to reach God's world. It reiterates that not many are interested in giving up their attachment to their body and this world.* Yet, they would want to experience divine powers, immortality and unending bliss. God lets us do what we want, for our happiness is of prime importance to Him. If we are happy here, and don't seek a change, we can be in the mortal worlds forever.

It is good that human population is growing, as so many will get a chance to attain immortality. Even the gods in heaven envy our existence (as an afterthought, they realize that a human life is better). Azhwar says it is natural for humans to attain immortality *"vaigundam puguvadu maNNavar vidiyE'*; "reaching the eternal abode of God is a precept/destiny for the humans on earth" but we seem to be going against our nature when we miss the opportunity to reach our eternal home despite acquiring a human life.

Que—what about all the magical/mystical powers and stories we hear about, does God perform miracles to attract us?

Ans—In simple terms, anything we can not perceive or understand is magic for us. When we understand what it is, it is not magic anymore. We see magicians perform magic acts; they also create mass illusion. They do it as an art, for a living. It is a skill level that comes with practice. We know that magic is performed to gain fame, popularity and finally to make money. Only humans would do all these acts for personal goals. Man can do magic because the 'soul' originates from God and even the magic by men is god-enabled, dwelling in every soul. Inanimate things cannot do magic. It is atma that is capable of doing magic and not our bodies.

I know a real life story about the power of 'mantra', as narrated by my mother. My mother's great grandfather, Sri Bhashyam, who lived in Srirangam possessed amazing powers enabled by God. It seems, when they could not attend the temple 'sevakalam', he and his Srivaishnava friends, would participate mentally in the service to the Lord from where they were. They would assemble at the bank of river Cauveri and Sri Bhashyam would chant some mantras, tossing up 'one ana' coin, and in return he would collect steaming hot 'aravaNai prasadam' offered to the Lord, in his hands and he would share it with everyone. True devotees, though possess incredible powers, would not use it for gaining fame or wealth nor would they misuse to harm others. They would live a simple and glorious life.

If man can do magic, God can do super-magic. The very fact that we and the universe exist, is already an evidence of God's magic. Man's magic is an illusion, make believe. God's magic is real. The way earth is positioned, enabling life to exist and flourish, is real magic. The fact that God has caused humans with such capabilities and so many species in different bodies, functioning differently, yet co existing in a world that provides for every need of every species, is great magic. Each person, each and every animal, each one of them in their respective bodies, having distinctly different characteristics, physically and emotionally, *each one having non-second DNA*, cannot be anything but magic. Even greater magic of it all is that we still cannot figure out the fundamental principles on which our universe is caused, and the way it functions. Everything that God does is magic, but beyond our understanding.

God's magic is real and does not vanish after the act; human magic is illusory. But God would not indulge in doing magic for gains like us. *God has no goals except our well being*, He has nothing to achieve for Himself. He does not have to perform any special effects to attract us. But that does not mean He cannot perform mysterious acts. When He does, it would be beyond our comprehension, to witness or understand, as everything about Him is divine and everything about us in this body is material, except ourselves.

We know of instances in the life stories of divine souls, God performing divine acts to protect them but they were not magic like the magic performed by human magicians. They were acts of God in support of His true devotees.

We know the story of Purandara dasa—how the disappearing diamond nose ring was instrumental in his becoming one of the great devotees of the Lord

We know how the Lord turned around for Kanakadasa to see the Deity in Udupi, and even today we can see the Lord's Idol in Udupi only from the back entrance.

We know that Krishna protected Draupati by providing robe, when Dussasana attempted the unforgivable sin. Krishna exhibited His divinity in every act He performed during His incarnation.

We know the life story of Prahlada who was rescued by the Lord personally each time Hiranyakashipu attempted to have him killed.

We know from Christianity how Moses gets the divine power from God to part the red sea that enabled people to pass through, the ocean giving way.

We know of Jesus Christ's resurrection, revealing that He was the son of God.

There is a story in Kenopanishad. The gods felt that they were the most powerful and independent, feeling supreme, thinking they can do anything. They had just then defeated the asuras in a war. They were convinced that it was their prowess that brought them victory in the war. They did not realize that it was Supreme God's powers that enabled their victory. But owing to the effects of the three gunas (sattva/rajasa/tamasa) and ego, they were deluded into believing that each one of them was independently superior and powerful.

3rd khanda expounds how they were made to realize that their powers were enabled by the Supreme Lord and that on their own they possess no powers.

3-1   When the gods were installed with powers in the worlds, it was Brahman (the supreme Lord) that verily achieved everything for the gods. But the gods felt glorified thinking that it is their doing and their glory.

3-2 Brahman knew of their egotism; He verily appeared before them (as a yaksha, bright as a thousand suns). They did not know what He might be. (God appears in the form of a yaksha to remove their false pride. He was visible in the form of a bright light, but beyond their comprehension)

3-3 The gods said to fire "find out what that yaksha is" who ventures out to know the yaksha

3-4 He goes to the yaksha who asks him "who are you? He replied "I am agni, I am jAtavEdA" (one who grants the benefits)

3-5 "What power do you possess? asked the yaksha, agni said "I can burn up all this that is in the world"

3-6 The yaksha placed before him a straw and said "burn this". Agni tried with all his power, he could not burn it.

He returned to the gods and said "I could not know what this yaksha is"

3-7 Then the gods said to vayu 'find what this yaksha is' he said 'so be it"

3-8 He went to the yaksha who said to him "who are you"? vayu said 'I am known as vayu or MAtarisvA(air)

3-9 'What power is there in you? The yaksha questioned. Vayu said "I can carry away all this that is in the world"

3-10 The yaksha placed before him a straw and said 'take it up' He tried with all his might but could not carry it away. Vayu then goes back to the gods and said "I could not know what this yaksha is'

3-11 The gods said to Indra 'know what this yaksha is, Indra said, so be it and approached the yaksha who disappeared. (the yaksha disappeared lest Indra's pride be broken in the presence of his subordinate gods)

3-12 Indra came across a resplendent woman adorned with many ornaments; it was the Divine Mother. He asks her 'what is this yaksha?' (Divine Mother appears before Indra to do him a favour and by her supportive response Indra thought she probably knew all this and asks her about the yaksha)

4-1 she said 'it was Brahman. Attain glory in the victory achieved by Brahman". On account of her revelation he came to know it was Brahman. She explains that Brahman appeared before them in the form of a yaksha to dispel their false pride of possessing all the powers. If they shed their ego that is the true victory they would have gained.

4-2 that's how these gods—agni, vayu and indra were ahead of other gods who were first to know of the Brahman, who appeared in the form of yaksha

They knew they saw Brahman at close proximity, as revealed by the Divine Mother. They realized that they possessed no powers on their own and they functioned as empowered by God.

Scholars contend that Mother Sita re-establishes the power of the Lord in Ramayana, when She holds a blade of grass in front of her when Ravana comes to appease her in the Asoka-grove where she was held captive. She holds the blade of grass to indicate that without the power of the Lord, all are powerless and cannot even move a blade of grass, let alone accomplish greater feats.

Que—what about the stories about spirits, ghosts. Do they exist?

Ans—it is said that spirits and ghosts are also souls who would have to wait to acquire a body and would be left to roam around in the interim. They are what they are due to their own doing. They are unable to function without a body and are eager to acquire a body; in that state they are restless. It could have been because they were responsible in ending their lives unnaturally, having retained so many unfulfilled desires in them that is driving them to acquire a body. Eventually they will go through the process of getting a body based on their karma. Whatever they experience as spirits or ghosts, longing to acquire a functional body, is the suffering they experience as an effect of their karma, either for taking their own life or losing their life at a time of having extreme desire to live on, retaining unfulfilled desires at the time of leaving the body.

There are also countless numbers of souls that are floating in space but they are not ghosts. They will acquire their next body in the normal course.

Que—even man has been able to clone some animals, is it not creating life?

Ans—Has man created anything out of nothing? No. By cloning, man has not created life. Man is instrumental in using the potential life to acquire a body. He has not created the life cell. Life is already forming and taking bodies. All that man has done is aiding life to acquire a body due to his curiosity to see if life cells can develop into a body and has discovered that it does. Life existed even before man started cloning experiments. It is similar to our growing paddy and other food crops. We have neither created the seed nor the earth nor other ingredients that are essential for growing our food crops.

However, we have to realize that the original soul in the person who has passed away cannot be cloned. They can only clone the preserved life cells and not the original soul. The cloned life cell would be a different soul which is one of several trillion cells in his body and not the Soul of the person.

It is important to realize that if we clone life cells from Einstein's body, we would not have cloned the real Einstein which is the soul. The cloned body would neither have the knowledge and intelligence of the original soul that was called Einstein nor be able to come up with theories he came up with.

We do have some of Lord Ramanuja's body preserved in Srirangam (tAnAna tirumEni). Can we clone his cells to become Ramanuja again? No. it would be a clone of his body and not of the divine soul Ramanuja.

Que—Are all those who worship, good people? Does God help those who pray? Similarly, does He ignore those who do not pray?

Ans—The popular assumption that those who go to temple, church and other places of worship are good people is relative. You can be a good person merely doing good things to others, does not matter if you visit the places of worship or not. It is not proof of one's goodness by going to places of worship, but good people do also visit the places of worship. In short, *not everyone who worships is a good person, nor all those who don't worship are good either.*

As declared by Krishna in the Gita "**samoham sarva bhUtEshu** . . . . "I am same to all beings, there is none hateful nor dear to Me, but those who worship Me with devotion abide in Me and I do abide in them".

It is clear from the above verse that God is same to all. However He is close to a true devotee. But a true devotee would not seek favours from God, except to serving Him.

It is important for us not be misguided into thinking that we can do anything and the moment we seek God's forgiveness, our sins would be gone. If it is true, then we would never want to be good people. If God forgives us for our sins, we would not have the laws of karma/consequence. And we can keep doing sins for eternity and the only thing that God can do is keep forgiving us. There would be infinite numbers of souls, each one committing infinite sins and probably even God would have to work overtime to successfully forgive each one's sins. Surely this cannot be true. We use forgiveness as a means to forget pain or hurt caused by someone. By saying we forgive; but the concerned person cannot escape consequences for his wrong doing. We would not be punishing him for his wrong doing nor would God. God would let the laws of karma do its work. We have not set the laws of karma to declare that we forgive. Forgiveness is an expression of kindness, that we do not hold a bad incident against a person and try to harm him in return. If we retain the burden of revenge in our mind, we are hurting ourselves. By forgiving, we remove the thought of avenging and that makes us feel better. It is for our own good that we forgive someone's wrong doing. But he or she would have to face the consequences of his wrong doing, even if we have forgiven them.

Why then do divine psalms and verses mention forgiveness in their expressions?

Divine verses by Sri PrativAdi Bhayankaram Anna in his Venkatesa Suprabahatam—prapatti, "**ajnAninA mayA doshAn asEshAn vihitAn harE, kshamasva tvam, kshamasva tvam sesha saila sikhAmaNe**" "please forgive my mistakes/errors, done out of ignorance, completely, without residue"

We must realize that to err is human. Errors are not sins. We err in most things as there is no such thing as perfection when it comes to humans. Here the forgiveness sought is not for sins and evil deeds, but for the errors and mistakes committed in doing righteous actions. We do make mistakes even in doing good things. For instance, we may undertake to feed the poor on a particular day, which is a good deed; but end up providing them food an hour too late due to delays in preparations or if the food is too spicy, causing them discomfort. We can apologize to them for the shortcomings. This is an error in our execution of a good deed.

Would the divine souls commit errors? Surely not, but yet, they seek to be forgiven for any shortcomings even in a perfectly enacted routine of worship of the Lord. It is for us to understand and seek such forgiveness with the realization that we cannot be perfect. Even the greatest of expressions in praise of the Lord's auspicious virtues would not really express even a fragment of His real virtue. For, each of His infinitely infinite glorious attributes cannot be expressed in words, or grasped by the mind. Yet He accepts our deficiencies with benign grace as though every utterance is a tribute to His Glories. His acceptance of our flawed expression in itself is what the divine Azhwars and Acharyas consider as His nirhetuka krupa (unconditional grace).

Sri ALavandAr also expresses similarly—
> "*upachArApadeSEna krutAnharharmaYa,*
> *apachArAnimAm sarvAn kshmasva purushottama*".

This verse is an expression seeking Lord's forgiveness at the end of daily thiruvaradhanam, for any errors committed by us. We would have given Him the divine bath in water too cool or too warm; we would have been inept in carrying out the ritual part. We would not have prepared food offered to Him perfectly; it could lack some ingredients. We might not be totally involved by mind, speech and body in carrying out the routine, our mind wandering. All these are deficiencies in our action for which we seek His forgiveness.

Que—some spiritual scholars mention that all our sins would be burnt into ashes when we pray and worship God?

Ans—some of them misinterpret what is stated in Thiruppavai—5 "*. . . poya pizhaiyum pugutaruvAn ninranavum, tlyinil tUsAgum seppElorempAvAi*". The Lord would enable a true devotee to exhaust his past sins and would accept his noble karma, effect of which he does not have to exhaust taking more births. Thus God lets the devotee renounce the effects of his good karma or neutral karma, like the dust which easily gets burnt in the fire. However, there is no escape from bad karma which would have to be exhausted by experiencing the effects of bad karma. We cannot renounce bad karma. A devotee considers even punya karma as ignoble for it would keep him away from God—"*ivan puNyattai pAvamennirukkum*". *It is same as our owning lots of wealth which can be renounced but we have to repay our debts which cannot be renounced.*

There are many people in the world, living a good life, who do not believe in the existence of God. They do not expect any help from God. Though they are non believers, they are still doing well and are successful in life. It is purely due to their past and present karma, which is the reason they are doing well now and if they continue to do good karma, they will continue to experience good life. But they do not have the realization that soon as their good karma is exhausted; they have to account for bad karma, for karma is always mixed.

God is kind even in accounting for our good or bad karma. He gives us a good life for the most part so that a person who is used to a good life does not have to suffer more due to change in fortunes. A person, who is used to poverty for most part of life, manages better than a person who falls from being well off, and cannot bear the thought of being poor. Many people take their own life when they lose their wealth. Those living a great life may exhaust most of their good karma and their next life could be a problem.

So why do we need God if life can go on well without Him? Because, when we do not relinquish the claim for doership and fruits of action, we would have to face consequences which would be a blend of good, neutral and bad. So they could suffer during their entire next life. If we are devotees, then we would not have to worry about consequences, as we would relinquish both causes and effects.

We become what we seek

Sri Azhagiyamanavala perumal nayanar in acharyahrudayam

1-11 says
> *"ivai kittamum vEttuvELAnumpolE oNporuL*
> *poruLallAdavai ennAdE . . .*

In contention—the atma, who is divine and different from this material world; who is supposed to have control over the non sentient body, allows his body to convert him like itself, due to attachment to the body, assuming the self as his body. However, the supreme Lord, who is the master and controller of all creation, due to his inexpressible love for his devotees, grants them similarity with Himself.

We are superior to the matter of this world and our body, but we allow ourselves to deteriorate to the level of non sentient matter, like that insect which converts any insect as itself (kittamum vEttuvELanum polE . . .), this world has brought us down to its level, by our own doing. *If we are attached to matter, we get influenced by matter. If we are attached to the Lord, the Lord elevates us to His levels.* **When it concerns matter, it is our doing; when it concerns the Lord, it is His doing.**

In another sukti 2-104—he ends saying—
> *" . . . shadguNa rasAnnamAkki vAnorkku ArAvamudAnavArE*
> *muttumuNNA munnam pArittu uzhuvador nAnjilkondu*
> *peruga muyalum pattiyuzhavan krishiphalamirE"*—

Sri Nayanar explains the hardship the Lord goes through in providing for everything the jivatmas seek. Only He knows that the souls are better off with Him in the eternal world. In order to have them realize that the joy in the mortal world is trivial, momentary and may also cause pain and grief, He is ever waiting for the souls to turn towards Him seeking His grace, in devotion.

He goes all out in seeking every soul's well being like a farmer, in protecting his crop, giving it all the ingredients, nourishment, and support it needs to flourish in abundance so that it attains the purpose of its existence. The purpose of a crop is to fulfill the need for food. The purpose of embodied human souls is to attain immortality, experiencing divine bliss. Just as a farmer supports his crop, so too, the Lord supports the embodied atma, to attain His divine world, thereby granting them immortality and eternal bliss, which they missed forever, thus far.

Chapter Nineteen

―――◆―――

Death, Time and Yugas

Que—What is death, why do humans and even animals fear death?

Ans—Death is truly not the death for the Atma. It is the end of life for the Atma in a body. Soon as he obtains a body in this world, he is deluded into thinking that he is the body and becomes attached to the body, its functionality and enjoyment he experiences using the body and senses. He is never fulfilled with any amount of enjoyment and does not want to let go of the body even at old age. The atma keeps on desiring for more enjoyment using his body and senses. His attachment to the relationships he acquires here and the enjoyment he experiences with the relationships and material wealth of this world, prompts him to become ever increasingly obsessed to his body. We don't fear death alone. We dread losing our relationships, losing material wealth, losing anything we love to possess, anything that is beneficial and useful to us. We don't worry about people not known to us or not related to us, dying. We are selfish even in attachment; we like to retain anyone or anything useful to us. We fear death of even pets that we are attached to.

Similarly, even animals are attached to their bodies without the realization of difference between the soul and body consciousness. They fear death out of instinct. However, they meet their death in accordance with karma for they don't end their life like humans, either due to addictions or committing suicide.

We have also known of people taking their own lives. This is due to frustration for not being able to attain the desired; or when they fail to achieve their expectations. They cannot bear the thought of life without their possessions. People commit suicide for various reasons—some due to failures, some being unable to face reality, some owing to suffering, some by losing their wealth. Either wanting to live on or opting to end life—is a consequence of our attachment to life or missing to acquire what we desire.

Though most of us fear death, the soldiers and such others willingly accept to lay their life in danger in order to protect us. They prepare to overcome the fear of death, sacrificing their life for the survival of the others.

Fear of death grips us when we become attached to body and there is no fear, when we become attached to God, ever willing to relinquish the body.

Que—can a person take his own life if the degree of suffering goes beyond the level of his endurance?

Ans—one shall not take his or her own life, it would tantamount to killing; he would have to face the consequences by taking birth to **suffer extra suffering**. Taking one's own life or others' life is not a solution for whatever reason. We will be adding to our woes by doing so. Going through the suffering now is much better than facing more suffering in next life. After all, life is meant for living. Everyone who is born is any way going to die. So why should we pre-pone death which is a natural eventuality?

Que—What is time? When did time start?

Ans—in practical terms, time is a measure of events. Without events we have no need for time nor would we understand the concept of time. In the larger sense, time began for this universe with the formation of the universe. However time is beyond this universe for there was a time even before the universe manifested.

To understand it better—for me, time started when I was born and it ends with the death of my body. However, time existed even before my birth and so did I and will exist even after I am gone out of this body. *In fact our DNA carries the age of our body and there is a body clock in our DNA, though no scientific research has yet come up with studying body clock in the DNA.*

However, time is not same for all. It is a different phenomenon for different beings. Time is not absolute as it is again one of the powers of God.

Gita 10-33—
　". . . . ahamEvAkshayah kAlo dhAtAham viSvatomukhah"—

"I am Myself imperishable Time. I am the Creator, facing all sides"

Time can freeze without events, but even then time exists but in a suspended state or frozen state. We, the souls and the universe merge into the supreme Lord at the time of total dissolution, and then only the Lord exists. In that state, we would be in a state of suspended animation. Then time freezes for us, as well for the universe. However, time is relevant only to us, for the universe has no sense of time, being non-sentient matter.

Time is timeless, it is without beginning nor will there be end, because, it is part of the timeless God. God is unborn, without a beginning while everything else—time, universe, souls, matter, knowledge (Vedas)—literally everything formed out of God and will merge into God.

We on earth relate to time based on events that are relevant to us, such as the sun rise, movement of earth in relation to our sun, moon, and stars. Events that occur at local the level or cosmic level—every event is connected through time. All the events in every one's life is measured by time. If our life goes eventless, even then our birth and death are the two events that bring time into our lives.

Time can only move forward as we cannot change the past or visit the past except in our memory. We can come up with theories of traveling faster than light to travel back in time, but that can happen only in theory and not in real terms. *In real terms, even if we travel trillion times faster than light, we can still arrive only in the future by a trillion times faster than light.*

Que—what about the yugas (millenniums) and the quality of people in different yugas.

Ans—the 4 yugas—kruta, trEtA, dwApara, and kali—represent the nature and quality of karma by souls taking birth in these respective yugas. It is important to know that the nature and quality here refers to the embodied souls based on their karma and not directly the souls, as atma is divine and beyond this prakruti but is influenced by the guna and karma when embodied.

Kruta yuga is considered the yuga of 'satvika' (pious) natured people. This is the yuga of righteousness. All the people would be engaged in elevating their knowledge and devotion. All of them would complete their full life duration and also would live for 1000s of years. There would be no physical or mental disability nor diseases and ailments in this yuga. This is the yuga of purity and knowledge. There would be no crime or sins. All those who take birth would be radiating divinity, resonating knowledge.

Treta—is the yuga with majority of the people being pious and sattvik and small numbers with a blend of rajasik qualities. If we gave a rating between good and bad, it would be around 80-20. Even in this yuga people lived their full life duration without untimely deaths. God incarnated as Rama towards the end of this yuga. People would live longer even in this yuga. It is said that Lord Rama lived for about 11000 years during His incarnation and His father Dasaratha lived for 60000 years. Many nitya suris took birth to experience Rama and His divine qualities. This was also a yuga of righteousness.

Dwapara—is the yuga—with a blend of sattvik, rajasik and tamasik with a Good-bad ratio of about 60-40. Very few were born with disability and most of them lived their allotted life time. There were some bad elements in the society towards the end of this yuga. Krishna incarnated and a lot of divine souls (nitya suris) also took birth to be associated with Krishna to enjoy His divine acts. The last dwapara yuga was the 28th of this manvantara; ended some 5113 years ago. Values of dharma started declining towards the end of this yuga. Sri Pillai Lokacharya says it all in one sukti—

"*Draupati paribhavam kandirudadu— krishNAbhiprAyattAlE pradhAna dosham*".

The disgrace meted out to Draupati by the kauravas was an unforgivable offence and Krishna had decided that all the bad elements of that society had to be removed from the face of the earth, in order to cleanse the society of sin and defilement. Even Pandavas suffered punishment for allowing such an incident to happen in the guise of honouring terms of agreement of the gambling game, they were tricked into. They lost all of their next generation including 'Abhimanyu' in the ensuing war. Krishna saved only parikshit for he was the only one unborn when this unpardonable event took place and hence he survived with the dawn on kaliyuga. In comparison to dwapara yuga, the standards of dharma have declined several fold in today's society. The high values of a society are measured by the respect given to the women.

Kali—is the yuga with more people having tamasik nature. People would be born with disability, untimely death, child mortality; diseases and ailments would be common. There would be no order about doing one's inherent duties. Yet, this is considered to be the best yuga for true devotees to reach God, as there are no qualifications for being a devotee; everyone has equal opportunity and entitlement. Towards the end of this yuga, God would take birth as 'kalki' to grace the bad elements by removing them from the society and to protect those that would find it impossible to survive without His intervention. We have some 427000 years still to go for the end of this kaliyuga, which started some 5113 years back.

Towards the end of kali yuga, it would rain nonstop for a year and the next year would go without rains. It is termed as 'ati vrushti' and 'ana-vrushti'. The duration of nonstop rain and no rain would gradually increase and eventually the whole planet earth would be inundated by water and no human life would be possible, even thousands of years before the end of kali yuga.

And it would be kruta yuga again after kali-yuga.

Following verse gives us insight, how devotion is practiced, in accordance with the respective yugas.

Padma Purana (Uttara-khanda 72.25) states:

"dhyAyan krUtE, yajan yajnais trEtAyAm, dvAparE 'rchayan; yad Apnoti tad Apnoti, kalau sankIrtya kESavam".

"if we are devoted to God by meditation in Kruta-yuga, by performance of yajna in Treta-yuga or by worship in

Dwapara-yuga; in Kali yuga, we can attain God by chanting His (Kesava's) names.

There is no end to the consequences for a person who treats a woman with disgrace. We can assess levels of deterioration we have reached with so many incidents of rape and other atrocities against women going unchecked, unpunished. By the same token, woman shall also live a life based on 'pativratyam', purity and chastity and the same is applicable to men as well. We can see that the women hold the key in all successful families and likewise they have their role in the ruin of a family as well. There is a famous saying in Tamizh "*Avadum peNNAIE, azhivadum peNNAIE*"—meaning that it is the woman who makes or breaks. Wherever the woman leads a life of dharma and purity, the family follows the same values. When the woman errs, that is also a reason for the family to lose values of life.

Women are acclaimed as the better gender than men when it comes to affection, sensitivities, loyalty, devotion etc; while they are known to have their weaknesses owing to obsession, temptations from relationships as well. The glorious virtues come to them naturally, while they can also err due to momentary temptations. *Women are looked upon as a more respectful gender than men; for only a woman can be a mother, nurturing life, care and affection. Men should try to elevate their levels in these aspects if they want to be equals with women. The only aspect in which men fare better than women is in their physical posturing and brutal strength which is not a positive aspect. Kindness and compassion make women a superior gender and should retain their place instead of coming down to the levels of men by claiming equality with them.* This is not to escape from giving them equal rights. The truth of the matter is, gopikas are the supreme entities when it comes to devotion and they were women. The great Azhwars, who incarnated as men, imagined themselves as women to seek Lord's companionship. However, Andal, a mere 5 year old child, surpassed all the Azhwars naturally by being a girl, for she was able to reveal her divine affection for the Lord naturally.

It is also true that some women of the society are being deprived of fair treatment in their families. There is also a potential problem with some women; though they are respected, well treated as more than equals, they claim that they are dependents without power and freedom. There is a psychic problem here. They are unhappy because they are unable to control the men in the family and when the men don't heed to their influence, they think they are deprived of equality and freedom. In other words, they want to control the actions and behaviour of the men in the family and when that does not happen, they falsely accuse of being suppressed.

Chapter Twenty

Nature of devotees

Que—Who is a devotee? Is he a special person, does he do things differently, can you spot him?

Ans—A devotee is just another person; there is no difference in his physical appearance from others. He would be full of humility, kind and caring, very conscious in his actions, ensuring he does not cause any harm to anyone. He would be a happy person and would spread happiness to all those associated with him. He would be a responsible person, taking good care of dependants. He would be conscious of God's presence in him and would dedicate everything to God. He would also realize the presence of the same God in every living being and hence would not see any difference between himself and others. He would be oblivious to their physical difference. He would treat everyone with equal esteem.

Sri Pillailokacharya gives us a hint of a true devotee—'karmam kainkaryathile pugum'—reiterates the fact that a devotee would do all his nitya karma (daily-prescribed duties) and naimitika karma—(periodical obligatory duties) in service to God.

A devotee would be unselfish. When we say selfless, it means that we should help unconditionally without claiming credit for helping or for fame and popularity.

What if a devotee is a poor man, who is not well qualified and has no opportunity to become rich, how can he help others when there isn't enough resource for his needs? He is poor due to his past karma. Soon as he exhausts bad karma, he would get the opportunity to earn resources for a comfortable life. It is by conscious choice backed by his righteous deeds, why he is a devotee now. He would be happy due to his devotion, which would be beyond the reach of many rich men. That is what devotion can do to us. He would have no fear of consequences as he has braced himself to face any adverse situation which would be due to his past karma and would be grateful to God even in crisis. He would be constantly praising God's glory and thanking Him every moment in life for having bestowed a human life. We can understand how precious it is to obtain human body when we think of the number of humans on earth today in relation to the number of souls in one human body. If there are 7 billion people, one human body alone has some 20 trillion living cells, each cell having a soul in it.

Plight of Narada as a family man (samsari)

There was a conversation between Krishna and Narada. Narada suggests that he finds it hard to understand as to why the humans on earth cannot follow the path of devotion. To him, being righteous and devout is easier than being addicted to sense gratification and materials of this mortal world. Krishna confirms to Narada, it was not such an easy process to be devoted to God as the attraction of enjoyment and material acquisition for more sense gratification is such a tempting force, that even Narada would not be able to resist if he was one of the humans. Narada does not agree with that; goes on to say that he was beyond all these temptations.

Krishna employs His yoga maya—Change of scene—

Narada, as a young man, spots a beautiful damsel and falls for her instantaneously. He approaches the girls' parents and seeks her hand in marriage. With the girl's consent they get married. Over the years, they have few children and lead a very happy life together. Suddenly, one fine day, it starts raining heavily, nonstop for a few days and their town was inundated by flood water. The flood intensifies and Narada's wife and children are being caught up in the current of flood waters and were being swept away from him. He tries more than he could to rescue them but fails. He watches them being washed away by the flood and cries out to God for help in great agony. Suddenly he finds Krishna standing next to him and pleads with Krishna to bring back his wife and children as he was unable to bear their separation, for he really loves them more than anything else and was truly experiencing a great life with them.

He did not realize it was all an illusion. Krishna asks him to wake up to reality. He then asks Narada what caused all this attachment. Just moments ago he was wondering why the humans were so attached and involved in their mortal lives. He was not any different when in a similar situation as the humans. Some of the ordinary humans are still devout and lived a balanced life performing their obligatory duties and not obsessed with enjoyment and mortal relationships. Narada then accepts that God's prakruti and maya were indeed beyond anyone's control and it would be impossible for one to overcome, unless he was a devotee.

God gives His devotees more wealth!

There was a conversation between Krishna and Uddava, who was a brahma-jnani. Uddava asks the Lord how a devotee would get to know that He has accepted his devotion, for only the Lord knows when a devotee has attained the state of acceptability. Krishna mentions thus *"yasyAham anugrihNAami* **tasya vittam** *harAmyaham"* whosoever I bestow upon my acceptance, I take away his wealth". This is generally misinterpreted as—"once the

Lord accepts a devotee for granting immortality, He would take away all his wealth, rendering him into poverty". It is not the correct interpretation. We bring no wealth with us when born. Our only earnings are karma. We bring karma with our birth from earlier lives. We spend some karma and earn more karma during this life. All that we own here is karma (punya/good karma or papa/bad karma) and nothing else. When we die, we take the baggage of accrued karma into our next life.

The material wealth that we acquire during our lifetime cannot be taken with us into next life; we have to leave behind even our body. So, clearly, Krishna is not talking about the material wealth when he says 'vittam'.

When Krishna declares in Gita *"sarva dharmAn parityajya mAm Ekam SaraNam vraja, aham tvA sarva pApEbhyo mokshayishyAmi, mA suchah"* "give up all dharma surrendering unto Me alone, and I will take care of your karma'. Only He can enable us to exhaust all our karma. Karma alone is our earnings in this world and we on our own can never exhaust all our karma. We stand entitled to attaining Lord's world only when we clear all our karma . . . And this is what He means in saying that whosoever He accepts as a devotee, by His grace; He would make the devotee spend all his karma, to grant him immortality.

Glory of Bhattar's expression for the divine couple.

This is a conversation bhattar has with the Lord Namberumal of Srirangam, in his prabandham "Sri Rangaraja stavam—poorva satakam—14, he says-

> *"yadi mE sahasra vadanAdi vaibhavam,*
> *nijamarpayEt sa kila ranga chandramAh,*
> *atha sEshavan mama cha tadvadEva vA,*
> *stuti saktyabhAva vibhavEpi bhAgitA"*

One day, after Namberumal's divine bath (tirumanjanam) and adornments, Bhattar looks at the Lord in wonderment, feeling overwhelmed by His divine beauty. Reading his thoughts, Namberumal asks him "how do I look", "can you describe Me'? Bhattar nods affirmatively, admitting there was no doubt He looked divine and out of this world. He could describe His divine beauty if he was granted 1000 divine tongues, with infinite potential for expression. Namberumal was amused and grants him without question, what he sought. And having obtained 1000 divine tongues, he looks at the Lord from Feet to Crown atop His divine lotus face—and mentions to the Lord that it was not possible to describe His glorious beauty by speech or expression.

Namberumal pretends to be fascinated by his response, questions him as to why, then, did he seek 1000 divine tongues? Obviously, if he couldn't describe His beauty after possessing 1000 divine tongues, he surely knew it would not have been possible in the first place when he did not possess 1000 divine tongues. Or did he think it might be possible with 1000 tongues and now after obtaining the divine ability, he realized it was still not possible? Bhattar tells Him that it was not the case. He knew very well in the first place that it would not be possible to describe His gloriously divine form, or His infinite auspicious qualities, either with or without the 1000 divine tongues. Namberumal now seemingly curious by this answer asks why then did he seek 1000 tongues if he knew so, much before?

Bhattar confesses—"I sought 1000 divine tongues because, even to say that it was not possible to describe your divine beauty, I needed 1000 divine tongues. I could not say it with the material tongue and speech. *A normal human sense of speech was not worthy to be used to express that His beauty was beyond expression.* And that's exactly what the Vedas declare (taittiriyopanishad—manomayaparyaya—"**yato vAcho nivartantE, aprApya manasA saha**" The Lord could not help but feel overwhelmed at Bhattar's devotion and true adoration for Him.

One other day, the Lord seemed very pleased with Bhattar, He mentions to him that He has granted Him the 'parama padam' (the eternal abode) and asks him if he was pleased to know this? Bhattar does not show any emotion at this declaration by the Lord. Bhattar responded saying "I would accept this on one condition, if I don't find You in the same glorious form as here, and if I don't get to serve you like here, I might jump out of parama padam to return to your abode here. There is no greater place for me than being in your service. Sri Pillailokacharya describes the divinely glorious form of Namberumal's stature thus—

> *"tirukkayyilE piditta divyAyudhangaLum,*
> *vaittu anjal enra kaiyum, kavitta mudiyum,*
> *mugamum muruvalum,*
> *AsanapadmattilE azhuttina tiruvadigaLumAi*
> *nirkira nilayE namakku tanjam"—*

This sukti establishes that the Lord here in His most glorious form, is for our sake, to seek Him. He is our only refuge in this mortal world. He stands here for our sake with all His divine glories, to enable us to soak in His divine beauty and take shelter at His divine Lotus Feet. His presence here is purely out of His 'nirhetuka krupa' or unconditional love for us. The great acharya declares that *"thirumantrattin ellai nilai archAvatArattil kANalAm"*, meaning that the Lord in the archarUpam (as deities) is the epitome and essence of Thirumantram.

Bhattar also shares his conversations with the divine Mother—in his prabhandam 'SriguNa ratna koSam'—describing the divine qualities of the Lord and the Peria Piratti—he mentions to her thus—

> *"aiSwaryamakshara gatim, paramam padam vA,*
> *kasmai chidanjali param, vahate vitIrya,*
> *asmin na kanchiduchitam krutimitya dAmbva,*
> *tvam lajjase kathaya koyamudAra bhAvah"* . . .

Here he describes the magnanimity of the divine mother; that she is so generous in granting us everything there is to give, yet she seems dissatisfied and shy that she hasn't done enough for us.

"you have given infinite wealth, what is more, you have also granted the ultimate state of existence in parama padam and there is nothing more that can be given—and all this you have done for merely soliciting your grace with joined palms together (anjali) which signifies that I have nothing to offer to you, and your generosity is such that even after doing the most, you still seem to feel shy as though you haven't done enough, what can be said about Your magnanimity! There is no equal to your kindness!

The true essence of 'anjali' is to convey that we have nothing to offer, and the essence of prostration before God and Acharya is to convey that we have nowhere else to go.

Many of us cannot relate to God or His existence in our lives when obsessed with our bodies; and if we do, it is only for how He can be useful to us. If we have no need for God, then we assume there is no God. We are convinced with our pre-conceived notion that there is just one life, here and now and all that we need to be focused on is how to maximize our enjoyment and physical pleasures. But with little introspection, we could see and relate to many realities that we did not realize, were true.

Inexpressible Glory of Azhwan

We cannot understand devotion and compassion if we do not learn a bit about Sri Koorathazhwan. Sri Manavalamamuni who is the re-incarnation of Sri Ramanuja, declares that it is not possible to describe in words or speech, the inexpressible glory of Azhwan; "vAchAm agochara mahaguNa dEsikAgrya".

Similarly, ThiruvarangattamudanAr in his ramanuja nUtrandAdi refers to Azhwan (slokam 7) "**mozhiyaik-kadakkum perum pugazhAn** . . ."

His glory transcends all expressions in words or language for being beyond the reach of the mind and intellect. The same expression can be found in the Vedas about God. Vedas confirm that God's glory cannot be expressed, for mind and speech return without being able to reach His infinite bliss. It says thus—'*yato vAcho nivartantE aprApya manasA saha*'—the auspicious glories of the Lord are infinite and infinite cannot be comprehended by mind or speech.

Azhwan had transcended the prides arising from the three statuses that most others have failed to overcome; such as:
  ➢ vidya madam (pride of being most knowledgeable, learned),
  ➢ dhana madam (pride of owning lots of wealth) and
  ➢ abhijAtyamadam (pride of belonging to a great dynasty of nobility)

Azhwan is none other than the incarnation of the supreme Lord, who takes birth in kali yuga to serve Ramanuja as his disciple. Lakshmana's service to Rama is unequalled. Rama feels obliged and desires to serve Lakshmana during his incarnation as Krishna. Lakshmana incarnates as Balarama, the elder brother of Krishna. But Krishna fails in his goal to serve Balarama and decides to incarnate as Azhwan in kali yuga serving Ramanuja who is the incarnation of Lakshmana. Azhwan was born in the year 1010 AD, 7 years ahead of Ramanuja and ends his incarnation few years before Ramanuja so that he would be there in the divine world to receive Ramanuja on his arrival there!

Azhwan takes birth in a wealthy family, in a small village— Kooram, some 11 kilometers from Kanchipuram. His glory spreads all around by virtue of his kindness and philanthropy.

He had mastered the Vedas, scriptures, divya prabandham. He was a most erudite scholar, divine looking and rich as well and yet his humility and kindness had no equal. He is considered as the only one of his kind as there were none who had all the three superlatives in terms of wealth, knowledge and resplendent personality. Only the supreme Lord had these virtues.

Most would flaunt their might even if they were either only wealthy or only learned or only good looking, belonging to royalty. Just one of these virtues would be enough to unbalance them. He had the best of everything and yet he was a perfect Srivaishnava, kindness personified to the letter. The daily feast at his place (tadiyaradhanai) would go on till late afternoon. The sound of the bells on the main door of the feast hall was so powerful that it would reach beyond Kanchipuram.

Once, the divine couple, Lord Varadaraja and Piratti in Kanchipuram express their appreciation of Azhwan's glory to Sri Kanchipurnar (Thirukkachinambigal). The Acharya visits Azhwan to convey the impact his fame has made, and asks Azhwan to visit the divine couple for worship.

Azhwan feels low and down on knowing that it was the wealth in his possession which was a reason for the Lord to think of him and not his devotion or any other quality. It also meant to him that he should give up all his wealth and proceed to Srirangam taking refuge in Ramanuja. He distributes all his wealth to the needy and proceeds to Srirangam. His consort, Sri Andal accompanies him.

Ramanuja, who had heard of Azhwan's glory was ecstatic to see him. He spends his days serving Ramanuja. Ramanuja had thousands of disciples. Many of the disciples felt that Ramanuja gave Azhwan special status for no good reason. While others would be designated to do many chores, Azhwan was shown greater respect that befits only an Acharya. Ramanuja read their minds and decided to reveal to everyone why Azhwan was different. Just after the daily worship, it was time for lunch. Ramanuja directs Azhwan to fetch some banana leaves from the garden for serving food. Azhwan does not return. All of them start murmuring that Azhwan could not do even a simple task. Ramanuja and his disciples go after Azhwan to find out what caused the delay. They found Azhwan lying unconscious and a leaf, half removed and dangling with liquid oozing out of the plant. Ramanuja explains to them how Azhwan was indeed the greatest srivaishnava and different from the rest. Soon as he cut the leaf from the plant, he saw liquid flowing down as though the plant was crying and Azhwan was so kind hearted that he could not endure that sight and fell unconscious. In reality, it does not cause pain to the plant. But the sight of liquid coming out was enough to melt him down. Such was the extent of his kindness and compassion.

Ramanuja had undertaken to write commentaries on the Vedas and Vedanta sutras of Vyasa as wished by Alavandar. Azhwan contributed predominantly to this cause. To complete his Sri Bhashyam, Ramanuja wanted to refer to the 'bhodayana vritti' in the Kashmir library. They went all the way to the king of Kashmir and on testing their piety, erudition and in depth comprehension of the Vedanta sastras and on excelling the pundits of his court in debate; the king permits access to the 'bhodahayana vritti' in his library. The pundits, who were defeated in debate, were envious of their mastery over the subject and were unhappy about their king giving them access to the sacred 'grantha'. They set conditions that neither they could take notes nor would they be allowed to take the scripture out of the library. Even then the duo from the south seemed to make progress, which again bothered the pundits who planned to exterminate the two visitors. Learning of the impending danger, they decided to leave Kashmir.

However, Ramanuja was sad that after all the effort, they could not study 'bhodayana vritti' completely, nor would they be able to recollect everything from memory. It was then that Azhwan re-assured Ramanuja that while his Acharya was resting in the nights, he would spend the nights in the library by-hearting the entire grantha and could repeat word for word. And they complete the long term project of 'Sri Bhashyam'.

While establishing the nature of the 'jivatma' Ramanuja inferred that 'jnAtrutvam' was the primary nature of the soul and Azhwan begged to differ on this and explained to Ramanuja that 'seshatvam' or subservience to the Lord was the prime inherent nature of the soul and 'jnatrutvam' was an integral aspect of 'seshatvam'. Seshatvam signifies the jivatma's inherent relationship with the Lord who dwells in the atma as the antaryami as well. Seshatvam reveals that the Lord is the eternal Father of all souls and Ramanuja agreed. Azhwan substantiates his view with Nammazhwar's Tiruvaimozhi 8-8-1 "*adiyEnuLLane*" which re-emphasizes that the Lord is the antar-atma in the soul, who as the Master, empowers it to function and the atma is the natural subservient of the Lord. Similarly, we are the masters of our bodies which remains subservient to us, under our control and command.

Azhwan's marriage to the divine lady Andal in itself is an extraordinary event, revealing that Azhwan and Andal were the divine couple. They lived in divine companionship their entire life without the marital relationship of mortal humans. This is evident for Azhwan and Andal did not have children till Azhwan neared 80. Sri Parasara bhattar and Vyasa bhattar, their two sons were born of the divine will of Lord Ranganatha. Even that was an extraordinary event. Azhwan and Andal went without food a full day as it rained relentlessly. He used to practice 'uncha-vritti' (accepting food offered by others). However, the Lord in the temple did not seem to miss any of his feedings. The evening bells rang again in Ranganatha's temple to indicate that the Lord was being offered his evening delicacies. Andal thought for a moment that while her lord went without food, Lord

Ranganatha was having his offerings without hinder. Knowing her thoughts, the Lord commanded Sri Uttama Nambi in his dreams to immediately take the 'akkara adisil' (milk-rice delicacy) and full course of dinner the Lord was offered, to Azhwan at once, with full temple honour. Sri Uttama Nambi carries out the Lord's command and requests Azhwan to accept the bhagavat prasadam, narrating everything. Azhwan immediately realizes that it must have been Andal's doing and looks at her. She confesses to him and both of them relish the prasadam sent by the Lord Ranganatha. By the grace of the Lord's prasadam, she gives birth to their two sons. It is also why Bhattar is considered as the child of Lord Namberumal as specified in his tribute "*sri parAsara bhattArya, sri rangESa purohitah, srivatsAnkha sutah srimAn srEyasE mE'stu bhUyasE*"; he is known as 'srivatsankha sutah' or the child of the Lord Namberumal.

Sri Ramanuja was elated at the birth of the two Bhattar brothers and has Sri Embar bring them to him. Soon on holding the babies, he says he was smelling 'dwayam' coming from them and looks at Embar. Embar was pleased to know of the effect on the children and submits to Ramanuja that he chanted 'dwayam' into their ears for invoking Lord's protection on them.

The Chozha king who was the ruler then in the south, was a fanatic follower of Shaivism. Vaishnavism gained more popularity during Ramanuja's period which the Chozha king detested. He was advised by Naluran, a srivaishnava in his court, that if Ramanuja was stopped from spreading his influence, the spread of vaishnavism could be stopped. He suggests to the King to have Ramanuja sign a declaration accepting the supremacy of Lord Shiva. Knowing the impending danger to Ramanuja, Azhwan and other close aides send him to Melkote in Karnataka. The king orders his chief to have Ramanuja and his Acharya, Peria Nambi, brought to him. Azhwan goes to the king in the guise of Ramanuja. The king engages Azhwan in a debate on Lord Shiva as the supreme God. He hands him a written statement "SivAt parataram na-asti" meaning there is no greater power than Shiva"; asking him to sign as a token of acceptance. Azhwan answers back forthwith "dronam-asti tatah param"— meaning 1/2 of a measure is greater than that.

Sanskrit is a unique language; same word has different meanings based on the context of usage. Shiva also means 1/4th of a measure. So the counter statement by Azhwan that 1/2 of a measure was greater than 1/4th—makes the chola king realize that this was not an ordinary scholar. He could not have imagined anyone coming up with such a statement with total authority and finality. The debate ended there. Azhwan won the debate without even mentioning the name of Shiva, the God that was the matter of contention here. The king could not think of a suitable reply and hence gets enraged at his defeat.

He compels Sri Peria Nambi to sign his acceptance conceding Shiva as the supreme God or he would have his eyes removed. Peria Nambi stood steadfast forsaking his eyes, instead.

Azhwan could not bear the atrocious act of the king and takes out his eyes declaring that the eyes that have seen such an evil person shall not be a part of his body. Thus Azhwan was instrumental in preventing an encounter between the tyrant king and Ramanuja, for the evil king who was intolerant at the popularity of vaishnavism; would have stooped to any levels.

Azhwan composed 5 prabandhams in praise of the Lord— Srivaikunta stavam, Ati manusha stavam, Sundara bahu stavam, Varadaraja stavam and Sri stavam. The status given to these prabandhams is unequalled. To his credit it is said in his taniyan (tribute) thus "srivatsachinha miSrEbhyo nama uktima dhImahE, yaduktayastrayI kanTE yAnti mangaLa sUtratam". If we consider the Vedas as the bride for the supreme God, (Vedas are meant to reveal God's supreme nature and it does so in His service); the Sastras, puranas, divya prabhandhams of azhwars are considered as the adornments for that bride, while Azhwan's five prabandhams are considered the 'mangala sutram'—the necklace or tirumangalyam, which confirms the wedded status to the Lord. Without the 'mangala sutram' a bride does not get the status of a consort and all other adornments have no relevance without the mangala sutram. It is like the wedding ring in the western culture. A bride might be wearing other jewelry, but without the wedding ring or a mangala sutram, the other jewelry does not give her the status of a spouse.

Ramanuja then returns to Srirangam on hearing that the krimikanta chozha; the tyrant had died of neck cancer. Azhwan who spends some years in Thirumalirum solai, also returns to Srirangam and when they meet, their joy in each other's company could not be equated to anything we can understand.

Towards the end of his life Ramanuja and Thirukkachchi Nambi (one of Ramanuja's 5 acharyas) take Azhwan to Lord Varadaraja in Kanchipuram where he composes 'Varadaraja stavam' in praise of the Lord. The Lord expresses his desire to grant some boons. Azhwan does not ask for anything, when insisted he prays for Naluran to be forgiven from the eternal hell for his grievous sins. It was Naluran who was instrumental in Perianambi to have lost his sight.

The Lord was overwhelmed at Azhwan's benevolence that he cared for the redemption of even a sinner like Naluran and declares that anyone and everyone, associated with Azhwan, would be granted the eternal abode. On hearing this Ramanuja expresses great joy that he is also entitled to paramapadam, as he was related to Azhwan by being his acharya. Not that he needed anyone else's association for this entitlement. It was out of sheer uncontrolled elation about being associated with Azhwan that he wanted this world to know and understand the 'greatest-ness' of Azhwan. Ramanuja was unhappy that Azhwan did not seek to have his sight back. But Azhwan confesses that he did not wish to see anyone else other than Ramanuja and the Lord, which the Lord had granted him.

They return to Srirangam and Azhwan goes before Lord Ranganatha asking to be relieved from this samsara. Even Lord Ranganatha declares that everyone associated with Azhwan shall attain His divine abode. On learning that Azhwan has sought to leave this world, Ramanuja was distressed and questions Azhwan how he could even think of leaving him alone in this world. To this Azhwan contends that it was only right for him to be at paramapadam ahead of his Acharya so that he would be ready to receive the Acharya with all the glory and honour that befits him, on his arrival there. Ramanuja lives for 120 years and then re-incarnates as Manavalamamuni spending 80 years more amongst us.

Thus, Azhwan more than fulfills the wish of Rama to serve Lakshmana by his un-equaled service to Ramanuja. Azhwan incarnated here as though to demonstrate the wholesomeness and completeness of Srivaishnavism.

Quality of life in immortal body

The immortal body is divine in all respects and a soul acquiring that imperishable body becomes so powerful that he will have no limitations as to what he can do. It is still a soul in a divine body and not God, but being with God, soul gets many auspicious virtues (only good) that God Himself possesses. God grants them similarity with Himself. Even the intellect, mind and senses would be divine in the immortal world. God grants us everything He can when we attain His world, just as a father would allow his child to use all his belongings.

In the immortal world, there is no birth and death like we have in the mortal world; the divine souls are not born as an infant and grow old like us. There is no ageing process for the divine bodies. They possess powers to acquire and change their body or take any form they wish.

It is hard for us to comprehend the divine existence from here. You can imagine a superman without any weaknesses or limitations—that is the closest comparison, though the body of the superman we know is not divine. The divine body is not made up of bones, flesh, blood, muscles and tissues like a human body. It is a body that cannot be hurt, that will not bleed nor feel pain; it will not age, would not smell foul; all of them would be ever in prime state, experiencing ever growing bliss. There would be no element of fear for the soul in an immortal body. You don't need to sleep like us here; Azhwar calls them 'imayorgal' those who do not sleep. This is exactly what Nammazhwar says *"nalam anthamillador nAdu puguvir"*—meaning "you would attain the world of 'endless bliss'. It is the highest state of existence, without karma and consequence. They would not err like humans. They would be much above even the gods of the created world, Brahma included. They would be literally the divine children of that supreme God. While they would be focused on doing what would please their Father; the Father being the greatest and infinitely omnipotent, would be looking to please them in every new way possible.

In this world, even in happiness, we seek change. We do not like monotony. But reality of this world is that the good experiences are short lived and there is no consistency or change in goodness or increasing degree of goodness, which is what we seek. We keep experiencing a blend of good and bad, joy and sorrow. However, in the eternal abode, there is continuous change in the goodness of divine joy. It would not be repetitive or boring. There would be no monotony. The Lord is a natural scientist and inventor. He would keep coming up with ever new ways to involve the divine souls experiencing unending joy. We would be experiencing infinitely growing 'bliss' in infinite ways.

Every moment would be more divinely blissful. Sri Nammazhwar describes the divine bliss of the Lord in Thiruvaimozhi 2-5-4 as "appozhudaikkappozhudu en ArAvamudamE" The divine bliss of the Lord would be like the water in the river which is continuously flowing, you would never have the same water again.

In the mortal world when the Lord bestows overwhelming grace, the devotee would not be able to absorb the enormity of the Lord's love for him. Though there are no limits to how much He can bestow, the devotee has limitations as to how much he can take. It would be beyond the devotee's capacity to experience the grace of the Lord, who knows no limits when it comes to showering His grace on us. Sri Andal expresses this factor in Thiruppavai—22 (angaNmA—pasuram)

> "kinkiNi vAicheyda tAmarai pUppolE,
> sengaN siruchiridE emmEl vizhiyAvo,
> . . . . angaNirandumkond-engaLmEl nokkudiyEl"

She asks Krishna to bestow His grace slowly, bit by bit so that we can withstand the enormity of His limitless kindness for us.

Que—isn't immortality dangerous? If bad people attain immortality and become powerful, they could be potential threat to the peace in all the worlds?

Ans—no and yes.

No, when we attain immortality in the eternal world. There is zero chance of anyone going out of control, for a bad person would not attain immortality, nor would anyone change becoming bad after attaining immortality. Because a jivatma can acquire the blend of sattva, rajasa, tamasa qualities only in a prakrutik material body in the created world which influences the atma to delusion and false pride. In a divine body, the atma would be influenced by divinity and purity of suddha sattva and hence there is no scope for becoming corrupt. The nature of immortal world is divinity without defilement. The intellect, mind, sense and body are also divine. Everyone in the immortal world would be granted similarity with God. Any one becoming a rogue element is only when he is in danger of losing his status and no one has any fear in the immortal world of losing their status. The immortality of the divine world is irrevocable, and eternal. So there is neither the fear of losing the status nor is there any state better than what they are. Everyone is involved in experiencing divine bliss with the Lord and there is no question of any one transgressing their nature.

Yes—when we get a boon of immortality in the mortal world; there is every chance of becoming corrupt due to the power of temporary immortality. That's what a Hiranyakashipu or Ravana or many of those that became powerful as an effect of the boons they were granted. Association with the material world influenced by the blend of tamasa and rajasa gunas, would prompt one to want to remain immortal here. That apart there is still the fear of losing that status and hence would cause destruction to others in order to safeguard his status. We know how restless the lord of the heavens, Indra becomes when anyone engages in tapas or obtains powerful boons, fearing losing his own position, because Indra's immortality is not eternal nor is heaven the immortal world.

In reality, the immortality obtained as an effect of a boon in the created world is not really the true immortality. They are wrong in thinking that they are immortals. It is just that they live longer than others. Even the sapta chiranjeevis—aswattama, bali, vyasa, krupa, hanumanta, vibhishana and parasurama—are immortals for this tama (a cycle of 4 yugas) and they too would be gone with the dissolution of their part of the world.

Que—in the immortal world, are all the souls in men's bodies or are there men, women and all the species that we see in our world.

Ans—Poigai Azhwar explains the infinite powers of the divine souls. They can assume any form they wish to take, and in all these forms, their bodies would be divine, not made of the material bodies known to us. It is also to be known that the supreme Lord is the only Purusha or Man, all the souls including that of divine nitya suris, gods and goddesses are feminine in nature.

Mudal Tiruvandadi—53
"*senrAl kudayAm, irundAl singAsanamAm, ninrAl maravadiyAm nILkadaluL; enrum puNayAm maNiviLakkAm, pUmpattAm pulgum aNayAm, tirumArkaravu*"

The essence of the verse is that "Adisesha" (adi means first, sesha means subservient—"eternal subservient of the Lord") takes any sort of form to remain in un-hindered service to the Lord. The expression 'endrum' confirms eternality. He engages in serving the Lord be it in the immortal world or even when the Lord incarnates here.

From this verse, we can understand that the nitya suris or the muktatmas in the immortal world can take any form of body they choose. There are only one people—immortals in divine bodies of their choice. They can assume a form of a man, woman, an animal or a bird or any other form unknown to us, and when they do; their purpose is to serve the Lord in every sort of way. They may assume the body of a 'cuckoo' if they want to please the Lord with their sweet sounds. They may become peacocks dancing for the pleasure of the Lord. They look for infinite possibilities to serve the Lord.

Thus everyone in the eternal world experiences the boundless bliss of the Lord, endlessly, as said in the Upanishad "*tad vishnoh paramam padam, sadA pasyanti sUrayah*".

Conclusion:

How does it help in knowing the nature of the self and our relationship with God? How would that make our lives better? Would it solve all our problems in this world?

We seek to attain God because He is our true Father and the eternal world is our true home. Knowing God will give us the realization that we belong to that Supreme power and His world. All our problems here are self created and we have to find the solutions as well. Being a devotee would give us a better resolve to deal with problems. We are not becoming devotees to seek things in this world or becoming rich. This is a karmic world and we can achieve everything here by doing our duties righteously, for God would not interfere in this karmic world. God has provided us with everything we need in this world. If we are righteous, we can be happy here. Even the so called happiness here is a blend of joy and grief. Our lifespan is short and we have to keep going in circles in different bodies based on karma. When in poverty, we think we can be happy if we become rich, but after becoming rich, we would still not find the happiness we want. Wealth and resources can only keep our body comfortable, not the Atma. But it is the Atma that is seeking to remain ever happy. That is where we need God. With devotion, we can not only be successful in working to acquire wealth righteously, but also find that peace and joy in life till we die. We would not be born in mortal bodies again as God would take care of our karma.

When God grants us His world, we attain similarity with Him, and there is no going back once we attain that state.

The beauty is that everyone knows everything said here, because knowledge is the nature of the atma. Nothing is new or unknown. We often ask ourselves, why didn't I think of it? The problem is when the soul is engulfed by false knowledge of assuming the body as the self, which is when he loses the self realization. And merely knowing everything also does not benefit us. We have to practice our nature, righteously. The moment we do everything with consciousness of the soul, overcoming the falsehood of body consciousness, we can start feeling the Lord dwelling in us. It is easier and simpler to realize this fact than many other things we do.

We have to realize that each one of us is a pure Soul, originating from God. If we retain that purity of soul consciousness, we can never do anything hurtful, we can never be cruel. It is important to be kind and compassionate than attaining all other achievements. Life is bound to be a mixture of ups and downs, joys and sorrows. But it is this soul consciousness that will keep us in equilibrium, always. There is nothing more to achieve either in this life or for attaining immortality.

The Lord seeks our presence in the eternal world because we can experience the unending divine bliss He bestows on all the divine souls there. We seek to attain Paramapadam not because we can attain eternal bliss and similarity with the Lord, but because we can serve our eternal Father without interruption, pleasing Him in infinite ways. God cares for our well being and happiness, always. He is never concerned about Himself. Similarly, being His potency, we should not be caring for ourselves in everything. Our focus should always be about the joy of the Lord and of the others.

Sarvam Sri KrishnArpaNamastu